W9-CCV-645

GOD: AN OPEN QUESTION

The Lord looks down from heaven
Upon the children of men
To see if there are any that act wisely,
That seek after God.

Psalm 14.2

GOD: AN OPEN QUESTION

Anton Houtepen
Translated by John Bowden

continuum
LONDON • NEW YORK

Continuum

The Tower Building, 11 York Road, London SE1 7NX
370 Lexington Avenue, New York, NY 10017-6503
www.continuumbooks.com

Translated by John Bowden from the Dutch *God, een open vraag.*
Theologische perspectieven in een cultuur van agnosme,
published 1997 by Uitgeverij Meinema
Copyright © Uitgeverij Meinema, Zoetermeer 1997
Translation copyright © John Bowden 2002

All rights reserved. No part of this publication may be reproduced or transmitted in
any form or by any means, electronic or mechanical including photocopying,
recording or any information storage or retrieval system, without prior permission
in writing from the publishers.

First published in English 2002

British Library Cataloguing-in-Publication Data
A catalogue record for this book is available from the British Library.

ISBN 0-8264-5950-1 (Hdk)
0-8264-5951-X (Pbk)

Typeset by BookEns Ltd, Royston, Herts.
Printed and bound in Great Britain by Bookcraft (Bath) Ltd, Midsomer Norton.

Contents

CONTENTS

Preface

Is God still asked for? If we put it that way, the question immediately gets us off on the wrong footing, as though God were an article on offer in the market of our needs, in demand or not in demand, depending on the whim of the purchasers. In reality, what we have is the question 'God?' and the exclamation 'God!' The question is whether there is anything like an ascent to God and a calling by God, as Hieronymus Bosch depicted it in his 'Journey of the Soul', which is on the cover of this book. This question preoccupies those who ask it, because it requires them to make a choice: for or against any thought of God and thus for or against the very God who determines our thought. To think God away, in the form of atheism, proves to be just as much a lifetime project as to admit God into one's thought. To admit God into one's thinking means to open up one's thought – and all that flows from it, feeling and action – in asking for God.

Those who believe in God admit God into their thinking. That does not mean that in so doing they leave their experience, their feelings, their reason out of things or do nothing with them. Far less do they put a stop to their thinking at some point in order then to be able to move towards God in their thought. Those who admit God into their thinking reorganize their whole pattern of thought and every aspect of their life. Those who look towards God see themselves and the other, society and the cosmos, in a different light, in another perspective.

This book sets out to contribute towards this change of perspective. It is an account of ten years of reading and talking with students from the Erasmus University in Rotterdam, where between 1984 and 1994 I occupied a chair in fundamental theology sponsored by the Radboud Foundation. There I learned that it is good to talk about God with a degree of caution; not, however, at the periphery of thought but from within, from the heart of our economic, legal, psychological and philosophical ideals and aporias. At the heart of our ideals – what, for instance, we want to achieve in our profession or what we want to devote our lives to – we attain to the summit of our ability, the sublime. At the heart of our aporias we are conscious how sham our constructs are, but we can also test hypotheses. Often theology has spoken about God at too great a length, from the wealth and the harmony of its system and its dogmas, as if it had certain knowledge about everything to do with God. Or, recognizing that no certainties about God may be had, it has overlooked or even scorned the sum of knowledge attained in questions about God. The questions are central to this book: the questions about ways of thinking about God which are humanly possible and are viable ways out of our aporias. So this book does not discuss the whole tradition of systematic thought about God, but only its key points, where the question of God gives direction to thought. To the last the questions remain authentic questions: they are not like questions in a catechism, which must elicit a standard answer. And all the more attention is paid to the difficulties, and the objections that can be made to belief in God. I hope that this book may make a small contribution to fundamental theology.

At the same time, the theme of this book is a topic of ecumenical dialogue of the first order, a theme which sadly has been neglected. Over the past half-century there has been much talk about forms of the church, about the sources of belief and the tradition of interpretation, about ministry and sacraments. And, though to a lesser degree, there has also been talk about the interpretation of the activity and the message of Jesus, about his significance in the midst of other religions and about the nature of the salvation for human beings and the world proclaimed by Christians. There has been much reflection on the social and ethical implications of the gospel of the kingdom of God and on the Christian mission statement that goes with it. There has been just one dialogue about the content and interpretation of the classical fourth-century creed which comes from the councils of Nicaea and Constantinople. And there have been conversations about the historical points of dispute as formulated in the confessional writings of later centuries, especially those from the time of the Reformation. But there has been a deafening silence about God, about the destiny of human beings and the world, and about the relationship between human beings and God, although the deepest legitimation for the opposing confessions lies precisely here. Are not these differences about human freedom and its limitation by the will of God? About the place of the role of the man Jesus in the very life of God? About the life-giving and re-creative power of God in the biography of each individual and in the history of the peoples? After all, Christians share with one another the scarlet thread of the prayer to God, the 'Our Father', that comes from Jesus himself. This prayer is in turn a re-reading of Jewish prayer and no less also forms a bridge to Muslim prayer. On the eve of Vatican II, taking up a saying by Augustine, John XXIII remarked that as long as we pray this 'Our Father' together we are not strictly divided. This book sets out to prompt ecumenical reflection on the content of this 'Our Father'.

If prayer is the guiding thread for belief and vice versa – *lex orandi lex credendi* – then the question of God is the foundation of all theology, although this question does not coincide with faith or piety. So the title of this book, *God: An Open Question*, may be understood as a personal statement: it is impossible to talk about God without defining one's own position. In doing this the book is also an account of my own quest as a theologian. What have I found? That asking about God opens our ideas to God himself, the Eternal One, the Most High, as a question to us.

The plan of the book is as follows. After an Introduction describing the current situation, in four sets of three chapters I try concentrically to sketch out the contours of questions currently asked about God, to open up windows on the infinite, to get to the heart of the Christian confession about God and in the midst of the *de facto* pluralism of religions and agnostic culture to try out a way of thinking about God.

Chapter 1 sets out to be a theological sounding-out of the deeper causes and the significance of the secularization process, with all its ambivalences. Chapter 2 seeks to provide some insights into the complexity of the *de facto* cultural agnosis in the West. Chapter 3 discusses the desperate questioning about God in the midst of suffering, violence and injustice.

Chapter 4 shows how there are areas in life which are difficult to fathom without a reference to God: the emotions as basic forms of religion. Chapter 5 draws attention to the holy, to that which seems to us to be inviolable and incomprehensible, to which we want to bow our heads in respect: traces of God. Chapter 6 is about history, in other words about the contingency and gratuitousness of time which elapses, but in which things and people are also rooted and in which truth and justice are constantly sought.

Chapter 7 speaks of God as the one who creates and cares for all that is: Father, Mother, Shepherd, Saviour – and about God's providential action. Chapter 8 turns to the central fact of Christian faith in God: Jesus of Nazareth as messenger of God, as the form of justice, love and peace, and as the pointer to hope and meaning beyond the limits of death. Chapter 9 is about God as dynamic energy, holy Pneuma, the power of the Spirit.

Chapter 10 is about the manifold figures and names of God, the pluralism of religions and the truth that illuminates all human beings. Chapter 11 presents a model of thought which has already been tested by the much disparaged René Descartes: God as the infinite, who leads us into thinking about infinite things. There is then a discussion of some contemporary thinkers who have again explored God as an open question: Marion, Chauvet, Levinas and Jüngel. Finally, Chapter 12 reflects on the relationship between revelation and experience, faith and knowledge, and seeks to define a contemporary space for theology.

An Epilogue sums up the conclusions from these four sets of three stages – which can also be read step by step and in any order – and sketches out the contours of what a theology which again allows the question of God as an open question could mean for our agnostic culture.

Because this book describes the course of my thinking and the history of my reading, I have added a great many references, of course to support what I say but also to offer a glimpse into the theological kitchen. They are not necessary for the argument itself. So they should not deter readers: reading notes is rather like zapping on the TV or surfing on the Internet. They are so many windows or views which can broaden or deepen thought.

I am much indebted to Hugo Vlug, who as a student assistant has suggested literature with great care and enthusiasm. He has collected valuable information, corrected the texts and supervised the layout of the book. My thanks also go to my colleagues at the Inter-University Institute of Missiology and Ecumenics, who have tolerated with true evangelical and ecumenical patience my concern for the questions of fundamental theology in what has sometimes amounted to a monomania, and also to my colleagues in the faculty of the Erasmus University, who have showed fruitful scepticism towards these explorations on the frontier of philosophy and theology but never without the cautious and fundamentally philosophical question 'Who knows?' I am most grateful for this to the Radboud Foundation, which has given me the opportunity to bring theology and philosophy into dialogue with each other for ten years.

Finally, I want to thank my most critical following, Eelkje, Wibo and Arjan. It is a miracle that they have been tolerant for so long that time and again their plans have to give way to what they – rightly – think that theology is: a few footnotes to God.

Introduction
A Culture without God?

Between 1965 and the end of the twentieth century there was a massive exodus from the church in Europe which at a deeper level can only be interpreted as a leave-taking of the traditional Western form of belief in God.[1] With reference to God and the destiny of human beings and the world we can speak of a culture of agnosis, which has many ramifications. Although the term 'agnosis' is a neologism which will not be found in the dictionary, I am deliberately using it in this book rather than the customary 'agnosticism'. 'Agnosticism' stands for a basic attitude with a theoretical foundation which regards any reference to God as an impossible and unnecessary addition to or duplication of the content of human knowledge and which therefore wants to keep God out of science and politics.[2] Kant already remarked that human life needs to take its directives only from itself and not from heteronomous values and norms or from revealed truths, immune to criticism, which are inaccessible to our capacity for judgement. Fichte already remarked that God deserves to be inconceivable anyway, since with our thinking we never arrive at God.

Although this agnosticism is certainly an influence in our culture – it is the methodological starting-point for Western science – the actual leave-taking of God is not just based on theoretical reflection on the impossibility of knowledge of God or revelation from God, but on a far more diffuse process, in which God and reference to God have slowly disappeared from consciousness. There is a form of life in which God has been forgotten and we simply no longer

1

know about God. That can vary from no longer wanting to know about God, through a vague tolerance which allows others to think in terms of God, to the complete absence of any question about God. What is characteristic of all these cases of agnosis is that there is no longer any need of God.[3] In the West, this leave-taking of God in fact involves a departure from forms of Christian belief. But it does not involve Christianity or the forms of the church as such, as though there were a crisis only in Christianity or the church. The leave-taking of the Christian tradition is not limited to a reduced involvement in church life but takes place above all in the forms of daily life that we call culture:[4] all forms of behaviour, views, rituals and symbols which give our life colour, up to and including our death, all of which we regard as valuable and therefore hand on to our children in education and upbringing. Language, art-forms, scientific models, world-views, religious forms of expression, patterns of relationship: all that together 'forms' a culture, of both individuals and groups. It also stamps the collective institutions of peoples, nations and states. Culture in this sense is the configurative unity of all these actions. None of them can be 'got separately'. That applies to language, science and art, but also to religion. That is why taking leave of religion is also a far-reaching cultural process, and not just a personal choice. The stories and forms of the biblical tradition, God and views of God, the time-honoured values, commandments and ideals which are derived from the ultimate destiny of human beings as coming home to God are disappearing from the symbolic universe of the modern European. We may still speak of Adam and Eve, but who still believes in paradise? We may well think 'After us the deluge', but who still knows the story of Noah and his sons? We may well still celebrate Christian festivals, but who still thinks at Christmas of the beginning of the Gospel of John, where it is said that God's *Logos* has dwelt among us, and who understands that? How do we explain to our children that Easter and Pentecost belong together? Christmas trees and Easter eggs are all that is left of the whole system of belief that was hidden behind the course of the liturgical or church year and in it was translated into a rhythm of life. And that is not to mention more lifelike symbolism like fasting and prayer, the spiritual baggage of biblical models, scenes and parables which guided the choices made by conscience, or dealing with sickness, suffering and above all death. Nor is it to mention the values and norms that regulate the way in which we deal with the affluent society, science, technology and politics, which we can put together under the heading of public morality or cultural ethics. And then there are the forms of expression of the faith in church and society, the course of which is usually described by the sociology of religion in terms of progressive secularization, the end of confessionalism, and diminishing orthodoxy. In the middle of the 1980s in the Netherlands the point had been reached when as far as the institutional side of religious belief was concerned most people were outside the church. It was expected that by the year 2000, three-quarters of the population would have no connection with the church. That the political system, the public media and – as a last stronghold – education are gradually turning 'pink', as we like to say in our distinctive way, is the somewhat delayed effect of this farewell under the surface to the church, religious inspiration and – at the deepest level – to God. In no religion is God an abstract and detached article of faith which one accepts or not, or about which one can have reservations while hanging on to all other religious forms. In the long run all these forms then lose their foundation and their purpose. They become folklore and convention. God can be called God only by those who know that the whole of reality is bound up with God. It is not a matter of marking out or maintaining a separate hole or corner for God. True belief in God therefore associates God with human forms of life, in whatever way.

For believers, God is part of their culture. Values, norms, symbols, world-views and self-awareness are characterized by the idea of God: it reorganizes the whole symbolic universe, what Scheler and Tracy call the God-world-self complex. Thus taking leave of God in culture represents a completely new definition of the world and the self. Both belief in God and taking leave of God create another world and another self.

The hypothesis of this book is that the present-day cultural agnosis is in fact the far-reaching process of a change of consciousness: thinking differently, feeling differently, acting differently in all spheres of life, including its limits, birth and death. We may ask whether the term 'secularization' indicates the meaning and scope of this process of change sufficiently clearly. And we may doubt whether the many attempts from the church side to breathe new life into the world of religious symbols has plumbed sufficiently deeply the significance and depth of cultural agnosis. It seems too easy to put all the blame – as theologians and catechists, bishops and pastors have tried to do – on antiquated forms of liturgy and proclamation or to stake everything on allusions to human experience – usually understood in the form of a weak existentialism – or what is called the power of stories.[5] Beyond question preaching orientated on experience and narrative competence are both very important in making the religious tradition accessible and keeping it alive. But they fail where people no longer seek this access or fill their lives with other kinds of experience. It is even conceivable that the narrative structures of the religious ethic may continue to flourish – as in an admiration for religious art or an interest in religious music – but without any specific reference to God or the divine. In this connection pastoral theologians have even spoken of a progressive secularization within the church.[6] When that happens the beliefs, Bible stories and liturgical rites take on the function of a welcome change from an otherwise technocratic culture, a hermeneutical surplus over and above all instrumental action: in the end men and women do not live by bread alone. Religion, art, amusement and a sense of environment then belong to the same atmosphere, which gives colour to life as a distinctive domain of specifically human experience. God has no special place in it; all this is not directed towards God. Perhaps it gives people some support between cradle and grave and protects us against boredom or meaninglessness, but it does not support us in living or dying. It does not provide us with an *ars moriendi*, because it does not support us over death. Nor does it provide us with an *ars vivendi*, since it gives no direction to the project of our lives or to the collective project of humankind that we work on as peoples and nations in history. Although in the first instance it cropped up in opposition to the absolutizing of human ideologies like liberal capitalism or Marxist communism, the notion of what Fukuyama has called 'the end of history' admirably expresses what cultural agnosis has led to in the West at the end of the twentieth century: a timeless existence, a life by the day, one long exploitation of the here and now. Moreover, and this is also particularly shaming for élites, it leads to an unparalleled religious illiteracy: political leaders then quote the Bible in season and out of season, as if believers still swore by a fundamentalist and biblicist exposition. Professors of philosophy publish atheistic manifestos against forms of belief which did not survive the nineteenth century.

Now such a description may perhaps sound all too nostalgic, too much a comparison with a period which lies behind us. To those who have never known it – young people under twenty who were born in or after the cultural shift of the 1970s – this nostalgia says nothing. Many older people too, however, hardly regret their farewell to a rich Roman past or the pomp of civic parades. What

4

do we really lose if we delete 'God' from our dictionary, if instead of going to church on Sunday we listen to the omnibus edition of The Archers, wash the car, go fishing or join in the rituals of the tennis club? What difference does it make if churches are pulled down and replaced by yet another bank or even a mosque?

Those who regard the process of the evaporation of the church and the slow disappearance of belief in God only in cultural retrospect will perhaps experience the actual culture of agnosis which is dominant in large parts of Europe as a process of levelling down: in antiquity and the Middle Ages, religion and the church gave colour to existence: they introduced heights and depths, passions and emotions. God had to do with the questions of life and death, suffering and hope, love and hate, sin and punishment. The church shared in the ambitions of rulers and scholars, soldiers and financial magnates. All those powerful people who liked to use the name of God as protection knew that in their callings they were kept in check by God through bishops and theologians, councils and papal decrees. That even continued after the Reformation, though more and more domains of life claimed autonomy, and more and more citizens demanded their share in the social course of events. Even the Enlightenment, which advanced the autonomy of the individual and proclaimed freedom of religion, freedom of research, freedom of conscience and freedom of expression as human rights, continued to cherish religion and the church as the basis for moral action and as the foundation of the social order. If God did not exist, Voltaire wrote, we would have to invent him, even when it was only to protect his own property against thieves and to ensure that his own domestic staff would be more careful with the cleaning: the fear of God is the best political power and the employer's strongest sanction!

Two developments have undermined this last support of religion and the church and replaced it with new ideals of humanity, which introduced a positive passion into the lives of individual and community again, thus making nostalgia superfluous.

- The philosophy of universal history, which determines its own direction by the development of human thought in the footsteps of Hegel; its most prominent representatives were Ricardo, Marx, Darwin and Comte in the nineteenth century and all the ideological systems for the public domain in the twentieth. These can be summed up under the heading of the *feasible society*.
- The philosophy of contingent life which makes the experience of

the here and now the criterion for action, in the footsteps of Fichte; its most prominent representatives were Schelling, James, Dilthey and Nietzsche in the nineteenth century and all the psychological frameworks in the twentieth. These can be summed up under the heading of the *attainable self*.

Together, this ideal of the feasible society and the attainable self, of the *dominium terrae* and the self-sufficient individual, form the extreme consequence of belief in human autonomy. Both movements of thought – with all their cultural, political, economic, hygienic and ethical consequences – had a therapeutic aim: that of liberating people from powerlessness and fear, from the shackles of their soul which people had put on themselves and from the 'micromechanics of power' which the subjects themselves constantly reproduced (as Foucault observed). Here to a large degree they succeeded. Because God was for so long associated with the shackles of our soul and with the source of all power, we have dragged God into our process of liberation, and aimed our arrows at the divine as that which curtailed and oppressed us. So we have proclaimed the death of God with the trumpet of our liberation.

Our judgement on the *de facto* agnosis of our culture must therefore be a differentiated one. There is a trivial agnosis which has always existed and which, as Foucault says, fills our life with pleasure and usefulness. Alongside that there is a vindictive agnosis which consists in renouncing images of God that have taken their revenge on human life, especially what Delumeau calls '*la religion de la peur*'; these have associated God with the Western culture of shame. There is also a philosophical, epistemological agnosis, which regards the idea of God as an unacceptable, superfluous and therefore irrational addition to reality.

On the basis of this threefold agnosis, do we have sufficient reason, as Heidegger argued, to drop theology for a while and to stop thinking up God? Must theology be abandoned as a contribution to culture and as an academic discipline at the university?

I do not think so. Not only does a culture without God risk all too quickly filling the gaps in thought with new pseudo-gods, to whom life comes to be subjected – happiness, power, property, honour and pleasure – but there is time and again a tendency to give hasty and spurious explanations of the riddles of the world of an esoteric kind, and to offer all kinds of simplistic ways to salvation which are branded superstition and magic in the tradition of

6

rational thought. If we erase God from our thought, in the end all kinds of images connected with specific qualities of life which cannot be controlled and calculated escape us. Failing 'God', we no longer have any words for blessing and curse, necessity and happiness, origin and destiny, dedication and love. Even the best literary descriptions of these cannot replace the reference to God and the divine.

Those who look at the tradition of thinking about God rather more deeply, those who know the stories from the treasury of the holy scriptures of Jews, Christians and Muslims and the primal religious stories from Asia, Africa or Latin America, at the least also encounter a quite different face of God there: a God of blessing and favours, of freedom and love, of protection and healing, of comfort and repose, of peace and justice. And above all they find a God of crossing frontiers – visions, voices, miracles – which give a direction to life and society.

Now the reference to this other God – not a better God, but a better approach to the true God – is not immediately convincing. We have become sadder and wiser through our experiences of the God of fear and power who also had very good credentials in the scriptures. Are not all stories about God the echo of our human condition? Do we not project both blessing and curse, drama and happiness, constraint and liberation, on to God? Is not 'God', however depicted in images, a duplication, a reflection of our longings, our passions, our insight into the vicissitudes of history and of every human life? If we are talking about limit experiences, are these not reconstructions by our spirit which, when we must yield to the unknown – death, for example – just before the fatal moment brings out from the arsenal of images that we have built up what seems most likely to give us comfort in the hour of death?

Feuerbach already saw this very clearly in his day: our insights into our thought-patterns, as Kant and Hegel had developed and exposed them, also unmask the nature of our willing and striving, loving and hating, fearing and trembling. In all this we are simply anxious to save our own skins; we are led by self-seeing and self-lament, because we want to survive. God is often no more than another word for our urge to survive, a last support against irrevocable death. If God is thus the product of our thought, will and desire, then we should be leading ourselves up the garden path if we thought that we had to be responsible before God, *coram Deo*; or that we had to listen to what God said and to look to God beyond death. God, as the product of our thought, would be a phantom that we had to banish in order to be able to think purely, in pure reason. That would be an excuse for not being responsible for ourselves between cradle and grave, the only time that is given us, and for not devoting all our faculties to the highest possible quality of life and the greatest possible justice in society. It would be a hindrance to our personal development and to the exploration of our possibilities as men and women who form the tip of the evolution of all life.

Now it might seem – and some theologians have been quick to posit this – that the ideals of the feasible society and the attainable self have meanwhile been so damaged by the postmodern critique of universal history and the critique of the concept of subject that there is once again room for God and religion. But it is not as simple as that, because belief in God without reference to history and without the story of human beings as personally addressed by God is untenable within the Jewish-Christian tradition, and because postmodern philosophy is no less agnostic in principle than the modern tradition which it deconstructs: until recently, 'God is dead' has also been taken for granted as a starting point by the postmoderns. Only very recently has postmodern philosophical reflection again dared to tackle the question of religion.[7] It remains to be seen whether the question 'God?' can at least once again become an open question there.

It is certain that on the basis of the modern critique of religion we have drunk in doubt about God from our mothers' breasts. We are all too well aware of the human, all too human, elements in religious ideas. So even those who do believe in God carry around a heavier burden of iconoclasm and are more oppressed by the task of a negative theology than some past generations:[8] the God of our thought, the God of our stories, is not already the true God who must precede our doubt and our stories. All our patterns of thought about God, all our primal images about life and fantasies of the future beyond death are the result of the nature of the movement of thought itself, always in search of the transcendent, always biologized by crossing frontiers which finally founder on finitude and death. This meta-sense colours our culture: as Weber said, it has demystified the world, but even more it has demystified religion. Theology in particular contributed to this by historical-critical insight into the origin and development of traditions and the relationship between text and context. It has also exposed the pluralism of the truth, the contradictions and ambivalences of religious convictions, even within one and the same religious tradition. Therefore it was also mistrusted by the church magisterium and by large groups of believers, who were unable to go along with this subtle self-critical play of thought. In the nineteenth century, that led to a close link between popular belief and magisterium, fideism and orthodoxy. Fideism stands for the view that believing is a voluntary leap into the dark, on the authority of a revelation from God which transcends thought. Orthodoxy becomes synonymous with the acceptance of time-honoured doctrinal statements about God and the divine, and hardly any account is still taken of their historicity or of the possibility of change in them. At the beginning of the twentieth century this fideism resulted in the campaign against liberal theology and against the historical-critical reading of the Bible in what later came to be called the modernist crisis. On the Protestant side dialectical theology (Barth, Brunner, Tillich, Bultmann, Bonhoeffer, Ebeling, Cullmann, Moltmann, Pannenberg, Jüngel) took its starting point from this opposition to liberal theology, but through its marriage with existential philosophy and the philosophy of history, paradoxically this led to a deeper and critical insight into the nature of the human quest for God. On the Catholic side Vatican II took nineteenth-century criticism of religion seriously for the first time and made discussion of the nature of religious forms of expression a world-wide ecumenical programme of renewal.

Since then it has been impossible to deny that God can only be spoken of in this meta-sense: the one whom we call 'God' himself shares in the limitations of our thought. To think God therefore also means to think, to rethink, thought itself; in other words, constantly to remember that we are the ones who are thinking our God. Some theologians express that by saying that all our talk about God is metaphorical:[9] just as the metaphor, as a movement of language, makes our thought capable of moving from one field of attention to another, so too talk about 'God' is a movement of thought which shifts our attention to a field of meanings which has not yet been outlined. It breaks open the eternal present without taking us out of the way.

Something like this happens in poetry. When I say, 'The moon moves through the night like a silver mirror', I am saying something about the moon that says more about me and my mood at that moment than about the movements of the universe, the effect of mirrors or the course of the night. But it brings the moon, the seeming world and the experience of darkness together in a new field of meanings of which I myself form the centre as observer and poet, while at the same time it decentres me. The poetical metaphor takes me from where I am, away from other contemplations, and by way of shifting and displacing my perspective shapes consciousness and desire at the same time. Poetry and metaphor catch my attention; they open my thought, shape my conscience and confront me with myself. And because that is a lifelong and ongoing process, from all these metaphors I also form a scenario, a configuration of my life: my self-image and biography. In this way, for some people 'God' is one of the basic metaphors of their life. It is then said that talk about 'God' opens up new fields of meaning which remain closed to those who do not know the metaphor 'God'.

It goes almost unnoticed that those who want to think in such a universal-metaphorical way about God as I myself have done in the previous paragraphs put 'God' in quotation marks. However, that is yet another form of agnosis: namely that agnosis which has got over its vindictiveness and therefore has also seen through the proclamation of the 'death of God' as an impossible metaphor. 'God' as a metaphor for the unspeakable cannot and anyway need not be declared 'dead'; nowhere is it a limitation on our life, and literally it can do no harm. To put it even more strongly: where 'God' appears only between quotation marks, and becomes the appearance of all that is, the endless metamorphoses of being are confessed as the last support. This is precisely what forms the starting point of postmodernism as constructivism: we are the ones who have created our 'God' in accordance with our image.

Those who believe in God will rightly regard this as counterfeiting. If we want to keep God for thought, the solution of 'God' as a pretext for and a form of our agnosis will be unsatisfactory from the start. Theology involves expressing God beyond the mental expansion of metaphor. We want to remove the quotation marks from 'God'; we want to show – to show again – that although thought is to a large degree autonomous and limited by the laws of perception and language, in its reference to God it aims at fields of meaning which could not be reclaimed without God as a last point of reference. Therefore to admit God into thought at the same time means to reshape all our thought. Theology which wants to think God – without quotation marks – cannot avoid constantly interrogating the time-honoured ways of thinking in which there is no place for God just as much as the patterns in which space is in fact left for God, to see whether they are consistent and how important they are for human life and life together. That alone already justifies its place in culture.[10]

INTRODUCTION

The question of God cannot be robbed of its force either by the systematic pressure from firmly defined dogma or by the vague forgetfulness of God in the Western ideology of prosperity. The question is so strong that it directs our thought: in thinking about it we are taken over by it. But we must also invest in it to see what the yield is. The aim of theology is to readmit God into the domain of our thought by opening a number of windows on the infinite, and this book seeks to argue for this by actually doing it.

1

Taking Leave of God:
An Inevitable Process?
Sociological, philosophical and theological interpretations of the so-called secularization process

One of the most accessible sociological readings of the phenomenon of the declining attractiveness and plausibility of the religious traditions bears the label 'secularization'. From the middle of the nineteenth century on, philosophers, social scientists, historians and those involved in the study of religion began to claim that the idea of God and religious forms of expression were or were becoming 'obsolete' as a result of developments in science, technology and culture.[1] God and religion would disappear from the world, and only the *saeculum* would remain: the earthly, historical, empirical reality. The current in the social sciences which defended this thesis is usually labelled positivism. The name of Auguste Comte is associated with it. Others speak of rationalism and rationalization, referring above all to Max Weber.[2] The church and theology initially opposed this thesis vigorously, but gradually tried to qualify it by arguing that belief in God and the forms of religious life make a contribution to the further development of knowledge and the coming of age of humankind, provided that all elements alien to the world are rejected and God and religion really become 'worldly', 'secular'.[3] A good deal has been written in recent decades about both forms of the secularization (hypo)thesis – the one that is hostile to religion and the one that is well-disposed to it.[4] Certainly both have come under severe pressure. But the presupposition that God and religion have gradually become superfluous in culture deserves serious attention for more than one reason. Belief in God is not self-evident, nor did it drop from heaven: the religions of humankind have grown up in history and so they could also disappear again in the course of history. Everyone will concede that religions and churches have not been without significance for culture, but they have also been dependent on changing cultures. Is there an opportunity for religion in our culture, and what can the contribution of Christianity be to present-day Western culture?

If we are to be able to answer this question, first of all it is necessary to give a historical description and interpretation of the so-called process of secularization as sociologists, philosophers, historians and theologians have tried to fathom it.

SECULARIZATION: THE LOSS OF GROUND BY CHURCH AND RELIGION

In its most superficial meaning, secularization stands for the increasing loss of ground by the churches and religion that we can perceive in our churches, which are becoming increasingly empty, and that can be quantified very precisely by sociological investigation.[5] The statistics of declining involvement in the church are impressive enough as a cultural phenomenon: whereas in 1958 around three-quarters of the population of the Netherlands were still church members, in 1992 that had declined to 44%. The decline is even more dramatic among young people between twenty-one and thirty: from 80% in 1958 to 28% in 1992.[6] Among church members we see a steady decline in the number of Sunday churchgoers from 1965 on: in 1965 two-thirds of Catholics above the age of seven went to church every week; in 1995 that percentage had declined to less than 12%.[7] Between 1980 and 1995 the percentage declined from 23.7% to 1.8%. Of the around five million Catholics registered in the Netherlands, an average of around 600,000 go to church on Sundays. If we take church attendance every two weeks as an indicator of church membership, then around 18% of all Christians in the Netherlands are associated with the church. It is predominantly the generation above fifty which still goes to church. The involvement of young people is minimal. Of Dutch young people between seventeen and thirty, in

1991 only 11% went to church once every two weeks.[8] Although 80% of all children of Catholic parents are still baptized and two-thirds of them still present themselves for first communion around the age of seven, from middle school onwards participation notably declines. In urbanized areas like the suburbs the degree of involvement has declined to less than 10%. Churches are having to close and are either disappearing from the city landscape or are becoming museums of religious art. The number of parishes and communities is beginning to decline as a result of combination into larger units. The number of active Roman Catholic professional pastors (priests and pastoral workers) has declined from 9768 in 1963 to 2650 (1,700 priests, 200 deacons and 750 pastoral workers). Theological faculties are struggling with decreasing student numbers: between 1977 and 1992 the total number of students in the Netherlands studying theology at university declined by 27%. Between 1987 and 1993 the number of Catholic theological students declined by 21%, though after that there was some stabilization.

Association with the church in the sense of following a number of Christian rules of conduct also halved between 1966 and 1991, while the acceptance of toleration towards those of other views doubled.[9] Little precise information is available about religious practices in families, like reading from the Bible, prayers at mealtimes and personal prayer or meditation, but surveys indicate that they are declining and diminishing all along the line. When asked about the three most important spheres of interest in their lives, young people aged between fifteen and twenty-four in 1984 answered as follows: 51% mentioned sport as their top interest, 49% art and entertainment, 39% the solution of social problems like poverty and the violation of human rights, 35% a concern for the environment, 27% a commitment to science and technology, 20% an acquaintance with other cultures through travel and tourism, and 19% political questions. Among many other diverse answers religion scored only 4%.[10] That percentage was just as low in 1994.[11] The transfer of belief to the next generation is usually extremely difficult.[12] The exodus of Catholics from the church is almost entirely to be attributed to the generation effect: the older, more religious generations are being replaced by younger, less religious generations. Surveys among students indicate that religious upbringing or religious education have hardly any effect. Surveys of schoolchildren indicate that belief is not an important factor for them. When asked 'What does your faith mean in your life?' in 1994, 36% responded 'nothing', 27% 'a little', 22%

'something', and only 15% 'a lot'. Among students it proves that belief in God, where it is present at all, has become very diffuse. At best, above all in the younger age-groups, it can be said that there is rather greater uncertainty over matters like life after death or God as an aspect or 'field' of 'meaning'.[13]

The downward tendency mentioned above has continued in almost all the larger church communities, although there now seems to have been some stabilization. Figures from the Dutch Reformed Church and the Reformed Churches in the Netherlands show that the process of secularization took place earlier among the Dutch Reformed, faster among the Catholics, and last and also more slowly among the members of the Reformed Churches in the Netherlands.

Such lists of figures easily prove discouraging. They almost begin to act as a self-fulfilling prophecy: it seems like fighting a losing battle. Parents see that they are no longer succeeding in handing on their beliefs to their children. Pastors blame the church authorities. From the 1970s on, the central church government of the Roman Catholic Church has reacted to the development with a narrow conservatism: back to clear rules of behaviour for church members, a centralistic government, generally binding formulations of faith and a fight against dissidents, the nomination of bishops who are loyal to the authorities. Church leaders complain about theologians and catechists and focus on trust in doctrine and the magisterium. We all complain about difficult times and the bad influence of prosperity, progress and self-fulfilment, as if there is a culture which leads to darkness about God because it blinds men and women to transcendence: all attention is said to have been focused on concern for health, possessions, security and an assured future; on maximum pleasure and minimum suffering, and on as efficient use as possible of all the scientific and technical aids at our disposal.

Some lard their complaints with little sparks of hope: the church may be finished, but there is still plenty of interest in religion. New Age temples flourish in the cities; promises of wholeness by therapists are vastly successful; foreign religions arouse the curiosity of the media; discussions about values and norms, about the limits of life and death, the nature of our most intimate relationships and feelings, fill our television screens evening after evening and almost day and night, reflecting life as in a distorting mirror. They are a source of malicious pleasure, or comfort and support in barren times: here we have exploring the limits as entertainment.

Others point by way of compensation to developments elsewhere in the world, where the religions still dominate the scene. Islam is manifesting a renaissance in many countries of the world. Hinduism and Buddhism are not losing their following and are growing as a result of demographic developments. Roughly one in three inhabitants of the earth are Christian. Of these, two out of three live in the southern hemisphere and of them two out of three are under twenty-five: that makes 400 million young people who are Christians 'with no hard feelings', who expect hope and emancipation from their church. Protestants look with amazement and jealousy at evangelical and Pentecostal successes in Africa and Latin America and at the steady growth of conservative currents. Catholics note – some with envy and horror, others full of amazement and joyful relief – the millions who follow the pope on his many world trips.[14] The prior and the monastery of Taizé have been a permanent crowd-puller for more than thirty years. It is no longer conceivable for pilgrimages to Czestochowa, Santiago de Compostela, Lourdes, Fatima and Medjugorje not to feature in the travel brochures of tour operators. And the nicest touch of all is that all those so-called unbelievers clearly cannot get by without religious rituals and remain keen enthusiasts about the aesthetic aspects of the Christian cultural heritage. Museums of religious art, religious music and Bible courses for art lovers flourish as never before. The media now and then make God and religion a new hype: *My God!*

Even liberal and socialist political readers cry out in their turn that the Christian heritage and its values must not be lost if we do not want to lose the foundations of law and freedom, solidarity and hope.

Between the extremes of radical atheism and active belief in God, both of which have become rare in Europe, others see a growth in the anonymous and amorphous religiosity of the great mass of people: this is a gigantic religious market, a potential that must be guided in the right direction.

It is clear that even if we agree over the figures, the interpretations of the loss of face by the church and religion are very different. But a few things are certain: the forms of Christian life within Western culture are no longer taken for granted. In Europe active believers form a minority in society. The culture as a whole does not lose any sleep over the departure from traditional views of God. Many are making their own investigations of what is on offer in the religious market. No clear new 'great stories' are on offer. It is possible to pick and choose between movements and spiritual groups of all kinds, but they do not form a new broad pattern of values or meaningful wholes.[15] The many sociological interpretative models of this pluralism and this fragmentation certainly have a heuristic value. They make it possible to see more clearly how things are: a more individualistic lifestyle, a more differentiated offer of meaning, greater social tolerance, the adaptation of religion to modern society, the diminution of involvement in another, decisive reality and – albeit in a relatively small group – a drift towards alternative religion. They do not explain the leave-taking from God; rather, they seek reasons for the continued existence of this diversity of religious 'niches'. Nor do they still offer alternatives like Comte's sociological positivism in the nineteenth century and Weber's rationalization theory at the beginning of the twentieth.

SECULARIZATION: A LONG HISTORY

Owen Chadwick[16] is perhaps right when he points out that the problems which for some centuries have been denoted by the term secularization are not an invention of the seventeenth or eighteenth century, but already have their roots in the Middle Ages. We already find all the factors of the so-called secularization process – the conflict between faith and science, church and state, religious ideals and actual practice, but also less involvement in the church and critical approaches to the sources of faith – from the fourteenth and fifteenth centuries on. For that reason there was also no question of a complete Christianization or a *societas christiana*.

Stephen Sykes[17] goes even further and reminds us that from the beginning Christianity has been 'an essentially contested concept': conflicts immediately arose over the identity of the Jesus movement within Judaism and within the culture of Greece and Rome. Jesus' own fate and that of many of his followers is bound up with this conflict. The demands which religions make on people and the ideals that they offer can usually be met only by privileged individuals: 'shamans', 'clergy', 'religious'.

But in the Renaissance, the Reformation and the Enlightenment something happened in the head and heart of Europeans which put the conflict between Christianity and culture on a completely new basis. It is this conflict – with all its intrinsic ambivalences, as the different ways of interpreting them indicate – that can be indicated with the battle-cry and the watchword 'secularization'.

This is also the drift of Paul Valadier's urgent thesis in his *L'Église en procès*:[18] for too long, in the name of a false picture of God, Christianity has made common cause with the strong forces of culture (those with political, technological and economic power), rather than adopting a critical attitude towards them. When these began to follow their own, autonomous course, the church seized hold of the domain of the schooling and upbringing of citizens and got a moral grip on their conscience. Now that most people have thrown off this yoke of the church, it is important to restore the right hierarchy of values in the relationship between gospel and culture. This was also the task of the early church. Here modernity does not coincide with secularization, for this term presupposes as a starting point a kind of theocratic situation and ecclesiastical and clerical domination, nor does modernity coincide with atheism or the over-estimation of themselves by human beings. Modernity is about taking leave of false images of God, church censorship and the overestimation of themselves by human beings.[19]

Finally, there is the thesis of the missiologist Anton Wessels,[20] which has already been mentioned, that secularization in fact amounts to the failure of inculturation and that in Europe, too, belief in God down the centuries has been dependent on a virtually successful syncretism with the deeply rooted images, symbols and myths of popular culture. The leave-taking of God, religion and church is said to be caused by our fear of imaging which accompanied the European Reformation, and our contempt for 'myths' which accompanied the 'demythologizing process' of the twentieth century.

Thus 'secularization' is a comprehensive, perhaps too comprehensive, key term for what at least so far has been a typically Western concept and phenomenon; hardly any definition can be found which does not also contain an interpretation. J. Sperna Weiland writes cynically that it is 'one of those vague words which offer themselves where thought stops',[21] following a critique which A. J. Nijk already made in his book on secularization.[22] The sociologist David Martin has criticized the concept of 'secularization' because of the circular argument that it contains: 'God is dead. Therefore secularization must be occurring. Therefore secularization is a coherent notion.'[23] With historians of culture, too, there is a great danger of dogmatic presuppositions, as if secularization were an unavoidable and irreversible world-wide cultural phenomenon. But precisely because of the ambivalence of the terminology and because it is such a comprehensive umbrella concept, we cannot avoid definitions. Charles West tried to define it like this at an ecumenical consultation in 1966: 'Secularization is the withdrawal of all areas of life and thought from religious – and finally also metaphysical – control and the attempt to understand and live in these areas in the terms which they alone offer.'[24] Peter Berger was even briefer: 'Secularization is the process by which sectors of society and culture are removed from the domination of religious institutions and symbols.'[25] W. Hartmann put it like this: 'Secularization entails that particular ideas, insights and experiences which have been originally gained "in faith" and were bound up with faith come under the disposition of a supposedly creative human reason.'[26] In all these cases we have 'the diminution of relations with another, decisive reality', according to G. Dekker[27] – in society, in culture, and also in personal life (with all its religious, ecclesiastical and cultural forms of expression). Owen Chadwick, who has been mentioned above, defines secularization as '... a growing tendency in mankind to do without religion, or to try to do without religion', but at the same time points out that in this definition everything depends on the definition of 'religion'.[28] In every case the term 'secularization' is a slogan and at the same time a polemical term, but the uses of it are different, depending on the standpoint of the speaker. According to Lauwers,[29] a polemical term relating to the legitimacy of a division between church and world, church and state, develops into a term for elucidating the problems of the church in pastoral work and theology and, at a deeper level, into an almost unavoidable metaphysical and historical process of rationalization which is under way all over the world, as we already saw with Weber (and Gauchet).[30] J. Sperna Weiland also ultimately thinks that: 'Secularization is the transition, extending over many centuries, from a metaphysical experience and interpretation of reality to another experience and interpretation of reality which in any case is not metaphysical. Here that historical, human, finite world is the horizon of human responsibility and human destiny; or, to put it more briefly: secularization is the process in which with the falling away of all "higher" worlds only the historical, human finite world (*saeculum*) remains.'[31]

So there are plenty of definitions, but they are not yet explanations. They mark out someone's position. The term 'transition' is characteristic: clearly something has happened to us, but the transition cannot be described in terms of a *terminus a quo* (where and when did it begin?) or a *terminus ad quem* (where is it going to and when will the transition be complete?). However, a great many hypotheses about and interpretations of the causes have been produced by historians, sociologists, philosophers and theologians.

Some historians are inclined to give a quite precise date on which the process of secularization in Europe began: on 8 April 1646, Longueville, the French delegate at the Westphalian peace talks, proposed that 'for the sake of peace' the Elector of Brandenburg, who had to cede some of his territory to Sweden, the victors, should be compensated by the secularization of a number of areas which hitherto had fallen under church jurisdiction. Thus the process of secularization will have begun in the discussions about property between church and state. The terminology is said to take up medieval thought about the distinction between the profane and the sacral, the temporal and the spiritual spheres of jurisdiction.[32] *Saeculum est id quod extra claustrum*: the world is everything that lies outside the walls of the monastery, is the definition given in an eleventh-century work.[33] And the Testament of St Francis begins with the words *Exivi de saeculo*: I have abandoned the world, or left the world behind me.[34] Right down to present-day canon law, *saecularisatio* means removal from church office or, more precisely, the loss of 'clerical' status, or also the withdrawal of church buildings, monasteries and the like from their religious purpose.[35] So although the terms *saecularis* and *saecularisatio* are certainly older than 1646, the Peace of Westphalia which settled the wars of religion between Catholicism and the Reformation, the Spanish crown and the German rulers, marks the transition to the idea of the autonomous state and the division of church and state, if only for the moment under the dubious slogan *cuius regio, illius et religio* (whoever possesses the land [i.e. the ruler] determines what religion shall prevail).

Against this historical background we can at any rate understand that secularization is loaded with a certain solemnity. As I have already pointed out, it is a battle cry, a programme for action, first uttered by the Renaissance and then by the Enlightenment, which sought to put an end to the deadly embrace of church and culture from the declining years of the Roman Empire onwards, in the aspirations of Charlemagne, the Holy Roman Empire and Habsburg imperialism. Some scholars have spoken in this connection of the fall of Christianity as a result of the shift under Constantine; perhaps with the best intentions, Justinian had the faith of the church translated into imperial laws, and from the time of Charlemagne the faith could be propagated with violence. The history of investiture and of the Inquisition govern the form of the

20

medieval theocracy: with the bishops of Rome on the restored throne of David, which takes over the title 'Mother church' from the original church of Jerusalem. At the level of symbols, prayers, values and laws, icons and buildings the unity of *sacerdotium* and *imperium* becomes internalized.[36] The first specifically theological treatises on the church are about precisely these questions, which legitimate the jurisdiction of the church. Boniface VIII was merely the tip of a far broader and more lasting development. From this perspective, secularization means liberation from the cloisters of clericalism and the end of all dogmatic compulsion and violence.

Of course this is a coloured picture of cultural developments in the church between 400 and 1500. A theological interpretation of the history of Europe could also take another form: what happened was the exponential development of the visions that Isaiah and Paul had at their call: to be a light for the peoples, the inculturation of the gospel in the world of the Romans, the Goths, the Germans, the Franks, the Visigoths and the Slavs. New basilicas arose on the old sacrificial sites of the original religions. The former Germanic and Celtic feasts of the seasons were coupled with the commemoration of the Lord and the Jewish festivals, the Jewish fasts, the Jewish symbols of incense, light, music and song.[37] This was a miraculous incarnation of the Jewish heritage in ever new circumstances, just as of course that Jewish heritage was the result of many kinds of cultural influences from Mesopotamia, Egypt and Greece. Religions do not just come on their own, and the Jewish-Christian tradition does not escape this law. Human religions must live on the linguistic and cultural material that is to hand in order to weave a new symbolic universe from it. However, for Christianity a main thread is provided: everything that happened to Jesus, the content of the apostolic witness (Acts 1.21–22), what has been believed always and everywhere and by all (Vincent of Lérins). That is the scarlet thread, the rule of faith (*regula fidei*) which forms the unity and identity of the Jesus movement in the midst of all cultures.

However, there is something to be said for the first reading. The *regula fidei* has frequently to yield to secular interests, to the interests of the *saeculares*, i.e. the knights and judges, the rulers and liege lords, and the bishops and beneficiaries allied with them. Without the prophetic criticism of the *regulares*, the monks of Benedict, Bernard and later Dominic and Francis, the marriage of church and culture would beyond doubt have led the church into an even greater fall.

Twice in the history of Europe the thread of faith which keeps

21

the church still standing in the original vision of Isaiah snapped because it was pulled too far by the assimilation with culture: in 1054 because the Byzantines no longer thought acceptable the intrusion of German, Celtic and Arab elements into liturgy and confession and the exclusive claims of Rome to the cathedra of Moses and the see of Peter; and in 1520, because *sacerdotium* and *imperium* threatened to block sight of Jesus' fate and mission as the crucified Messiah.

After that, the twofold break bifurcated further countless times and was handed on like original sin with the export of European culture and the mission of the church to the newly discovered cultures of Latin America, Africa and Asia. Thus the *de facto* divisions of Christianity also coincide with the interlocking of the two 'swords', which was taken too far, and with a lack of self-criticism – *ecclesia semper reformanda* – on the part of European cultural Christianity.

The fundamental theocratic conception of the state – in which all laws regulating property, trade and security were deeply determined by the Law of God, itself under the supervision of the church (bishops, abbots, the pope) – then gave way, at least in the West under the influence of the Reformation, to an aristocratic and ultimately democratic idea of the state. In this the free citizens became subjects of their own law, and the identity of each state was the result of the recognition of its frontiers by others. That the earth is 'the Lord's', that all land is the grant of the Creator, that the ultimate purpose of life is defined by the gospel and that there is no salvation outside the church, hitherto symbolized by the omnipresence of church jurisdiction, the patchwork of monastic and diocesan immunities and the cultural supervision of moral behaviour by theologians: all this became brittle, frayed and fell apart into different disciplines.

Reformation philosophers of law like Christian Thomasius, and Enlightenment philosophers like Locke, Rousseau and Kant, further developed the notion of the autonomous state and the autonomous morality of the free citizen. Political leaders like Napoleon, Bismarck and the Russian czars confiscated everything that belonged to former areas of monastic immunity. Napoleon stabled his horses in the ruins of the abbey of Cluny, which was taken down stone by stone to provide the – expensive – cornerstones of the palaces of a new bourgeois élite. Later he imprisoned Pius VII in the Vatican and forbade the establishment of any monastery in France and Belgium. The *Reichsdeputations-*

hauptschluss of 1803 then stripped more than 300 abbeys, 18 dioceses and 4 archdioceses of virtually all their land and capital. For some decades the czars compelled all monks to live in the country and there to practise 'a useful profession'. The Russian Revolution and the Stalinist terror against the church simply continued this policy.

Meanwhile, after 150 years of opposition to this secularization under property law and the division of church and state which went with it, the church in East and West terminated its concordats and privileges virtually everywhere and with this termination found peace. Despite repeated attempts at restoration, within a century the typical European process of denominational pillarization, which attempted to compensate for the lost sphere of jurisdiction in other areas of culture (schools, health care, the press, party politics and even the sphere of sport, amusement and art), had become an anachronism as a result of de-confessionalization and the loss of any effects of the faith on culture.

We can lament this, be content with it, rejoice in the development or try to turn the tide. But it seems far more important to recognize under the superficial structure of this secularization of politics and cultural institutions an event which goes far deeper: the event of Enlightenment itself, the modern history of freedom, the birth of autonomous men and women who have come of age. Sociologists and philosophers have made it clear to us that at that deeper level secularization is an emancipating, liberating event. It means the emancipation of dissidents (as in the case of the English dissenters who got their opportunity under the influence of John Locke and as a result of the succession of William and Mary). It meant freedom of research for scientists, freedom of legislation for politicians and jurists, freedom of government for citizens, freedom of opinion for the press. Toleration, human rights, ecumenism, pluralism of religious convictions, freedom of religion and freedom of con-science: all this is the concrete fruit of the history of freedom in the West. Enlightenment means that human beings come of age, out of the tutelage which they had brought on themselves. Kant spoke of 'the departure of man from a self-imposed tutelage',[38] and indeed, as Weber pointed out, all areas of life were rationalized.

After the nineteenth-century opposition to the Enlightenment a great many twentieth-century theologians embraced the values of the French Revolution (freedom, equality, fraternity). Following Troeltsch and Weber, people like Gogarten, Bonhoeffer, Chenu, Metz and Schillebeeckx emphasized the fundamental secularity of

23

the Jewish-Christian tradition which fought against all false religion, any idolization of historical institutions, rites and formulae, and gave God alone the honour and the last judgement on history. That created the theological space for the coming of age and the true 'worldliness' of Christians (to use Bonhoeffer's term) and again brought to light the 'glorious freedom of the children of God'.

Encouraging as all this was, this development, too, was not without ambivalence. The Enlightenment is not the continuation of Isa. 49.6 with other means, although it made the same claim. 'The departure of man from a self-imposed tutelage' did not just bring freedom from the old idols, but also put new ones on a pedestal. Whereas up to the Enlightenment people thought that they were living *coram Deo*, i.e. under the eye of God as the last criterion of the good, after that they began to live as 'a God in the depths of their thoughts'. The hybris of the autonomous person is that he or she has replaced God's providential supervision of the vicissitudes of nature and culture with the illusion of human cybernetics, rather than trying to think of the two things together. The just criticism of an image of God that enslaved freedom led to a scientific atheism and later to a banal post-theism of scientific and technological rationality. It produced a mechanistic picture of the world in which analysis was tacked on to analysis, explanation on to explanation, without it being possible to indicate any meaningful connection which integrated the whole. As Eco remarked: there is no Plan, but only planning. Reality becomes friable; everything is hypothetical and open to criticism; there is no supporting desire and no subject supported by God. As Foucault remarks, it has exploded. Very little remains of the human person through whom God is expressed and comes to speak.

The humanistic atheism and the post-theistic humanism which have supported Western civilization since the Enlightenment, which – against the opposition of the church – produced the civic freedoms and anchored them in law, lacks a point of reference to support it, a criterion, an auto-immune system. Thus, as Cardinal Danneels pointed out,[39] the Western cultural system produces its own poisons: freedom degenerates into individualism and narcissism, which loses sight of altruism and alterity; tolerance leads to an unguided pluralism of values, to a confusing loss of direction and uncertainty; openness and communication lead to the exhibitionism of 'the argument' and 'chatter' into which the personal conscience is drawn: 'we are sated with speaking and deaf for the word' (as

Danneels put it). All over the world damage is done to the unassailable, unattainable mystery of God which rings out in the human person. Lesslie Newbigin thinks that we in the West have returned to a pagan culture and that the gospel must be presented anew to this culture as it was once upon a time: as a counter culture, as 'foolishness to the Greeks', especially through a restoration of eschatology and teleology. Human beings have a vocation before the throne of God. And by reflecting on the meaning of Christian freedom: powerful witness, without compulsion and violence, in exemplary Christian solidarity.[40]

Indeed there is no mistaking the fact that the system of freedom and progress has itself led to new violence and counter-violence, to a balance of terror, to competition from cradle to grave, to a micromechanics of power between individuals, groups, parties and nations. And it draws illogical, irrational, occult and esoteric reactions from people who have been crushed by this omnipresent logic and mechanics: the 'cultures of unreason' are rife and fill the shelves of our bookshops. They provide the scenarios for children's imagination in 'Fun Factory': the myths that we drive out and the fairy tales that we want to oppose return with unconcealed power as fearful monsters and spectres.

SECULARIZATION: IRREVERSIBLE?

Thus an uncritical reception of the process of secularization seems impossible. There is certainly a need for critical opposition, and perhaps we have a new *'casus* or *status confessionis'*. The evangelization of Europe is a serious task. But here we must learn from history and see how what Blumenberg has called the legitimacy of modernity[41] can be united with the critical force of the gospel.

The medieval synthesis of the *terrena non despicere et coelestia desiderare* (do not despise the earthly but strive for the heavenly) itself already represented a notable shift from the early-Christian and at all events Neoplatonic sense of life, as that characterized faith and spirituality until at least the eleventh century. Formerly the tendency was to say *terrena despicere et coelestia desiderare* (despise the earthly and strive for the heavenly). The Middle Ages could realize this synthesis by a specific reading of Rom. 12.2: *nolite conformari huic saeculo* (do not be conformed to this world) in the light of the next verse *sed reformamini in novitate sensus vestri* (but learn to perceive in a new way), or of the preceding verse: *ut exhibeatis corpora vestra hostiam viventem, sanctam, Deo placentem* (offer your bodies to God as a living, holy sacrifice, well-pleasing to God). They organized virtue and training for virtue (*paideia*) on the basis of classical ideals, but with a clear doxological focus – everything to the glory of God – and with a strong emphasis on the self-surrender of the crucified Jesus, which also included his body. Even then that did not lead to a complete identification with the gospel, but people were still aware that the partial identification was a perverse identification and a sin.

The same synthesis remained in the Reformation and the Counter-Reformation, for all the mutual differences over the medieval synthesis of the earthly and heavenly. In all kinds of variants for both those who were active and those who were less active in the church – and at that time there were also plenty of the latter – the question of life continued to be connected with the question of God as formulated by Augustine: 'What then am I, *my God*? What is my nature? It is characterized by diversity, by life of many forms, utterly immeasurable.'[42] The doxological focus and the fundamental involvement with the crucified Jesus remained the core of the Reformation protest against the scholastic synthesis of human freedom and the grace of God. For the Catholic Counter-Reformation it was just as important to rethink this synthesis, in which the interpretation of the Augustinian heritage (Jansenism) played a major role. Despite all the anthropological and ecclesiological differences between Rome and the Reformation, there thus remained a far greater agreement over the interpretation of the *saeculum*.

But the Renaissance and the Enlightenment gradually led to this synthesis of earthly and heavenly options being experienced as an antithesis. Thus the questions 'Who am I?', 'What is life?' and 'What is truth?' could gradually be detached from the essential content which Augustine had given them by the invocation 'My God!' Not only was the doxological framework of the fundamental questions of meaning lost, but also their context, which was in principle metaphysical and eschatological. The real 'concern' of reason proved to be not what is defined as person, life and truth in the life of God, but exclusively the autonomous self-determination of it by human beings.

Theology became anthropology and cosmology, initially still with God as the basis – God as the origin and primal goal of human beings and nature – but no longer with God as the Living One to whom life itself puts questions. The quest for human autonomy and the striving for the *dominium terrae* then quickly amounted to the leave-taking of the idea of God in personal living and in the pattern of cultural, political, scientific and technological life. Then God no longer had a demonstrable place in the spheres of nature or history, law and politics, or art and technology, far less in the spheres of heart and feeling, fear and emotion, suffering and death. God was excluded from all these domains, or rather, God was not mentioned in them at all. In post-theism God was neither confessed nor disputed, neither doubted nor affirmed, nor even discounted in a methodical not-knowing or agnosticism: organized atheism or agnosticism suffered at least as strongly from a loss of face and members as theism and religion. For that very reason secularization as a watchword and battle cry is an anachronism: the very designation of reality as *saeculum* at least still presupposed the idea of *caelum* (heaven) and *aevum* (time) as categories of our perception and modelled the rhythm of our life on them. What could still be secularized if no rainbow was spanned over cradle and grave, field and harvest, land and people; if the name of God was no longer evoked, and blessings were no longer looked for from any church? Wasn't Augustine's remark, 'How shall I find You, if I am without memory of You?',[43] applicable here?

Research by psychologists and sociologists of religion shows that most Europeans no longer believe in a God who personally intervenes in their lives. They live *etsi Deus non daretur* (literally, just as they would if God did not exist), but without the force which that word still had as a protest against enslaved human autonomy (in Grotius and Bonhoeffer). They no longer orientate their lives on divine, absolute commandments; they do not turn to God in prayer, even for help; they no longer explain the historical and physical process by means of the first cause and final purpose. And those who still call themselves believers do not significantly deviate from those who call themselves non-believers in the orientation of their lives, amusements, the way in which they spend their time, their views of the future, patterns of consumption or images of sickness.

'God is dead,' Nietzsche made his 'madman' trumpet, but by his own confession he was too early for the definitive departure, although he already began the *Requiem Aeternam Deo*.[44] It would be another century before this became a universal sense of life, and was really communicated to church and theology.

After a century of powerful opposition, with an appeal to divine revelation and the church's magisterium, documented in mission, evangelization and revival; in denominational segregation, emanci-

27

pation and Christian politics; in the pressure on confession and the infallibility of dogma (1825–1925),[45] there followed fifty years of surrender, a turn towards the world, a recognition of the faults of the church, liberation from religious pathologies, a return to the sources of tradition and a renewal of the language of faith: 'God is dead, long live theology! The churches are the tomb of God, long live the church outside the church!'[46] In a miraculous metamorphosis, after antithesis and opposition, the churches and Christians strove for a new synthesis of the church and the world, started by Brunner and Tillich, Bonhoeffer and Gogarten, on the ground of the Reformation. This was taken over by Chenu, Guardini and Rahner on the Catholic side, received by the World Council of Churches after New Delhi in 1961 and by Vatican II, and further systematized in ecumenical unanimity by Gollwitzer, Moltmann, Pannenberg and Jüngel.[47] The synthesis is, according to the title of a book by Jüngel, *God as the Mystery of the World*.[48] God is the deepest mystery of the world as it is. God is not necessary nor an X factor for the *saeculum*, cosmos or *humanum*. But God is more than necessary, gratuitous freedom, surplus of love, future; God is the essential *arreton*: the indefinable, incomprehensible, inexpressible.[49] I shall synthesize these attempts later in this book.

So present-day theology no longer speaks of a God who enslaves human beings or of the theocratic pretensions of the church. Fundamentalist reactions seem more like rearguard battles and regressive phenomena.[50] But only conservative groups and churches are growing. Clearly the alliance with the Enlightenment and the theological critique of religion (Gogarten, Barth, Bonhoeffer, Tillich) as a response to the religious critique of modernity no more makes Christianity credible than did the obsessive opposition to the Enlightenment in the nineteenth and beginning of the twentieth century. All along the line we have to note that neither the theological opposition to the process of secularization nor the theological surrender to it have been able to turn the tide. The evaporation of the church and the departure from religious meaning and a hierarchy of values seem to be steadily increasing. As sociological investigations show,[51] 'God in Europe' is a diminishing factor. Indeed from the beginning of the 1980s there has been a loud call – *ex cathedra Petri* – for 'a new evangelization of Europe', 'a new humanism with God',[52] 'Common Witness',[53] and a vital and coherent theology.[54] The theme of the Eighth Assembly of the World Council of Churches in Harare in 1998 was 'Turn to God, Rejoice in Hope!'

The question is whether such a re-evangelization is possible and what the conditions for it should be. Though Nietzsche was premature in his call 'God is dead', does not our 'Long live God!' come all too late? Cannot the humanism that we advocate, gasping for breath, racing against the clock and shuddering at our technological capacity, do just as well, or even better, without God?[55] Or does belief in God and reflection on the idea of God add something irreplaceable to the question of the survival of the earth and humankind? Does it in fact make any difference to anthropology to ask 'Who am I?' in the quest for our identity, or to ask, 'Who am I, *my God*?' as Augustine did?[56] Does it make any difference to prop up the quest for true humanity with the 'Our Father'?[57]

CONCLUSION

That process of the evaporation of the church, the departure from traditional ideas of God and the forgetfulness of the biblical epic which we stubbornly but anachronistically continue to call secularization, is an enormous challenge to church and theology which could also become a *kairos* from God, a reprieve. What is more attractive than to re-read the tradition with a renewed sense of our narrative competence; to rethink metaphysics now that we can see the limits of physics so clearly; and to reform the church, now that we see that in so many changed contexts and non-Western cultures, forms of the church are on offer to which neither the dust of centuries nor the violent bloodshed of centuries of the exercise of power in the name of God cling? But in that case we have to recognize both the opposition and the surrender which successively characterized the mainstream of theology in the nineteenth and twentieth centuries as inadequate reactions. We must no longer dress ourselves in the emperor's new clothes: those who do not take the process of secularization seriously, and think that the nineteenth-century opposition to it must be continued with other means, forget how much faith and theology have gradually been stripped by the dominant culture of rationality; those who take the process too seriously, and think that the twentieth-century acceptance must be continued even more radically in a new alliance of the ideals of humanity with the power of the gospel, are prematurely supposing that our nakedness has been clothed. Neither opposition nor surrender is an adequate reaction. What we need is a critical loyalty, a theology 'beyond secularization', and forms of faith and church which can work as a ferment within the autonomous ideals of *saeculum*, *politicum* and *humanum*. How can we bring God and religion back within the domain of thought? What windows are available to us which can make a view of God once again possible in our culture?

2

The Many Colours of Agnosis
The complex roots of taking leave of God

If the notion of an inevitable secularization will not wash, what is the basis for *de facto* taking leave of God in our culture? This question is not so simple to answer, above all because the leave-taking from God has been so massive and so deep: any reference to God as something or someone behind reality, let alone to 'My God' or 'Our Father', already sounds like a voice from a strange world. There are I and you, we and the world, and within it many riddles and secrets, but no 'Third Party', no 'Other', no 'Superior Being' distinct from the reality which is known to us; no criterion, guideline or conscience other than the laws that we have made ourselves; no judge of living and dead. Of course we also recognize values and purposes for life – we even make very great demands on upbringing, work, comfort and leisure – but there are no 'higher purposes'; there is no 'journey of the soul', let alone a 'salvation history'.

We already saw in Chapter 1 that most people in Europe 'have no need of God'. Although that is not based on an inevitable historical process, as positivism predicted, it does involve the idea of God itself and not just the religious forms of expression. So although we do not have a militant atheism, we do have a widespread agnosis. This whole new situation of a more obvious unreligious, post-theistic[1] starting point must have consequences for the way in which theology and catechesis discuss the question of God. A first requirement is that we introduce the necessary nuances into actual agnosis.[2]

31

There is a trivial agnosis which has always existed and which fills life with pleasure and profit. Alongside that there is a vindictive agnosis which consists in renouncing images of God which have marred the pleasure in human life, especially what Delumeau calls 'la religion de la peur', the religion of fear, associating God with the Western culture of guilt and shame. There is also a philosophical agnosis which regards the idea of God as an unacceptable, superfluous and therefore irrational addition to reality. This agnosis has assumed the form of a critique of the metaphysical concept of God in theism. This criticism of theism is essentially bound up with the concept of modernity, with the secularization thesis and positivism. Finally – though this needs separate treatment – there is a far more aporetic and enigmatic agnosis which cannot reconcile the idea of God with the bitter riddle of the suffering caused by disasters, wars, sickness and death and all the evil that people do to one another (see Chapter 3).[3]

TRIVIAL AGNOSIS

I have already remarked that belief in God is not a matter of course. It is not so difficult to banish any notion of god or gods. In this sense a deliberate atheism is not a modern phenomenon. Although the great Greek philosophers like Plato and Aristotle regarded atheism in the sense of the denial of the existence of a supreme or first eternal and religious Idea or Spirit behind all the vicissitudes of reality as irrational and immoral, there were others like Aristophanes, in his satire *The Clouds*, who already wiped the floor with this 'God of the philosophers' and in so doing to the present day have easily won over the mockers: scepticism and doubt about the order of things and the meaning of life is not so difficult to express. An attitude that says 'Let us eat, drink and be merry, for tomorrow we die' has very old credentials. Both the Bible and the Qur'an know of the temptation to swear by everyday life, to experience its short duration and to try to get everything possible out of it. We find traces of that in the later books of the Bible, in Ecclesiastes, Jesus Sirach and Wisdom. We also constantly come across the seduction of this agnosis in the Psalms. Psalm 4.8 speaks about the pleasure of people who stake everything on the harvest of grain and grape. Psalm 20.8 speaks about those who seek their power in chariots and horses. Psalm 5.10–11 speaks about people who rebel against God and know no norms of truth. God is invoked against those who forget the poor (Ps. 9.19), against the corrupt generation that does violence to the weak (Ps. 12.6,8), against those who pervert the law, and usurers who mock God and the commandments (Ps. 10.3):

The wicked boasts of the desires of his heart,
and the man greedy for grain curses and renounces the Lord.
In the pride of his countenance the wicked does not seek him;
all his thoughts are, 'There is no God.'

This is expressed in the famous complaint in Psalm 14:

The fool says in his heart,
'There is no God.'
They are corrupt, they do abominable deeds,
there is none that does good.
The Lord looks down from heaven upon the children of men,
to see if there are any that act wisely,
that seek after God.
They have all gone astray, they are all alike corrupt;
there is none that does good, no, not one.

So for the true Israelite, belief in God means sobriety and sensibility about our actions, responsibility. Psalm 14 speaks of 'those who devour the people'. Agnosis in the sense of 'taking no heed of God' is tantamount to morally irresponsible action. Moral indifferentism – out of caprice, says Psalm 17.4 – and belief in God cannot go together. Consistent and trivial agnosis and moral indifference often will. Psalm 14 already speaks of the masses 'who eat up my people as they eat bread, and do not call upon the Lord'. In our culture, too, we find the everyday, trivial easy-going approach which is satisfied with 'bread and circuses' and also the flat morality of self-interest which respects nothing, which exclaims 'our people first' and shuts its eyes to the fate of refugees, women on social security, asylum seekers, the enslaved, prostitutes. Over against this are those who allow their consciences to be addressed by God and follow the law of God (Pss. 15.2–5; 16.7; 17.3; 18.22–25). Of course that does not mean that all unbelievers suffer from moral indifference. Certainly not all those who 'believe in God' are by definition moral heroes and saints. But banishment of God from reflection out of self-interest, utility or pleasure will affect above all the weak, the poor, the modest. Isn't it an unmistakable historical concatenation of circumstances that the leave-taking of God in Western culture in the name of progress, science and technology has created a void in international relations and blurred the limits of power? The death of God – in the sense of a dry-eyed leave-taking of the ecclesiastical and religious sheet anchors of public morality – has made the great economic systems of capitalism and communism founder on the boundless injustice and caprice of élites. That churches and believers have sometimes made common cause here and in any case have been too late in reacting critically does not alter the fact that the fundamental agnosis of the market, the banks and the civil service has had a pitiless effect on the fate of the peoples of Asia, Africa, Latin America and Eastern Europe.

There is also a less dramatic, more everyday agnosis: the agnosis of the citizen who derives all his values from self-interest: the culture of the emancipated European city-dweller, who swears by art, amusement and scholarship. Friedrich Schleiermacher, on the threshold of the nineteenth century, addressed such people with much foresight in a famous philippic:

> From of old faith had not been every man's affair. At times but few have discerned religion itself ... Now especially the life of cultivated people is far from anything that might have even a resemblance to religion. Just as little, I know, do you worship the Deity in sacred retirement, as you visit the forsaken temples. In your ornamental dwellings, the only sacred things to be met with are the sage maxims of our wise men, and the splendid compositions of our poets. Suavity and sociability, art and science have so fully taken possession of your minds, that no room remains for the eternal and holy Being that lies beyond the world.[4]

Finally there is the agnosis of the 'full diary'. Daily concerns demand so much time and attention in a complex society that as a result the idea of God withers and becomes unnecessary ballast. In this connection Dorothee Sölle speaks of a 'banal atheism'. Sociologists speak of a 'hedonistic-utilitarian complex of values'.

Such terms are dangerous, because they too quickly pronounce a value judgement. Theologians and preachers all too easily derive pessimistic views of culture from them, which have to serve as the background for a call to conversion and a return to the 'God of the fathers'. However, it seems that much more is involved. The verdict on our contemporaries also applies to ourselves. It is better to postpone it.

Could it be that the actual picture of God which has grown up in Western culture is itself part of the cause of the leave-taking from God?

VINDICTIVE AGNOSIS: RELIGIOUS COMPLEXES OF FEAR AND GUILT AS ARGUMENTS AGAINST GOD

In his book *Sin and Fear*, Jean Delumeau[5] has described the intriguing history of the development of the Western culture of guilt and shame from the High Middle Ages to the French Revolution. In so doing he has implicitly typified the Enlightenment as a leave-taking from this culture and the image of God that goes with it: God as a strict and punitive judge, as an all-seeing eye which scrupulously notes all the sins of the bedroom, all the intrigues, all the shadow sides of human life, and writes them down in the book of final reckoning. The work of Eugen Drewermann[6] is one long complaint against this religious culture of guilt and the image of God that underlies it. A great many people who grew up in this culture of guilt and had difficulties in wrestling with it seek their salvation and gospel in the school of Maslow and his humanistic psychology, and in the religious offshoots of it in spiritual movements like New Age.[7] In his studies of the doctrine of the atonement in Anselm and Calvin and in his book *Believing by Daylight*, Herman Wiersinga[8] has tried once and for all to prune away from the undergrowth of notions that obscure the view of God the offshoots of the idea that human beings have infringed God's honour and that this requires satisfaction by the sacrifice of Jesus – who 'pays the price' in our name. Here is a quotation:

> One cannot dismiss ploys involving hell and damnation as a caricature of malicious journalists or as the folklore of pessimistic islanders. Sin and damnation on the one hand and grace and salvation on the other together form the model with which generations of Christians have been brought up down to our own time. They have thus become so familiar with these notions that while they have got rid of the faith (as some of them say), they have retained a sombre sense of life.[9]

In this 'religion of fear' there was not only conflict and competition between God and human beings but also a quite dualistic theodrama in which God and evil were involved in a constant fight. Here Evil is personified in the figure of Satan, the devil or the antichrist,[10] and sin is regarded as a collective doom of all human beings or even of the whole creation, which only the elect can escape, through God's gracious election. The doctrine of the two ways or the two kingdoms – derived from the largely

35

apocryphal apocalyptic literature from the first centuries BC, taken over here and there by the New Testament and further developed by early church writings, Augustine and Luther – has transferred the internal conflict of God between anger and mercy, grace and punishment, to the sphere of history and to the domain of human interiority. Thus conflict and being of two minds becomes a quasi-divine characteristic of history and of the human project. In Hegel's dialectical philosophy and in Marx's class struggle this theodrama gets its secular, cultural and social counterpart. It is the notion of this dualistic theodrama, taken up in all kinds of popular belief and deriving from Persian, late-Hellenistic, German and Slavonic myths, that time and again has drawn the picture of God, contrary to all theological and official church clarifications.[11]

Although no mention of such a theodrama between God and his adversary at the heavenly court can be found in the texts of the early Christian creeds, and although time and again the church spoke out against such dualism, the theodrama did come to form part of the Christian notion of God. It entered the baptismal liturgy, especially through baptismal catechesis:[12] 'forsaking' Satan and all his works began to form part of the liturgical questions asked at baptism when the newly converted were received, and later also at the baptism of children. It was expressed in the iconography of the Middle Ages: in the notions of the devil as a frightful monster and in the notions of the apocryphal doctrine of the fallen angels. But it had already been expressed at an earlier stage, albeit in a more spiritualized form, in the ascetic literature about the fight against the powers of evil, for which later portions of the New Testament provided the ammunition. The Devotio Moderna, the Reformation and the seventeenth-century reform of the church spun out this theme further and gave it a theological foundation with the doctrine of God's double predestination: God determines the battle against evil beforehand and knows its course; he predestines some to salvation in heaven and others to destruction in hell. The Catholic (Counter-) Reformation, with the enormous influence of Ignatius of Loyola's *Spiritual Exercises* and the spirituality of Alphonsus de Liguori (1696–1787), disseminated in popular catechesis down to the twentieth century, had a similar effect on Roman Catholics. The spiritual life of Christians is depicted here as a constant fight against evil, as a 'love in fear' which is constantly bowed down by the loss of 'the state of grace' and thus eternal salvation, and which regards the whole of church life and the spiritual life as decisive for heaven and hell: 'Those who pray will be blessed, those who do not pray will be lost'

(Alphonsus). This culture of spiritual combat, and the fear of failure that goes with it, have filled the collective unconscious with many unhealthy feelings of guilt and shame. The idea of God is governed by this. God is constantly looking over our shoulders like a supervisor. For those in authority – parents, teachers, church and political leaders – God becomes a stick behind the door. God himself becomes a partisan God with more enemies than friends, the model of intolerance towards all those who deviate from the true faith. But God is also divided in himself, in a constant battle with his adversary, the *diabolos*, just as in reaction human beings are constantly being led astray to choose the wrong side and sell their souls to the devil (the Faust motif). What had crept into the Jewish culture of the intertestamental period as extrabiblical and un-Jewish and to which the New Testament preaching was strongly opposed – the thought that human beings are subject to the power of an evil spirit and that God would come off worst against the opposing forces of darkness – continued to live on as a battle cry within the Christian doctrine of the atonement. The asceticism of the early monastic movements and the writings of the desert fathers, along with the slumbering influence of Manichaeism, which Augustine was never able completely to escape, configured the Western form of Christianity as an ongoing battle against the devil. Belief in God was infected with the legacy: evil became 'the Evil One', right into the heart of the Christian prayer, the 'Our Father'. Article 12 of the Dutch Confession of Faith might be regarded as a summary of this belief:

> He [God] also created the angels good to be his messengers and to serve his elect. Some of the angels fell from this exalted state in which God had created them into eternal corruption, but the others persisted through God's grace and remained in their original state. The devils and the evil spirits are so corrupt that they are enemies of God and all that is good. *With all their might, like highwaymen they lie in wait for the church and each of its members in order to destroy and to devastate all through their deceits* [my italics]. They are therefore condemned by their own wickedness to eternal damnation and daily await their terrible torments. Here we detest the errors of the Sadducees, who deny that there are spirits and angels, and also the error of the Manichees, who say that the devils originate from themselves and are evil by nature, not that they have become corrupt.[13]

Consolation is announced in Article 13, the reference to God's providence and fatherly care, with which 'he holds the devils and all his enemies in check and they will not be able to harm us without his permission'.[14]

That human beings are incapable of good and that matter and the body are full of corruption and impurity has been hammered into them from the fourteenth century on: by penitential preachers and dealers in indulgences, by Reformers and Puritans, by Jansenists and other rigorists. Article 14 of the Dutch Confession has had an influence right down to the twentieth century:

> Human beings ... have deliberately subjected themselves to sin and thus to death and the curse by hearkening to the word of the devil. For they have transgressed the commandment to live that they have received, and through their sin they have departed from God who was their true life. *So they have corrupted their whole nature and thus deserved bodily and spiritual death. Having become godless, perverse and corrupt in all their doings, they have lost all the admirable gifts that they received from God. They have kept only weak traces of them, but these are enough to deprive human beings of any excuse* [my italics].[15]

In Article 15, which is about original sin, this is presented as:

> *a corruption of the whole of nature and a hereditary evil with which even little children are infected in their mother's womb ... It is not even completely destroyed or wholly exterminated by baptism, since sin always stems from this corruption, like water that wells up from a poisoned spring* [my italics].[16]

Of course in the same confession of faith there are also numerous calls on believers not to have an exaggerated fear of God: we need not cover our shame like Adam before God (Article 23); we do not need any special intercession from the saints to turn to God (Article 26); believers need not fear God's judgement (Article 37). But in spirituality the first articles continue to have a lasting influence. The same is true of Question and Answer 5 from Sunday 2 and Answer 8 of Sunday 3 in the Heidelberg catechism: 'I am by nature prone to hate God and my neighbour'; 'Are we then so corrupt that we are utterly incapable of doing anything good and inclined to all evil? Yes, unless we are reborn by the Spirit of God.'[17] In the literary tradition the question has almost become the answer, as if the Christian confession implies that human beings must be denied any status of goodness or satisfaction.

Of course it was not much different in the Catholic tradition. There was no intention of teaching the absolute loss of natural goodness and responsibility in human beings, but human beings had to suffer all the more if, after being baptized, they succumbed to sin again and lost sanctifying grace. The term mortal sin tortured the conscience as an almost inescapable doom, even of small children. For many people the confessional, the seat of the church's mercy and forgiveness, became a place of torture, where unless you confessed everything you ran up more and more debts on your soul.

For centuries, contempt for the world (*contemptus mundi*) and constant reflection on human mortality went hand in hand in the culture of asceticism. The strict world of the monks became the model for Christian life, in which the striving for power, honour and private possessions, sexual satisfaction and a concern for posterity was presented as being of less value than the struggle for spiritual and physical mortification. 'Earthly values' thus had to yield to the 'evangelical counsels' (the vows of poverty, sexual continence and submission to the rules of life according to the gospel in the community); the 'religious' were thought to stand closer to God than did the ordinary 'citizens of the world'; the earthly 'kingdom' or 'rule' of the secular authorities was thought to be closer to the devil than to the 'heavenly kingdom' or 'rule' of the church, and the former was always called on to serve the latter. These cultural scruples, which according to Freud were pathologically exploited by Christianity, then, according to Delumeau, led to a cultural neurosis: the intolerable seriousness of falling short of the norm. The justification of the sinner, intended as a comfort and blessing for weary toilers, itself became a dogma about toiling: who is righteous before God and when? The sacrament of confession, meant as a mitigation of the penance of the early church and as a symbol of God's mercy, became a terrifying duty, the performance of which could decide between eternal life and the eternal punishments of hell. We can still read in the most recent *Catechism of the Christian Church*:

> To die in mortal sin without repenting and accepting God's merciful love means remaining separated from him for ever by our own free choice. This state of definitive self-exclusion from communion with God and the blessed is called 'hell' … Immediately after death the souls of those who die in a state of mortal sin descend into hell, where they suffer the punishments of hell, 'eternal fire'. (nos 1033, 1035)

Granted, no. 1036 adds that here and in Gospel texts like Matt. 7.13–14 – about the narrow gate to salvation and the broad way to destruction – we have a call to responsibility, that God does not predestine anyone to hell,[18] and that the verdict on human beings is passed by God alone. But the terror is always there for anyone who is still in any sense familiar with the tradition of the term 'mortal sin'. Although the words 'devil' and 'Satan' do not occur in the index, evil is again personified in the exposition of the last petition of the 'Our Father':

> In this petition, evil is not an abstraction, but refers to a person, Satan, the evil one, the angel who opposes God. The devil (*diabolos*) is the one who 'throws himself across' God's plan and his work of salvation accomplished in Christ. 'A murderer from the beginning ... a liar and the father of lies' (John 8.44), Satan is 'the deceiver of the whole world' (Rev. 12.9). Through him sin and death entered the world and by his definite defeat also creation will be 'freed from the corruption of sin and death'. (Roman Missal, Eucharistic Prayer IV)

Although it is confessed with scripture that in Jesus 'the prince of this world' has been overcome (John 14.30), the motif of the battle against the devil from the apocalyptic tradition (Rev. 12.17), as a lifelong fight against the personified evil of God's adversary, thus also continues to play a central role in Catholic belief and spirituality.[19] Thus verses about the devil continue to circulate in the idea of God, and visions of the devil populate the symbolic universe of obsessed women, even in the practice of psychiatrists. Such belief does not make people healthy, but forms the background to vindictive agnosis. It may then well be that the supreme deception of the devil – the belief that he does not exist – has had even more diabolical consequences than the belief that he is a power opposed to God. It has infected the picture of God as a God who constantly lures human beings into ambushes by means of his fallen angel, the devil, who 'goes around as a roaring lion, seeking whom he may devour' (I Peter 5.8). For centuries monks and priests have begun the night with this verse from the Bible: it is read at compline (the evening prayer of the daily offices and of the breviary).

Of course, such sweeping judgements on a past culture are always one-sided and made after the event. If we definitively forswear the devil and banish him from our culture and our imagination, we need not deny either the seriousness of human wickedness or the reality of psychological disturbances. Men and women are overpowered by their feelings, paralysed by evil, by fear and negative feelings. Dark powers and forces sometimes seem to govern fate. The sinful desire and the powerful attraction of evil are time and again made a theme in the Bible. This happens in the story of the first human sin in Genesis: the transgression of boundaries by Adam and Eve (Gen. 3), Cain who kills Abel (Gen. 4), Abraham who exploits his wife (Gen. 12), the disputes over property between Abraham and Lot (Gen. 13), the tribal wars (Gen. 14), the jealousy of Sarah and Hagar (Gen. 16), the sexual exploitation of foreigners (Gen. 17), incestuous relations (Gen. 19), the expulsion of Hagar (Gen. 21), the deception of Jacob (Gen. 25). The description of evil as incomprehensible, as the result of oppressive dilemmas, as the fruit of aporia, is striking: you cannot have everything; you must often choose between two evils, and evil soon becomes a habit and a culture. So God says to Cain in Genesis 4.7: 'If you do well, will you not be accepted? And if you do not do well, sin is crouching at the door; its desire is for you, but you must master it.' However, none of this justifies any personification of evil as an evil power. Rather than arming us against such personifications and unmasking their malicious sources within the symbolic universe of culture, the Christian tradition has encouraged and sometimes even exploited them. So far it has hardly dissociated itself from them, despite all 'demythologizing': original sin and the primal struggle between God and evil, God and the power of evil, form the most stubborn common basic metaphor or basic configuration of Western Christianity and of religion in general.[20] A certain vindictiveness among those who have experienced it as nauseating is all too understandable: God has not gladdened the youth of many people. For centuries, in the eyes of many the church has undermined human fulfilment and respect for natural life, for the body and the earth as God's gifts of creation. According to Nietzsche, Christian spirituality has turned human beings into submissive slaves, who in order to escape evil and hell have to dance to the piping of the clergy and submit to the authority of the church and the government in its service. Women above all have suffered under this regime of fear of the bodily and the inferiority of anything connected with sexuality.[21] The church's doctrinal statements about anything to do with sexuality and procreation are still overshadowed by the culture of guilt and shame that I have described. They breathe fear and an effort to dominate; they fear eroticism and love poetry; they preach continence in place of the art of love, they take celibacy as the norm rather than the growth of good loving relationships. It is precisely here that we have the roots of much of the vindictiveness against belief and the church which is hidden behind the massive European agnosis.

At a deeper level all this has darkened the view of God: strife and violence are internalized in the very idea of God; the crusade against evil – with all its lamentable historical implications and legitimations – is sanctioned by it; domination, power and the will to power are made divine properties which have displaced enjoyment, loving care and tender intimacy from the image of God. In technical theological terms we have to say that the forensic image of God which emerges from this culture of guilt and shame has displaced the doxological and axiological image of God or at least distorted it. Rather than connecting God with the human values of the good life and human dignity (*axios*, *dignitas*) and with the glory (*doxa*) of all that is attractive and appeals to the senses, or with the abysmal depth of our finitude, our freedom and our aporias, we have associated God with the public domain (*forum*) of the power of government (*imperium*) and jurisprudence (*iustitia*). We have now gradually taken our leave of this God of power and will, the God who is 'finally right'. Can we without vindictiveness look for a God of love, freedom, growth, enjoyment and mystery?

RATIONAL AGNOSIS: GOD AS THE UNNECESSARY DUPLICATION OR PROJECTION OF HUMAN POSSIBILITIES; THE CRISIS OF CLASSICAL METAPHYSICS

God's existence, normative power, supportive function and personal attractiveness no longer form the starting point for the symbolic universe of our culture. The belief in a supportive power is in fact declining rather more slowly than belief in a personal God who cares for us – after all, there has to be something like this – but the answer to the question where and how this supportive power can be localized or thought about remains vague, if any answer is given at all. No *locus Dei* can be found any longer in the midst of the cosmic forces, and in so far as we had localized God there, he has been shown up as a 'God of the gaps', leaving aside the sparse attempts at a new concordism. In the field of psychological forces – subject, person, ego, consciousness, heart, conscience – which are intrinsically less visible and measurable, God has been able to maintain himself even longer, but since neurologists have called this the 'central control unit' and we have been able to map the genome of our cell-dividing mechanism, a place for God is disappearing even there. There are those who still see a solution in a return to the all-embracing One of Plotinus, Nicholas of Cusa and Spinoza, to the holism of Dao and New Age or to an eschatological ontology:[22] God is not yet, but he may manage to become something like that. However, there is no essential difference between an X factor in the midst of all the other factors which define subject and object and an all-embracing X factor which cannot be unmasked as a projection or a cipher that has to support all the difference. God is not a necessary component either in the thinking subject (*res cogitans*) or in the thought-of object (*res extensa*), nor in the unity of the two. The idea of God does not add any epistemological value to our capacity to differentiate, even if, with Levinas and some post-moderns, we reflect on the limit experience of existence and nothingness, the awakening of the subject from formless being. Any trace of God that we think that we can perceive in the caverns of being – in situations of fear, solitude, boredom, suffering, the distress of death or near-death experiences, which Kierkegaard and Tillich and more recently Levinas have attempted to find – remains ambiguous.[23]

Some have sought the leave-taking of God and the causes of opposition to theism in a fixed and static metaphysic of being and in the philosophical idea of God which identified the name of God with the 'Supreme Being'. Heidegger above all prompted a marked philosophical mistrust of the idea of God as a kind of last support in reality with his criticism of 'ontotheology'. Heidegger thought that theology wrongly denied the Being itself of things by beginning to speak of all that is as *essents* and pointing even to God himself as the highest *Essent*. Here the self changes from a dynamic indication in verb form of all that is, with all the contingency, historicity and mobility that is to be found there – he prefers to call this *physis* – into a static and abstract general substratum of all that is, of which God is then said to be the highest Fulfiller and all-supporting Origin and Ground, as a truly 'Supreme Being': the Absolute or Being *par excellence*.[24]

This 'Supreme Being' underwent a further defining metamor-phosis at the end of the seventeenth and beginning of the eighteenth centuries as a consequence of more recent scientific insights into the fundamental structures of the universe, especially the discovery of the laws of gravity. Newton, Malebranche, Descartes, Fénelon and Leibniz are said now to have given a further mechanistic colouring to this God as 'Supreme Being', who through Aristotle and the renaissance of Aristotle brought about by Scholasticism was above all thought of in terms of 'First Mover': now he was God as the original force behind all the laws of nature. The step to the deistic notion of God by the physico-theologians, and also to the pantheism of Spinoza, in which God and the natural order become identical, is said to be just the next phase in a long-drawn-out process of the assimilation of belief in Yahweh to the world-view of modern physics.

The identification of 'the God of Abraham, Isaac and Jacob' with this new 'God of the philosophers' is said to be the cause of the loss of belief in God. A return to Pascal's awe at the mystery of the contingency of nature and history is said to be the approved means by which we can find God. The Jesus story is said itself already to imply a criticism of the philosophical 'Supreme Being'. Jewish philosophers like Levinas with their critique of ontology – the doctrine of the being of things and their last necessary ground in Being itself – are said to be able to help us.[25]

Levinas and others are certainly right in arguing for a different picture of God which takes more account of the vicissitudes of human history and of the personal biography of every human being, a picture of God which does not coincide with something like a 'Maître et Possesseur de l'Univers' or 'Fine-tuner' of the universe. Indeed, belief in the God of Abraham has nothing to do with this kind of physical and quasi-metaphysical explanation of God. It is an unnecessary duplication of what after all we already know about the structure of the cosmos: that a good deal in it has not yet been explained and that human beings have very little to contribute to this universe. As Heidegger already pointed out, you cannot dance or sing, sacrifice or pray to this God who still has to keep filling the gaps in our knowledge.

However, to take leave of Aristotelian metaphysics as the foundation of the idea of God does not by definition mean abandoning a frame – a specific window – from which it would be possible to think of God, the cosmos and human consciousness together, or abandoning a project of philosophical theology. A mere reference to the contingent-historical emergence of Jesus – in opposition to the God of the philosophers, which de Boer opts for in his re-reading of Pascal and his critique of Descartes – does not help us much. It is a repetition of moves which Lessing already unmasked and which have also constantly been rejected in the mainstream of theological tradition, moves which put faith and reason too far apart from each other, to the detriment of both. Those who without further questioning wager on the figure of Jesus of Nazareth, because of his extremely human belief in God or his philanthropy, gloss over one of the basic notions of Christianity: that this Jesus is the revelation, image and form *par excellence* of the living God and that the core of his message and activity is a reference to the will of God – the kingdom of God. Thus a reference to Jesus certainly does not make the question of God superfluous, but actually raises it, certainly if it is confessed that though Jesus was done away with by human beings he 'is seated at the right hand of God' (as the Nicene Creed puts it). I shall go into this question more deeply in Chapter 8. It is sufficient then to point to the terminology of the early followers of Jesus, who did not hesitate to call him the Logos of God: the one in whom God speaks, in whom God communicates with us, in whom the true and the good take form. So, according to Paul as well (Acts 17), a living God should have a connection with our thinking. Paul argued for a *logike latreia*: a rational service of God (Rom. 12.1). Anyone who sees God and thought, faith and reason as a priori enemies or rivals no longer has any criterion for distinguishing between faith and superstition. Any conversation about forms of faith and formulations of faith, ideas of God and religious practices; any explanation of faith to unbelievers, any form of ecumenism and dialogue and any form of testing preaching within the church by the historical testimony of the scriptures would become superfluous. Theology would then truly degenerate into rhetoric and fideism; preaching would degenerate from a tentative plea for the invisible God into a sheer art of seduction by visionaries or a notarial exposition of the foundation documents of the tradition.

It is therefore essential to have a framework of thought within which it continues to be rational to talk of God, even if at this point we find the classical metaphysics inadequate. The difficulty is of course that it was classical metaphysics that formed the framework into which many notions of God were woven: God as creator and preserver of nature and as the criterion and guiding thread of history, God as first cause and last purpose of the universe, God as the supporting force of all that is. Does the leave-taking from classical metaphysics also necessarily mean a leave-taking from all these properties and qualities of God?

This is what Habermas[26] claims, and he regards it as progress. He thinks that if religion still has functions, it has these functions on the basis of its connection with the new values of reason: that we can communicate with one another. Religions clearly belong to the forms of communication which people have needed hitherto. But

45

really that is a detour, a duplication. Thus theology, too, is none other than a 'dispensable encouragement of communicative competence'.[27] Indeed post-metaphysical thought does not dispute any theological assertion and does not even challenge religious reflections; however, it regards both theology and faith as a needless detour and in this sense as meaningless.

More important than this rationalizing and demystifying of world-view and self-awareness is the demystification of religion itself. Comparative religion, the psychology of religion, exegesis and hermeneutics of the texts of the tradition, historical insight into the course of the religious tradition, have also demystified the phenomenon of religion itself as a possible concomitant phenomenon and provisional stage of human development which may not necessarily make a lasting impression. We have seen that 'God' too is a hypothesis.[28] Hence the plea of some for a modest departure of academic theology into the field of religious studies, albeit at the same time with a recognition of the possible critical, ethical and aesthetic power of religion, expression of faith and reflection of faith within religious systems and churches. Of course this last is logical: if there are no churches or religions in which there is music, then there is little room for the academic investigation and teaching of theories about the music of religions, other than as the archaeology of religions.

Here it seems very likely that in our post-theistic culture theology is singing its swan song, a dirge to God. To prepare for this, theology now scrutinizes the grammar of the religious argument and seems limited to that. The advantage would certainly be that it could offer better explanations to unsuspecting visitors to museums of religion in the twenty-first century than is the case in most museums now.

To say this is to complain and accuse at the same time. I am very well aware that indeed another theological programme must be sketched out. I remarked that I regard taking leave of a self-evident belief in God as a *kairos* and a reprieve for church and theology. That needs to be clarified, and I shall do this in a last section.

AGNOSIS AS A MORATORIUM: A REPRIEVE FOR CHURCH AND THEOLOGY

In a collection of articles entitled *Identity and Difference*, in 1957 Martin Heidegger already put forward a proposal for a pause in thought, a moratorium on the idea of God in philosophy and theology.[29] This philosophical and theological pause did not amount to a call to separate faith and knowledge permanently, although Heidegger certainly did not see the possibility of any good relations between the two. His was a far more radical call: for a complete uncoupling of the idea of God from thought, even in theology. This was precisely what the 'God is dead' theologians intended, under the slogan of wanting to live and do theology *etsi Deus non daretur* (Grotius, Bonhoeffer): a theology without God or at least without using any of the ways of thinking about God adopted hitherto.

Forty years later, have we reached a point at which we should discontinue the pause in thought? Has the idea of God in the meantime not undergone so many purges, for example by the attention to the nineteenth-century critique of religion and the acceptance of the Enlightenment, and by the self-criticism of theology which has become one of its most important tasks, that it could again become part of thought: part of a new way of thinking in which the critique of Enlightenment theology could also be echoed, but without any nostalgia for the former antithesis?

There is no denying that Jewish-Christian theology in the period of antithesis against the antithesis which began with Gogarten and the move of the church towards the world and which culminated, for example, in *Gaudium et spes* and the optimism of Uppsala, has in many respects made a liberating contribution to the culture of the *humanum*: hermeneutical theology has liberated us from dogmatism; political theology has made a connection between the fight for human rights – the ideals of the Enlightenment – and the gospel of God in the Old and New Testaments; liberation theology serves to continue to make those who have not yet been able to profit from the ideals of the Enlightenment subjects of history and bring them emancipation; ecumenical theology is putting into the practice the ideals of tolerance, osmosis and convergence which Locke, Lessing and Kant still had to purchase at the price of being accused of heresy; feminist theology is breaking through patriarchal thought-forms, forms of language and powerful institutions, also against pressure from church leaders. Rather than being the quiet teachers of their people, theologians have now become revolutionary activists and expect the church to be more the cocaine than the opium of the people.

Welcome though all this is, it is not enough. It is difficult to live permanently on antithesis and critique alone, and antithesis to the past makes any reflection obsolete in the long term. If the theme of 'God' is not to disappear from the annals of human history, then positive arguments also need to be adduced for mention of the name of God.[30]

Reiterating the traditional ways of thought, for example the so-called proofs of the existence of God, as Hans Küng has tried to do in his *Does God Exist?*,[31] does not seem to me to be the best way of doing that. These proofs of God or 'ways' were patterns of argument, derived from the then *artes* of logic, rhetoric and mathematics, on the basis of articulations of faith which were already presupposed. Such articulations of faith escape us by virtue of our cultural agnosis. They still exist, in text and image, but they no longer form the hinges (the literal meaning of *articulus*) of our lives.

However, it cannot be bad to continue to remember these old ways of thinking, because they map so well the classical theism that I described above. There were four or five of these ways of thought (*viae*) towards God:

- the cosmological order calls for a first cause of causality;
- the dynamic of history calls for an ultimate purpose and perspective of all that happens;
- the phenomenon of the diversity of things calls for a supporting ground, a formative principle that is found in the One Being itself, in which all potencies are fulfilled and which therefore necessarily exists;
- the order of action and striving for the good calls for a driving force, a moral imperative, a last justice; the effective cause of all religion.

Cosmology, eschatology, ontology and axiology, ordered after Aristotle's theory of the four causes, together define the symbolic universe of the Jewish-Christian tradition. The ideas that philosophy – natural philosophy, the philosophy of history, metaphysics and ethics – has developed in this sphere seem to fit in with the content of this tradition, and therefore these arguments also functioned as usable analogies for religious experience. But because in the process of secularization all values for action, all being of *essents*, all goals of history and all causes of nature are seen as self-supporting, autonomous systems, the whole effect of their analogy collapses. Everything that theism asserted and regarded as valuable – that God orders the cosmos, guides history, supports entities and directs the conscience – is regarded in post-theism as improbable and superfluous. Whereas believers will continue to say that the whole of reality is full of signs of coherence, teleology, truth and value, unbelievers will point out that this same reality proves to be chaotic, fortuitous, a semblance and a lie, and that the only order, direction, certainty and truth always comes about through the culture of rationality which leaves aside any irrational, a-rational or supra-rational basis of explanation. Believers too are not ashamed to adopt this standpoint. The proofs of God no longer work, because there is no longer any question of *quod omnes vocant Deum*, as Thomas could still conclude at the end of each of his *Viae*.

However, the comparative method as followed by apologists from diverse periods of church history does not seem to me to be a better way. These apologists tried to indicate the noetic surplus value of the starting points of the gospel and belief in God over against the surrounding culture: the Stoics have their virtues, ours are better; the Hellenists have their *Logos*, we have a better one; Plato has his Ideas of the good, the true, the beautiful, we have better ones.[32] That always amounts to the dominant trend in philosophy or culture being taken into the service of theology or church doctrine, without any answer to the question why these trends themselves did not arrive at the idea of the Christian God of salvation. Twentieth-century philosophers end up here being canonized as anonymous Christians.

The best and most obvious way seems to me to be the way of reflection on the practical and theoretical values of Christianity for present-day culture, the surplus value of which can only be proved experimentally and which is also only offered to be tested, '*ad experimentum*'. Neither authority nor compulsion, neither rule nor sanction, will be able to impose these acquired values, although it cannot be a bad thing if elements from them are also disseminated as 'civil religion', and if their experimental evaluation is also recognized in laws and public argument.

I think that a number of fundamental notions and values from religious experience are lacking in the four ways to God, which were derived as analogies from philosophical reflection, and in the method of comparison, in which theology likewise allowed itself to be guided by whatever thought-system was at hand. At any rate they were under-emphasized. They are precisely those values which prevent the connection of things from being purely mechanical, which prevent the purposefulness of history from being another word for determinism, which prevent the truth from being imposed inexorably and harshly out of a static securism and the values simply being the values of those who offer the most or have the power.

It seems to me that exposing such values from the traditions' own symbolic universe, bringing the new out of the old, within the story-telling community of Christianity, is the narrative task of theological teachers. Their speciality consists in a knowledge of the archives of the symbolic universe of believers; their task – wherever they live and however they are paid – is that of a selfless and non-violent service to human culture by pointing to God as a critical force, an added value which does not aim at the comparative and which does not get bogged down in antitheses but leads to fulfilment. I think that theological teachers now have a breathing space for this task and that they are better equipped for it than ever before. And the church, now that it has been robbed of all its theocratic privileges and now that here and there it is beginning to become a factor of liberation in autocratic cultures, needs to and will value this positive service from theologians. But how can that be achieved?

CONCLUSION

In the midst of the phenomenon which has produced the 'legitimacy of modernity' by itself and despite Christianity, according to H. Blumenberg, or possibly also through Christianity, according to M. Weber and K. Löwith,[33] the human person has not progressed in keeping with his or her own feelings in life, relationships and society. The capitalist ethic of progress and work, the Marxist idea of a planned welfare state, the supportive trust in mathematical skills (measuring, counting and constructing), the fundamental equality and participation of all men and women: all that may be the harvest of the Enlightenment. We certainly must not take our leave of it too quickly, even in the name of postmodernist criticism.[34] And yet we sigh again under -isms: secularism, utilitarianism and individualism as by-products of the Enlightenment and the quest for human autonomy.[35] And although we continue to rate immaterial values – health, education, good relationships – higher than material provisions,[36] it is precisely at these points that the 'education of the human race' is far from complete and we have to lament many harmful technological and social developments. The quality of personal life is far from having been secured by the apparatus with which we have surrounded ourselves; it even blocks our view of living life and produces unemployment, whereas others no longer have any time to live.[37]

Religious agnosis is merely the symptom of a cultural agnosis which goes far deeper; it consists in the aporia of the narrowing of our perspectives when we are actually trying to broaden our minds. As Fénelon already observed about many of his contemporaries: we are like armchair scholars who are so taken up with texts and experiments that life itself, our body, our senses, the space in which we are and even our awareness of ourselves escape us, and with them any view of God.[38] Couldn't we conceive of a bodily religious experience which penetrates heart and kidneys, marrow and bone, a view of God which liberates us from fear and blinkers?

3

The Despairing Question: Where is God?

WHERE IS GOD?

Dachau, D-Day, My Lai, Srebrenice millions of dead in successive waves of hatred and violence; terror, catastrophes, daily violence against people for pleasure or profit. Where is God, where does all this misery come from and how can we be rescued from it?

It is the question of God, not just as the prayer of bewildered and desperate believers – where are you, God?[1] – but also as a *cri de coeur* of many non-believing contemporaries in whom repugnance at irrational human behaviour can only be turned into a curse which despite them points to God. To whom else can we attribute this collective madness of violence? But at the same time that creates the problem of God's existence: if God has to do with this evil – and with so many other disasters and so much suffering – how can there be a good and almighty, a gracious and righteous God? And if God has nothing to do with it and can do nothing about it, then what in heaven's name is God good for? The philosophical and theoretical question of God's existence: *must we or can we accept the existence of God: an Deus sit?* thus acquires an existential sequel: *what does it matter and what does it matter to me that God exists or possibly does not exist: utrum Deus sit?*

I sketched out the trivial and vindictive answer to that in the previous chapter: 'God need no longer exist', for some people because they simply banish God from the world in which they live and no longer encounter God in their ways of life (trivial agnosis, 'what you can't see doesn't exist'); for others because they have only experienced God in the form of shame, guilt and fear (vindictive agnosis: 'God as the great bogey man'). Then we saw that rational and philosophical arguments have also been advanced against the idea of God, in which God is declared a superfluous hypothesis.

According to Hans Waldenfels,[2] our culture is perhaps determined not so much by this argumentative-analytical agnosis which cannot accord God a place within the categories of our experience[3] as by an aporetic-enigmatic agnosis, that cannot reconcile God's existence with the experience of the night side of life. Right at the beginning of his theological handbook *Summa Theologica*, Thomas Aquinas mentions these very two arguments against the existence of God.[4] His answer to the problem of evil (which he takes from Augustine) is that God still brings good out of evil, or that God allows evil in order to do something good. Thus the violence of nature ultimately contributes to putting everything on the right lines. This answer amounts to the idea that evil, in so far as we ourselves are not guilty of it, is really a trick of perspective: human beings cannot see everything, as God can.[5] The only evil that we can get our fingers on is human failure, which falls short of the measure of the good: *privatio boni debiti*. The rest is in God's hands and we must leave it there: God can write straight with crooked lines. Flowers also grow on war graves. And new life can appear from birth pangs. We find this line up to the beginning of the eighteenth century, in such different thinkers as Spinoza, Leibniz and Fénelon.

After the Enlightenment, philosophers were no longer willing to accept this argument. Voltaire protested against it after the 1755 earthquake in his famous novel *Candide ou l'optimisme* (1759),[6] and Rousseau thought that the only solution to earthquakes was to move to safer places. Kierkegaard and French existentialism made the sharpest complaints about the simple acquittal of God by saying that everything is for the best; this also happened in Jewish philosophy after the Holocaust. This pious acquittal of God and the excuse that suffering represented the growing pains towards the good became the theme *par excellence* of sarcastic mockery of the image of God and the sharp critique of religion by Bloch, Camus, Unamuno and many others. It meant the end of a theoretical argument – theodicy – which sought to harmonize the idea of God and the experience of evil.

TAKING LEAVE OF THEODICY

The term 'theodicy' (from the Greek *theos* and *dikaioun*: the justification, i.e. the acquittal of God) is a discovery of the New Time. Leibniz made the use of it famous by his *Essais de Theodicée*, which was published for the first time in 1697 and in the 1710 edition had as a subtitle: *Sur la bonté de Dieu, la liberté de l'homme et l'origine du mal* (on the goodness of God, human freedom, and the origin of evil). This subtitle clearly indicates that the problem is a complex one, involving a number of arguments at the same time. Leibniz wanted to maintain the unity of both faith and reason against Pascal and Bayle, who had begun to play the two off against each other. For Bayle, and in a certain sense also for Pascal, there are two realities: God and revelation on the one hand, and human beings and reason on the other. With their reason human beings can study only the connection between particular phenomena, always only 'saying something about something' (Aristotle), always knowing only 'details'. They cannot survey the whole. Perhaps God could do that, but because God himself is all-embracing, human beings cannot know the existence of God nor even how God deals with this totality. Hence Bayle's scepticism about all theology, and Pascal's awe at the infinite space of the universe and the unfathomable depth of matter. Leibniz thinks that reason perceives the individual and knows it in its connection with the whole. Any separate fact is separate only by being permanently 'maintained' and 'defined' by the intentionality of the whole. We could not isolate any individuals or facts without giving them a place in a greater whole. Leibniz thinks that this 'definition' or 'maintaining' is another word for what is meant by God's providence. The greatest problem for Leibniz is the manifest clash between this divine providence, will and governance and human freedom. He solves it with a reference to creation by God, who can realize the good only in freedom and who therefore has to 'risk', to 'reckon in', human misdeeds and sin. Christian Wolff, Shaftesbury, Alexander Pope and Herder all took the same line as Leibniz. They were opposed by Bernard de Mandeville (*The Fable of the Bees*, 1714), Voltaire, Rousseau, Locke and Hume. All of them began to make a radical distinction between faith and reason. Theodicy became a task for believers. Philosophers have to limit themselves to anthropodicy: to what relates to the development of freedom, the challenging of evil and the education of the human race.

Of course the problem is much older than the name that Lebniz gave to it: how does one deal with the experience of evil and suffering, misfortune and injustice, and how can this be reconciled with the confession of God's goodness or the power of the gods? According to Milton Yinger, the core of all religion lies in this question and its possible answer.[7] Of course that is first of all a problem for believers, as for example the biblical book of Job demonstrates, and also many Psalms: how can the promise of salvation and blessing which is associated with calling on the name of the one God, YHWH, be reconciled with the actual doom and injustice that affects so many people? How does the idea of a special bond between God and Israel accord with the military, economic and political disasters of Israel over the course of the centuries?[8] And above all, how can the appeal to a good God be reconciled with the evil that affects good people in particular?[9]

A BELIEVING THEODICY?

What a believing theodicy implies is well described in Job 1.22: 'And in all these things [Job's misfortunes and the disasters that overcame him] Job did not sin or charge God with wrong.' So in a religious context theodicy means first of all not accusing God falsely, not foisting on God things for which we ourselves are responsible. Of course that applies to crime and violence against others and the abuse of nature. But it also applies to failing to recognize the dangers of nature, taking risks and above all putting others at risk. Accusing God consists of disclaiming responsibility for one's own fate, not accepting the fragility of existence, using the idea of God to escape one's own pain and suffering.

The question is: must God be involved in what is called 'the problem of evil'? The problem of evil is primarily a human problem, shared by both believers and unbelievers: the experience of suffering, pain, sickness, misery and death as contradictions to life in which by nature we seek repose, enjoyment, health, satisfaction and fulfilment. But life cannot be lived without pain, sickness, violence and death. And even in the battle against it we produce further fragmentation. So we need to begin by recognizing the real character of evil, the structural nature of which is woven into existence, and by sharing the bewilderment at it. At a mass grave, nothing good can be said, nothing can be waved away. When a loved one dies, only mourning and tears are left.

55

When the tears have dried and we are left with the loss, we can perhaps affirm the fragility of life, and not only human life. In order to live, all living beings must make use of other life, subject it, use it and consume it. By living we ourselves are also shrivelled up. And not just that: through our urge to survive we also threaten the life of others, and by our precautions against death – through science, technology, economics and politics – we cause shock waves of devastation elsewhere in nature.[10] The horror remains, even if we see that it can hardly be different, and even for those who believe that there is life 'with God' for human beings after death. So there can be no question of mitigating evil, even with an appeal to reason (our lives are all bound up together) or an appeal to God (God has ordained it like that: human beings yield, God commands). Rather, even in the name of God there needs to be bewilderment, a failure to understand and a refusal to accept, real opposition and the reduction of suffering, lament and complaint, a protest if need be against God, as we find this in the Psalms, the prophets and the book of Job. Only when the real existence of evil again becomes a question to dwell on, a deep chasm of offence, indignation, a profound question 'Why?',[11] is there a chance that God too can again become an authentic, open question. As Job says, because he cannot restrain the anguish of his spirit and the bitterness of his soul (7.11):

I loathe my life;
I will give free utterance to my complaint;
I will speak in the bitterness of my soul.
I will say to God, Do not condemn me;
let me know why you contend against me.

Does it seem good to you to oppress,
to despise the work of your hands
and favour the designs of the wicked?
Do you have eyes of flesh?
Do you see as man sees?
Are your days as the days of man?
. . .

Your hand fashioned and made me;
and now you turn about and destroy me.
Remember that you have made me of clay,
and will you turn me to dust again?

Why did you bring me forth from the womb?
Would that I had died before any eye had seen me,

and were as though I had not been,
carried from the womb to the grave.
Are not the days of my life few?
Let me alone, that I may find a little comfort
before I go whence I shall not return,
to the land of gloom and deep darkness,
the land of gloom and chaos, where light is as darkness. (10.1–5,
8–9, 18–22)

How does one escape from the aporia of suffering and death, so
unfairly distributed in the world (21.7–34; 27.14–23)?

If I look for the underworld as my house,
if I spread my couch in darkness,
if I say to the pit, 'You are my father',
and to the worm, 'My mother' or 'My sister',
where then is my hope?
Who will see my hope? (17.13–15)

The theological defence against this claim and accusation, expressed
in the book of Job[12] by the pious moralist Eliphaz, the scrupulous
lawyer Bildad, the respectable citizen Zophar and the youthful know-
it-all Elihu,[13] already contains all the later rationalizations of the
aporia. No human being is wholly righteous (4.17; 5.14); human
beings themselves cause all kinds of unhappiness (5.7); the trials and
punishment often have a positive effect (5.17; 36.8–11); suffering can
be a way of rescue and a warning (36.15); crime never pays, and one
day a reward will come (15.20–35; 18.5–21; 20.5–29). There is also a
movement from misfortune to happiness: God's ways are sometimes
wonderful (5.9); God time and again gives new happiness and life
(33.29–30); no one is right in the face of God (9.2; 25.4); God's wisdom
is unfathomable (11.6), God alone can see all things (22.12), it is
senseless to argue against God: 'God remains God. Must he say, "I
have made a mistake; I was there"?' (34.31). The Almighty One who
rules over the violence of nature can only be righteous (37.23–24). But
Job answers:

But what does reproof from you reprove?
Do you think that you can reprove words,
when the speech of a despairing man is wind? (6.25–26)

But I have understanding as well as you;
I am not inferior to you.
Who does not know such things as these? (12.3)

Even now, behold, my witness is in heaven,
and he that vouches for me is on high.
My friends scorn me;
my eye pours out tears to God,
that he would maintain the right of a man with God,
like that of a man with his neighbour. (16.19–21)

Behold, the fear of the Lord, that is wisdom,
and to depart from evil is understanding. (28.28)

It is precisely the appeal to God's omnipotence – God, who ensures that human beings have all the happiness in the world – which dooms both human beings and God to impotence (23.16). God should act in accordance with human wishes; human beings should call on God in vain to guide the ordinary course of events with 'miracles'.[14] The dogma of fair retribution – that God always rewards the good and punishes the evil – leads to the greatest injustice: those for whom things go well are said to be blessed by God and those who are maltreated are said to have God's curse to blame for this. To cry out, 'Tough, your fault', is in fact the height of godlessness, as is also the notion that faith in God must become evident from human success. The attempt to avoid evil – crime, dangers, catastrophes, injustice – bears witness to true wisdom and true respect for God.

'YHWH's answer' in Job 38–41 is one long-drawn-out hymn of praise to the good creation and to the course of affairs within it. That things also go wrong in the creation is no argument against God. The whole Jewish tradition begins from the actual ambivalences of nature, history and human life. As well as drinking water there is also bad water (II Kings 2.19); as well as fertile fields there is also barren land (Num. 20.5). There are always rotten figs to eat (Jer. 24.1), thin cows among the cattle (Gen. 4.13). There are days of misfortune; there is the affliction of death and a host of misdeeds for human beings. One term stands for all these things, *ra', ra'ah*: evil, the un-thing, the non-sensical. And witness is borne that God creates both the things and the un-things, both good and evil (Isa. 45.7–12; Amos 3.6); they are often inextricably entangled and in any case impossible for human beings to sort out. Anyone who wanted to do that would be like God: like Eve and Adam he would become a victim of his arrogance, would have to slink away in shame, experience perpetual pain and difficulty, and undergo death. In this ambivalent situation, thought in terms of a mixture of things that we do and which happen to us – the whole connection between cause and effect[15] – is the still mythical ground where people trace the hand of God in the concrete experience of misfortune and happiness, affliction and satisfaction, and even in sin and guilt. In that sense we can perceive a gradual development in Jewish scripture towards an uncoupling of suffering and guilt which is only completed in the New Testament, but which takes full form in the prophets – for example in the songs of the suffering servant, who is nevertheless God's beloved – and already in Job.[16] We can also say that if there is any question of divine retribution and thus of a dogma of retribution, this is always in a context of rescue from oppression and injustice. It usually takes the form of the appeal: 'Do not let the evildoers fare well. Woe to the evil, they will have to answer to God for it! Woe to the enemies of the people!' Belief in God's justice must not be used to perpetuate the specific fate of human beings in misery, to make them pariahs and outcasts. Therefore the theologians in the book of Job who think that good and evil, blessing and curse, can be calculated in terms of the dogma of retribution, and who want to put all the blame for misery on human beings, are told: 'My wrath is kindled against you . . . for you have not spoken of me what is right, as my servant Job has' (42.7–8).

Indeed, Job is also called righteous, although his name (*'iyyob*, *qittol* of *'yb* = be hostile) means enemy, adversary, accuser. Clearly one can still be presented as the model of the righteous man if one complains and accuses, opposes and resists God. Belief in God thus does not exclude but includes protest against suffering and the struggle against evil. Noah, Daniel and Job are regarded by Ezekiel as the three great righteous men outside Israel. In James 5.11 Job is a model of steadfastness. In I Clement 17.3, Abraham, Job and Moses are cited as the saints of Israel. Various churches are dedicated to them. The Qur'an honours Job's memory in Surahs 21 and 38. Bloch mentions Job in the same breath as Moses and Jesus as a model of the true hope, which does not disguise suffering, and which even contrary to all the existing theological ideas about God maintains a plea for truth and uprightness of conscience as the supreme guideline for human action.[17]

THE THEOLOGICAL THEODICY

Now despite the warning to the theologians in the Job story, a theological argument was developed over the centuries which then became the very occasion for the Enlightenment critique of religion.

This is because the human search into the sources of evil cannot be silenced, and also because a debate with philosophical solutions which seem incompatible with the monotheism of the Abrahamic religions is unavoidable. The Enlightenment critique of religion took the form of presenting the traditional theodicy in an ironical way ('Look what the supposed God does in history and how little this God can achieve'), but twentieth-century theology finally attempted its own theodicy in the form of a critique of theodicy ('how foolish it was to address such questions to God'). The history of this complex argument has been described many times.[18] Max Weber divided it into a rough universal typology of 'rational theodicy' which he thought applicable to all religious systems.[19]

First and foremost there is the Persian-Assyrian *dualism* which decided on the existence of two forces or powers, one for good and one for evil, guided by two conflicting gods: a god of truth, light, purity and goodness and a god of darkness, lies, pollution and evil. This notion has its offshoots in Mazdaism, Manichaeism and in different forms of Jewish and Christian Gnosticism. Even the main line of Judaism, Christianity and Islam did not remain wholly untouched by it, as is shown by apocalyptic ideas and remnants of belief in the devil and magic.

There is a second form, exemplified in the Indian doctrine of karma – streams of which remain within Hellenism, since the teaching of the Pythagoreans and that of the Stoics are related – which might be labelled *fatalism*. There are good and evil chances (*fatum, fortuna*), in principle equally accessible to all, but of which individuals make different use. It is a matter of determining one's own fate, out of reasonable self-interest, according to the wisdom of the masters, in order to find peace with one's true self in life (thus for example among the Stoics: *heimarmene, ataraxia, secundum naturam vivere*), if need be through the stages of several biographies (in all forms of belief in reincarnation), or by long and diverse lives gradually rising above all desire and finding repose in the eternal nirvana.

A third option was for some kind of divine *retribution* through which the unequal opportunities and unequal fate of mortals will be put right. Weber distinguishes three forms here: an earthly paradise for the people or the religious group at the end of history, which may or may not be the evolutionary or revolutionary result of a gradual diminution of affliction by trusting in God's law and covenant, for which all generations strive depending on their abilities; an individual retribution in a supra-historical other world, in which all are personally rewarded for their good deeds and punished for their evil deeds (possibly helped by intercession, mediation and satisfaction on the basis of the merits of others); and a form of retribution which is put wholly in God's hands, on the basis of an eternal council or predestination, an option which comes from absolute submission to the sovereignty of God in good and evil days, and which borders on determinism.

This terminology is certainly too crude. Schillebeeckx[20] gives a more historical but not specifically chronological typology in eight models: ontological dualism of good and evil (Mani and Marcion); evil as a lack or a deviation from the good (*privatio boni*) (Augustine); evil as the destruction of an original harmony (*harmonia praestabilita*) (the Stoics, Leibniz and also many forms of the Christian doctrine of original sin); evil as the result of a false perspective (Wolff, Pope); evil as not caused by God, but allowed (*permissio*) for testing (Thomas Aquinas); evil as an exclusively human problem (*homo homini lupus*), the consequence of rivalry and class struggle (Hobbes, Rousseau); or, the good as a human project of evolution or revolution, continuing with one another in a creative dialectic (Hegel, Darwin and Marx); evil as a punishment for unbelief and good as a reward for the elect (the group theodicy e.g. of Gnosticism); and finally, suffering as a punishment for sin, as inherited guilt (the strict notion of retribution, which is likewise often bound up with the doctrine of original sin).

The disadvantage of such typologies is that they do not take sufficient account of the connection between theodicy and anthropology, soteriology and eschatology, and with it the underlying image of God. The common presupposition of all these models is that a consistent image of God depends on a logical and if possible a causal explanation of the suffering actually experienced (through harm, pain, loss, injustice and inevitable death), whereas the idea of God in most religions does not in fact serve to explain suffering but to teach how to endure it and, as far as possible, to combat it.

The crucial question of theology is not how we can harmonize belief in God and suffering in a conclusive systematic explanation of the world but how, despite the experience of evil, we can still believe in God without abandoning thought, without choosing the way of irrationality. That is precisely what moved Immanuel Kant, as we shall see, and why he definitely wanted to put a stop to all forms of theodicy, with reference to Job. However, Kant continued to be dominated by the premise of the logic of the universe which must be in tune with the logic of God. Therefore all that was left for him was the postulate of the practical reason for God: God as the source of the categorical imperative to do good. He abolished the fear of God from the domain of autonomous reason, and maintained the task of avoiding evil as the only certainty of faith.

This whole concentration on consistency and logic,[21] and within it on causality as the most important basic metaphor for the relationship with God,[22] means that essential aspects of the idea of God which were on the agenda of the discussion of the problem of evil in theology before there was such a 'rational theodicy' get forgotten. We can see them in Augustine, in Thomas Aquinas, in Pascal and even still in Leibniz, Descartes and Kant. Now that we no longer appeal to the former – the logic of the universe – in connection with suffering, we drop the question of a logical God and we can re-read the tradition from the idea of a surprising God. God is different, utterly different, from what we should expect, says Augustine. God reorganizes our logical thinking, not to make it illogical but to transcend the logic and to seek a broader, deeper rationality.

A RE-READING OF THEODICY AS AN OPEN QUESTION TO GOD

So we cannot avoid a re-reading of the great line of the theodicy argument. Here we must necessarily keep to the major key points.

Epicurus

Epicurus coined a sharp formulation of the classical question *Unde malum?* (Where does evil come from?) to which the theological – and in part also the philosophical – theodicy sought to give an answer:

> Either God wants to remove evil from the world,
> but He cannot do so;
> or He can do so, but does not want to.
> Or He does not want to and cannot,
> or He does and can.

If He wants to and cannot, He is impotent.

If He can and does not want to, He does not love us.

If He neither wants to nor can, He is not the good God and moreover is impotent.

If He wants to and can – and that is the only thing that is appropriate for Him as God – where then does actual evil come from

and why does He not remove it?[23]

Now from the Enlightenment on, many have read Epicurus' questions as an argument against the idea of God: the experience of evil is said to show that there is an internal conflict in the very idea of God. So because of the phenomenon of evil, God cannot exist. Those who read Epicurus in this way forget that, following Heraclitus, he wants to demonstrate the conflicts and antinomies of existence. In fact his question is not fundamentally different from that of Job or the Jewish scriptures as a whole. What he wants to demonstrate – and this is the core thought in all his fragments – is that it is impossible to make head or tail of the way things go in the world, that there is more chaos than order, and that the story of cosmic harmony must be taken with a pinch of salt. What he disputes is not God or gods or religion as such but the idea of an all-determining or all-guiding logic of the universe or 'providence'.

Nevertheless a logical argument has flared up over Epicurus' questions. There are two key issues: How can a good and caring God be the same as the one who causes, wills or allows evil? And how can the promise of salvation and blessing for human beings be fulfilled by God despite evil?[24]

The first focus found its focal point in the theological adoption of the Hellenistic idea of God's providence, which began to form part of the treatise on creation, the second in the doctrine of redemption (soteriology and eschatology). However, the division between these arguments is quite a late development; it is one of the causes of the failure of a theological theodicy and even of a crisis in the believing theodicy. A theodicy which seeks an answer only to the first type of question easily gets entangled in the problems of causality and freedom and in questions of rivalry between God and human beings. Here it provides conceptual explanation and clarification, but does not show any understanding of the experience of misery, nor does it solve any problems. A theodicy which is focused above all on the way out of the problems, on deliverance from evil, on liberation from misery and the healing of wounds, too easily passes over insoluble suffering, the aporia and powerlessness with which evil confronts us; or it takes refuge in exclusively supra-historical or at best collective historical solutions: 'Only be still, only wait, all will be new, heaven and earth'; or, 'The victims of now are the growth substance of the salvation of the future.'

If the argument about creation and providence on the one hand and about redemption and fulfilment on the other are to be plausible, they must therefore show a connection, without denying suffering or glossing over evil. We shall see that this connection is especially guaranteed in the Christian doctrine of God's threefold being. However, the connection has not always been seen so sharply in the history of theology, often because theologians have been too defensive when confronted with currents which destroyed the consistency of faith in the one God. In the Graeco-Roman world of the first four centuries the Jewish Jesus movement had to contend with a widespread fatalism which attributed the chances of life to a gracious fate or to evil powers. For many people religious life consisted in sacrifices to the good gods and conjurations against the evil powers. Thus it was based on a fundamental dualism which was also configured in the myths and tragedies into a universe of symbols.[25] Plato's philosophy was a true therapy against this division of reality. His thinking gave a teleological order to experiences: despite evil, something glimmers through of the good in all that is; what matters is a right perspective, a right policy. But sufficient reasons remain for doubting this great story. It indeed creates unity and direction – and in this way makes sense of existence – but it underestimates the riddles, the shadows, the developments against the grain, the decay and the abyss of the suffering of victims caused by evildoing and violence. Hence the scepticism, the dysteleology, of Epicurus and others. Hence, too, the hypothesis of a metaphysical, eternal and unmoved master of the universe in the great Hellenistic intellectual thought-systems of Aristotle and the Stoics, who can remain at a safe distance from the ups and downs of the earth, in absolute *autarkeia* (God is self-sufficient, and does not need the world or human beings) and *apatheia* (God cannot suffer, or be touched by suffering).

Plotinus

In the face of this Aristotelian and Stoic apathy of the gods, in the face of Plato's teleology, which branded evil the not yet good or the less good (*privatio boni*), and in the face of Epicurus' scepticism, which sees the good as the exception rather than the rule, Plotinus, as an 'exegete of Plato',[26] tried to find an intermediate solution.

He takes over the following patterns of thought from Plato:[27] the influence of the gods – servants of the One – extends to the smallest particles of the cosmos. Each particle has its own place in the whole, is there for the sake of the whole and thus is in the service of the One. Within the cosmos human beings are the playthings of the gods, but they play a special role on the cosmic scene: they strive for the good. And they will be rewarded, just as the reverse, the doing of evil, will be punished. The cosmos itself is a mixture of *Nous*, the intelligible world, and *Anangke*, physical necessity, the fixed forces and patterns in matter. The world itself did not come into being through *logismos*, i.e. as the result of consideration; rather, the influence of the *Logos* on matter has made the existing world the best conceivable world: we could not have made a better one even by reflecting on it. That does not alter the fact that there is more evil than good, more misery than happiness.

Plotinus takes the following insights from Aristotle's *Metaphysics*. All that is, is dependent on a highest principle or *arche*. Plotinus calls that the One (*to hen*). This principle governs the order of all things in the whole (*mian ten suntaxin eis ta hola*). This principle consists of *Nous* and *Logos*. All life takes part in the same energy and consists in activity, shared with the *Nous*. The *Nous* is thus certainly not at rest, *otiosus*, but eminently active: *actus purus*. The *Nous* is constantly making a stand, in the service of the One, in the fight against chaos, fragmentation and decay. The cosmic order consists in the management of the different factors or causes which are connected through the *Nous*, just as an army commander orders his troops. Human beings can know from the form of the appearance of things – the phenomenon – that there is such an order (*hoti*) but not why it is there or what it is ultimately for (*di hoti*).

Plotinus argues against the atomists and Epicurus, who attribute everything to chance and will have nothing of any *Nous*, any *Logos*, any *arche* or *telos*. He also argues against Epicurus and the Gnostics, who think that the universe is the product of an evil builder (*kakon demiourgon*) or the outcome of a fallen *Nous*, a corrupted world soul, as a second force alongside the originally good *Nous* or as a second phase of an originally good creation (compare the views of Mani and Marcion). He rejects the Gnostic distinction in evaluation between the fragmentary world of the senses, which is thought to be bad, and the intelligible, supra-sensory world, which is regarded as the only real and authentic world. The one world order is the product of the one *Logos*; it is truly filled with wisdom (*sophia*). The evil that we experience is the result either of the limitations of matter – the material with which the *Nous* must work and within which the *Logos* operates – or of the evil actions of living beings. The providence (*pronoia*) of the *Nous* leaves responsibility to human beings. Those who impute evil to providence commit the sin of anthropocentrism and outline a picture of the world in accordance with human insight. The difference between good and evil entities, between events which bring blessing and events which bring affliction, and between good and bad behaviour, is thus not in conflict with the *pronoia* of the *Nous*, but the product of perverse human evaluation: human beings who want to have a different syntaxis from that intended by the *Logos*, and who construct for themselves causal and chronological notions of the cosmos as a product in time. Greater insight, more courage to accept suffering, more political responsibility in order to combat evil: those are the ingredients which Plotinus recommends for maintaining belief in providence even in difficult times.[28] Here all the emphasis is on combating evil; there can no longer be any question of a tragic fate.[29] We must suffer dying and even murder in a relaxed way; after all these are part of life.[30] In life we are no more than actors who play a temporary role, although it is important to play the role as well as possible: let the one who wants to save his soul save it, and do so in the time of the body!

Augustine

Augustine, who may be called the founder of Western theological theodicy,[31] utterly shared in this way of thinking. He had to oppose the late-Jewish and early-Christian dualism of Mani; the *deus otiosus*, the passionless, unmoved, eternal author God of Aristotle and the Stoics; the Neoplatonic docetic monism of Plotinus; and the activism and perfectionism of Marcion and Pelagius, who each in his own way had an exaggerated notion of the liberation for freedom of the perfect good brought about by Christ. In Book VII of his *Confessions*,[32] Augustine gives the result and the synthesis of his quest for the relationship between God as the supreme Good and the reality of created things in which we distinguish between good and evil, or at all events between better and worse. It is clear that the picture of God also changes with each view of reality. Here especially, the relationship of God to place and time and the view of the being of things is involved. Then in this chapter Augustine also offers a metaphysics in a nutshell and shows that the question 'Where is God?' is a crucial question for theodicy: those who invoke God after defining their standpoint about things quite apart from God no longer make any contact with God. The bond with God is already given with the being of things, even if we regard some things and some events as bad. Augustine does not want things to be bad as such: Genesis says that God created everything 'very good' (Gen. 1.31). Indeed he writes a hymn of praise to creation in which the dangers and shadow sides, the riddles and death are certainly there, as we already found in the Psalms, as Job had already done before him and as Francis was to do after him: there are the sun and the moon, day and night, heaven and earth, the clouds and the sea, the mountains and the valleys, rain and hail, water and fire, the beasts of prey and the domesticated animals, young and old, life and death. None of all this is the supreme good, and nothing is wholly bad. What we regard as negative, bad or evil is in fact always a question of deficiency, shortage, corruption, damage,[33] just as sickness is the absence of health and loneliness is the absence of friends, and just as a catastrophe is a disruption of the normal course of events and sin is a failure to achieve the norm of perfection to which God has called human beings. If the being of things is seen statically, good and bad things are independent substances and dualism lurks: the notion that there are two separate forces at work, one for good and the other for evil, or even two kinds of substance – matter and spirit, truth and lies, pain and pleasure – each with a 'Supreme Being' at the head, a God of good and a god of evil, side by side, as Mani taught, or one after the other, as Marcion supposed.

The starting point can thus only be the concrete one reality with all its chaos of things good and bad. But in that case how does this ambivalent reality relate to God? Not in a pantheistic manner, says Augustine, as though reality were a kind of sponge that had soaked up God's presence, so that God was equally and as it were physically spread out in everything, be it good or evil. Nor in the way of the God who looks on at a distance, who as architect or engineer has thought up the blueprint and now makes the workers – the forces of nature, human free will – carry out the work, who guides it now and then or explicitly makes things go wrong in order to spur them on to better work. But God does this in such a way that there all existing things are directed towards the good, are made to strive for growth and become the best that they can be, an *ordo ad deum* which emerges from our estimation of values: then we prefer the good to the bad, the attractive to the ugly, the truth to lies. Although here Augustine makes grateful use of Plato's theory of the eternal Ideas which find (only) their reflection in reality, he emphasizes the reality content of truth, goodness and beauty, and protests against thinking of evil as a substance. Evil is rather a human perspective, characterized by fear, and a derived inauthentic mode of being, characterized by sin. Here there is a fundamental asymmetry between the direction given in creation towards the true, good and beautiful and what is actually the fragmentary realization of them. For even what we experience as negative is never without any value: its existence makes up part of all that is. And we should neither want nor be able to lack that whole: it is that of which scripture says that God regarded it as 'very good'. Thus Augustine, with Plato, directly opposes the scepticism of the Epicureans, who denied any orientation on the good, any teleology.

But he does not go along with Plotinus when the latter denies the notion of a creation in time, or only has an eye for the whole. God may be eternal, but the cosmos is not. Therefore God must also be the creator of time, of the order of the sequence of things and the generations, their division and the determination of their place in space. Both are real and not a mistake in perspective; there is nothing like an intelligible, i.e. imaginary, world of which this world is simply the shadow and semblance. No, this concrete world and these concrete human beings are themselves an emanation of God's glory, an image of God (*Confessions* X). Thus Augustine totally rejects Plotinus' flat Platonism, which smoothes everything out; everything shares in the eternal reality of the *Nous* in equal measure. But he also rejects the notion of a *deus otiosus*. There is a history of God's creation, there is a salvation history; God goes along with his creation and cares for it; God is not apathetic. God has a plan for creation, namely its consummation and richer fulfilment: we do not yet know what we shall be.

The second thing that Augustine rejects in Plotinus is his excessive emphasis on the responsibility of each individual: as if all disaster should be blamed on human beings – that has already been rejected by Job and by Jesus – and as if human beings themselves had to and could save their own souls. The Christian idea of forgiveness and redemption by God is opposed to this. Therefore Augustine points to God's concern for the weak, to Jesus' renunciation of power, and to the fact that the forgiveness of sins brings more happiness than exercises in virtue and therapy for traumas of the kind advocated in Neoplatonism and Gnosticism.

Finally, he also rejects Plotinus' view of bodily and earthly life, as if it were only a game, a 'play' or a 'child's game', and death were simply a change of role. The life of every human being is unique and a unique opportunity and calling for each individual, which determines friendship and communion with God in a life after death.

Therefore Augustine restores evil to human proportions within the 'theoretical order' of ancient cosmology: as *privatio boni*, evil is not *fatum*, blind fate, but a limitation to be overcome. Both catastrophic and moral evil become tasks for freedom. Rather than blaming God for something, human beings must take their hands out of their pockets. Here God does not leave them alone but gives help: *auxilium*, *adjutorium*, the grace of support and ultimate redemption, through Christ and the church in the *civitas Dei*. Häring raises the question which has constantly resounded since modern times: is this not a theodicy which puts the burden on human beings? It may unburden God, but is it not too heavy a burden for human beings?[34] If evil is made a deed instead of a doom,[35] is that not then a choice for the strong against the weak, the victims, as it is in Plotinus? Has Augustine's view, with offshoots down to the Reformation and Jansenism, with good reason – for Augustine himself seeks evil in human fear – led to guilt complexes and fear of God's judgement, which in turn have led to aggression against the human self? Did Augustine understand Job?[36]

Thomas Aquinas

Augustine's views remained decisive throughout the Middle Ages. In the midst of all the vicissitudes of nature and history, of which God is the creator and preserver, it is the vocation and task of human beings to act in accordance with the will of God towards the kingdom of God and in so doing to perfect their souls (*perfectio*), through suffering and death, in an ongoing fight against sin. Here the *exitus–reditus* scheme, derived from Neoplatonism, the doctrine of the journey of the soul, is the starting point and basis. We have come from God, like the whole creation, and we also return to God, whereas all other matter and all other living beings only arise out of matter and return to it: they are for the glory of God and to help human beings. Human beings must strive upwards towards the divine light and ensure that they do not live like animals and in so doing lapse into a less than human state.[37] Human happiness consists in a right insight into these conditions of creation and an orientation on God, the *ordo ad Deum*, which will be consummated in the eternal encounter with God, the *visio beatifica* after death.[38] Boethius' *De consolatione philosophiae* had already stood the theodicy question, 'If God exists, why is there still evil?', on its head: 'Is there still anything good, if God does not exist?'[39]

Thomas Aquinas likewise produces a similar argument: '... if evil exists, then so does God. For there would not be anything good if the ordering in the direction of the good, of which evil forms the hindrance, did not exist. But such an order would not exist if God did not exist.'[40] Thomas begins by repeating Augustine's insight that everything that is, is good because it is created by God: *ens et bonum convertuntur*.[41] Geyer calls this the 'ontological depotentiation of the negative'.[42] Levinas and de Boer were to attack this position vigorously, because it already gives the pure existence of things a surplus value. However, Thomas does not mean first of all that we have no reasons, no norms, so that we cannot report anything at all when we see reality as related to God.[43] Good and evil are predicates, not 'existences', despite all appearances to the contrary. They are always the result of contrasts or comparisons. Here evil is always measured by the good, as an absence of the good.[44] And even evil, in so far as that is intended, still derives something from the good that is necessarily bound up with it: otherwise human beings would not want it, for no one wants evil as such.[45] If we consider the whole of creation, it is even an enrichment and a good that there are such things as *corruptibilia*.[46] God can also make something good out of so-called evil.[47] Without evil we would lack all kinds of good things: in this way Thomas reverses the thesis of Anaximander, who thought that there is nothing good, because the good always comes into being at the expense of something else.[48] It is the very perfection of fire that is the cause of the consumption of air and the burning of matter![49] But God is not the cause of evil, because in God there is no tendency to non-being: there can be no defect in God, God wills to be pure good.[50]

Within this insight, Thomas raises the question of evil in the framework of ethics, i.e. the doctrine of happiness and the analysis of human action that can lead to happiness. The goodness of the creation puts the human beings who make use of it in debt. Human beings have a responsibility to leave it intact and as far as possible by their behaviour and freedom to match its perfection and harmony. The sheer deficiency is not yet negative: the finite as such is not evil. Evil consists in the perverse strivings of the finite, when this does not strive for the optimum. The good is worth striving for: *bonum est appetibile*. Evil is not *appetibile*; as such it cannot be the aim of the will or of being as a whole, because in that everything strives for perfection.[51] No, the human being alone has the freedom or not to strive for the optimum. God cannot and will not have it otherwise, by virtue of his Being, and nature cannot do otherwise, because of its inbuilt purpose or *entelecheia*. Only human beings can go against their nature and interrupt the striving of nature. So only in human beings does the deficient become evil. Evil must therefore be defined not just as *privatio boni* but as *privatio boni debiti*: the withholding of the good that is due.[52] In Thomas this is translated theologically as hindering or withholding the good that is due to the creator. This is the nature of the deficiency of created things which are imposed on human beings as a punishment, but which they can make worse through guilt. In that case human beings lay themselves open to punishment because they neglect their innate talent to seek their ultimate goal in God. Being open to punishment is worse than being punished, because in it we experience ourselves as bad, and that is the worst evil.[53] So the worst evil is not catastrophic evil – not being able to do what one wants – but moral evil: not wanting what one can do. Life is a gift of God which must be ordered on God, out of gratitude. 'Salvation' or happiness consists in this life attaining its goal. Theology is the doctrine of human salvation in the service of God. All that furthers this salvation (technology, science and politics) then belongs – materially – to the themes of theology but – formally – only in so far as it brings about human salvation, in other words in so far as it leads to the truth. To seek the truth is a form of striving for happiness.[54]

Thus Thomas' doctrine of evil and of the attitude of God to catastrophic and moral evil does much to rid people who cannot do what they want of guilt and strongly determines the punishment of those who do not want what they can do. His thought reminds the strong of their responsibility and does not impute any sense of guilt to the weak. However, for the fate of those who suffer outside their own guilt and even outside the guilt of others, his argument remains unsatisfactory: God needs defects to enrich the creation and to make the differences possible! There is little room in Thomas' thinking for tragic evil. God becomes above all the God of a morality of achievement. The Reformers were to find this doctrine of human merits unsatisfactory and in conflict with the biblical idea of God, here in connection with the misery of their days and the beast in human beings.

Luther

Martin Luther and the other Reformers in his footsteps radically dismissed any form of theodicy in which human beings tried to call God to account for catastrophes and for moral evil. It is often said that they replaced the justification of God by man with the justification of man by God. Human beings as creatures have little to offer God: everything happens by virtue of God's sovereign will. God also sees through the human will (the heart), and does so by virtue of divine providence, which also fathoms reason (thoughts). So there is nothing for human beings to do but to live in conscience and awareness with God before their eyes and in obedience to the word of God in the scriptures. Their freedom is essentially subject to God's will. But human beings can rebel and go opposite ways, and indeed have done so, from Adam and Eve on. That makes them uncertain: how do I stand, what must I do, how will things go with me at God's last judgement? Why do I do what I do not want and live in accordance with my desires? Why do I not succeed in doing what I should want, but constantly fall short? According to Luther – in vigorous debate with Erasmus and the humanists of his day, who in the footsteps of scholasticism emphasized human freedom – human beings do not have free will, although we have freedom of movement and freedom of thought and action. We are fundamentally bound by human defectiveness, by an innate tendency to evil which is rooted in us and a constant failure to attain the ideal of the kingdom of God. We do not attain what God wants of human beings, as this is laid down in the Law of God, the Commandments of Israel, and the evangelical counsels of Jesus in the Sermon on the Mount. So human beings are in God's debt, and only God can justify them by his grace, by ridding them of guilt and sanctifying them in order to make them worthy of God. Only belief in justification by God, despite human sin, gives us the certainty of God's gracious concern. This is the summary of the whole Bible, the core of the gospel of Jesus Christ which liberates us from the doom of the Law and reveals God to us as a gracious God.

But Luther and the Reformation do not resolve Job's old questions in this way. The personal certainty of faith does not resolve the impotence of human beings in nature and history, nor does it answer the question of the relationship between natural contingency and the divine purpose of history, the course of which is absolutely firm because of God's sovereignty. There remain for Luther two kingdoms, domains or regimes: the actual course of events, which must be guided by the politicians with laws and penal sanctions and by the professional dedication of people in all spheres of life; and the divine ideals of which the church makes use through preaching and sacraments, the help of God's grace and the call to a sense of vocation and conscientious action. Luther and the Lutheran tradition could not avoid a certain dualism between the two and there was a danger that Christians would be neutral or quietist with respect to the historical events and decisions.[55] The dramatic consequences of such neutrality on the part of Christians towards the historical and political course of events became evident in the twentieth century in the period of the Nazi regime and the Second World War. Only the ecumenical movement overcame this neutrality and this dualism of history and salvation history.

The problem of human freedom as freedom of choice and freedom of initiative and thus the question of human responsibility for science, technology and ethics which Luther, too, does not deny and which were directed more sharply in a humanistic direction, has also not been resolved. Thus Lutherans after Luther, including Leibniz and Kant, could become the founders of the concept of human autonomy and the ideals of the Enlightenment. The term and model of a 'rational theodicy' come from Leibniz, and from Kant the rational deconstruction of any theodicy: thus in two centuries the inner conflict and aporia of Luther's thought led to radically different pictures of human beings and God which are still influential in our day.

Leibniz

Gottfried Wilhelm Leibniz, who was born in 1646, shortly before the end of the Eighty Years' War, and who died in 1716, forms the transition from the Augustinian heritage – he himself was a Lutheran – to 'modern' philosophy and liberal theology. This gives a central place to the autonomous, questioning, researching and experimenting subject rather than to an 'order of grace', an 'eternal counsel of God', a 'journey of the soul' or a 'salvation history'. The main concern from now on is human salvation and happiness and the fight against anything that can oppose that. There was a scientific quest for cohesion and proof and for universal mathematical models: necessary truths, clear images, formal arguments. Together with Descartes (1596–1650), Spinoza (1632–77), Hobbes (1588–1679) and Malebranche (1638–1715), Leibniz is reckoned as being in the school of so-called 'rationalism'. These figures are also called the philosophers of the early Enlightenment. They all want to order reality in such a way that the order of knowledge corresponds to the order of being. But that can be done only if we can indicate why each actual movement (clashes, relations between persons, activities) must be as it is and cannot be otherwise. This attempt has also been called 'panlogism': the logic of the universe corresponds to the logic of our thought, and a causality of purpose corresponds to the causality of work. Causes and reasons, the natural and the moral order, are interwoven. That this is the case can only be the consequence of a divine plan for human beings and things, orientated on the universal harmony of God's will and human reason. It is a matter of acting in accordance with the supposed will of God. God himself wills nothing and does nothing outside the world order. We ourselves cannot devise any event which does not follow the rules. Even a miracle does not happen outside the world order, because what we call natural laws merely form a divine custom from which God can deviate for a stronger reason; but even then he observes (other) natural laws. This regularity of God becomes the proof of God *par excellence* for the pupils and descendants of these founders of rationalism in the eighteenth century, the so-called physico-theologians. For the sake of belief in God they thought that they could profit from glorifying the building of the spider's web, the beehive, the behaviour of ants.[56] Their 'natural theology' became the target of the mockery of theologians and atheists alike. In the previous chapter we paused over this modern critique of 'theism' as one of the backgrounds to philosophical agnosis. But this did not do full justice to their intentions. They wanted to save religion and also Christianity from the sphere of the irrational and the infinitely religious purpose of philosophy and the whole of human knowledge and potential activity.

Indeed what Leibniz aimed at with his theodicy[57] deserves a theological re-reading. Not all his ideas are a priori unusable. In particular Leibniz's refusal to accept a double truth, that of faith and reason, deserves a closer look. He talks about this in a chapter about faith and reason which precedes his theodicy. He also returns to it in his *Discourse on Metaphysics*.

By separating the domains of the worldly and the divine rule, Luther's Reformation, along with the mistrustful attitude of the Roman Catholic magisterium to new scientific methods and discoveries, had prepared the ground for a division between faith and reason. It seems impossible to know God other than in the faith that God himself awakens. In that case religious ideas no longer have any 'factual' character: creation, the fall, revelation, the Law of God, communion with God, redemption, sacrifice, reconciliation, etc., then form, as dogmas and axioms, a priori a world of their own which only in the second instance – and so to speak through a misunderstanding on the part of the church or science – clashes with things like natural laws, logic, historical and causal knowledge. 'They live by grace of the life that created them, namely the religious life,' says Leibniz. Faith then becomes a way of looking, a way of speaking. It does not provide analytical knowledge. Therefore statements of faith, too, are never hypothetical but absolute. On the other hand, reason provides knowledge only of natural and historical data, which can be tested by research and experiment. Indeed Hobbes, Bayle and Locke opted for positing that faith is 'beyond reason' and that it does not provide knowledge for the scientist which he cannot find in a better and clearer way without reference to God or faith.[58] Leibniz thought that this division, which in fact in the long run proved fatal for the relevance of faith in Western culture, was an invention of the devil.

Leibniz[59] takes the newly discovered laws of mechanics as the starting point for his thought. The whole of reality consists of substances which clash with one another. We can legitimately make assertions only about these substances, or rather: our thought that makes such assertions and the thoughts that we can have about certain things can never be detached from the substances. Everything that we assert about them 'rests' somehow in such a substance, which thus functions as the vehicle of all properties and the source of all predicates: *omne praedicatum inest subjecto*. Thus there are not two worlds, one of thought and one of things, as Descartes argued, for thought is always thought about something, which in one way or another is an aspect of a substantial reality. Leibniz gives the name 'monad' to this substantial reality, the smallest possible nucleus, which is the source of all possible assertions and the vehicle of all aspects – Kant would mockingly call it the thing in itself, *Ding an sich*. Thus present, past and future always form predicates of concrete substances, and also define their place in respect of other substances in the universe. Moreover the structure of the universe is composed in such a way – that is its *harmonia praestabilita* – that this is reflected down to the smallest substances. Each particle forms an impression of the universe as a whole and can exist only in connection with it, just as every point on an infinite line or a crossing of lines 'dominates' all the lines of force that emanate from it, although the point itself knows no extension and occupies no space. It is the same with monads. They form the centre of an infinite number of relations and definitions. God forms the supporting background to this connection of part and whole. How? Through what Leibniz calls the principle of potentiality. Every monad goes actively in search of the whole. As well as the atomic structure of the particles which cannot be divided further, in each part and between all particles there is also something like a force of cohesion, comparable with the feeling and desire and will of human beings. That is the primal force, the *appetitio*, with which things cling to one another. Everything partakes in this force, and one cannot devise anything that has no part in it. Thus everything is also valuable because God has a feeling for it all, down to the smallest detail: God 'sees' and 'feels' the universe from every possible perspective. So God creates unity in the diversity of things and ensouled substances without being exhausted by them or specifically settling somewhere in them.

From this perspective there is no such thing as evil. That arises only from the perspective of human freedom, which is said to will something different from what actually happens. But the actual course of events, with all its apparent faults and imperfections, proves to provide the best possible world. So even Adam's fall was a *felix culpa*, because this led to the incarnation of God's Son, with all the blessed consequences that followed. Moreover, a world in which evil happens but which also knows freedom is better than a world in which everything happens of necessity and automatically, as it must. Nor can one argue that there is more evil than good in the world, because quantity and quality cannot be compared: whereas the possibilities of the good are infinite, evil has its limitations.[60] Furthermore, Leibniz rejects out of hand the statement that God's sovereignty, omnipotence and providence exclude any freedom and thus any reason for guilt and punishment: God creates the human will, the hallmark of our freedom. Although what we do thus happens in accordance with God's providence, we take the initiative; we do things because we want to. There is an absolute necessity only for what actually is, what cannot be other than as it is, as in the laws of nature or mathematics. In what we want to realize in freedom we make use of the necessary things, of consequences and effects. Therefore the slogan *ora et labora* – pray and work – is not a contradiction at all.[61] So God can order things in such a way that sometimes evil consequences arise out of processes of nature or human activities. Just as human beings do not intend these evil consequences but take them into account, so that is no shame on God. In God too there is a prevenient will and a consequent will. Although God always wills and intends only the good, sometimes he must in consequence also allow less good things, with a view to his ultimate will and intention.[62] It is like a ship on a river: it gets its speed from the river, but the cargo reduces that speed. Yet the cargo has to arrive somewhere. In other words, God has to fit in with the checks that he has, and these include among other things the law of inertia and the inertia of the human soul. Here Leibniz refers specifically to Augustine and to Thomas Aquinas,[63] but also to Arminius and Duns Scotus.[64]

It is clear that Leibniz and his contemporaries were mesmerized by both the limitations and the boundless possibilities of human freedom with regard to the laws of nature, which were being tracked down. The principle of inertia, the laws of gravity, the laws of thrust, the connection between acceleration and force, the insight into mass and weight, amplitude and pendulum; the discovery of the circulation of the blood and the way that the heart acts as a pump; the discovery of the microscopic world in biology which so fantastically seems to be ordered by the same laws as the macrocosm which people caught sight of through the telescope; the new possibilities of cartography and geography, which made the precise measuring of distance, definition of location and navigation possible: all this, together with the certainties of mathematics, ultimately seemed to banish all that was chance and arbitrary. Leibniz and his contemporaries were not blind to the shadow side of the violence of nature and human misbehaviour, but with the whole tradition they put all their hope and trust in God's infinite purposes, which had to be even more certain than the forces of dynamics. At the same time they were matter-of-fact enough to see that this could be achieved only by causes and motives and thus with counter-forces and restraints. For them, God is the one who can achieve the maximum effect with the minimum labour and is always concerned with the reconciliation of opposites and the harmony of the universe. In this sense Leibniz also argued for tolerance, ecumenism and a policy of peace, and he was also the founder of eirenism. His metaphysical arguments finally had the sole purpose of deciding the controversy about grace and free will, election, justification and merit, which stamped his time.

Thus he observed that the exclusive emphasis on God's righteous and sovereign government makes God an arbitrary despot: 'For why should we praise what he has done, if he would be equally praiseworthy for doing quite the opposite? Where would his justice and his wisdom be, if there were only a kind of despotic power, if will took the place of reason, and if, in accordance with the tyrant's definition, what the most powerful wanted was on that account just?'[65]

Conversely, those who think that God could have created the world better than it in fact is – which was the view of Duns Scotus and the nominalists, but also of Leibniz's contemporary Male-branche and some Jansenists – arrogantly set themselves on a judgement seat above God's throne. Those who are not content with what God does prove to be discontented subjects and rebels. Leibniz confesses: 'God does nothing for which he doesn't deserve to be glorified.'[66] But that is not the same thing as tranquillity or quietism. Thus we must be calm about what has happened and is now past, but when it comes to the future we cannot sit with our hands on our laps, waiting to see what God will do. It is a matter of acting 'according to the presumptive will of God'.[67]

Kant

It is at this last point that Kant's critique begins. How do we know this 'presumptive will of God'? For centuries this had been derived from the Bible and established by the teaching authority of rabbis and church leaders. But after all, the biblical authors and the scribes, the church fathers and the bishops, surely had no other means of knowledge than experience and reason?

According to Kant, all philosophical attempts to harmonize evil with the will of a good God must be regarded as failures.[68] In fact a great deal happens in the world which has no purpose, which one cannot in the remotest way claim happens in accordance with the 'presumptive will of God'. Thus moral evil is clearly in conflict with God's holiness as Lawgiver and Creator: the violence of nature which causes so much suffering is clearly in conflict with God's goodness, with which he is thought to care for his creation, and the disproportion between sin and punishment – the unfair treatment of sinners – is clearly in conflict with God's justice as a judge. One cannot solve the problem by playing these properties of God off against one another, as if, for example, because God is good one ignores his righteousness, or vice versa.

Kant thinks that the notion that God's wisdom is of another nature than human wisdom, or that our understanding is too limited to see into God's ways, is the end of all morality: in that case one can no longer speak of doing God's will. It is just as bad to say that evil is caused by human limitations as such. In that case there is no longer any responsibility for evil: we cannot do otherwise. That also applies if one thinks that God does not will evil but simply has to allow it because of the limited possibilities of human beings and the world. Then too we can do nothing about moral evil: it simply becomes a natural disaster.

In this last case, catastrophic evil as the cause of death and affliction, it is not much of an argument to say that such suffering is only semblance and that sorrow over the dead is short-sighted because we wrongly want to remain alive come what may or because many would no longer wish to live in such circumstances. In fact no one wants to come to an end at such a moment and in such a way. Nor is it much of an argument to say that suffering and pain hit harder than enjoyment and pleasure, since in that case the question arises why God has intended this unhappy and undesirable situation for us. In the end the promise of a future happiness after this life is implausible; why does there have to be all the suffering as a proof of it? Who is better as a result? Neither God, or he would have to be a sadist, nor human beings, unless they are masochists.

Finally, in connection with the lack of righteousness in God: it is not true that evil punishes itself, for example through remorse. There are criminals enough who seem to have no burden of remorse. Nor is it true that suffering always furthers a virtuous life. Nor does it help to appeal to a kind of restoration after this life: why should the divine wisdom – the presumed will of God – turn out to be other at the heavenly court than what is laid down in the natural law and the universal sense of justice? But at this precise point we experience the clash between our moral commitment and the actual suffering that nevertheless comes upon us.

So not a single philosophical theodicy succeeds in making the actual experience of evil correspond with the idea of the moral wisdom of God's governance of the world, although we cannot prove the opposite – and thus the non-existence of God – either.

Physico-theology arrives at a certain insight into the artistic construction of the universe, and insight into practical reasons suggests that universal rules of behaviour are woven into creation. But we have no idea of the connection between being driven by natural necessity through an Author-God and at the same time being thought to act in freedom. This is a contradiction in terms.

Really theodicy should read the will of God from nature. But in that respect nature remains a closed book: we do not know its course. There is only one book, according to Kant, that gives us insight into God's purposes, and that is the book of Job. Here God himself, as Lawgiver, states his purposes, and Job, when faced with God, refers only to his experience and his conscience. Thus Job does not base ethics on his faith, but his faith on ethics. That is the only authentic religious answer if religion is to be more than 'gaining favour', namely a good way of life. Thus the key to dealing with suffering and sin lies in truthfulness and faithfulness. Human beings are good enough to will the good, but they are intrinsically inclined to threaten themselves and others in doing so.

Thus, according to Kant, the judgement on good and evil lies in human beings themselves. There is no philosophical or theological bench of judges which can pass a verdict on the presumptive will of God. There is only the experience of suffering and misdeeds. The only judge is our own capacity to judge and – but Kant cannot yet give it this name – the narrative competence of the one who suffers – like Job – or the one who sins: we can perceive one another's complaints and cries of woe in so many stories of suffering; we can confess to ourselves and others in order to acknowledge our mistakes and shortcomings and to ask for another chance.

Christians with a less vindictive antipathy to the biblical story than Kant and with more insight into the narrative force of tradition will let the passion narrative of the righteous Jesus and the penitent confessions of the unfaithful disciple Peter or the persecutor Paul count in their complaint to God, which is inevitable if they are honest, and then quickly refrain from putting God on trial. Here it is human beings themselves who are in the dock.

CONCLUSION: THE THEODICY QUESTION AS A SYMPTOM OF PASSION FOR THE GOOD

However, the re-reading of the theological theodicy argument has yet another consequence than a reference to the truthfulness of the conscience and the humility of human beings towards God. The very question which resounds in theodicy reveals something of the good's own power of blessing; it discloses the passion of human beings for the infinitely good. Where does the question of the origin of evil come from if not from the presumption of possible good? Where else could this possible good be located than in God? That is a variant of the twist which Boethius already gave to the story: how could anything be good without God?

The whole human project of religion and science, art and technology, is based on this passion for the good. If we say that human beings are wise and experienced and also refer to experience and wisdom ourselves, then we are talking about ways to the good that have gradually been found.[69]

The question of evil – why is there evil, why do I do evil, why does evil happen to me? – is a predication of my passion for the good, for what heals, makes sound, makes happy. Experience – experience remembered, experience told of – as something that happens to us resists our constant flight into forgetfulness. We can evade the passion for the good by such questions as: What difference does it make? What does it help? All is semblance, all is relative, there is no substance, no relationship, no subject but only a predicate: you are what you say. But the surplus value of what happens to us is shown in the face of the suffering other, and also in the sense of guilt of the perpetrator that I am, even if I want to acquit myself. Levinas and Ricoeur are both right here: l'appel and l'aveu are two basic motifs of experience, parallel to the complaint and accusation which are there in the sight of the suffering other: the complaint leads to the appeal, the accusation to the confession, l'aveu.

Here, as Häring rightly observes, the distinction between good and evil assumes a hermeneutical function.[70] Evil cannot ever be localized anywhere, for we cannot divide reality into parts where evil can be localized and parts where good can be localized. All the 'places' which have been noted for this in the course of history – matter, the body, the other, time – are just as much forms of what we experience as good. Nor is evil a substance which can be 'somewhere'; it is the quality of things as they are, in their connection as process or system. Both in its catastrophic and its ethical dimension evil is always bound up with freedom and choice. Even if there are victims, that too is the consequence of free human choice: their own if they have chosen the risks; that of others who are out for their own advantage; that of society as a whole which is guided by perverse aims (relating to the ecological disasters which threaten us); the economic injustice that arises in the division of society into the rich (in opportunities) and the poor (in opportunities); the sicknesses which arise from bad habits or inadequate medical care. This interweaving of evil with the human freedom (of choice) does not do away with the experience of the tragic: there is much suffering about which 'nothing can be done'. However, the recognition of this does not exclude a constant challenge to it: thus the 'tragic' in particular assumes a hermeneutical function in the direction of the good. How can something like that be avoided and what can we do about it?

All experience and all life is thus an experiment with ourselves: inspection, critique, examination, a demand for improvement – always in search, as we are, for the good and the beautiful, the *kaloskagathos*. The question of theodicy is an aspect of this *eros* which drives us and can never become an object: evil cannot be removed from the world, but in the midst of all that is evil and sinful there is nevertheless a desire for the good and whole, as a creative event which constitutes our persons. The Jewish-Christian tradition has called this *eros elpis*: hope. This hope is the answer to the complaint and accusation of tragedy, finitude, sickness, guilt and death. It restores a shine to existence, it changes the shine into a glitter, it turns sin into a renewal of life.[71]

Thus thought too – the quest for wisdom, philosophizing – is driven by a pathos which continues without ever being caught up with, as Blondel remarked. Coherence and direction are sought in this pathos. It is not dissemination but recollection, though that can never happen without difference, dialectic, configuration and exchange. Existence is a tragicomedy which cannot be completely mapped out either by the comedy-writer Aristophanes or by the tragedian Agathon: when they both fall asleep, life goes on and corrects their drunken intoxication.

Therefore the lesson of the long history of theodicy is that we cannot master the shadow sides nor experience the light without shadows. In the midst of the shadows, however, people reach for the light: we find that in the light of the ever-new day, in the light with which we ourselves see and in the light in the eyes of others. The cosmic forces (Newton's light), their modulation in personal freedom and the awareness of and dedication to the shining other: these are the three powers against the darkness of nothingness, of tragic fate, of death.

The question is: does *thanatos*-darkness finally win out over the light? Death is the strongest argument against the existence of God: my own, unavoidable death, but above all also the death of the other whom I love or the deliberate murder committed by those who kill for motives of pleasure or utility, and finally the threat of the death of all life in the entropy of the cosmos.

So the choice is not between God and fate, God and nature, God and life – fate, nature and life are all compatible with God.[72] The choice is between God and the existence of death.

After a weak defence against Kant in the footsteps of Hegel (for example in Teilhard de Chardin), theology has long given up its attempts to trivialize evil in order to be able to acquit God. The modern answer of theologians, which I gladly follow, is that God is present in the very question of the why, in the aporias that we experience, in complaint and lament against violence, in the reason which combats violence through technology and consultation, through dialogue and reconciliation, through mercy and the offer of another chance. God is a God of the living, not of the dead; a God of peace and not of violence. There is no violence in God.[73] Thus God is purged of blame and any human flight from responsibility is cut off. At the same time the temptation to look for 'a better God' is also cut off: if God exists, this world with all its ambivalences, catastrophes and human crimes is God's creation, God's own work, handed over to human beings to make it a place which can be lived in. We find this respect for refractory reality and this realism about human possibilities and responsibilities in the creation theology of recent decades.

But even then two questions remain, which seem to me to be questions of fundamental theology *par excellence*:

- If reason is involved in our opposition to violence, rationality in the best meaning of to each his own (*ratio* = rationing), then why still God? Does not the hypothesis of 'God' in this answer prove superfluous? Does what happens as a result of autonomous reason make a difference?
- If it is a matter of complaint and accusation, or liberation and responsibility, then what about punishment and retribution, what is to be done with the fight against evil which will not succeed without violence, what about the forces and passions which push us beyond the limits of reason? Is God involved only with half the world, only with its sunny side and not with the night side? Is God in fact only with the good and goodness? And does not that mean the return of a two-worlds scheme, against which the monotheistic idea of God rightly rebelled?

In the following chapters I want to show that if we accept the ambivalences and paradoxes as given, windows can nevertheless be found in life which offer a prospect of the good, the holy and the sublime, of historical growth and becoming, of becoming a subject in the presence of God, which rob suffering, fate and sin of their character of doom, precisely through the prospect of God.

4

Traces of God: The Human Emotions
Desire, trust, protest and forgiveness

The Russian novels from the period just before the great upheaval in 1989 – which began from a complete atheism but gradually rediscovered the need to identify with the religious[1] – described against the background of the rotten Soviet system the experience of the void, the difference between having and being, between the gratuitousness and unpredictability of happiness and love, as Buber, Marcel and Levinas did earlier in the West. They wanted to see all the planned, technological, economic, bureaucratic aspects of the world in which we live once again filled with what for example Ilya Ehrenburg calls 'a culture of the emotions': the questions of guilt and repentance, fear and sorrow, desire and wonder, dedication and ecstasy. It seems that what was true of the Eastern bloc – the imprisonment of culture in an extremely limited form of rationality, anxiety about daily rations, the labyrinth of procedures, the endless comparison of planning and result – has increased just as much in Western culture, not as a result of an imposed party ideology or as the result of a shortage but through the complexity of the means by which we wanted to get a grip of our life. Is there still time to dwell timelessly on things, time for uncalculating outlooks, for the reparation of guilt, for protest against the ordinary that is the planned course of things? In short, is there room for those apparently useless, time-consuming things which are connected with our emotions?

Heidegger and Arendt[2] had written earlier about the changed sense of time in Western culture. Time, as *temps*, *tempus* (clock time, measured time) – which is no longer related to *saeculum* (generation, lifetime) and *aevum* (duration, the succession of centuries) – becomes the all-defining *mensura* (measure) and *regula* (criterion, guiding thread) for life: like a ticking alarm clock 'now-there', 'now-then', 'now-here'. Heidegger calls this the vulgar concept of time which lacks the depth-dimension of time that is given us to live in. Although we spend the greater part of any period of twenty-four hours in simple actions without a material product – walking, looking, eating, talking, listening, making love, playing, sleeping – according to Arendt all our attention is paid to the work that we have to do or the recognition – wages, honour – that we want to achieve by it. '*Homo faber*' is threatening again to become an '*animal laborans*': a drudge who no longer has any time for the highest human activity, for what Heidegger calls 'authenticity'. People labour at their work even when they are unemployed – indeed, precisely then. We come to grief on the very machines with which we have surrounded ourselves, the machines for production, communication and transport. The space for symbols which enlarge the spirit is reduced by the attention that all this facilitating material constantly demands of us. Our work (*labor*, *labour*) and the product of this work which brings us respect (*opus*, *oeuvre*) determine what we call our diary, our agenda, whereas most of what we actually do consists in different kinds of occupations (*actio*, activity) which cannot be put in a diary: the purely lifelike patterns of movement, play, language, imagination, attention and involvement which together determine life. Instead of being a moment of dating (giving time) and taking time (free time), our own lifetime, the *nunc stans* of each movement, the decisive opportunity that we have in the present to choose freely becomes the course of time (time elapsed) and not having time (working time). This reversal is not just a sociological or psychological phenomenon but a change which is inherent in Western thought and implies a loss of being: our internal clock – which should ensure that we fill the time given us as well as possible and mark out the journey of our soul well, leading to a fair distribution of action and contemplation – is thus set to the external instruments for measuring time. Instead of having an eye for the mysterious possibilities of every beginning of time – Arendt calls that our natality, our capacity for taking the initiative – or realizing how each moment brings our existence closer to death – the real temporality of *Dasein* according to Heidegger – we adapt ourselves only to our own counting – and our own watch – so as to lose no time in accumulating obligations which pursue us from the past.

Thus our sense of time is formalized through organization and planning and mechanized by a multiplicity of spatial movements: the time that we need to get from one point to another. Control panels and computers – fax and Internet – replace relationships; urban anthropology is characterized by infinite displacements, role patterns, services, pigeonholes and agreements. Although our official working hours are less, for large groups the amount of free time available is reduced to a minimum. The social costs of the urban stress which is generated in this way are almost incalculable, let alone the personal suffering that arises out of them. It seems certain that increasing criminality, stress illnesses and the need for therapy are the result of this urban lifestyle.

According to R. Girard, this stress is further increased by the sacrificial crisis in which we find ourselves as Western society. According to Girard, the driving force of human action is not desire as such (*libido*), far less the nostalgia for all primal forms of being human (*archai*, archetypes, according to Jung), but the rivalry of the rival, which is at the same time a model and an obstacle for our desire. This rivalry must be tamed by 'diverting' the fears which are its breeding ground. The fear of the death which can come to me at the hand of another; the fear of being crushed by someone else in relationships or work; the fear that whole peoples have of a rival economic and social order, all these could be 'diverted' as long as rivals still came to an agreement through a shared third party. God and religion performed this function of the shared third party with sacrifices, rituals, sacraments, festivals and myths. According to Girard, now that that has vanished, violence lurks, and the logical results are the cold war, career pressures, competition and stress, which are the order of the day.[3]

The key question posed by culture to religion and theology would then be whether they can offer a picture of God which will withstand the religious critique of modernity, because it no longer stands in the way of human fulfilment and autonomy and because at the same time it offers us the instruments, the metaphors and the rites which are meant to restore our meaning in life and prevent the development of violence.

In particular if it is true that the marriage of violence and power with God and the church in the history of Europe and America and the Slavonic-Byzantine world has been furthered by Christianity and that secularization is a legitimate reaction to this abuse of violence and power – and there is much to say for this argument when we see so many wars of religion, burnings of heretics and crusades – this question of an image of God in which there is no violence and which can provide armour against violence is extremely legitimate.

The Czech president Vaclav Havel wrote in one of his famous letters:

> If we are to make life in this world at least to some degree bearable, we need a way of being human which knows an orientation 'behind' and 'beyond' this world; a way of being human in which every 'here' and 'now' is related to the infinite, absolute and eternal. An unconditional orientation on the 'here' and 'now' closed in on itself makes every tolerable 'here' and every tolerable 'now' an empty wilderness and finally colours it with blood.[4]

THE AMBIVALENCE OF THE CRITIQUE OF THE ENLIGHTENMENT

Is the fragmentation of metaphysics and the erosion of the church in the West itself the cause, or one of the causes, of the tensions, the conflicts, the stress, the depressions and the violence in our Western world? Must we describe the period of the Enlightenment, which even as believers we have now entered as over-enthusiastic latecomers, as a time of the darkness of God, as such different theologians as H. Berkhof, L. Newbigin, J. Ratzinger and K. Wojtyla have done?

Or is it rather the case that, as H. E. Richter has argued, we are suffering from a God-complex and that we have read the image of God that we have abandoned into our own consciousness: the God of power and logic, of will and law, of autarchy and apathy, of patriarchy and the art of government, now incarnated in the ideal image of the strong ego, the domination and the death urge which characterize our culture as a Faustian culture: human beings as the fallen angels of former times, feverishly setting out once again to plough from the earth the heavenly garden that was once permanently closed to us? And having grown weary of our own counting and measuring, must we then hand ourselves over to Dao and New Age; have ourselves rocked to the tune of holism; gape in admiration at auras and reckon in chakras?

I think that such conclusions are premature, that they too easily fall in with the criticism of the Enlightenment which for a generation has become good form in the land of the philosophers.[5] The French Revolution certainly involved much bloodshed, and after the American Revolution a great many Americans sold their souls to progress. The autonomy of the subject has led world-wide to a boundless narcissism of both individuals and nations and hindered the solidarity without which freedom and equality are only half the story. But at the same time reason has combated a great deal of violence, shown up false myths (like those of race, gender and nature), encouraged a respect for truth by free investigation, rooted the dignity of all human beings in a charter of human rights and given form to responsibility in democracy and participation in all spheres of life. We shall have to defend these fruits of rationality against any guru, imam, rabbi, apparatchik or pope: 'Down with all attempts to reverse our coming of age!'[6] This rationality consists essentially in the appeal to arguments and the quest for truth, in the sense that no one may be sacrificed to it by violence.[7] What Evans has described as 'the cults of unreason', in which violence and power take on a sacral aura, are more dangerous than the 'goddess of reason'. If within religions violence and power are surrounded with a sacral radiance, both reason and faith are abandoned, because neither will tolerate violence. That is the pure insight of two centuries of 'Enlightenment'.

But at the same time there is also a void as a result of the exclusive reference to human autonomy. God, too, has disappeared behind the oppressive and polluted horizon of our 'making and breaking'. It is not so easy to judge what is cause and what effect, but the state of things needs to be examined honestly.

The *locus Dei*, which the ancient Near Eastern, Hellenistic, Arab and European culture sought in the order of things, in the chain of causality and the logic of the universe, has escaped us. It has been taken over by particles and forces, codes and rules, disciplines and systems, all regulated by the equipment of our spirit, knowable only as measured, counted, weighed and analysed, as quantum mechanics has made clear to us. Modern biotechnology conjures this up before our eyes in all its horrifying perspectives a makeable human being. The *locus Dei*, which was previously felt in our innermost self and which responded to the name of 'soul' – our deepest self, directly bound up with, created from and determined by God – is now replaced by the experience of the deepest self as the centre of attention, what psychology calls the central control unit, a container of pleasures, caught between cradle and grave, determined by the map of everyone's genes and, who knows, guided by the suprachiasmatic core of the hypothalamus.

There seems to me no longer to be any reason to connect ego or cosmos, *res cogitans* or *res extensa*, with God. As a liberal English preacher already prayed in the nineteenth century: 'Dear God, if you exist, save my soul, if it exists!'

Our milieu is no longer anywhere *milieu divin* (as Teilhard de Chardin still thought); our innermost self is no longer hidden in God (*intimior intimo meo*, according to Augustine and the whole Christian tradition). The idea of God cannot withstand the critique of theism and the charge of projection either as a cosmic principle or as a psychological source.

THEOLOGICAL REACTIONS

What can theologians do in this cultural situation? How can they make the vision of God shine out, make the rumour of God audible again, as it shines out and can be heard in the scriptures, in the lives of prophets, apostles, martyrs; in the activity and the visions of Jesus? The Christian faith wants to show and not just to hold it to be true that a human life according to the standards of Jesus enters the very reality of God. It wants to show that God is Father, Mother, Source of cosmos and self, in whom we live, move and have our being (Acts 17), of whose family we are (I Peter 1.4; Ps. 8), who penetrates our marrow and bone (Ps. 139), whose heirs we are, daughters and sons (Eph. 1.1–23). All that may be the product of human imagination, but it does express something for which men and women have given their lives, by which they have ordered their lives, and which they have accepted as determinative for their lives, not thinking of themselves. And that in our deepest self and in the birth pangs of creation the Spirit of God itself speaks with sighs which cannot be uttered (Rom. 8) surely colours the existence and course of things in history in a real way and not just 'by way of speaking'.

How can we think this God without fabricating an idea of God which is of human making (*le dieu disponible* of deism), for, as Augustine put it, *si comprehendis, non est Deus*: if you understand, it isn't God. A god who could perhaps be expressed in an understandable way could not be God, but only the sum of human perspectives, values, needs or interests. How can we relate to this God, and how can this God relate to us without making God an 'X factor' (*deus ex machina*, God of the gaps) which can be captured time and again? For in that case it is a matter of choosing to live *etsi Deus non daretur*. How can we relate to this God without remaining stuck in the field of language and sign, symbol and metaphor, for that presents the risk of a theology which degenerates into a 'grammatology' of religious argument and God-talk? How can we relate to this God without contenting ourselves with a vague reference to religious feelings and sentiment, because since Nietzsche, Freud and Sierksma that exposes us even more sharply to the charge of religious projection and infantile illusion? And finally, how can we do this without failing to do justice to human freedom and responsibility – for we have had enough of a 'religion of fear': God and human beings are not rivals?

Theology has the task, in the light of present-day human experiences, and drawing on the commemorative experiences which have been handed down to us in the scriptures, of attaining to ways of thinking about God which not only make God thinkable but also make life liveable; which allow God to be tested and tasted (*frui Deo*) as the secret beyond the void and which arm us against the poisons of our autonomy. Over the past twenty years theology has attempted to do this by appealing to our freedom, our activity, to *le projet humain*. We have been able to read that God is a God of freedom, future, setting out, rebellion. God is a God of governance, counsel, involvement, solidarity. Religion is not the opium but rather the cocaine of the people. Peace, justice and the integrity of creation lie within our reach if only we want them, following the God of the exodus. An incredible amount has changed for the good as a result of this way of thinking about God in political theology and liberation theology.

And yet people switch off, wondering what the added value of the idea of God is over and above the intrinsic value of the struggle; what the peace of God adds to the peace of the nations; what is the real character of Christian justice over and above the justice of humanity and human rights; how the World Council of Churches is really different from the United Nations; or, as Hans Küng aptly put it:

> Why, then, believe in God? Why not simply in man, society, the world? Why in God and not simply in human values: liberty, fraternity, love? Why add trust in God to trust in ourselves, prayer to work, religion to policies, the Bible to reason, the hereafter to the here and now?[8]

PASSION: STORIES ABOUT WEAL AND WOE, VALUES AND EMOTIONS

Another way is perhaps on offer which avoids these false dilemmas and shows them up to be false. Life is more than activity and project, planning and necessity, making and breaking. The life that we lead is always led and lived; we share in life and also share it out. Despite our freedom we are woven into all the contingencies of existence, from cradle to grave; we receive the light and the air in which we see and breathe. We live gratuitously, far more than being determined. For the most part our behaviour is non-instrumental: behaviour which is not guided and which we ourselves have not learned. Rather, we are determined by this passionate and participatory side of our existence. But this very insight, and the experience of it that we have, fall short. And for God to be bound up with this side of our existence would dissuade us, keep us from theology, preaching and catechesis.

But now that other ways are proving dead ends we have to try it, provided that we are aware of the warnings from the past. I want to do that, not as a last necessity, but from the core of biblical belief in God itself, as I think I can test that from the stories of the past. These are stories of people in fear and hope, sorrow and joy, longing and opposition. The very name of God – YHWH – is bound up with cradle and grave, pleasure and mourning; with fields and harvest, hunger and thirst; with house and hearth, love and hate; with the city gate and law, trust and protest. God – YHWH – is engaged in a permanent emotional lawsuit for the weal and woe of human beings. And Jesus appears at feasts and parties, by the well and in the market place, among friends at table, in mourning and at weddings. The gospel of God in the Old and New Testaments is full of emotions; it is a gospel for our human emotions.

Of course there are the mighty acts of God, but surely not as brute facts. There are the words of God, but surely not as the disclosure of concepts and the communication of truths. The Word of God, God's own logic, which is reflected in God's actions, is mediated through the emotional experience of nomads in search of pasture, of people who argue over their frontiers, of dynasties which seek each other's lives. But it is also mediated through the experiences of Adams and Eves who do not know what to do with their garden; of Cains and Abels who cannot control their rivalry; of Moseses and Aarons whose laws and rites get too big for them;

of Davids and Goliaths who have to tame their power; of prophets and wise men who in the course of events want to turn in protest against injustice.

The gospel of Jesus takes the form of an appeal and a parable, a rise and a fall, reconciliation and suffering, execution, perplexity, rebellion, enthusiasm. And it is the very experience of God's refreshing, seething *Pneuma* which helps paralysed apostles back on their feet, makes them shift their limits, constantly maintains their solidarity (*koinonia*) in suffering and death, to the ends of the earth (*oikoumene*) (Matt. 24.14).

THE WAY OF THE EMOTIONS

The symbolic universe of the Jewish-Christian tradition is full of emotions. But what are emotions?

A long philosophical and theological tradition has reflected on the fact of our emotions, as the real stirrings of our soul, as the real powers of being (to use Tillich's term) of God and gods. Above all when psychology – to which this domain is contracted or which has claimed it for itself – gained its independence, this whole area of life and the symbols of life were to some degree removed, marginalized from systematic thought about God and human beings in theology and philosophy. The domain was assigned to the vague sphere of spirituality or mysticism and tolerated under strict church super-vision, as devotion for simple people or as a hobby for charismatic groups and conventicles. It was sometimes also reserved for women: in the negative sense as the effeminate and the unmanly (when men still had the say), or in the positive sense as the creative and the warm, as the feminine answer to the cold rationality of male culture (when women got a say).

But not least in philosophy and theology there have been those who have occupied themselves with the sphere of human emotions: Plato, Aristotle, Boethius, Böhme, Pascal, Spinoza, Schopenhauer, Kierkegaard, Nietzsche, Bergson, Scheler, Plessner, Simone Weil, Simone de Beauvoir and really – though sometimes in a much more rationalistic way – all existentialists. And among the theologians Augustine in his *Confessions*, Peter Lombard, Thomas Aquinas on the passions, Martin Luther, Gottfried Arnold, the pietists, Schleiermacher with his theology of 'feeling', and, in the twentieth century, to mention just a few: Paul Tillich, Romano Guardini, Jacques Pohier, Johann Baptist Metz and Dorothee Sölle.

Since the seat of the soul was transferred to the brain, in the Western tradition this whole philosophical and theological reflection on the human heart has been side-tracked and in reaction has found its way into spiritualistic and anti-rationalistic channels. So some rethinking seems urgently necessary.[9]

According to Nico Frijda, in his extensive study of the emotions,[10] emotion is 'the inner determinant of non-instrumental behaviour' or 'the external expression of behaviour that finds its reason only in the person itself', but which nevertheless by definition has the function of appeal, stimulating a readiness for action and relational interaction. We speak of emotions where human behaviour issues in a surplus, in a lack of purpose, which nevertheless seems to be utterly purposeful at a deeper level. As laughing and crying, anger and pleasure, disgust and sighing make clear, they have a liberating effect. These inner determinants have many forms of expression, physiological and psychological, like tremors, moods, promptings, some of which are uncontrollable, apparently only a product of arousal and which thus can hardly be called human actions in the classical sense of *actus humanus*. But together they form non-intentional structures without which action, relations and communications would be impossible.

This passionate side of being human – for that is the specific realm of the emotions: what happens to you – is a sphere in which the bodily and the spiritual still form one domain, in which the animal and the human still border on each other and are related to each other (without ever being identical): human characteristics which do not coincide with subjective feelings and moods but are deployed fully in the sphere of inter-subjectivity and communication, for which they seem to provide the prime raw material from their deeper, more universal level. No wonder, then, that this passionate element is filled and loaded with language and symbols. It is very striking that believers and unbelievers connect the cry 'God' with it.

However purposeful, emotions evade any thinking in terms of causality. They are orientated on non-instrumental behaviour: what one can achieve with weeping and laughter stands or falls with its authenticity, as that which is not intended, wanted or caused.

Emotions are aroused by relevant events, when the interests of the person are involved. They are the result of the interaction between the real or the foreseen consequences of an event and the interests of the subject. They are also the forms of reception, the inner assimilation of the gratuitous and the contingent. They are regulated only in an interplay with the universe of symbols, which moreover they themselves produce. Their surplus character – which also distinguishes emotions from games and dreams, two other sorts of non-instrumental behaviour – becomes evident from simple examples. Eating is purposeful, instrumental behaviour, but eating well, having a feast, dining, is emotional behaviour. Mating is purposeful, instrumental behaviour, but petting, making love, is emotional behaviour. Burying someone is purposeful behaviour, but mourning, weeping, saying goodbye at someone's grave is emotional behaviour. Emotions define the difference between utility and enjoyment, between *uti* and *frui*, between *scire* and *sapere*, between loss and lack, damage and guilt, crime and sin. If we apply this to religion, then we have the difference between prayer as muttering and prayer as a *cri de coeur*.

According to Darwin the emotions are no more than useful, hereditary or learned habits, perhaps rudiments from earlier stages of evolution, which can ultimately be reduced to useful preparations for efficient behaviour. Sexual arousal is then simply a preparation for intercourse; the tensing of a muscle in anger the preparation for a leap or a vengeful blow; blushing for shame a form of mimicry or protective behaviour; and so on. That is an instrumentalist, rationalist reduction of emotion.

But emotions are not purely expressive arbitrary feelings and moods either, simply experience or arousal, far less pure will or desire as an independent phenomenon without any object. Reason is not absent, but remains pre-reflexive, pre-active and as such passionate. Language is one of the instruments, the cultural vehicle with which we also communicate with one another emotionally, according to time-honoured patterns, which moreover are strongly defined by the context. So in our emotions we become moved, which is what the Latin word literally means.

THE CHRISTIAN RELIGIOUS EMOTIONS

As I have already indicated, the Jewish-Christian tradition shares with other great religions a field of religious language which is strongly orientated on the emotions. Fear, desire, trust, curse, lament, joy, fill this language field. The central notion of grace, with its many interpretations,[11] sums up many of these emotions. Through this grace we are moved, as by God's own grace and gratuitousness. We can enjoy it, because God has given it to us to enjoy. God creates pleasure in human beings: that is our grace, which breaks through physically in our emotions. It is precisely in the field of the emotional and the relational that a relationship to reality reveals itself which in Christian terminology calls up, summons the name of God – YHWH, Abba.

It is the sphere of the blowing, stirring, breathing, brooding of God's spirit, *Pneuma* and *Ruach*, which comes over us and takes possession of us. God is in the passion, and this passion is itself in God: that we are given, born, reborn, received, accepted, taken up, finally transported away from all that is necessary and determined, the contingencies of finitude to which we are nevertheless called. We need not be charismatics, mystics, exalted hysterics alien to the world, neurotic enthusiasts, to test this way of thought: Kant already gave his programme of thought the motto *sapere aude*: dare to taste and to test.

It seems to me essential for the Jewish, the Christian and the Muslim tradition to test this way to God, to put markers on it, to develop a Christian culture of the human emotions in this calculating, cybernetic age.

I can see that four such ways of thought have already been tested in theology and philosophy: the ways of desire, trust, protest and forgiveness: these are basic human emotions which supply the basic metaphors of our belief in God.

Thomas Aquinas distinguishes two groups of emotions: those of the *appetitus concupiscibilis* (love/hate, desire/loathing, enjoyment/sorrow; each time distinguished by its positive or negative variant), and those of the *appetitus irascibilis* (hope/despair, daring/fear and anger, in different variants). I sum up these two groups under the headings desire and protest. But in more recent psychological accounts, attentiveness and concentration are also regarded as emotions, as is that consolidation of existence in trust which is opposed to stress or depression. It seems to me that there are also philosophical and theological foundations for emotion described in this way: the *frui Deo* itself, the *contemplatio*, the happy experience of *satisfactio*. I sum that up under the heading of trust. And finally – though the division is not exhaustive – there is the special emotion of vengeance and rancour, which has a different character from hate, and the corresponding emotion of the forgiveness of sins, which restrains vengeance. R. Girard in particular in his work has identified this emotion as the foundation of human society. For Thomas *fiducia* (trust) and *misericordia* (mercy, the disposition to forgive) fall under the heading of *virtutes*: he does not regard them as *passiones*, but as a form of purposive activity. It then becomes more difficult to maintain their character as grace. To a large degree the later dispute over grace was in fact about the difference between *passiones* and *virtutes*.

Perhaps it is illuminating in this connection also to speak of values: it is then a matter of structures of thought and action, experiencing and telling, which give direction to life, principles of ordering which define where we allow ourselves to be driven emotionally, when things 'touch' us, and at the same time arm us against aberrations and threats to the meaning of our lives. So in this concept of value an interaction takes place between virtues and emotions, between *virtutes* and *passiones*. This is a complex of ways of thinking, feelings, values and indications for action at the same time, which I shall call a life form.[12]

Like looking for meaning or concentrating on non-instrumental action, the way of this life form is a real alternative to, counter-weight to, correction of, the technical rationality which seems to choke the fabric of our existence.

I think that in sketching out an adequate picture of God, theology can draw four life forms from its archives and at the same time link up with a philosophical critique of culture. In my view these forms take us beyond secularization and perhaps back to the memory of God which according to Augustine is a condition for understanding God. They form the core of our Christian prayer as that has taken shape in the 'Our Father'. It is precisely this basic Christian prayer which combines faith and praise with emotions and values; it combines faith with ethics, doxology with axiology. It appeals to the human emotions of desire, trust, protest and forgiveness, and it directs the scale of human values to the comprehensive greatness and nearness of the gracious God.

The life form of desire

The narrative of the scriptures, from the garden of Eden to the new Jerusalem, is not a historical narrative or a prediction of the future but a witness to a constant and eternal desire to which nature, history and human hope bear witness. That longing is more than the untameable desire (*eros*) for harmony, for equilibrium, for company, for satisfaction, which characterizes all life as Plato has described it. It is certainly deeper and broader than the desire or passion (*concupiscentia, libido*) which arouses our ardent desires and brings us to sexual ecstasy, although the metaphor of desire, from the Song of Solomon to the mystics, often draws on this source. The longing in the scriptural narrative is also more than just Spinoza's *conatus essendi*, Bergson's *élan vital* or Tillich's 'courage to be', i.e. the pressure towards self-fulfilment and self-preservation which characterizes beings as such. It is more than the dynamic process that we call nature, in which a certain purposefulness or teleology seems to be innate despite all strokes of fortune.[13] The desire to which scripture bears witness embraces all this, knows it all, but weaves out of it God's own desire for salvation and healing, grace and liberation, fulfilment and redemption. God himself longs for an association and a bond with the human being who is blessed; God himself is the love which reveals itself in traces of love between creatures, and it is this love which keeps alive the song of desire for *shalom* – peace and justice. This love does not act out of need or necessity but out of a sheer delight in love and life, peace and contentment. It is also sometimes given to people. In any case it is given to us as a sense of the ultimate criterion of the good and the true which itself can and must be associated with utility and law, obligations and rules.

In the prayer of those who serve God this ultimate longing rings out as a basic emotion, even before we have found words for it or complained about our needs. This ultimate desire (Tillich spoke of 'ultimate concern') is a *locus Dei*, a 'place where God is found', in other words a place where God allows himself to be found, communicates himself to human beings and allows himself to be 'tasted' and 'tested'. Therefore the tradition also says that prayer, as an expression of this ultimate desire, is a sigh of God himself in us. As long as this resonance with God's ownmost desire is not yet present in human prayer, there is not yet prayer but only complaining or muttering. But if this is the case, then praying helps us and is heard even as we pray. Anyone who prays 'Hallowed be thy name' has already done that; anyone who prays 'Thy kingdom come' has already taken the first step on the way to God. Anyone who cannot yet pray 'Our Father' or 'Thy will be done' can already move towards God by way of desire, detect traces of God in the desire for *shalom* and the commandment for righteousness which is expressed by the desire for justice in the face of the other.

A long theological tradition which leads from the prophets of Israel via Jesus of Nazareth to Gregory of Nyssa, Augustine, John of the Cross and Pascal has coupled the view of God with this human desire for the good. Those who say 'God' are saying with a stammer, perhaps cursing and sighing, as believers and unbelievers at the same time, that they long for the good. Those who say 'God', even in the form of a curse, are proving that they can desire as human beings. Those who as human beings can no longer desire, those who in human terms have 'arrived', can no longer say 'God'. For those who are cynics or sceptics, for whom everything is hallucination or illusion, those for whom the appearance is the nature of all change, of all life, there is no God. Scripture says that their belly is their God. 'Mammon' is the only one to whom one can then still say 'Amen': God's name is identical with the milling round the edge of the coin, the sign of the exchange value of possessions, consumption, production and cast of one's own worth, expressed in the equivalent without added value of gold or silver. That is the way in which gods have also come into being (the Indo-Germanic *guta* means moulded). But to say 'God!', whatever meaning it may have later, is at any rate to deny the ultimate importance of the moulds of our own value. As Jewish monotheism, belief in YHWH, pronounced over cradle and grave, field and harvest, land and people, house and hearth, is, as K. Waayman points out,[14] a desire that spans the whole of life, that relativizes all penultimate values and puts them in the wider context of good, purified desire. From then on belief in God is not a projection of our own worth but a longing for worth in a greater whole and an unmasking of any projection of our own worth.

Thus those who say 'God' reverse relationships, know other values than those which are determined by the driving force of rivalry. What are these? Scripture calls them fruit of the Spirit which abides (Gal. 5.13–24; 6.8; Rev. 14.13): love, joy, peace, patience, friendliness, goodness, faithfulness, gentleness, modesty. They are the values which exclude violence and killing, which both honour Abel and protect Cain, which try to do justice to both Sarah and Hagar, which bestow a blessing on both Jacob and Esau: the values of peace, safety, justice, healing and the cancellation of debts; the values of a purified desire.

This life form of desire as a way of thinking about God excludes any objectifying of God. 'No one has seen God at any time,' and 'whoever sees God must die,' says scripture. '*Quae supra nos, nihil ad nos*' ('What is beyond us has nothing to do with us'), said Socrates on the point of dying. According to Jüngel, God is the one who is worthy of desire, not the one who is necessary.[15] According to Gregory of Nyssa in his *Life of Moses*, the true vision of God consists in our looking for God, not ceasing to desire God.[16] God is the one who is worthy of absolute and incessant desire. What does that mean in our post-theistic culture?

The phenomenon of desire itself is not God: projection, dream, ideal, all that may be a condition for talking about God but it is not God himself. God is not exhausted by the categories of surmise and desire. God is more than the human will and the human heart. God does not coincide with our religious feelings, needs, symbols or systems, nor even with our 'natural desire to see God' (*desiderium naturale videndi Deum*), if we could accept that.

Nor does God coincide with all that we desire. That remains within the sphere of the attainable. God himself is unattainable: we cannot tailor God to the measure of our desires or our concepts: *Si comprehendis, non est Deus*, as Augustine said.

So real desire for God cannot be split off either as a phenomenon or as an object of life as it is lived: it takes over the whole person, it stamps him or her a 'subject before God's face' and at the same time forms part of God's own self. As Augustine put it: 'Our heart is restless until it finds rest in you'; all that we do, all that happens to us, is brought into God's innermost self. The innermost self of a person, our inner room, our conscience, our heart and soul, our person, is taken up into the very being of God, becomes part of God's own essence, glorifying his name from cradle to grave, with the flock or at home, at the city gate and in all that anyone's hand finds to do (Deut. 6). All that ever was and shall be is from and to the longing self of God: anyone who ever lived, lives or shall live, lives from and to the longing self of God. To put it more strongly: the self that we experience, our apparent independence, is an experience which we share with God himself. Luther was right: all that we are, we are *coram Deo*. The co-ordinates of our existence – I, you, we, thinking and doing, language and sign, yesterday and tomorrow – become real only by being rooted in and directed by the reality which is this God and which thus creates religious devotion, brings it into existence, 'by grace', because God himself has pleasure in people. The process of life itself, desire upon desire, which come to consciousness in human beings, is therefore itself rooted in and orientated on God: *gloria Dei vivens homo, vita autem hominis visio Dei* (that human beings live is to the glory of God; that we see God is life), as Irenaeus of Lyons remarked.

Of course the prayer of the believer is deeply changed in character as a result of this life form. 'God' is invoked as the one who comes (Jüngel: 'God's being is in coming'; Pohier: 'God must keep coming in order to be there'). Prayer itself becomes a hymn of desire which does not fail when the direct effect does not come about and which does not coincide with the psychological experience of desire either. It is directed towards the living, loved Other, who supports and tests all other desires. Prayer as an expression of the life form of longing meets the criteria for true longing: it cannot even be prayed for. So prayer is a school of true humanity.

What could there be against accepting the legitimacy of enlightened reason and associating this life form of prayerful desire as an antidote to its excesses, by way of an auto-immune system against injustice and violence?

The life form of trust

Desire is never completely fulfilled, but it does know moments of peace. At such moments we experience the emotion and the value, the life form of trust. There is love to which there is a response. There is the experience of trustworthiness and trust. Despite all the mistrust and lack of trust which surround us in the culture of suspicion that we have constructed – everything assured, everything made safe, everything shut up – we still live primarily by trust. Even the most untrusting person has to trust now and then. Despite all mistrust, a fundamental trust appears in the practice of life. In science, politics, ethics and communication this fundamental trust is the condition for the very possibility of progress, planning, management, success. People go by what others have found, argued, determined, said. Not, of course without testing or without a critical perspective. But not without accepting a number of presuppositions, especially that people want to be taken at their word, that a fundamentally similar logic is followed, that people are prepared to allow arbitration in cases of contradiction or conflict or to postpone judgement. Language itself contains such implicit rules; it is the vehicle of trust within a language group. Only alien language creates a situation of mistrust which calls for translation and trustworthy interpretation.

Politics – despite all the conflicts of interests and differences of evaluation – works towards a common administration, as long as there is a basis of trust between the government and the people's representatives. Here the voice of the majority decides, but account is taken of the opposition. Trust is put in question only when differences of opinion and possible policies can no longer be reconciled. Where this trust is completely absent, as in a dictatorial regime, the whole culture suffers under general mistrust in the exercise of government.

When it comes to ethical decisions, for example those about the life and death of terminal patients, but also in the ethics of our relationships or attitudes towards possession, this trust again plays a decisive role: the trust of the sick person in the helpers around, the trust of relatives and friends in one another and in the medical carers, the trust of the doctors in their medical knowledge and apparatus, the trust of two lovers in respect of each other's lives and well-being, the trust of owners in the existing law of property and the protection of their legitimate possessions, the trust of the poor and those in need in social support and welfare.

That really applies to every minute of our daily life. Life in the city would not be safe for a hundred yards without this trust. Parents and children are dependent day and night on this trust. Trust as a gift is the support, as it were the stream of energy vitalizing culture. The critical authority that watches over this has the task of guarding against any escape into false certainties of institutions, authority and dogma: the subjects responsible for these institutions, authority and dogma must never be lost sight of, since only they can guarantee that the institutionalized trust does not begin to turn against itself: Big Brother is watching you! Only an open society in which those who support the institutions and those who make the law or the dogma remain accountable, so that the institutions, the law and the dogma remain flexible, can guarantee such trust. It is precisely because a fundamental affirmation – *emunah* – of human life in the world is possible as 'human', i.e. with an eye to a number of specifically human constants, that there is freedom, and human beings can constantly also reassess their ethical, political and cultural choices.

Erikson put this well: 'By trust I mean what is commonly implied in reasonable trustfulness as far as ethics are concerned and a simple sense of trustworthiness as far as oneself is concerned.'[17] According to many developmental psychologists, this trust rests on 'basic trust' which, if all goes well, people get from parents and above all from the mother. But at the same time it is a basic structure of our knowledge, our planning and our hope, to which we also refer in others. In the midst of all the uncertainty about existence and fear, isn't that a gift of God which for us rests in God's own care? Isn't it a way of thinking about God through which we may have and bring up children, even in the awareness of the possibility of an absolute catastrophe? And isn't it why, while we can destroy the world, we nevertheless do not do so?[18] Isn't the church community the fundamental community of trust in which we encounter one another unarmed, come together at the one table as sinners and saints, and are reborn naked from the bath of life, wishing one another peace over and above all social limits.

So those who say 'God' are expressing trust, as Jesus says 'Abba', 'Amen', also and precisely in the midst of all god-forsakenness: those who say 'God' are taking a position as children of God, enjoying the freedom of the children of God, knowing that God takes pleasure in men and women, and does not want the death of sinners but their life. This trust is our ration for every day, as the daily bread that is given us, and this bread – our life – is also given, granted, us. Isn't that an experience of grace, of gratuitousness, to the depths of our being, an experience of natality,[19] and thus an experience of God which overcomes fears and death and which at the same time avoids and banishes murderous actions?

Shouldn't this culture of trust, rooted in God, be able to overcome the defeatism and depression of so many people and thus contribute to a real combating of 'urban stress' in our urbanized, secularized culture: an antidote to the excessive organization of self-confidence in the culture of autonomy which we have inherited from the Enlightenment?

The life form of protest

Sometimes desire and trust turn into the emotion of protest. We encounter chaos, catastrophe, defeat and resistance; and injustice, guilt, suffering and sin. We instinctively protest, out of pure emotion, against the evil that comes upon people, in the name of justice. In so doing we even accuse God; we ask God to turn the tide: lead us not into temptation! The experience of God, we say, belongs in the category of experiences of happiness: only those who seek happiness will find God. But on our way we find suffering, injustice and death: not only our own pain, injustice and death but also the death, the pain, the injustice of the innocent other, the victim (Levinas) and the loved one (Proust).

Because we ourselves have dirty hands, the innocent other also accuses us: the poor, those who are discriminated against, the forsaken. But who other than God keeps this protest going? Who other than God accuses us – through the suffering of others – calls us to conversion and resistance? Who other than the one who is the ultimate righteousness gives us the criteria for action, for humanity? Granted, God is not the same thing as humanity, but who other than God makes humanity possible, keeps it alive, keeps it going, when human beings so often behave in a bestial way? Granted, God is not the same as our conscience, but who other than God keeps that conscience going as a sense of knowing together (*con-scientia*), despite all confusion and being misled about good and evil? Isn't it the real message of the story of Adam and Eve that access to the knowledge of good and evil remains in the hand of God and that no autonomous choice or direct revelation can guarantee the mediation of good and evil?

Certainly God does not coincide with the fight for liberation – as if this fight could ever be an end in itself – but who other than God keeps this ideal of liberation going despite the oppressive pressure of self-interest and the status quo and despite the caprices of the rulers? Who other than God could tame the beast in human beings? Who other than God will protect Cain? Who other than God can put an end to human rivalry and violence? Only God, in whom there is no violence, who does not need to measure himself against anyone – either against human beings or against any evil power: thus the church has always stood firm against any temptation of dualism – only God can purge our resistance to injustice or vengeance and self-interest. It is God who reconciles the opponents with one another in the victory over injustice.

Thus God is a liberating God whom we test and taste in our opposition to injustice and evil. It is not for us to be the executioner or the judge, or to legitimate our activity as executioners, but to maintain our opposition against any assimilation to what is usually the case. That happens in our complaint against injustice and our accusation to God about the injustice that happens; God himself joins us in the complaint and we join in God's plea for those who have been robbed of their rights. Only in this way can we win the legal case that we keep making against God about evil – how can God do evil to good people? – and at the same time overcome it. That happens in prayer, which in its original form is a blessing for the other who has been robbed of his rights. The Hebrew word for blessing, *barak*, means 'to stand up publicly for someone, to make a plea, to intercede for, to defend'. The Latin word for prayer, *prex*, *preces*, is really the booty from war which needs to be offered to the gods. So Christians have found their *prex* permanently in the surrender of the crucified Jesus and thus have made their praying a plea against all sacrifice. In the celebration of the eucharist – *eucharisteia, berakah* in the name of Jesus – in hope and opposition to injustice we encounter God himself, who intercedes for us in Christ.[20] Of course this fundamentally changes the prayer of believers: God is not asked to break through the order of causality for some self-interest or even for the general interest: far less is God called upon to do this to consolidate one's own self-confidence. The cry 'God!' is uttered for the sake of the others who are robbed of their rights and the believers who suffer. As a result one's own scale of values is deepened, internalized and, if need be, radically changed.

How could this kind of prayer conflict with the project of autonomy? But at the same time: how is this project of autonomy qualitatively defined so that the prayer of believers as a non-violent court of justice – at the same time a public ministry and advocacy – keeps alive the public awareness of the infringement of human rights, the exploitation and oppression of others?

The life form of forgiveness

Last of all I see the way of forgiveness, seventy times seven. Only human beings can forgive one another, put an end to the chains of vengeance and violence, and give one another new opportunities. Paul tells the Romans that the strong should support the weak, not by making themselves strong but by involvement and tolerance, by respect and renouncing judgement and retribution (Rom. 12–14). That is not heroic, not courageous as the Stoics understand courage. It is courageous in the way of God who spares the weak and leads to glorification (cf. II Tim. 2.22–24; I Tim. 6.11; Gal. 5.22).

If we human beings forgive one another, we do so not simply with an eye on God, so that God forgives us (cf. Matt. 6.12), but because of God, who gives the power of forgiveness (cf. Rom. 5.6 and 12.1–21), who makes the good happen through toleration and forgiveness.

No single law of physics or biological evolution, no single psychology of fulfilment or of restraining the oppressive drives forms a basis for this disposition to forgive. Nor is it brought about automatically in people. It is not part of any utilitarianism: if forgiveness is offered only in order to receive the same attitude in return, as is fitting in a culture of courtesy, where excuses are good form, religion loses its religious depth-dimension.

Nietzsche rightly saw that forgiveness is indeed an essential part of the morality of Christians. But it is not a low and lax morality of compassion or resentment at unfair distribution. It is the answer, rooted in God himself, to the vengeance to which human vindictiveness can lead and the only effective weapon against the terror of rivalry and fear to which the Superman is exposed. Indeed, after the death of God, it is not really possible. For who other than God, who gives human beings freedom, even to evil and death, can forgive most deeply and make forgiving possible, breaking through the circle of *do ut des* which determines the contractual sphere that has dominated our society since the Enlightenment?

Hannah Arendt has written notable things about this alternative life form of forgiveness. For example, political sanctions and penal law are in no position to repair the social evil that there is in those who perpetrate evil, which surpasses by far the damaging consequences, however serious, that there might be. Only forgiveness can also give 'reparations' to the perpetrator himself, together with the victim, who has the sovereign possibility of forgiveness, as believers would have it, in the name of God.[21]

The circle of revenge is part of the philosophy of the contract, of reciprocal self-interest. According to this philosophy we require retribution for damage suffered; we cut the ties that we have entered into because we cannot make good through forgiveness; we refuse to restore church communion because we dare not repair breaks. Neither in Christianity nor outside it does this circle of retribution lead to God. But those who break through the circle experience the God who tames vengeance, who silences Lamech's song of revenge (cf. Gen. 4.23–24 with Matt. 18.21–22). Their call to God, their prayers, are the internalization of the will to forgive because they also relate to the enemy and the rival, the persecutor and hater. Those who are not ready to pray for their enemies cannot love them either; they cannot do what according to the gospel of Jesus is more than habit, but 'the one thing needful' that is required of Christians in any culture.

Therefore the 'Our Father' asks God to forgive us 'as we forgive others their debts'.

CONCLUSION

The profound process of secularization has not made these four life forms impassable as ways to God and ways from God. Conversely, these four ways do not deny the positive consequences of secularization either. But they do go beyond it in attaining a deeper level. They arm the humanity of autonomous human beings against the poisons that are produced by the system of their freedom.

These four life forms and ways of thinking about God which unveil the transcendent mystery of our existence make us understand, express, experience; at the same time they demonstrate why belief in God is untenable without a faith community. God can be thought of and experienced only in a concrete alliance of desire, trust, protest and forgiveness.

For too long we have sought God as an object among objects, on the wavelength of quantity and causality. We have described God's transcendence in the comparative of our mechanical logic: First Mover, Ultimate Goal, Perfect Being, Greatest of the Powers. In this way we have made God a factor – an all-embracing factor of nature and history. But neither the God who is first Cause, almighty but unmoved Mover, nor the God who is the End and the Horizon of our existence, has survived the religious critique of modernity.

After that we have sought God as the subject of subjects: Legitimator of our freedom and fulfilment, Driving Force of autonomous human beings, a God in the depth of our thoughts. However, the I-culture which resulted from that is just as little bound up with God, nor has God's transcendent Self been preserved in it. Autonomous human beings have banished God from their hearts. The critique of religion by experts on the psyche has exposed the religious myth as an obsession and constriction of the healthy self.

But a present God who keeps the culture of our emotions pure, before whose face we live and who makes us live graciously – in longing, trust, opposition and forgiveness – in pure quality and gratuitousness, can be thought of and above all thanked. This God is more in the emotions of humanity than quantity and causality. And there is more in our feelings about ourselves than the emptiness of unlimited freedom. Where our thought – and by that of course I mean more than just the cognitive aspect of our thinking – becomes thanksgiving, the doubt and the risk of the void can be taken to have been overcome.

The function of church and theology 'beyond secularization' could be precisely that. As far as theology is concerned, this function cannot be replaced among the *artes*. Now that the sciences are no longer its handmaid, as in the Middle Ages; now that it need no longer be the handmaid of the sciences, as after the Renaissance;

now that it has given up its obsessive opposition to the ideals of the Enlightenment, there is a *kairos* for theology to serve men and women with the story of God. And as far as the church is concerned, to the degree that it is willing to take its modest but specific place in culture as a narrative community, it will share in this opportunity.

5

The Holy that may not be Violated: A Sight of the Divine
Quests beyond postmodernism

In the famous stained-glass window 'Jacob's Dream' in the Fraumünster in Zurich Marc Chagall has given special form to the vision of Genesis 28. Whereas in Jacob's dream according to Genesis 28.12 angels were going up and down a ladder to heaven, Chagall made them human figures pushing one another up and down a spiral ladder. That produces a chain of people of whom Jacob himself forms a part. In a picture of the world which has taken leave of angels and demons, and in which the contact with heaven is left to all kinds of 'cults of unreason', in Chagall's view there are still people who reach out for the divine and the eternal: people who transcend themselves by reaching for something that drives them and by so to speak pushing one another up.

When Jacob wakes up in the Genesis story, he exclaims: 'Truly, God is in this place and I knew it not. This can be no other than the house of God and the gate of heaven.' He then erects a sacred stone to mark the awesome place and attaches a promise to it: that he will devote 10 per cent of all his income to sacrifices. This is the primal story of the sacred and the sacral, which is separated out in the midst of all the ordinary historical, profane, temporal, spatial and fortuitous characteristics of the place where we stand: a dedicated stone, sacrifices, promises for life. *Sacer* and sacral, derived from the verb *sanciri*, also literally mean none other than that which is defined and hedged in, marked, special, extra-ordinary.

But what is still holy? As children of the Enlightenment we have taken leave of holy places, holy books, holy days, holy trees and animals and even of holy men and women. We have forsworn the sacral, understood as that which is marked by a board saying 'No admission'. Recently, a development worker told me about his experience among the Baka pygmies in southern Africa, when Western chainsaws came to fell their giant trees for our hardwood soundproofing and window frames. Of course the workers concerned did not know that for the Bakas the trees formed the sacred homes of all their forefathers: every tree ring was a mark and an anniversary of the living who had preceded them. There was no end to the tears of the pygmies which accompanied the noise of the chainsaws. In India Jain monks preserve an old custom which goes back to the precept of Buddha to spare all living things, even worms and ants. When they go down the street they sweep it clean before them with a besom so as not to tread on any insect or to do harm to any fly. 'Because man has compassion on all living beings, he is called the holy one, the one who is *ariya*' (Dhammapada, 200 BC).

There was a time when we could call God 'the Holy One'. And one characteristic of the church was that it was called the one holy church. With Paul we could call believers the saints and the church the communion of saints. Now only Mormons dare to give themselves this title: the Church of the Latter Day Saints. Who still experiences life as sharing in the holy things of God? Who still lives with the idea of a heavenly court where all the saints shall meet before the throne of God? Whose heart still warms at the canonization of exemplary figures from history?

The process of secularization has not only disenchanted the world, i.e. rid it of superstition, myths and paralysing fear – and who can have anything against that? – but has also sobered up religion itself. That causes problems. Historical criticism, the psychology and sociology of religion and the crisis of metaphysics in philosophy have broken up all the characteristics of the phenomenon of religion – its sacral foundation – in unholy iconoclasm. Critical reflection on the phenomenon of man has even exposed the notion of a special *humanum* as a construct of historical, psychological, sociological or philosophical generalization of partial phenomena. In the postmodernist fury of deconstruction not only the image of God in human beings but also the image of human beings themselves has fallen apart in smithereens. Everything is profane, i.e. transparent: it is what it is, and that is that. What can still be holy in this way?

In this chapter I shall first demonstrate, by means of some reflections by Jürgen Habermas, what the consequences of this iconoclasm are for our Western culture. Then I shall show that what we call 'the holy' does not by definition coincide with the sacral and ritual, as Habermas – and so many of those engaged in religious studies during the nineteenth and twentieth centuries – have interpreted it. The term 'the holy' has itself undergone all kinds of metamorphoses, depending on the function that it had in philosophy and religious studies. But an important widening and nuancing of the concept also has to take place in the history of religion, simply because of the Jewish-Christian language field. Emmanuel Levinas takes up such a nuancing in one of his Talmud Lectures, published under the title 'From the Sacred to the Holy'. I shall use his view to demonstrate some aspects of the experience of 'the new holy', which is far from having disappeared from our culture and which can take us beyond postmodernism.

TAKING LEAVE OF THE SACRED ACCORDING TO HABERMAS

According to Jürgen Habermas in his *Theory of Communicative Action*, the Jewish-Christian religion as a structure for thought and action in Western culture, as a provider of values and norms, of metaphysics and ethics, has gradually gone over to, been replaced and dissolved by, modern structures of consciousness. The Enlightenment marked this transition:

> ... that the socially integrative and expressive functions that were at first fulfilled by ritual practice pass over to communicative action; the authority of the *holy* is gradually replaced by the authority of an achieved *consensus*. This means a freeing of communicative action from sacrally protected normative contexts. The disenchantment and disempowering of the realm of the sacred takes place by way of a linguistification of the ritually secured, basic normative agreement; going along with this is a release of the rationality potential in communicative action. The aura of rapture and terror that emanates from the sacred, the spellbinding power of the holy, is sublimated into the *binding/bonding* force of criticizable validity claims and at the same time turned into an everyday occurrence [my italics].[1]

This evocative statement expounds Kant's famous statement about the Enlightenment from 1784 – the departure of human beings from self-imposed tutelage – in a different way from Kant himself. This approach was taken earlier by Feuerbach, Nietzsche, Weber and Freud. According to the time-honoured thesis, the unfolding of human autonomy and freedom was hampered by the restrictive bonds of belief in God and religious practices and authorities. Secularization, as a phenomenon of desacralization, is an indispensable condition and an unavoidable connotation of the process of increasing rationality. The religious myth loses its function of legitimating power, manipulating (the patriarchal) order and putting a brake on free investigation, freedom of expression and freedom of conscience. The 'death of God' is a condition for the birth of the person who is truly human because he is powerful; who is no longer subject to anyone and is no longer afraid of any devil. Such a person therefore also knows equality and equal status in all forms of life and society. Additionally we bid a massive farewell to the ritual practice of sacrifice, feast, prayer, commandment and contemplation and replace it by binding agreements and texts which also ensure us new cohesion and new forms of society.

However, Habermas goes a step further and adds two elements, the first confidently, the second hesitantly. First he gives a concrete indication of how the myth of God and religious practice are coming, or have already come, to an end: not through the unmasking of their restraining force but by being replaced with something better, which is liberated in the leave-taking from the sacral. Insight into the 'spellbinding' force of the sacral makes room for the 'binding' force of communication.[2] The communal spell with which the holy kept all imprisoned has been broken. Now there is only face-to-face attention to one another. There is no longer a signpost pointing upwards or into the distance; the signpost is now mutual agreement, reciprocal responsibility. According to Habermas, the conversation itself, which takes place at the destruction of the temples, and in which according to Nietzsche fear and nostalgia, mourning and uncertainty still dominate, becomes the vehicle of new freedom and trust: from now on human beings, who previously lamented their distress to the gods, lament their distress to one another. Anyone who referred to divine authority must now verify it to others; anyone who bore witness in the name of God must from now on try to convince with arguments.

That is not just a subjective action or an individual undertaking but a 'metamorphosis of structures of consciousness'. These are found objectively, in language and sign, in laws and conventions, in trends and fashions. Therefore everywhere formal authority with claims to divine authority or legitimation on the basis of old privileges is replaced by 'democratic leadership': truth is no longer seen as absolute certainty about states of things, but as a consensus of those who take part in a conversation about goals and means for attaining the optimum. As Rawls argues, the good that we seek in ethics is none other than the result of assessments, arrived at by argument, of the balance between the least suffering for the fewest people possible and the greatest happiness for the most people possible.

The second addition that Habermas makes to the modern critique of religion is the element of 'expressing in language'. Of course conversation and communication which come into being after the destruction or disappearance of the holy need language. However, for Habermas this is not language as such but one function of language: language as a means of criticism. The holy, too, had its own language. But the particular language of the holy and of religion does not tolerate any contradiction. It is ultimately irrational, and anything but argumentative. One can pray to God, but this prayer does not become a conversation. What remains, now that God is no longer the one who is addressed or the one who addresses, is reciprocal conversation between human beings, and the most important bridge to truth and consensus is criticism, contradiction, the palaver. It spreads into politics, education, the media. Laws come into being only after consideration by all those involved; or they can remain limited to government regulations through so-called self-regulation. In education, only what is generally discussed holds. No one need keep silent any longer; all may say what they have in their hearts. The new priests are the journalists with their interviews, who have seduced reading matter from the mouths of anyone who wants to say anything. There are public debates on all the old basic values: sex, birth and death become the subject of a public argument. All those without a voice get a voice. It is no longer possible to speak without having a say. But Habermas still hesitates: the aim of communication remains action, praxis. In the end it cannot be a matter of the palaver itself. Ultimately that too falls under Heidegger's critique of 'chatter'. As Foucault has shown us, making criticism an everyday matter and the possibility of criticizing things itself leads to disciplining, practices of argument which in turn can be manipulated by élites and ideologists.

It seems to me that Habermas' project of rationality as

argumentative communication must in the end come to grief on precisely this 'expressing in language'. The farewell to the ritual practice of sacrifice, feast, prayer, protocol, commandment, etiquette, adoration, contemplation, and the replacement of all that by binding agreements on the basis of consensus leads to new limitations of autonomy. We get tangled up in the web of our reflections by the exponential growth of bureaucracy, the culture of meetings, mobility, the telecommunications system, academic publications, in which all over the world there are problems of congestion and in which a new type of illiteracy and a new power élite is growing. In the long run this damages democracy and the true progress of the *humanum*.

What Foucault has called the endless possibility of criticizing things leads to a fragmentation of culture and a loss of trust: political bureaucracy leads to a tangle of regulations and formulations in the plural where in the long run communication takes place between computers; the ambivalences of language lead to Orwell's double-speak and to what Havel has called the great ideological lies: texts tumble over one another, so that anyone who wants to find truth must first deconstruct the texts, as Derrida argues, or at least note in what truth game they can be used, as Gadamer points out. But in that case, what is consensus and how do we ever arrive at authoritative consensus statements and canonical texts? And if everything is up for discussion, from where do the conversation partners then get anything like 'value' and 'meaning'? Or does the value and the meaning of life go no further than the duration of a good conversation or an hour of therapeutic playing around with the language of our dreams? Where does conversation lead to, other than to constantly new conversations? Where does the primacy of action really lie?

And conversely, why is there the abiding experience, which cannot be suppressed, of that which lies outside language, which cannot be spoken or put into words, which is not yet concentrated thought? Why does reality resist becoming a fable, stubborn as it is (H. Berger)? Why does the truth finally win out over the language of lies, or, why do we seek criteria for speaking the truth or testing lies?

Of course it is true that the Enlightenment illuminated much religious darkness and much church twilight. Perhaps the reference to reason does represent a kind of redemption of religion from its own darkening. Perhaps Enlightenment is indeed a kind of self-redemption of God, a revealed vision of what religion really is, which illuminates from within and which has been given to human beings by God himself. Perhaps the disenchantment of the world is at the same time in fact a disenchantment of religion.

But why should religion, if it has illuminated and redeemed itself with the help of reason, language and communication, then need to disappear? Doesn't taking leave of the sacral, of power and fear, lead, rather, to a truer picture of God and concept of God which is more positive towards human beings? Doesn't the concentration on the mutual ties which take the place of any tie to the one God (*religio* as derived from *religare*, bind) first of all lead to true intersubjectivity and only after that to the identity of the autonomous subject? Isn't attention to the face-to-face first of all rooted in the lighting up of the face of the other, the sufferer, the victim, instead of in the narcissistic reflection of the preoccupied self? Doesn't attention to those who are injured, the victims, lead to a better sense of the holy as that which may not be violated or attacked than the former emphasis on the totalitarianism of the burnt-offering which was offered to God or gods and on the opulence of the holy of holies, the temple in which God is inaccessibly enthroned beside the royal court? Isn't the sheltering of refugees and strangers closer to worship in spirit and in truth (John 4) than keeping the impure and strangers outside the precincts of the temple and forecourt? Isn't the truly holy the sanction against injustice rather than the sanctioning of power and privileges for a clerical élite? Isn't the Jewish-Christian tradition of prophetism the internal Enlightenment which in this religious tradition time and again sounds out as a light for the *goyim*, i.e. the nations or the unclean, the pagans? As the Jesus movement, doesn't Christianity live by following someone who himself was cast out of the sphere of the holy, was cursed as impure and crucified outside the holy walls of the city, by a clerical élite and because of a critical remark he made about the temple? (Even if this reading of Jesus' arrest and execution in the later Gospel narratives is untrustworthy by the criteria of any objective historical account, the reading is still of great importance as an echo of the thought of the first generation of Christians: original Christianity has an idea of holiness which knows neither temple, altar nor priests.)

Habermas' critique of the religious forms of expression of former days, characterized as 'ritual practice', can thus be affirmed by Christianity from within, and if this is Enlightenment, then the Enlightenment is thoroughly rooted in Christianity itself, as

115

Gogarten and Löwith argued in the twentieth century and Hermes and Günther argued in the nineteenth century. In that case there could be no question of an original antithesis between faith and reason, as even the First Vatican Council (1869–70) emphasized, despite its powerful opposition to the Enlightenment.

Moreover, Habermas cannot avoid also using certain contents of the former religious forms of expression in his views:

> Among modern societies only that which can introduce the essential content of its religious tradition, pointing beyond the merely human into the realm of the profane, will also be able to rescue the substance of the human.[3]

> God becomes the name for a communicative structure which compels people, on pain of losing their humanity, to transcend their fortuitously empirical nature by encountering one another indirectly, namely through an objective which is not themselves.[4]

Is this just a nominalist interpretation of religion? Is the name of God a code word for the objectivity of the other, which breaks through my selfhood, opens it up, and so makes me aware of that which is greater than myself, that which transcends my fortuitous, conscious and perceivable existence? Or is this transcendence which lies in alterity itself a sign, a communicative symbol, of something else, which transcends both the self and the other and thus again points us towards distances and heights and depths which we cannot comprehend, either as I, as you, or as we?

Habermas thinks that if religion still has functions, it does so on the basis of its alliance with the new values of reason, but that is really a detour, a duplication. That also applies to theology: perhaps it does further the capacity for communication, but in that case that is a superfluous detour: 'a devious encouragement of communicative competence'.[5] Indeed Habermas' post-metaphysical thought does not challenge a single theological assertion, nor does it challenge people's religious reflections; however, it regards both theology and faith as a needless detour and in this sense as 'meaning-less'.

But Habermas does not back up this claim. It therefore seems important for theology, given its agreement with the project of the Enlightenment as Habermas describes it, nevertheless to show the distinctive value domain and potential of meaning in religion, in this case Christianity.

THE APORIAS OF HABERMAS' CONSENSUS THEORY

To begin with, it can be stated that the option for an exclusively discursive ethic and a consensus theory of truth lacks plausibility at some essential points:

- How can compassion and solidarity with the victims of power ever be reached through consensus? In striving for the optimal and in establishing a consensus there will always be losers: whence the need also to be concerned about these losers?
- How is 'solidarity with the not so clever and the illiterate' possible if they themselves have no voice within the discursive argument and have no influence whatsoever on what is decided about them and by whom?
- How can what has gone irrevocably wrong and thus can no longer be discussed be coped with except through the possibility of forgiveness and reconciliation? But these things cannot be compelled, nor communicated in argument: they rest on a one-sided self-limitation and surrender to the transgressor.
- Where must the consensus get its aims from, if it is not to become the dictatorship of the majority, the trends, the party? Is there a criterion which in fact transcends the *de facto* unanimity of the like-minded? Can we do without such a criterion, far less the possibility that lies, crime and injustice get the say through majority decisions, as historical Fascism in Europe has demonstrated? And even if this comparison is exaggerated and one thinks that this Fascism cannot be repeated, have we nothing to dread from the always limited possibilities of communication among men and women, which do not always avoid group dictatorship and the right of the strongest. In the name of whom or what is a correction then possible which puts misunderstandings right and clearly can take revenge on self-interest in the formation of a judgement? Doesn't the theory of the separation of the powers and the independence of the judiciary pose strong counter-arguments to the plausibility of Habermas' reference to consensus? What is really celebrating a victory when law celebrates a victory: isn't it the rhetoric of the advocate or public opinion with its viewing figures?
- How can the contingent and unexpected, the meta-ethical and metaphysical, find a place in communication? On what basis can the original, particular and unique suddenly gain the force of

117

conviction? Where is the reality which permanently evades all arguments and descriptions and which so often robs of its rationality the process of argumentation and paradigms that does take place?

- How does aesthetic experience, which after all is contingent and unique, work before it becomes commonplace and fashionable, when taste and fashion do not after all decide about this experience?
- Where is the reality of what lies outside language – like birth, death, the course of the cosmos, the laws of gravity – which escapes all arguments and descriptions but which also proves decisive in the outcome of the conversation?
- What is left of the 'utopian qualities' of human tradition, the desire for what has not yet been thought or seen, the apparently impossible, which nevertheless one day becomes reality?[6]

In all these domains, precisely what I would want to regard as the truly holy triumphs. In later articles, Habermas has himself recognized these limitations to his theory and thinks that the categories of the holy and the religious cannot for the moment be dispensed with.

THE NEW HOLY

Religion does not yet seem to have disappeared, even from the popular press. Newspapers report on fundamentalist groups which grow so strongly that their membership even affects patterns of political loyalty in some areas. There are advertisements for meetings and courses about all kinds of Eastern religions. Gregorian chant makes its way well up in the charts alongside reggae and rap. The 'Body, Mind, Spirit' sections in bookshops grow steadily larger, and books about code hidden in the Bible can be found on airport bookstalls. John Paul II is the subject of constant reports, and Alpha courses can be found from London to Tallinn.

So is there still room for the holy? Does it form a possible category for thought which in a culture of agnosis and a society focused on profit and pleasure could mediate between an inconceivable God on the one hand and the equally inconceivable absurdity of a nihilistic, vegetative existence on the other? After all, we want health, law and happiness, and direct technology and politics in this direction. We cannot survive without rules and procedures, but we clearly want to do more than survive. We want quality of life: human rights, the acquisition of possessions, education and schooling, care of the weak, tenderness and freedom. Clearly a number of things are 'holy' to us, so that we canonize them in a hierarchy of values, an axiology. It is this axiology, the canon of the holy, which forms the key to our existence, the core of enjoyment and ultimately the test of our happiness.

Before we can expose this 'new holy', what is 'holy' to us, in more detail, we need to free the current concept of 'the holy' from its inevitable historical strait-jacket.

THE METAMORPHOSES OF 'THE HOLY': A SEMANTIC CLARIFICATION

In the philosophy of religion 'the holy' was first of all used as distinct from, or as a distinction from, 'the profane' (thus Eliade).[7] But this distinction proves to be no more than a 'hermeneutical horizon' or 'transcendental a priori' which is so defined by the context and so polyvalent that as a principle of differentiation it has become obsolete. What still distinguishes holy from profane texts, holy from profane buildings, holy from profane heroes, holy from profane art, once the will to know or the use of pleasure becomes the criterion of what has value? Both in the utilitarian-productive and the hedonistic-consumptive complex of values there is no longer any place for this transcendental a priori, except as a metaphor for the highest profit or the greatest enjoyment: what is holy to the producer or consumer. The canon or standard of this is defined and made by advertising and trends.

'The holy' (as a synonym for *mana*: the numinous and the power that emanates from the rite) was established by phenomenologists of religion (like R. Otto[8] and G. van der Leeuw[9]) who were in search of an umbrella term for religious experience which could combine both monotheistic and polytheistic religions and also agnostic and atheist world-views. But the wealth of comparative religion which has grown out of this, which seeks a common denominator or origin of all religions, has already long since given way to more differentiated approaches. Granted, this 'coupling approach' has been customary as a quasi-empirical 'structure' or form for religion (thus Durkheim), as a scheme or design for investigations in the sociology of religion. In Durkheim's 1912 definition:

> A religion is a solid system of beliefs and practices relating to holy things (i.e. separate, forbidden), beliefs and practices which unite in the same moral community, called the church, all those who belong to it.[10]

Theologians and psychologists of religion to the present day object to this reduction of the phenomenon of religion, which seems to cut out its very core, namely entrusting oneself to something or someone. The beliefs and practices mentioned form simply the symbols or signs of religion.

Simply as a consequence of secularization, for a long time 'the holy' has been used as a functional concept, to indicate what determines the quality of society for individual and community.[11] In so doing it has restrained violence,[12] chaos and lawlessness,[13] and, in a meaning which has more negative connotations but which is just as functional, it has prevented true communication which does not want to be more than communication (among others, as we saw, in the case of Habermas).

It is, finally, used in a paradoxical sense as a collective term for all experiences of transgression which are necessary for the realization of the self along the lines of the sacred as 'taboo' and 'prohibition' in Freud, Lacan, etc. It still can be found in Georges Bataille in this paradoxical meaning.

Thus even as a scholarly construct, 'the holy' has undergone all kinds of metamorphoses[14] in both content and function. Where people were no longer aware of its character as 'construct', it has also been elevated to a metaphysical or ontological category (e.g. in Otto but also in Heidegger) and has inserted itself between God and human beings almost in the role of a demiurge. In recent theological schemes along these lines, there has certainly been an argument that 'the holy' should be introduced as a kind of middle term between the concept of 'meaning', which is felt to be too anthropological, and the idea of 'God', which for some is a bridge too far.

Does this make sense? Can productive theological use still be made of the concept or the experience of 'the holy'? Can a new anthropological mist be dispelled for the sake of communicating the idea of God? I think that it can. I shall show this in two moves. First of all I shall draw attention to the enormous differences in three word-fields which underlie the one term 'the holy': on the one hand the word-field *hieros-sacer* and on the other the word-field *hagios-sanctus*; *hosios-chassid* forms a third dimension. Then I shall turn to

Levinas, who in his Talmudic lectures has worked out the difference between 'the sacred' (*le sacré*) and 'the holy' ('*le saint*').

HIEROS, HAGIOS, HOSIOS

The distinction between the word-fields *hieros-sacer* (*kohen*) and *hagios-sanctus* (*kadesh*) is particularly important. The first word-field in fact stands for all that is striking and special which regulates human life through fate or tradition. In both Semitic and Hellenistic culture, *hieros* is the hieratical: the dwelling place of the gods and the ark of the covenant, the head and the bed of Zeus, the bow of Heracles, the chariot of Achilles, the seed of Abraham, the law, the transgression for which the death penalty is inflicted. And also the cosmic forces: the light, the earth, the land, the rivers; and the cultural associations: the cities (Hierosolyma, Jerusalem), the political laws and governors, the places, the times, the rites, the temples and the servants of worship, the priests: *hiereis*. From this sacral complex there emanates an enormous ordering, guiding force through fear (*tremendum*) and fascination (*fascinans*), and in precisely this way religion can also derive its analogies for the idea of God from this arsenal of images and symbols: God as patriarch, prince, ruler of the cosmos.

The second semantic field – around *hagios* – stands for all that is exemplary and perfect, that generates respect and discipleship of its own accord and is free of injury, shortcomings, impurity and sin (cf. *communio sanctorum, sanctificatio*). It denotes the venerable for which one has respect, for example God's dignity and compassion (*kadusya*). The holy God is concerned for the people, dwells with them, protects the weak, and is therefore inviolable and above all violation. But in that case God also calls for respect for the inviolable and for the avoidance of violation and sacrilege. So in Psalm 24.3 the purification and cleansing from guilt which may be expected from human beings are also bound up with this: 'Who may stand in God's holy dwelling place? He whose hands are clean and whose heart is pure.' In contrast to *hieros*, *hagios* is rarely used in the sphere of temple, cult or taboo, but usually for what is of high moral standing and the divine as the most perfect, for the dedication of life to the true and the good. This is what is said in a prayer which is at the heart of Judaism and Christianity, which has been handed down in the 'Our Father' in the petition 'Hallowed be thy name, thy will be done': the two petitions are complete parallels.

The third word-field for 'the holy' – that around *hosios-chassid* – points to the experience of being blessed and elect, being spared, finding happiness and fulfilment. Piety and holiness are not found first of all in taboo, ritual or moral purity, but in a relationship of trust with the divine, in the attainment of true and constant happiness, even despite suffering and death. The saints are those who find grace in God's eyes, in whom God has pleasure, who can share a roof with God.[15] In his book *Original Blessing*, Matthew Fox in particular has called attention to the distinctive meaning of the category *hosios-chassid* in the Jewish-Christian tradition.[16] As so much religion is associated with taboo, prohibition and a constant fight against evil – from which we must be redeemed and saved – in his view it is a distortion of the positive experiences of happiness and blessing, peace and integrity that one also finds in religion. The truly holy must not be sought in either the hieratical taboo, the moral prohibition or the pedagogical struggle for perfection, but in the sphere of basic trust, joy in life, the experience of 'salvation' as spiritual and bodily health. It is clear that here he is appealing to a modern hierarchy of values. The danger here is that the contrast experiences of pain, grief and death are filtered out of the sphere of the religious.

In the theological tradition of Judaism and Christianity the choice of one or other word-field has had major consequences for the sense of the holy. Dangerous one-sidednesses in the image of God and the image of human beings are associated with each choice. The choice of *hieros* leads to cultic distortions, to clericalism and temple ritual. The choice of *hagios* can give rise to Puritanism and moralism, as has often happened. The one-sided emphasis on *hosios* neglects the night side of reality.

Thus for example Karl Barth[17] in his doctrine of God, in complete accord with the Calvinist tradition, points out that God's holiness has to do only with the second word-field. He strongly emphasizes the difference from Rudolf Otto's 'the Holy'. Otto wanted to expose the 'numinous', as *mysterium tremendum et fascinans* – against Kant – as being more than just the morally good: it is what gives one goose pimples, what goes through 'marrow and bone' and 'strikes one dumb'.[18] Otto really wanted to give religious experience an 'objective' foundation, like Barth, and against Schleiermacher and Feuerbach: religious experience is not a feeling of pure dependence which can be dismissed as a projection of human shortcomings but insight into the complete inaccessibility of the *mysterium tremendum et fascinans*. The 'numinous' is the object side – that which comes to us. Here Otto wants to do justice to the experience of God's holiness, for example in Ex. 15 and Isa. 6, but he misses his target because he seeks the core of religion and of the holy not in the word-field *hagios* but in that of *hieros*, a temptation which the Jewish-Christian tradition in fact finds it difficult to withstand.

But the danger of one-sided distortions also lurks in Barth's antithesis to 'the Holy' as a construct of the study of religion. He makes 'the holy' the attribute of God's overwhelming otherness and perfection:

> ... that God, as He seeks and creates fellowship, is always the Lord. He therefore distinguishes and maintains His own will as against every other will. He condemns, excludes and annihilates all contradiction and resistance to it. He gives it validity and actuality in this fellowship as His own and therefore as good.[19]

Here an almost moralistic idea of 'the holy' peeps round the corner; it is projected on to God and is more Neoplatonic than Christian. This ideal of holiness as spotlessness[20] has also been the dominant ideal of *sanctitas* in the Catholic tradition: keeping clear of everything that causes moral impurity. It is closely related to the levitical tradition: holiness as purity and completeness. The New Testament dismissed this idea of 'holiness': for the pure all is pure (Titus). It is not what goes in at the mouth that makes a person unclean (Mark 7.15–16; Matt. 23.25–6). Those who are not perfect will be acceptable to God: the lame will walk, the blind see, lepers be cleansed (Luke 4.18–22).

This *sanctitas* as *puritas* and *perfectio*, as a striving for the sublime, is and has been an equally devastating metaphor for the Christian view of God and attitudes towards God. When Bataille and others seek the experience of the holy and the sublime in transgression, dissipation and degeneration, this must be seen against the background of the religious struggle for spotlessness and perfection.

FROM THE SACRED TO THE HOLY: THE CHOICE OF EMMANUEL LEVINAS

Is it possible to mark out the distinctive nature of 'the sacred' (*le sacré*) over against 'the holy' (*le saint*) without getting into a moralistic/puritanical current, without lapsing into the sphere of the hieratic and ritualistic understanding of 'the sacred', and without lightly choosing only the sunny side of existence? Can this be done in such a way that religious experience can shine out in the midst of and in all the profane? Not as what Eliade calls 'hierophany' or 'kratophany' (which time and again associates arbitrary phenomena of the 'separate', 'special', 'miraculous', 'irrational' or 'powerful', associating the divine with 'magic', but then keeps losing sight of them again by 'disenchantment'), but as precisely belonging to what is normal, rational, ordinarily human and good.

Levinas has shown a way here in his Talmudic lectures of 1971, published in his *Du sacré au saint* in 1977.[21]

Levinas sums up the whole world of taboo, fate, magic, of the irrational and the esoteric, of merits, good works and sacrifices, under the term 'sorcery'. That is the category of 'the sacred', the religion of need, which wants to put reality in our hands. By means of Talmudic commentaries on Ex. 19.13; 22.18; Deut. 20.16 and 18.10, Levinas first of all expounds the difference between conjuring tricks (illusionism) and superstition in the Jewish sense. The latter is an action done with evil intentions, aimed at deception; conjuring tricks are deliberate illusion and nothing is going on here. The conscious world of the 'as if' in dreams, imagination and illusionism is usually a human possibility. But where real magic is concerned, there is a real goal to be attained, an alteration of reality by inauthentic means. That infringes the purposes and the honour of God. The holy – the course of things as this has been ordered, the meaning of things in their own nature – is destroyed: a transgression takes place, as for example in the case of religious bestiality (Ex. 22.19). Human beings and animals do not normally, i.e. in the Jewish sense according to God's purposes, have sex with each other. A transgression of this order for higher purposes in magic is an attack on the true mystery of things, all 'created after their nature' (Gen. 1.12, 21, 13, 25). The truly holy is something like 'unmixed essence'. Levinas asks himself whether such an idea of the pure true being can function in a world which has not yet been completely desacralized. The sacral – in the sense of 'the sacred' – constructs a kind of mystery on the other side of reality.[22] As if things could be prestigious, something quite special, like the cedars of Lebanon with which the temple was panelled. The sacral wrongly makes certain quite ordinary things important and the magician suggests the same thing. Magic is a niece, indeed a sister, of the sacral; the sacral always verges on magic, however pious the form that it takes. It lives on appearance and maintains the appearance:

costly temples without visitors, sacrifices as a sign of social prestige. There is a clear boundary between the magic of the sacral and the innocence of the illusionist. Levinas gives the example of a man who with a spell can fill a field full of cucumbers and with another spell can harvest them. As long as he does no more to the public, this remains a conjuring trick, but if he begins to sell them at a pound a piece it becomes magic, and according to scripture he can be punished. Levinas sees something like this happening in the modern economy, where imaginary cucumbers are being sold for great profit, for example on the stock exchange. Or where female charms are treated as selling tricks in business. Superstition, 'sorcery', becomes manipulation of people if we become indiscreet about the mystery of things:

> Sorcery is in fact looking beyond what it is possible to see. Sorcery is the curiosity which manifests itself where one has to lower one's eyes, indiscretion with regard to the divine, insensitivity to mystery, clarity projected on that which needs to be approached with shame, some forms of 'Freudism', perhaps also some demand of sexual education, and finally certain forms of sexual life itself, perhaps even some demands of 'science for all'.[23]

Where culture suffers from scientific superstition and no longer sets any limits to the openness of all things and the possibility of criticizing them, sorcery comes into play. This superstition is present, not in the pagan other, but in the heart of religion. In the Jewish people, too, it is the desire for transgression as such, transgression as an experience of the unique and sublime. Levinas thinks that a fundamental magic has arisen in modern Western culture, as a result of which people can no longer take one another at their word and everything degenerates into ideology, into the semblance of the 'not-said': we call it this but we mean that. Some authorities of the truly holy or of unfalsified life must remain, in the face of the danger of a culture of suspicion, of general mistrust, a general impurity and complete hypocrisy. That also calls for ritual, but the kind of ritual which does not again create holy times and places for itself – in the sense of being outside human life as a kind of alternative order in respect of the ordinary and everyday – but transforms the whole person in our ordinary, daily life. The sabbath, the festivals, the fasts and the prayers – those are the important rituals here, because they involve the whole body: through rest, the kick of the festival, the hunger of the fast and the gesture of complete submission that takes place in prayer. But those who go outside the way of the true, outside the given nature of things as they are willed by God, are in fact in search of another god. As if there should be such a thing outside God ... Moreover these are not manipulations of technical ability as such, but a refusal to take into account their limitations, which find their symbol in the sabbath. Not only Israel but also the other cultures and the secularized West keep falling victim to this 'religion of need' and the desire for the sacral. Therefore the prophetic call is to the really 'holy': the holy God shows his face in the inviolable face of the suffering other; he reveals his glory in the threatened and defenceless. And also in the symbols of life: the sabbath, the feasts of liberation, the pilgrimages, the covenant of love and trust and the forgiveness of sins.

So the truly holy and the mystery of God are to be found in that which is absolutely worth desiring, that which is freely given, the inviolable,[24] which defines the limit of the human. Here we encounter 'the Most High', 'the Eternal', 'the Holy'.

THE HOLY: A MATTER OF CARE AND REVERENCE

Even in a completely secularized culture which rejects 'the sacred' in principle, there is room for the experience of this 'new holy' (I have taken the term from Vergote).[25] It is not necessary to look for this in transgressions (Bataille), which are only the other side of the taboo. It can be found, rather, in the experience of limits, from which we shrink, not out of fear but out of reverence and awe. This reverence and awe assume communal forms (and not only in arguments):

- a concern for the fragile environment in which we live – against the dissipation, the pollution and impoverishment of life;[26]
- a concern for truthfulness, consideration, dedication, communication, democracy – in the face of corruption, violence and dictatorship;
- a concern for justice, human rights, peace – in the face of poverty, discrimination and armaments;
- a concern for the quality of our relations: equality, tenderness, freedom – in the face of sexism, usurpation and slavery;
- a concern for health and imagination in sport, play, amusement, art – in the face of any flat hedonism and trivial consumerism.

These 'concerns' are not a just a matter of moral convictions, rational goals for self-fulfilment or chance values of Western culture, but a matter of 'the mystery of things' and 'traces of a liberating God' (to use Borgman's phrases). They are rooted in the nature of things themselves and decide on the quality of humanity. God's 'Ten Instructions' (the Decalogue, the Ten Commandments), which are a summary of the Jewish and the Christian ethos, fulfil a similar function: they are the creed about the climate in which we live and the cultural profile at which we aim. They are intended as rules of behaviour for humankind and in this sense are also universally valid. Some of them are derived from earlier laws for society from Mesopotamia and Egypt. But by being directly linked to belief in YHWH they have taken on a specific content which also colours the specific rules for behaviour. Indeed the first three commandments cannot be separated from the last seven, as often happens. Religion and behaviour are interwoven. The content of this creed or cultural profile of Jews and Christians can in fact be better described as 'ten values for the holy'. To show how they work in this direction we have to translate them anew. I shall do that by linking the Decalogue from Deut. 5.6–21 and Ex. 20.1–17 with the ten 'Affirmations' of the World Council meeting on Justice, Peace and the Integrity of Creation in Seoul, 1990.[27]

TEN VALUES FOR THE HOLY[28]

I.   Those who want to lead a meaningful human life must not be guided by self-interest, prejudice, inherited rights or values they have devised themselves – all these are idols and demons which lead people astray – but by the one God, from whom and to whom is all that lives (Deut. 5.6).

The world belongs to God – all forms of human power or authority are subjected to God and are a human responsibility (Seoul I).

II.   Nothing that exists is worthy of being venerated as God, but those who reject God bear the consequences, even to subsequent generations (Deut. 5.8–10).

The earth is God's – all forms of property, possessions or behaviour which represent injustice to others or which destroy the environment are an infringement of God's glory and damage the image of God in human beings (Seoul VIII).

127

III.   Those who call on the name of God need to act accordingly: God sees through any frivolous reference to God, all false religion out of self-interest (Deut. 5.11).

Human rights are given by God. Guaranteeing them is the hallmark of the fear of God (Seoul X).

IV.   Work is not the last goal of our life: all those who work have the right to rest; friends and family have the right to attention; and it is good to remember regularly that time is given to us by God as an opportunity of grace (Deut. 5.12–15).

The earth and life are holy and loved by God. Our work and our activity must reflect God's own joy in the sabbath (Seoul VII).

V.   One generation needs to be concerned for another, for all are children of God. That is the condition for a stable peace and a balanced society (Deut. 5.16).

Every society must guarantee respect and dedication to the progress of human life in love in accordance with the will of God. The death of children from famine and the curtailment of future opportunities in life are a denial of God's purposes (Seoul V).

VI.   All deadly violence is forbidden (Deut. 5.17).

God most loves the victims of injustice and violence (Seoul II).

VII.   It is wrong to abandon one another's partners and to dishonour them (Deut. 5.18).

Men and women are created in the image of God. Therefore they must not behave dishonestly (Seoul IV).

VIII.   It is wrong to appropriate things without having worked for them (Deut. 5.19).

The earth is God's. None of our possessions is our absolute property. There are things which cannot be bought. The market value is not the norm for our trade and activity. Wealth at the expense of others is theft from the poor. There must be justice in respect of property and possessions. The worker is worthy of his hire, but those who can get no work must share in the prosperity (Seoul VIII).

IX.   It is of the utmost importance to live in the truth (Deut. 5.20).

Truth and truthfulness form the basis of a community of free men and women (Seoul V).

X.   The desire for more possessions must be kept in check, since it damages love of neighbour and is the root of all evil (Deut. 5.21).

We shall no longer learn war or threat or the desire for profit, so that all can live happily under their own fig trees (Seoul VI).

This catalogue of values describes what is holy to us and on the basis of what we may call people holy: holy people are those who live by these values. They describe the co-ordinates of true human self-respect – in the personal, relational and social extensions of our bodily and historical existence. At the same time they describe the structures of a way of existence which serves God, and the themes of Jewish-Christian worship and prayer. They explain the human way of living as 'the image of God' and form 'the criteria of the kingdom of God', the 'abiding fruit of the Spirit' (cf. Gal. 5.13–26).

CONCLUSION

As long as the church and theology seek the holy and the divine elsewhere – in terms of power and planning and a good outcome (providence); of election, judgement, reconciliation and retribution; of revelation, magisterium, discipline and hieratic, sacerdotal forms of temple liturgy – the universal doubt about the Christian faith will remain, even if that faith is stated and packaged better. Without a connection to reverence and respect for the inviolable and the holy values of life, faith remains on the outside and declines into ritualism, finally becoming 'sorcery'.

As long as culture and science have an eye only for the use of pleasure and the will to know, and consequently persist in a utilitarian pattern of norms and values, based on agreement and negotiation, people will seek refuge in all kinds of esoteric forms of religion, though these will lead them, without their wanting it, back into the world of magic in which they must refer to a presupposed other, alternative, world of meaning. Here communication with the argument of rationality is impossible and also unwanted, so that we flee into underground cellars and secret societies. Or we flee into the postmodern game of meanings, into communication for the sake of communication, into relations for the sake of relations, into pure slavery to the contingent.

Therefore attention to the truly holy as it has been described here is of essential anthropological importance, not only for those who believe in God but also for secularized citizens in Western culture. Recollection of them is not just a provisional remnant of metaphysics, as we heard Habermas say, but a powerful step beyond postmodernism. To return to Chagall's picture: we share in pushing one another up.

6

Can God be Found in History?
The open space of the possible

THE QUESTION: WHERE IS GOD?

Where is God? That is an almost irreverent, sometimes desperate hope. It is really *the* question about God, which connects nature, history and human existence, and links them to the living God. Even as a sceptical question it is a question full of aporia and longing, a question of the prospect of God. So far, there has been a remarkable silence on the question in the ecumenical dialogue between the churches, as if all Christian traditions agreed on this point. Is the great concentration of ecumenical dialogue on the church, on redemption in Christ or renewal in the Holy Spirit perhaps itself an excuse for this crucial question to believers, which resounds from the lips of so many who do not – do not yet or no longer – believe? Or does the silence about the question of God arise above all out of ignorance and perplexity at the very different answers which the world religions give to it?

NO TRACE OF GOD

Those who want to localize God look in vain for co-ordinates. God cannot be fixed at any point in space or at any moment in time. So the question 'Where is God?' cannot be answered within time and space. Our agnostic culture dismisses the very question of God as meaningless. As we saw, at its deepest level secularization means that people want to restrict themselves to the *saeculum*, i.e. the limitation of nature, history and existence in time and space, and precisely in so doing regard the question of God as meaningless. People already have their hands full with questions and answers within time and space. Believers and unbelievers, those who do and do not believe in God, can also get on very well with one another here. If we are honest, we realize that we can get on for a very long time without ever speaking of God. Some people, like those in New Age circles, who find this restriction to time and space too narrow and too cold, fall back into old forms of pantheism. But their solution, which identifies God with all that is, was and will be – *deus sive natura* – is too clearly born out of necessity to be credible. Karl Barth already remarked, 'If God is everywhere, then God is nowhere.' But God cannot even just be somewhere, sometimes here and sometimes there. No entity, not even the totality of entities, coincides with God, but it is even more arbitrary to read God in 'somewhere' between the lines, or to make him end up in a vague, comprehensive space (as Jaspers does with his 'the All-embracing').

The idea of God itself – and thus not just our agnostic culture – in fact prohibits us from locating God anywhere. And at the same time it commands us to confess a real relationship between God and all that is: God is everywhere and in all things worthy of worship.[1] In the biblical account of the faith of Israel, which is at the same time the source of the faith of those who follow Jesus, God, though always unseen, unnameable and incomprehensible,[2] is nevertheless the main agent in a historical drama: God is brought on stage acting – saving, blessing, guiding, judging, questioning, speaking – in the midst of conflict and peace, human hope and despair, in the midst of the vicissitudes of things. God is invoked, called on here. As the scriptures imagine God, God is also the one who directs himself towards and judges all human beings, all peoples. And God leads, guides and tempers even the forces of nature, if necessary. However, the account of the scriptures which bears witness to this appearance of God is not a journal or a protocol, but a story full of human configurations in many different contexts. This configurative narrative of God has been deconstructed in succession by comparative religion, historical criticism, demythologizing, existential philosophy and the literary criticism of postmodernism. The consequence is that more than ever theology is called on to make its talk about God plausible, even before a single page of the biblical narrative is read, if it is not to limit itself to the household of faith, or from the beginning fade into the grammatology of the biblical argument, the literature of the phenomenon of religion.

DOMAIN, DIMENSION, DYNAMIC?

The solution to the paradox of God's present absence has for centuries been sought in a distinctive domain of God: heaven, supernature, eternity. Modern variants of this speak of a separate dimension, which lies several fields higher than our known dimensions of space and time.[3] Others give the hypothetical stereometric figure of the hyperoid as an analogy: this is a supra-dimensional polygon, the properties of which can be demonstrated by hyper-fast computers. All these solutions try to demonstrate more or less in a geometrical fashion; they appeal to what Marion calls 'calculating thought'[4] or to what Horkheimer calls instru-mental thinking,[5] which so constricts us in our attachment to space and time. Perhaps it helps this or that mathematician to think beyond his or her tautological play of lines and theory of functions and in so doing to grasp again the whole, the order and the connection which are woven between the lines as an equilibrium of forces, as a quite distinctive dynamic that transcends analysis. Fénelon already remarked that God can be found only in the movement or dynamic which makes it impossible for us to think of a whole without being able to define that whole as such, for example the cosmic order or even a spider's web. It is the same here as with the category of 'movement'. This approach dissolves the paradoxes of Zeno, which were based on the fact that we think only in bits and pieces: the arrow which cannot reach its target because each time it must first cross half of the remaining distance, and Achilles and the tortoise who for the same reason reach the finishing line at the same time. However, movement itself cannot be divided into such moments; it escapes analysis and deconstruction. Thus God as God-in-movement makes the many moments, authorities, factors into a dynamic and coherent whole.[6]

All these analogies certainly have a value in making belief in God part of our picture of the world. But they fall apart if with the Christian tradition we look for God in need or expect God on the other side of the grave. If our whole world collapses on the frontier of life and death, or in a great catastrophe, we have few domains, dimensions, wholes or dynamics. In Auschwitz, the question 'Where is God?' could no longer be answered 'Everywhere', or with a reference to Spinoza or Fénelon. Nor will that ever be possible after Auschwitz. Any thought in terms of coherence and harmony falls apart on the broken life of so many people, the radical oppositions between the autochthonous and the allochtonous, whites and blacks, the painful unravellings of civilization, the balance between generations and sexes which has been destroyed, the threat of a fatal nuclear fission of all that lives, the violent but unavoidable entropy of the universe, and the radical finitude of every individual.[7]

SALVATION HISTORY: THE MIGHTY ACTS OF GOD?

Another solution is sought by associating God, not with the whole of historical reality, but with specific moments of history. Thus history becomes part of a salvation history by the marking moments of the *magnalia Dei*, the mighty acts of God. Now and then, sometimes, God is said to play a main role, or at any rate to have played a main role, in history: at the beginning and the end of the cosmos (creation and judgement); at the beginning and end of religion and the religious covenant (revelation, the return of Christ); at the great turning points of history, as in the appearance of Abraham, Isaac, Jacob, Moses, Joshua, David, Jesus, the apostles. And perhaps also in the days of Constantine, Charlemagne, William of Orange, Luther and Calvin or even in those of William Booth or one or other of the forefathers of the many Christian denominations which each went in search of light for itself in the nineteenth century, not to mention those who saw God at work in Frederick Barbarossa, Napoleon or Hitler. The objection to this line of thinking is that in such a way, both inside and outside the Bible, God can too easily be harnessed to tribal interests, even if the tribal interest is religion. Why should Hagar and Ishmael have to come off worse than Sarah and Isaac on divine authority? Why should Jacob's descendants have been blessed more than those of Esau? Why were the conquests of the kings of Israel praised as acts of God, but their losses always attributed to their sins? How can we still read Saul's massive massacre among the Amalekites as a mighty act of God, done through the hand of Saul?

Haven't the victors always cried that they had God on their side? Isn't the interpretation of history in terms of light and darkness, good and evil, what is willed by God and what is hostile to God, by definition arbitrary and blasphemous?[8] When at the time of the

134

First Vatican Council of 1870, after the proclamation of the dogma about the competence of the pope to make definitive statements in particular cases, a thunderstorm burst over St Peter's, for both supporters and opponents that was a sign of God from heaven. Was it a blessing or a curse? Every day hundreds of thousands of people are in search of such signs of God for their lives. What is the difference between those who have interpreted such signs as pointers to God as described in the scriptures of Israel and those who now do that through astrology and horoscopes?[9] In the midst of ambivalences, darkness and nihilism, what more do we really have than a story about traces and signs of God? What more do we have than God by way of speaking, God as *dramatis persona* or *deus ex machina*, in short 'God' in quotation marks? Any talk in terms of the action of God is always by definition only the description of events which have been read as the action of God: God cannot be traced as agent in the midst of all other agents and factors, even if we call some events miracles. Any reflection about God in history is confronted with this question. Indeed we see that what are set down as the mighty acts of God – for example the exodus of the Hebrews from Egypt – as an epic of Israel have taken the form of praise, festival and liturgy in the celebration of the Passover. To a considerable degree, moreover, the *magnalia Dei* are meta-historical promises and expectations, as within the framework of creation, redemption and consummation of history and the promise of resurrection and eternal life. We can say that God guides, directs and tests history and thus gives meaning to our actual fate as a chance that has been given to us, as a vocation and destiny, but we cannot establish God in history; God does not occur in it.

GOD: THE SOURCE OF OUR BELIEF IN GOD?

Or – a third way of establishing a *locus Dei* – is it perhaps the case that in our story about God, the Eternal One somewhere speaks to us, that God himself addresses us in the narrative about God, in that we are brought to the idea of 'God'? That is the old way of God as the source and voice of our conscience, our awareness, our feeling and our will or desire. This God of the human heart can also continue to be of service in suffering and misery, in complaint and accusation. The fact of the believing tradition itself is then the sign of God's presence. But here too the question arises whether all this is perhaps sheer imagination, an echo and duplication of our own self-awareness. Since Feuerbach we cannot just lightly step over this question.

HISTORY AS THE CENTRAL POINT OF OBSERVATION

Theologians have always had difficulties in choosing between these three possibilities of the God-self-world complex (Scheler, Tracy):[10] God in nature, God in history or God in the human self(-awareness). Every choice produces dangerous one-sidednesses, as e.g. H. Berkhof has made clear.[11] Despite all the problems that it involves, he finally opted for making history the central point of observation,[12] from which nature and the human person also come into the picture. Here is a quotation:

> The category of history is more fruitful and more comprehensive than the others. It can take in the categories of existence, future and evolution. This cannot be done the other way round, or if it can, it more easily goes wrong. And without this framework of salvation history, existence becomes ghostly, evolution deterministic and the future utopian.[13]

So nature, too, needs to be seen as history and the human person – any individual, any people, any human generation, all knowledge, all consciences, all desires – is at the same time the product and the source of a historical dynamic. There is no human self, no identity of a people which does not go through time, in which there is not a journey of the soul; in which there are not all kinds of historical adventures and wanderings; in which at the same time we incur scars and leave our characteristics behind. Be that as it may, religion seeks to connect God with this way through time and to put all the vicissitudes of human beings and the cosmos in God's hands. Part of the content of the idea of God is that nothing can escape God's attention and that everything that happens takes place before the face of God, not as chance and caprice but 'to the glory of God' and 'for human salvation'. The vicissitudes do not just end up in good fortune, but contain an invitation to happiness and responsibility. The reference to God makes that history more than the mere course of things. It is also the result of purposeful action by human beings, for which we are responsible; there are things which cannot be, even though they happen regularly. There are things which remain valuable, even if they perish. History is

136

therefore also the cumulative experience and recollection of all that is good and valuable, the wisdom and happiness of centuries, together with the memory of its black pages. Belief in God means not accepting that the whole of this centuries-long dynamic of the coming into being of matter and the evolution of life should be finally written off as a remnant with no value, as rubbish, so that each generation is 'dung on the field of the world', a step towards the prosperity and happiness of the next. Therefore the idea of God means an accentuation and intensification of the idea of history: the modes of time – past, present and future – are the forms of perfection of God's own biography which spans time, adapted to human historicity and the bodily existence of human beings. God himself writes history and therefore writes no one off. In the Jewish and Christian tradition that means trusting God, 'who keeps faith for ever'. Such a view of history is not a matter of course in the midst of our aporias and in the face of death. Many people will not get much further than Achterberg's famous poem:

Man is for a time a place of God.
If you take this away from anyone
there remains a graveyard with a stone,
under which lies that which had come to
this consummation, this abrupt conclusion.
But God goes further, goes beyond him
in his millions. God is never alone
for he consists of a surplus of life.
For him we are a full can of petrol,
which he leaves behind empty and without regret ...[14]

Those who put human beings and God on a time-line in this way themselves make human life a brief episode in the biography of God. The alternative is that every human life at every moment is filled with God and that its meaning is not defined by utility or purposefulness. To ask about God then does not mean that we are asking about the final result or the good outcome: first of all there is the eternal present, and every moment can be experienced as the point of intersection where we encounter God. But after all, if it should stop at that one moment, if there was no expectation of anything to follow, every day would be dead time, perhaps free from craving, but then also without hope and desire. Without ongoing history, every today would in a moment turn us into stone monuments.

Judaism, Christianity and Islam have opted for a historical analogy for the encounter with God, whereas the Asian and Afro-

American religions opt more for the eternal present. However, both choices are one-sided and full of aporias. Thus the biblical epic is not just a historical narrative and Buddha's path of wisdom is not unrelated to the concrete, including the political course of affairs in human history. Therefore there is a guideline for both: to follow the path of the wise, to seek traces of truth and lasting happiness in the fleeting time of life. For Jews, Christians and Muslims, however, there is a signpost: God is out there before us.

GOD NO OUTSIDER

There are yet other reasons why theology cannot lack a historical perspective. There is first of all the internal logic of the Christian confession. To begin with, there is the praise of the creative God who has not become an outsider in the further fate of creation. As the classical liturgy puts it in its opening prayer: 'Our help is in the name of the Lord, who has made heaven and earth, who does not forsake the work of his hands' (Pss. 124.8; 138.8).[15] Then there is the fate of Israel, from the exodus through the exile to the diaspora and the building up of present-day Israel, which is interpreted by Israel itself as a covenant history, and to which Christians, too, cannot remain neutral. Thus the history of the concrete religions and their historical evolution becomes an analogy to God's involvement with men and women.[16] As a special aspect of this there is the abysmal crime of religious violence between and within the different religions, which comes to a clear climax in the Holocaust: a theology after Auschwitz surely cannot put the concrete history of the religions – and with it the history of violence in the name of God – in quotation marks.

However, that also applies to the history of good, the history of hope and the prospect of God. So we have to speak historically about the Christ – God's long-awaited Messiah – and Christians cannot avoid beginning with Jesus of Nazareth, whether they prefer a christology 'from above' or a christology 'from below'. But the work of the Holy Spirit, too, can only be described as the work of Christ through time, for example as the history of the mission and the apostolate of the church. Thus God himself – as economic Trinity – also writes history,[17] and always does so with human beings. Finally that ends up in the judgement, the eschatological consummation of every human life and of human history. Romans 8 prevents us from forgetting the glorification of creation here.

God's revelation takes place in this whole course of God through history, disclosed to us through the tradition of the Christian faith,[18] in which Christ is recognized and confessed as the meaning of history.

But that is something different from a utopia which turns out well. Historically speaking, things did not turn out well for Jesus either. Historically speaking, things cannot turn out well for anyone, or for the cosmos as a whole. Above all the apocalyptic tradition constantly reckons with a fatal course of history, in which only a few escape. Even Genesis, the first book of the Bible, already knows the end of history: the flood, the destruction of Sodom and Gomorrah, the dispersal of the peoples. The message is that God knows how to distinguish good from evil only at the limit of death and the destruction of the world, and utterly continues to stand on the side of the good. And above all, that the course of things and the passage of the ages really grieves God, expressly because the biography of human beings – children of God – is part of 'God's own life', from which we go and to which we return: according to the confession of Christians, in the footsteps of Jesus who, although a victim of history, entered the very life of God, as he came forth from it.

THEOLOGY OF HISTORY

Thus believers cannot do without a view of time, times and history in time if they want to get a glimpse of God. But it is dangerous too quickly to declare one's own perspective a universal theory and to want to trap God in concrete historical developments.

Christian theological reflection knows many interpretations of the course of history and all kinds of turning points in it. The biblical narrative of the exodus is one of the oldest examples of a philosophy of history: the fate of a group of migrants, freed from a situation of injustice, wandering in search of a fixed place to live in, written down after they have settled permanently in order to remind them of their origin, so that they are always ready to travel again. This is the epic of Israel, a people tossed to and fro between Zion and diaspora. It is the story of David, a shepherd boy on a king's throne, to whom nothing human is alien, called by God to establish justice and to create unity, no more than that, and in this way a king after God's heart. It is the story of Jerusalem's exiles, full of homesickness for their former land, accepting their fate, in service among the peoples, prophetically comforted by God's judgement on all domination. And finally it is the story of Jesus: a history of the rise and fall of God's own messenger, a crucified man who lives and reigns from the shameful symbol of injustice, the cross, his blood shed like that of so many prophets, but rehabilitated by God, the true king of the Jews, the true shepherd of the people, liberator Messiah only through discipleship and never again through violence. And the story is subsequently told by his disciples, by converted followers like Paul, by the old visionary of the Apocalypse in refractory times.

But then, very soon, it is also portrayed by people like Eusebius of Caesarea, who could not resist declaring the semi-convert Constantine a saint, addressing him as the messenger of God, bringer of peace. And by Augustine of Hippo, whose view is far more subtle: the conflict between two worlds, the earthly and the heavenly city, until God himself takes over the helm. Or by Joachim of Fiore, who sees the world empires of his time perish, until a thousand-year realm of peace comes. Many later figures have praised their own revolution as the beginning of that thousand-year empire, if not with violence, then with more democratic means: Melchior Hoffmann and William of Orange, Frederick the Great and Napoleon, 'the American dream' and Lenin's paradise for workers in the Soviet Union. And perhaps last of all, the ideal of a 'One Power World' (Bush Snr.) or 'One European Home' (Gorbachev, Kohl).

Theology at the same time knows a long tradition of criticism of such a religious and ideological glorification of human utopias or boyhood dreams. Athanasius already warned against identifying human claimants to salvation – like the Roman emperors, who were fond of having themselves called 'saviour' (*soter*) and who even did not shrink from the qualification 'godlike' (*homoousios*) and 'Son of God' – with messengers of God. In fact early Christian dogma, which reserved the titles 'Son of God' and 'of the same substance as God' for Jesus, is an explicit criticism of this kind of identification: 'If someone says to you, here is the messiah, or there he is, do not believe them' (Matt. 24.23–24; Mark 13.21; cf. Luke 17.23).

In the twentieth-century ecumenical movement, too, both the seduction and the critique of the utopian can be heard time and again, above all in connection with questions of social and political justice and the interpretation of the idea of the kingdom of God.[19]

THE CATEGORY OF 'HISTORY' IN ECUMENICAL DIALOGUE

Many sub-divisions of the theological tradition depend on the view of history. It also seems to generate confessional differences. It was soon discovered in the ecumenical movement that a shared view of history is the condition for a close Christian *koinonia*. At an ecumenical conference in 1959 on 'The Meaning of History',[20] Protestant, Anglican and Roman Catholic historians and theologians (including H. Kraemer) came to conclusions which since then seem to have been normative for the theological argument.

By comparison with the Graeco-Roman view of history, which interprets the facts of nature and culture in the framework of divine power, fate or justice (*dike*) (thus Thucydides, Polybius, Livy and Tacitus),[21] the Jewish-Christian interpretation of history gives a central place to freedom and God's *telos*. History is going somewhere, and we are responsible for it. Certainly we are subject to tragic and often catastrophic laws of nature and bound to the limits of space and time, which also determine the finitude of life, but within them we have a free space, what Bloch calls a vacuum of the possible, in which another scheme or scenario guides us: that of the Torah and of the criteria of the kingdom of God. Freedom, challenge, desire, relationship, love and *Logos* predominate in that scenario. Without this kingdom of freedom, history becomes a pure course of events, the chronology of a ticking watch, the geometrical order of one instance after the other of the same thing.

In the face of all fatalism and determinism, the Jewish-Christian view of history puts forward the concept of the *dominium terrae* (Gen. 1.26–28), that of a responsible society and the personal call and destiny of all men and women. In the end all this is under God's judgement, but this judgement already pervades our decisions, just as God himself also pervades all natural events and the course of all history, though it is never possible to localize God anywhere or to identify God with the phenomena which press in on us. Thus the idea of God, the view of nature and history as a divine '*oikonomia*', and the view of the freedom and responsibility of the human person are correlates. Gratuitousness is the binding element of this correlation: God does not force himself, does not force anything or anyone, and does not allow himself to be forced. And on the other hand God's action of blessing and sparing (*charis, gratia*) does not destroy nature; it leaves contingency and the laws of nature intact, but with a view to the glorification of human beings and

God's own glorification – *gloria dei vivens homo* – brings them together into a new configuration, a new scenario. It is given many names: covenant, salvation history, redemption, new creation, consummation, kingdom of God. This Jewish-Christian view of history has left its stamp on Islam and also on the humanistic culture of the West. Its roots may go back to Egyptian, Mesopotamian, Indian, Persian and Chinese wisdom, but only this view of history has developed its own group and sense of community, which in principle is universal: open to all peoples, not bound to caste, language, race, sex or fixed patterns of culture; open to change and reinterpretation, and thus open to hermeneutics.

But in this scheme of history many questions remain about the interpretation of the facts of nature and history, of what can be explained in terms of causes and reasons, or is to be striven for in terms of values and goals. There cannot be freedom on all sides; it is limited in communal patterns by discipleship and faithfulness to God's law, but even within that there is room for interpretation.

One of the problems of interpretation – which is already a theme in the biblical narrative itself – is the question of the course of history. It presupposes a linear development through time, perhaps an evolution, an ongoing improvement and a good outcome to history and a perfection of changeable and ambivalent nature. The contrast which is often made between a more cyclical view of history – which above all has an eye to the circular course of the seasons, the generations and the cultures – and a more linear course – which points to evolution, progress, perfectibility and the accumulation of knowledge – is a false one, certainly if it is meant to indicate the difference between Hellenistic and Jewish thought or that between religion and the true service of God. There are also problems of interpretation about the place of human beings – like the exercise of the *dominium terrae*, the dominion of the earth. But it is quite certain that in the Bible, from Genesis to Daniel, from Mark to the Apocalypse, the question of the course – the origin, the meaning and the outcome – of history is connected with the vicissitudes of human beings. Paradise and flood, the building up of Israel and the exile, the praise of God's cosmic wisdom and the almost cynical complaint about the transitoriness of nature and history, all relate to the place of human beings, their responsibility and God's judgement on their lives. The biblical argument about the forces of nature and the history of the peoples nowhere has a purely cosmological or historiographical purpose; it has an eschatological and anthropological focus: attention is focused not on the initial or final phase of the cosmic big bang, or on the rise and fall of world empires, but on the quality of the human response to the divine determination in days good and bad.[22]

GOD IN NATURE AND HISTORY

The study report *God in Nature and History* (1965), which was also accepted by Faith and Order in 1967 as a contribution to the Uppsala assembly,[23] also contains many useful thoughts for a Christian theology of history. It is about the reconciliation of the Christian confession with the modern scientific world-view and the historical insights into the origin and development of the Jewish-Christian tradition: how is belief in God's active presence in nature and history to be maintained? In this document, nature and history are seen as two lines along which God's ultimate purpose with creation is realized. This insight is expressed in Israel's discovery of the covenant of God with the earth, with all human beings, and especially with the people of Israel. In Christ this covenant is endorsed and renewed in the direction of God's new creation, in which sin, suffering and guilt will be overcome:

> Christ is ... the new man who leads the process of history to its ultimate goal ... The old adamic humanity was the starting-point of history; a new pneumatic humanity, built around the new man, the resurrected Christ, is the goal of history ... All this gives us the image of one great movement from lower to higher, going through atonement and salvation and so directed towards its ultimate goal, a glorified humanity, in full communion with God of which goal the risen Christ is the guarantee and the first fruits.[24]

However, all this is realized in down-to-earth forms of matter, the biological struggle over existence, bodily drives, an existence marked by sickness, guilt and death.

Christians need not fear the analyses of Marx, Darwin or Freud, any more than they needed to oppose Galileo: as creatures we share in all facets of nature, of evolution and the history of the peoples. God's salvation is achieved in the face of social and economic injustice and political skirmishes. God's salvation is realized only in history, a universal history in which the special history of Israel and of Jesus functions as moments of disclosure. It is to this history, our concrete history, that God has committed himself. Christian eschatology is not escapism:

The new earth will be this earth renewed ... Since there is some kind of continuity between history and consummation, the suggestion of a contrast between history and consummation is to be rejected. Of course the human mind is here at the limits of what can be thought and said. Nevertheless it should be boldly stated that the alternative, consummation as a timeless motionless eternity, is alien to the Christian faith. The historicizing of life has been experienced as God's own liberating work. The end of such a work never can mean its abolition, only its glorification, its preservation in a wider context of life. The idea in the New Testament that mankind in the consummation will reign with Christ (Rom. 5.17; II Tim. 2.12; Rev. 3.21; also Luke 19.17) seems to express this conviction. Consummation will mean a new and far more thorough-going display of man's freedom and dominion.[25]

But Christians need to resist any seduction to interpret all kinds of historical phenomena or institutions as 'signs of the times':

There is one great Sign of the Time and of all times: Jesus Christ and none besides Him.[26]

In 1967 there were still many pitfalls and traps here: *God in Nature and History* was received with a great many critical comments, above all from the Lutheran side, where there was a concern to avoid any suggestion of a possible synergism of God and human beings:

We need to determine with more clarity in what sense, if any, it can be affirmed that our cultural achievements will be used as building-stones for the kingdom of God.[27]

If we thought that it was exclusively up to human beings whether God achieved his rights and his kingdom, God would be left out of account. If we think that God and human beings work together in a complementary way – the term used is then synergism – it becomes impossible to make anything of God's omnipotence and sovereignty. Moreover, it can never be established which is God's share and which that of human beings. But if in reaction we see God at work only where human beings have nothing to contribute, we lapse into a primitive image of God, into paganism. In a reflection on the value of scientific and technological knowledge, Berkhof says:

... at this point the Christian community ... has continued to think in a pagan way; in other words, it has started from the view that the power which nature exercises on us is another name for the power of God. It saw God act in the floods and in the lightning flash. It did not see God in the dykes and in the lightning conductors. The Old Testament makes a radical shift: God does not stand behind nature over against human beings, but behind human beings over against nature.[28]

The cultural achievements which together with the course of nature determine history are thus no less alien to God than the gradual development of the idea of God and the religious forms that we call revelation or the human words that we cherish as Holy Scripture and as the Word of God. So the Christ event too is embedded in a long evolution and the incarnation, so to speak, does not drop out of thin air, nor is redemption in Christ completed in one day.

God also works for good through the good works of human beings. God and human beings cannot be rivals. According to P. Schoonenberg, 'What God does more, human beings do not do less, nor vice versa.'[29] This view of the working of God in history that we find in Reformation and Catholic theologians forms a firm bridge between the Reformation and Rome. The character of this view of history with its orientation on the future also brings together the theology of East and West. Salvation from God is more than the repair of a break or the restoration of a fall from the past. It is a gracious turning of God towards creation, passing through ruptures and pitfalls – God's condescension – in which human beings are encouraged and renewed to put greater trust in their calling, so that they live a life that looks towards God (*theosis*), a life that renounces the drive for heaven-storming perfection and the development of fatal utopias. But at the same time this life knows about responsibility and freedom: the course of history lies completely in human hands. Belief in God as the signpost for history is therefore itself constitutive of the course of things.

That is reason enough to spend a life in critical dialogue with the ideals of the time and thus theologically to begin with the signs of the times. That must also be, first and foremost, because human beings themselves live in historicity, since 'it is not yet revealed what we shall be' (I John 3.2).[30] Human beings hanker after God all through history and through life, and human life is built on hope for the future: not as a deterministic extrapolation of human nature or of history now, but because of the forces 'which work on and are applied to both from outside, and give us reason to expect such a future'.[31] Thus history is not a chronological course in the direction of end-product or end-time, but the ongoing and current passage of a creative dynamic of present, past and future. The eschaton or the last day is not a limitation on historical time but the removal of limits from it, and so it cannot be fixed on a time-line either: it is always time and soon too late; it is constantly topical in the irrevocable passage of time.

So there can be no question of a naïve historicism. The nineteenth-century concern with the history of religion and the approach to the biblical text in terms of theories of its development was a reduction of the biblical material to biblical history and a certain distortion of the narrative patterns produced by the question of what the real historical value of the information was. That stamped the source or revelation claimed in these writings as a museum piece: there is a closed revelation, to which one can only refer back and of which the scarlet thread is formed by a succession of witnesses, from Adam to Abraham, from Moses to Jesus, from Paul to Timothy, and that's it!

Nor can it be a matter of an unhistorical actualism, as if only the here and now counted, with no sense of responsibility for the morrow or for future generations. Anyone who says 'God' is looking towards God's eternal present, in which one day spans a thousand years.

HISTORY AS OPEN FUTURE

Thus history stands for the open future, freedom, responsibility and human fulfilment. This intermediate level also makes the term 'salvation history' more accessible to modern thinking. Salvation history as a retrospect, as talking after the event about contingent historical events – the exodus from Egypt, Jesus' death on the cross – can instead easily be suspected of being an ideology: particular facts are selected and others are left out (as in Exodus the catastrophe which befell the Egyptian army or the original inhabitants of Canaan). The exposition of events – Jesus' execution as willed by God – often causes all kinds of misunderstandings. But salvation history as a perspective takes the events from the past as signs, pledges, guarantees and guidelines of God's purposes. It is a 'covenant history', to use Berkhof's term:[32] God goes up with human beings in their history. Here we have the power of the Spirit, which gradually transcends and conquers sin, evil and death. In this sense the historical fate and historical message of Jesus as the Christ is not *passé*, is not an episode of profane history, to which salvation is to be attached chronologically, but an epiphany of God's eschatological purposes which has kairological significance.

HISTORY: MORE THAN THE SUM OF MOMENTS OF ENCOUNTER

Does that then mean that nothing counts other than living each moment at the deepest as a moment of grace, in supreme concentration and contemplation of God as *intimior intimo meo*, which finds its pinnacle in the mystical relation with God? Although there are many advantages in expressing the connection to God in terms of partnership, relationship and encounter, as has happened since Buber ('in the beginning was the relationship') and Brunner, very radically with Bultmann but also with Schillebeeckx (*Christ, the Sacrament of Encounter with God*), the question arises whether the option of encounter does not finally rob faith of any content:

> If the only question is the encounter between God and human beings, and all that can be objectivized – also including human beings as part of nature and as persons who act in history – falls outside this encounter, then faith is robbed of all elements of the reality of nature and history that can be experienced.[33]

Thus belief in God presupposes a real connection between God and created reality:

> We have a God who is more than 'the voice which resounds eternally'; more than the guarantor of our existence; more than the other pole of a relationship. We have a God who binds himself to our blood-warm and rebellious existence as human beings in the world for life and for death, who penetrates there, almost perishes there, saves it, transforms it and creates new possibilities. The inner unity of Act and Being (cf. Bonhoeffer) which emerges there is the reflection of salvation itself; it consists in the fact that the Creator enters his creation, that *salvation becomes history* [my italics], that Jesus of Nazareth is the Christ and the sixty-six books of the Bible are God's word to us, that the 'outside me' (*extra me*) and the 'for me' (*pro me*) are opposite sides of the same coin, that the Spirit penetrates the hidden corners of our psychological existence, and makes

our bodies a sacrifice well pleasing to God, and that in the consummation we await a new earth in which righteousness dwells. And the central point of all this is the incarnation of the Word, in which it has taken the form of a servant and has become objectifiable, in which God has made himself object to the death, indeed the death of the cross. The salvation that emanates from there is salvation for our reality of guilt and suffering: it goes over into objectifiability and takes the form of a book, a doctrine, an institution, a human word, water, bread and wine.[34]

But all that stands under the sign of provisionality; it calls for fulfilment and consummation in the eschaton. Eschatology there-fore also presupposes the fulfilment – the final end – of nature and history. They are more than the discarded stages of a burnt-out rocket. Berkhof thinks that the biblical message of the vision of the kingdom of God also presupposes this consummation.

CHRONOS AND *KAIROS*

But how can this consummation be read off the Christ event? How can the 'new time' that has dawned in it permeate the actual course of rise and fall? How can the *kairos* of God's grace that has broken into our history form part of our *chronos*? Or rather, how can everything that is subjected to *chronos* and thus to finitude and death begin to share in this *kairos* which transcends, overcomes, finitude and death?

Of course there is first of all the dualistic answer of an ever-increasing conflict between light and darkness, good and evil. In Chapter 2 we already saw the pernicious consequences of this way of thinking, which is also not very plausible from an empirical-historical perspective.[35]

However, there is also the answer that time becomes *kairos* by means of the stories of responsibility and hope which we produce in time and tell to one another. Paul Ricoeur above all has deepened this notion in his hermeneutical philosophy. In his view we must pause longer in order to deepen our concept of culture and history and to be able to understand history as the place where God can be found.

THE NARRATIVE PATH OF PAUL RICOEUR

The narrative path of Paul Ricoeur[36] offers an attractive alternative to the excessive fixation on history as a chronological course of time and an exclusive concentration on the actual significance of the self-constructed present which threatens in semiotic approaches. In his hermeneutics Ricoeur is carrying on a fight on two fronts: he is disputing the idea of an unmediated understanding of the intentions of the text by studying the historical intentions of the author. That is the romantic hermeneutics which defines all texts in terms of the information that they convey. The other extreme that Ricoeur wants to challenge is a structuralist hermeneutic which reduces all texts to their momentary effect on the reader and thus has an eye only for the performative functions of the text. Ricoeur is also giving the poetic force of the text an archaeological and teleological effect: if it is to become a criterion and standard, a canon, the narrative configuration does not derive its evocative force solely from the semantic logic of its performance – the internal consistency of the story with all its actants – but also from its capacity to express an original reality of life – the prefigurative dimension of any mimesis – and its capacity to bring about something in readers and hearers, players and onlookers: its refigurative effect. What is brought about is therefore more than an agogic or diegetic event: it is dependent on the dramatic depth of the underlying prefigurations. Although fiction and remembrance are the two forms and ingredients of any good narrative, whether novel, fable, parable or historical account, in the end the narrative success is not determined by the intention of the narrator but by reference to a drama which is effective underneath it, which touches narrator and hearers equally. Three times in his trilogy *Time and Narrative* Ricoeur returns to this marker on his narrative path, which he terms '*scrupule*'.

Nevertheless, it would be fatal to understand this dramatics exclusively as a recollection of dramatic events from the past. That is how we have often understood salvation history – in all its dramatic effects as liberation, redemption, justification, adoption as sons of God. That is also how we have often understood the work of God in Israel and in Jesus which is attested to us in the scriptures. We then live by the covenant concluded at that time, as heirs. We live from the life of Jesus given once for all, at that time on Good Friday. The whole of Christian life is then the constant anamnesis of what has already happened. The reverse side of this, apostasy in actions which are not well-pleasing to God, the stoning of the prophets, the rejection of the Son of Man, also took place at that time. Now all that remains to us is the ritual memory of this covenant of salvation realized once and for all. However, for Ricoeur the dramatics remains in what is still possible, in the teleology of the subject; granted, this is not yet anyone, but it can become so in the light of God's creation. Kevin Vanhoozer in fact characterizes Ricoeur's work as a work which bears witness to the passion for the possible: it is a philosophy of hope.[37] But the biblical writings in particular lead us, like those involved then, in the direction of this hope. The Bible is the historically trustworthy witness to an untameable desire, a permanent expectation of God's blessing.

At this point Ricoeur's thought runs parallel to that of Karl Rahner.[38] Jesus appeared as one who was saved, as one who put unconditional trust in a *telos* that transcended his subject, in a surplus of being. The nature of this surplus, hidden in the infinity of God, forms the scarlet thread of the biblical quest from Genesis to the Apocalypse of John. If that is no more than a human construct, no more than pure fiction, however effective, then we come out of it cheated. But if it is promise, based on God's *telos*, then there is a firm ground for our hope (Heb. 11).

HISTORY AND IMAGINATION: TWO ASPECTS OF THE NARRATIVE, TWO FORMS OF PASSION FOR THE POSSIBLE

History is the study of human behaviour in the past in the form of staging. Any historical event which is narrated is likewise staged as a merely fictitious story. Any event can at least be staged as the end of a chain of events or as their beginning. The total chain of events can no more be mapped precisely than all possible consequences of the actual event. Thus in its turn the history that is written – history as story – is always also coloured by fiction.

But a difference remains. The difference does not lie in the character of fiction as a poetic construction by comparison with the empirical and descriptive character of historiography: both fiction and account, argument and course, make use of constructions, metaphors, associations and connections. Both also seek to communicate something and produce an effect on the reader. The difference lies in dedication to the sources and intersubjective testing of the sources. History and narrative both presuppose a hermeneutical community and a public audience. But history at the same time presupposes a hermeneutical community which regards itself as vehicle and mediator of the heritage of the past. Theology cannot abstract from this hermeneutical community: it is like a good scribe who brings out of his treasury both old and new.

The second difference is more serious. It has been emphasized above all by Hans Frei[39] in his *The Eclipse of Biblical Narrative*, in which he accuses Tracy and Ricoeur and all other mediating theologians from Schleiermacher up to and including Tillich and Bultmann of betraying the person and cause of Jesus. If the whole narrative structure of the scriptures is taken up in their character as parables – the parables as a poetic staging of life in the direction of God's kingdom and Jesus as the most perfect parable of humanity – then the whole biblical hermeneutics becomes an instance of universal hermeneutical rules about the transfer of values by means of texts from the past. The Bible is then one of the many classics of world literature, and Jesus is a unique narrator with a unique narrative competence, but nothing else. What happened to him and what he himself intended – in the account and the poetry of his disciples – becomes a scenario of humankind, in principle no different from that of Socrates or Buddha or Muhammad, Mahatma Gandhi or Albert Schweitzer. Frei therefore wants to go back to the literal meaning of the scriptures, to the contingent-historical character of God's self-revelation in scripture and the unique event of God's coming among human beings in the person of Jesus.

Although I share Frei's questions about Ricoeur's and Tracy's project and think that with the inextricable interweaving of the God-world-self complex that they presuppose we no longer have any criteria with which to decide between human 'wholeness' and 'salvation from God', the therapy offered seems to me to be more of a regression. An appeal to the literal meaning of the scriptural witnesses fails to recognize the inevitable poetic or construct character of any witness which cannot bow to proofs or to the consensus of all witnesses. The scriptures are about controversial events. They are carrying on a court case, with a number of pleas. But they do not contain any court proceedings or the results of journalistic research. There are bizarre stories, which take a miraculous course, from Cain and Abel, Abraham and Isaac, Jacob and Esau, Moses and the people, David and Uriah, David and Bathsheba onwards. There are stories of prophets who are stoned and of Jesus who was crucified. There are stories of disciples who denied and betrayed him and who nevertheless were transformed into pillars of the church. In the midst of the dramatic history of the peoples a small people gathers together its experience with its God and proclaims this God as the God of the universe. In the midst of the colourful Greek, Roman, Celtic and Germanic religious pluralism, the community of and with Jesus brings into being a common worship, an ethic of equal rights and a common vision of God's governance. Here the source events of the Exodus and Sinai, of Golgotha, Passover and Pentecost, play an abiding role; never, however, only in the literal sense of a historical 'cult legend', but rather as the abiding source of a questing confession.

CONCLUSION: A PLEA FOR A BIBLICAL THEOLOGY ON A HISTORICAL BASIS

The structure of the biblical ethic is fundamentally historical in the sense that specific people with sometimes bizarre biographies are configured as concrete witnesses, prophets, messengers of the mystery of God and see themselves refigured as such, as is indicated by Paul's account of his conversion. In the likewise historical and contingent collection of these witnesses with universally human instructions for action so that they become Law, Prophets and Wisdom in the canon of Jewish scripture, we are given a historical fact which defines the identity of both Judaism and Christianity; its form as source text is permanently normative for all later interpretation and commentary. The very quest for a standard text of the scriptures as source text – the so-called basic text – legitimates a historical-critical approach to the texts and also makes this necessary. A biblical theology in the original meaning of this term is vitally necessary, so that we know and retain knowledge of as many as possible of the historical circumstances on the basis of which the critical establishment of the basic text can take place. *Mutatis mutandis* this also applies to the scriptures of the New Testament.

A second argument for maintaining the historical approach to the biblical text is the actual history of its tradition, its selection and canonization. Especially as a result of so-called canon studies a new type of biblical theology is making an appearance which, through an emphasis on the pluralism of texts and the semiotic approach to each part of the text separately, never indicates the process of stratification by means of which one narrative is handed down and another is not. The scriptures that we have are the last version of many textual schemes which have been put together and selected by critical users in a process which is not yet complete.

A third argument is the epoch-making character of the idea of God and the forms of religious expression in the Old and New Testaments. Although the scheme of rise and fall cannot be used as an all-embracing pattern of history, there are different emphases in the idea of God in the history of Israel and the church. In her book *A History of God*,[40] Karen Armstrong has indicated the importance of an honest account of the pluralism of ideas about God within Judaism and Christianity, and also in Islam. However, this epoch-making character calls for choices. The choice of Christians is indissolubly bound up with the choice of the Jew Jesus and his idea of God as a provisionally definitive form of God for the human approach to God.

A fourth and last argument lies in the notion of a personal encounter with God, inherent in the Jewish and Christian idea of God, or of going to, being received by, coming home to, God as the one from whom we also set out. Therefore history is not just the account of a course so far, but also the hope of a sequel beyond our horizon. The epic of Israel looks forward to such a utopia: the gathering of the people in Zion, the reconstruction of the dry skeletons in the valley of death, the worship 'in spirit and truth' in the restored temple of Jerusalem, the coming on the clouds of the Son of Man, who will speak out above all injustice. Christianity has taken over this expectation of salvation and filled it with the vision of the Son of Man who will draw on it and act like the figure of Jesus: at his name every knee shall bow, all must follow his commandments. In place of a *nebula fidei* – a God behind the clouds, a vague cloud of witnesses who have seen visions, a mysterious phenomenon like a cloud by day and a fire by night – a historical person emerges as guide and pointer to God. The scarlet thread of his biography becomes the *regula fidei*. Biblical theology needs to clarify how he, the Son of the old people, must be the Son of God to the end, who fulfils the promises to the patriarchs, the wisdom of the kings and the admonition of the prophets.

These four motifs again and again wager on the therapeutic force of the epoch-making sense that history is transcended, corrected and made whole only by ongoing events. The category of history has come to stand in a somewhat misty evening light as the result of the philosophical critique – by Fukuyama and Lyotard – of the concept of history. Can the Christian view of history withstand this? At all events, it can do so better than the Marxist or existentialist utopias to which Fukuyama and the postmodern philosophers are opposed. For Jews, Christians and Muslims God is not a God of the Great Narrative; God is not an abstract and speculative meta-idea who has to guarantee the cohesion of everything, the continuity of the laws of matter or a good outcome to the cosmic hubbub, but one who is involved in all the little stories of human beings which are woven together and which become what – in configurative language – we call salvation history. I also include in this configured salvation history the later ideas of faith: confession, liturgy, dogma, catechesis and spirituality, which certainly reflect the culture that happens to be present, but which have also contributed towards shaping it and which fill the symbolic universe of both believers and unbelievers. That is not a fixed doctrine, not a dead language of faith, but a constantly developing and constantly corrected living language. However, configurative language remains alive only within the *koinonia* of those who look towards God and who in the name of Jesus bow their knees to the One and Eternal, 'Adonai Abba', 'who remains faithful for ever and does not abandon the work of his hands'.

7

God who Creates and Cares: The Father of All Human Beings
Fragments of a liberating theology of creation

GOD IN NATURE AND IN SPACE-TIME

For our modern senses, nature and history with all their causes, forces and motivations form a single whole, just as body and soul cannot be separated from each other. We speak of physical, psychological and physiological processes, of an environment in which we live, and, where human beings are concerned, with psychosomatic connections between what we want in freedom and what we can do, bound up as we are with bodily energy and the natural forces of gravity. We look feverishly for correlations between currents in the brain and thought-processes, genetic patterns and behaviour, traumatic memories and current psychological suffering. It is not that we have found many explanations, far less that we have usable guidance mechanisms to hand. But after all, we have so much insight into the complex connection between nature and nurture, between our fragile freedom and the limitations of our own bodily ecosystem, that it has become impossible for us still to believe in the existence of a soul or spirit which has been inserted into human beings and will be split off from them again, or of independent 'pure spirits' like angels and demons. Because, at least in the West, we can no longer envisage anything like a separate effective 'spirit', detached from matter and the body, we cannot make anything either of God as a 'pure spirit', as previous generations did.[1] A way of thinking which began with the ancient Greeks and found its climax in Hegel has thus largely become unusable. Already in the school of Pythagoras there is a heavily populated atmosphere in which human beings live. The whole space of the invisible and the intangible consists of many levels or spheres and is full of forces and powers, angels and demons. It is the space of the divine universe, within which material things and living beings then crystallized, shaped and formed in accordance with divine outlines and ideals. According to Plato, these are all to be derived from the eternal values of truth, goodness and beauty. It is the task of all that is to reflect these ideas (*mimesis*), to long for them (*eros*) and finally to return to them, leaving all matter and transitoriness behind. Human beings are also aware of this task. They need to be concerned for their souls: human life is a journey of the soul, like that of a divine rider on an obtuse horse. In reaction their body is then that horse, which must be led in the direction of the good, chastized and trained, just as the form of the work of art must be fought for in the material. Matter and also the body is the brakeman in the firm service of the soul and, on close inspection, its prison in which it is enclosed as long as we live.

GOD'S CREATION: AN ALTERNATIVE TO DUALISM

The three monotheistic religions of Judaism, Christianity and Islam incorporated this Platonic thought-pattern into their idea of God and gave it world-wide currency. It also linked them with the Asian and Afro-Australian religions, although there the accents were put in different places. At the same time in principle, with the doctrine of God's creative and caring action, it has combated the dualism of matter and spirit, body and soul, nature and supernature, which threatens in this thought pattern. That embraces everything: both earth and heaven, body and soul, visible and invisible. All that is, is created: angels and demons, powers and forces, matter and life, cosmic nature and earthly history, the species and individuals, indeed even good and evil, life and death. The creative God has to do with all that is, all that was and all that will be: with the 'spiritual' as well as the 'material', with the 'lowest' as much as with the 'sublime'. That is the basic dogma of any monotheism.

So within this belief in the creator God no space can be

conceived of which is not filled with God, nor a God who has to limit himself to a part of space, namely the space of the 'Spirit'. God has to do with all 'spaces', all 'spheres' to which our capacity for thought and our thought system can extend. But God never coincides with any of these 'thought spaces' or 'universes'. God is said to be 'omnipresent', but he can never be 'localized': whether in holy places, in holy times, or in a separate space outside time.[2] Concepts like 'heaven', 'hereafter' and 'eternity', which in the tradition are thought of as God's 'dwelling place', cannot be expressed in co-ordinates of place and time; indeed they are quasi-temporal and spatial metaphors which try to escape the way in which we think in terms of time and space. Anyone who first of all connects God with such escape clauses puts God outside the reality of earthly existence as it is experienced, cuts the tie with God as a source of all life and makes religion a complicated system of necessary connections between the inhabitants of the earth and a distant and alien superpower. Such a Supreme Being must then be invoked in many ways, be worked on with sacrifices and constantly kept friendly so that it is near to people. In reaction such a Being will then be accused, criticized and rejected when it is too late for help in hopeless matters. This idea of God makes God secondary to what is. It attributes being to *essents* and makes God a kind of supreme *Essent*. Here the very being of things hangs in the air and God becomes a human creation, a factor of all that is within the categories by which *we* determine what is and how it is.

A REVERSAL OF PERSPECTIVE

The only remaining possibility for giving God a place within thought in terms of time and space, which is now our lot, is to reverse the perspective: God is nowhere within space or time, but space and time play themselves out, unfold, 'within' God. That too cannot be thought of without metaphors, as already emerges from the quotation marks within which we must now put 'within'. But in any case this is a better solution than putting a 'God' within quotation marks within our time and space. For now God has to do with the whole of reality from 'within', i.e. from himself and in himself. Theologians have coined the term 'panentheism' for this altered perspective. What is meant by it can be made clear from a simple analogy, derived from the experience of our bodily functions. If I talk about 'myself' or about my 'I', I am talking

157

about my whole body, my whole life, though nowhere am I 'in' it, nor does 'my life' coincide with any moment of my life. Unless I suffer from particular psychological disorders, I understand myself to be wider than my body:[3] my 'horizon', my 'reach', my 'memory', my 'network' of relations and even what others think of me, my 'name and fame', all make up part of my 'I' as a person, as 'consciousness' and as 'centre of activity'. I am in fact an 'extended person' with a changing range, who gradually unfolds. I can also from time to time withdraw into myself, among other things by changing roles from the public to the private domain. And conversely, I constantly hand myself over to others: what others think of me, what they do with my words, actions and ideas or their remote consequences can no longer be controlled. So I in fact again let go of the space which I 'occupy' in freedom in my constellation as a person and make myself and others free for new experiences. Thus the human person grows through his or her experiences, constantly corrected here by interaction with the growth of others. By analogy, God can be thought of as the 'I' who has to do with all facets of reality, albeit in his own time and way. Precisely for that reason, God can also be spoken of as a 'person': not of course as the individual person whom we know and experience as someone who acts, speaks, hears, touches and tastes in a bodily way, but as the extended person from whom we derive the analogy. Moreover it is typical of all analogies referring to God that the differences always prove greater than the agreement, as a medieval council already established.[4] Thus God can be taken up as the perspective of thought and action without coinciding with our ideas and without being a needless duplication of our actions. Precisely in the sphere of the personal, where human beings are at their best, where they show themselves at their greatest and attain their widest range – caring, helping, cherishing, respecting all that lives – God comes into view, as the source and the test of human care and love. Precisely for that reason God is worshipped as creating and caring, and all human creating and caring takes on a divine halo, because God has to do with that which is dearest to us: the personal dignity of the human being who respects and reveres all that lives, who gives expression to the sublime, and who precisely by so doing grows into a personality. The creator God cares for creatures as parents care for their children: mothering, fathering, cherishing, feeding and guiding. Scripture says that God is someone who is always there: YHWH. According to Jesus of Nazareth, God is the Father of all human beings, who knows what is good for us.

Nothing and no one escapes God's attention: God's 'omnipotence' means that God has 'to do with' everything.

GOD: FATHER, SON AND SPIRIT

Within Christianity the fact that God 'has to do' with all that is, with all that lives, and especially with human beings, has taken on a specific threefold structure which is specifically connected with belief in the central significance of Jesus of Nazareth as an icon and form of the invisible God. Because it is said of him that God has dwelt in him among human beings and that although he knows himself to be wholly bound up with the will and the work of God, he nevertheless also addresses himself to God in questioning and supplication and even in despair, the question arises of God's covenant and bond, God's presence, will and activity, before, in and after Christ. These were present before Christ in the religious quest of Israel and the surrounding peoples, which led to the monotheism of belief in YHWH. In the activity and the message of Jesus, God shows people the way to a new experience of God-with-us, and belief in YHWH goes beyond the limits of Israel. After his death this enlarged belief in YHWH had to give an account of itself to Judaism, which did not go along with this movement, and to the other religions. Although the respect for Israel remained, and the other religions were used as bridgeheads for the new YHWH faith, they were challenged to have their experience of God corrected and supplemented by making the acquaintance of the faith of and in Jesus, the one who was specially sent and anointed by the Spirit of God, whose way is the truth and the life for all men and women.

This threefold activity of God, his *oikonomia* – before, in and after Jesus – corresponds to God's deepest being, which consists in relationship to the whole of time and space and to the whole historical process of matter and life, nature and history. Only the analogy of a plural or polyphonic personality is sufficient to give a picture of this personal relationship of God to God's 'world': the triune God (*Trinitas Dei*, Trinity), Father, Son and Holy Spirit. At the same time the threefold form of address to God as the structure of Christian prayer ('Glory be to the Father, and to the Son, and to the Holy Spirit ... through Jesus Christ, our Lord, who lives and reigns with you in the unity of the Holy Spirit'), as the watchword of Christian identity and as an articulation of the Christian creed, serves to make the necessary connections: with the God of Israel,

159

YHWH, Adonai, called 'Father' by Jesus; with the God of Islam, called Allah by Muhammad; and with all the other names for the secret of the all-embracing breath of God or Atman, which is experienced in the Asian religions.

Perhaps it would have been better if we had introduced rather more structure within the threefold talk about God. There can be no question of three separate, successive 'forms' of God. At any rate it is clear that both the Father and the Spirit span the times and bring the peoples together in one worship 'in spirit and truth'. However they may appear on the scene – as cloud and fire, as voice and wind – YHWH and his Spirit are one in their presence among human beings and especially among those who call upon him and praise him. Only the Son becomes present in a lifelike way, as a human being among human beings. Paul (Rom. 1.4) says that he was made Son by the Spirit of God. The Father and the Spirit, equal in origin, thus represent YHWH's creativity and dynamic, God's descent and hidden dwelling among human beings. The Son is God manifest among us, who leads us to the Father in the power of God's Spirit. In him the movements from God to us and from human beings to God cross, the coming of God and the going to God. So there is certainly no question of three gods, nor of a divine team of three, nor of a metaphysical dialectic of the One which bends itself back on itself again through the antithesis of the Other.[5] There is the same God, who manifests himself to human beings in different ways. To make these three differences independent as three separate divine subjects is to put the situation too strongly. To say that these are only different forms or roles of God is too weak. So the tradition speaks of three persons or hypostases which permeate one another and whose outward working is communal.

Over the course of the centuries much confusion has arisen over this threefold structure of Christian faith in God, to the scandal of Jews, Muslims, Buddhists and also some groups of Christians – the Unitarians – who saw a threat to the unity of God in this notion of God's so-called trinitarian being. And not everything was completely clear even among those who could find themselves in the picture of God that I have sketched out: there has been a great dispute over 'the one God in three persons'. Thus the Christian idea of God has itself become a hindrance to belief in God. One cannot escape this by speaking at an abstract level only about the 'deity' (*deitas*): the concrete, historical determinations of the different contents and meanings of the idea of God in the Jewish, Christian and Muslim tradition are then left out. Moreover, it is not enough, as we have done in Chapters 1–6, to seek traces of God without touching on the specific characteristics of God as Father, Son and Spirit. There is no such thing as an abstract 'deity' alongside or above the active God of the order of salvation who is called Father, Son and Spirit.

However, the unity of God must continue to be maintained in the face of polytheism. Where God appears in the outside world there is one and the same will and working. As the medieval theologians put it, *opera dei ad extra sunt communia*. Of course in our theological reflection we can then expound this will and working in three articulations, as the creeds of the church also do: in the threefold scheme of creation, attributed to the Father of all humankind; of redemption, regarded as the work of the Son who has dwelt among us in Jesus, the well-beloved; and of the sanctification and fulfilling that we experience as the inspiring, live-giving work of the Holy Spirit, which creates community. But from the perspective of God there is the one history of salvation, God's continuous soteriological action in bringing about the salvation of human beings. Therefore the scriptures also speak of the share of God's Messiah in the work for the creation 'from before the foundation of the world'. And in the fourth century the church father Athanasius could declare: 'All that has been said of the Father can also be said of the Son, except that he is the Father' (*Contra Arianos*, III, 4). So we also confess that the same Holy Spirit is from God who overshadowed the primal source of life, who sent the prophets in times of disaster and crisis to awaken Israel to new life, who caused Jesus to be born from the Jewish girl Mary as Son of the Most High, who at Pentecost set the disciples in movement beyond all frontiers of language, and who arouses mercy, love, humility and friendliness in men and women. Thus all that is good comes about through the power of God, through God's 'two arms of the Spirit and the Son' (Irenaeus of Lyons, around AD 180).[6]

Even most modern theologians would assert that God's action in the cosmos and in the world of human beings (= history) cannot be parcelled out.[7] But that is not because God's unity is closed in on itself, but because nothing in reality – if monotheism is to remain consistent – can exist outside the one God, however and wherever it is also attributed to God. And it is based on the fact that we can think of God only as related to us: 'The structure of God's being is also his movement of himself towards us,' remarks P. Schoonenberg,[8] and E. Jüngel says that 'God's being is in coming.'[9] If that is the case, then it equally applies to all that Jesus Christ meant and did and to all that is attributed to the working of God's Spirit. At the same time, however, the structure of God's being is also a challenge to God, a power of attraction, a calling and gathering in the direction of God's kingdom. From Genesis 1–3 up to and including Revelation 19–21 the story of the creator God is at the same time the story of human liberation – redemption, ransom, reconciliation, justification, sanctification, deification. And the story of liberation which comes to its historical climax in the person and fate of Jesus begins with the wisdom from before all times and lasts until the judgement at the end of time. Equally, God's life-giving Spirit as the breath of God spurs people on down the ages towards love, solidarity, the holy and the communion of saints: the Pentecost event is the fulfilment of the old prophecies and the beginning of a mission and movement of the witnesses to God's creative will for liberation which embraces the world and the centuries.

In the meantime, I suspect that in our days we have the greatest difficulty with what is taken for granted by theology in the system of faith – the trinitarian economy of salvation as this is narrated in the scriptures and articulated in the praise and the creeds of the church. Some of this difficulty stems from alien speculations which have developed down the centuries around this system of faith. Anyone who is talking about 'one God in three persons' already has a good deal to explain: this cannot be a plurality of persons according to our human nature and understanding. God is not something like a three-headed governor of the world or a three-headed occupant of the spaceship cosmos. On the other hand it is also too simplistic to speak of three 'roles' of God, as the theologian Sabellius already attempted to do in the third century. Rather, here are three perspectives or aspects from which we get on the track of God: from Israel's belief in YHWH, the one God of the whole cosmos and of all peoples; from the person and the message of Jesus of Nazareth, who shows us the true face of God's love for humankind; and from the discovery of believers of all times and all places that God is near to them with life-giving energy and with a fantastic call to do good.

However, the tradition of God's Trinity is meant to be rather more than a threefold way of looking at God and experiencing God. In it God himself is depicted as an interplay of relationships, as between Father and Son, Son and Spirit, Spirit and Father. The names and titles of God lead to inevitable problems of understanding. They are not about family relationships, procreation or

162

dependence. The Father does not bring forth the Son, and the Son does not produce the Spirit, although we always speak of the Spirit who proceeds from the Father and of the Spirit who is sent through the Son (John 14). The God of Israel is the same God as the God whom Jesus calls his 'Father', and that is the sole reason why Christians call God 'Our Father'. The God of the peoples is the same God as the God whom Jesus calls the Breath and the Wind of God, who will blow on his disciples and inspire them to do the will of God. So no one can turn against the God of Israel or the God of the other religions in the name of Jesus, for it is the same God. Conversely, no one can turn against the God of Jesus in the name of the God of Israel or in the name of other religious experiences, for it is the same God. And no one can say that God has dwelt among us and that in Jesus' life God has shown himself to be Lord and Master, except through the power of God's Holy Spirit (I Cor. 12.3).

So of course when God is called Father or Jesus comes to be called the Son, we do not have marks of gender. And although Hebrew uses a feminine word – *Ruach* – for the breath of God and Greek uses a feminine word – *Sophia* – for the Wisdom of God, this does not denote a feminine element in God. Those who talk about God's care for human beings can use both fatherly and motherly metaphors, as scripture also does, but that does not make God an androgynous reality or a kind of ideal parental couple. The one God stands above any polarity or complementarity of gender which characterizes our contingent existence as living beings, and at the same time, according to Gen. 1.26, in our sexual differentiation we form an image of God. The relationship of human beings to God and God to human beings is like our attachment to the inimitable, unrepeatable other with whom we can never fuse, however intimate we may be with each other: it comprises involvement and freedom, distance and intimacy. As Augustine put it, it is closer than close, *intimior intimo meo*, and at the same time at an unbridgeable distance: *superior supremo meo*. It is the source and goal of our longing heart: *cor meum inquietum, donec requiescat in te*.

Unfortunately, over the centuries, God as Father and Jesus as Son have taken on masculine features: because God was called Father all fathers behaved like God, as Mary Daly commented. Because a man was called the Son, only males could lead preaching and the liturgy in his name. Here the laws of analogy are grossly transgressed and God's threefold being is harnessed to the chariot of the cultural desires and standpoints of one sex. It would have

163

been better had males themselves exposed this heresy and had not needed to wait for twentieth-century feminist theologians and self-confident women. It is incomprehensible that Christians who confess 'We are of God's race' have made their marks of gender the subject of disputes in the church and religion, completely in conflict with the message and the activity of Jesus and his immediate disciples and witnesses.

The recent theological plea that God's threefold being should be approached from the perspective of the human quest for God in the concrete course of the history of religion – and thus not from outside, as if the articulations of belief in God reached us from the outside – certainly does not solve all the problems. But at any event it does leave room for the recognition of our aporias. It allows God to be God; it allows God as an open question to our thought which nevertheless arises from the thought itself to remain valid, rather than prematurely cutting off the question. Moreover this coupling of the idea of God with the specific course of the religions makes it clear that religion in all its forms aims at a threefold reference: to nature, as that in which all our lives are embedded; to the vulnerable fate of the individual, who is ground down by injustice and violence that cries out for justice and for a true advocate for the victims of injustice; and to the dynamic of consolation, mercy and compassion which forms community. Thus Father, Son and Spirit are not just metaphors for human needs, not just projections of dependent, infantile human beings. They are divine hypostases, which extend to us as a challenge in nature and history, as the unexpected guests at Abraham's tent by the oak of Mamre (Gen. 18), the subject of Rublev's famous icon of the Trinity.

THE CREATING GOD

Even then there are certainly no fewer aporias when it comes to ideas of God's creating care. The most common is that all ideas are conditioned by culture. Thus in the West we have to make use of concepts and symbols which are derived from the Euro-American cultural field. An intercultural dialogue about the theology of God's creation – for which the 1991 Assembly of the World Council of Churches in Canberra made a powerful plea – is vitally necessary, but alas it is still in its infancy. Nevertheless I hope that what follow are thoughts which can also be acceptable to Jews and Muslims.[10] For one of the first demands made on a theological argument about the creator God is that he should be *Creator* for all those who believe in God. Precisely as Creator God, God cannot by definition be imprisoned in religions or churches. A God who was God only for a particular group of believers or who had no difficulties with those who do not believe in God would always remain a tribal God, a rival of other tribal gods or in competition with anti-divine forces. Precisely for that reason the biblical book of Genesis sketches out God as the maker of all human beings, the guardian of all peoples, the protector of both righteous and sinners, of both clean and unclean animals, of the elect and the rejected. Moreover God is conceivable only if not just human beings and peoples but also the cosmos and all of nature are regarded as his work, down to the smallest particle and the most infinitesimal cellular matter: precisely because it is created, it is stamped as meaningful and good, even if by definition it is not already perfect. In particular, that last plays us false. There is the bitter riddle of the tragic, the incomplete, the malignant in all that is. We can no longer say so easily, 'Whatever is, is right' (Pope) or '*Omnia inquantum sunt, bona sunt*' (Boethius). Nature is too cruel for that; our life is too volatile; violence is too crude; death is too harsh. Precisely because of that, many people, as we saw, have switched off at the very first article of the church's creed, which praises God as the Creator and Guardian of the universe. Can such a good creator God still thrive in our bitter experiences with nature and with ourselves? But there are still a large number of other aporias which we have to take seriously: belief in a creating and caring God is not so obvious.

THE APORIAS IN BELIEF IN THE CREATING GOD

I cannot clarify better the first aporia of our faith in the creating God – as that is articulated in the first article of the church's confessions of faith down the centuries – than by recalling some verses from Francis's hymn to creation, better known as the Hymn of the Sun. In Guido Gezelle's version, they run:

> Most high, all-powerful, gracious Lord ...
> Yours alone is the praise, the glory, the honour
> and all blessing.
> To You they belong
> and no one is worthy to pronounce your name.
>
> Praised be God by lady earth, our mother,

who feeds us
and guards us,
and gives us all kinds of fruits
and painted flowers and herbs ...

Praise and bless my God with grateful mercy,
honour and serve him with great humility ...

For most of our contemporaries this hymn of praise to creation enters a language field which is very remote from everyday experience. What for Francis was still obvious – wonder and reverence for nature – is given a conditional sense by Gezelle in his work: 'If the soul listens, everything that lives has something to say ...' He already saw that an extra effort of thought and will was necessary: a listening soul. For most people of our time this experience of a nature which speaks of God, let alone praises him, has been lost, however willing an ear they may have for it and even if we leave aside our ambivalent experiences with nature. Unlike Augustine, and also unlike e.g. Bacon and Pascal, we modern technical people no longer regard nature as a reader with stories of meaning and destiny, but as a workbook, with instructions for its use. It is a book which is opened for sober analyses with a view to production and exploitation. Poetry and contemplation are for dreamers or at best for Sunday, when the work has been done.

It is thus getting less and less possible to experience the direct relationship between all that is living and dynamic in nature and God, and the direct relationship between human beings and this nature. By what we call the process of secularization, God has been displaced from the natural world: there we find fields, minerals, building material, leisure parks, roads, houses, factories. Through industrialization, human beings too are displaced from this same world: the world in which they live has been colonized (as Habermas puts it) by instrumental thought (to use Horkheimer's term); what surrounds human beings – their environment – can be expressed in terms of utility, economic value, scarcity. Human beings themselves as a working force become consumers and pollute the environment; they become an economic factor, a residual value. Already in the 1930s Martin Buber, Karl Jaspers and Georg Lukács saw the connection between this 'objectivization', 'reification' and 'instrumentalization' of the world in which we live and taking leave of God. The natural world in which we live becomes the object of human knowledge and ability. God becomes by definition unknowable and consequently also meaningless for the knowledge of nature. If the God of the deists – the God of the very first beginning of creation or the last tractive power of the universe – is unmasked as a physical and metaphysical stop-gap, God is definitively declared dead. And human beings confront nature in just as autonomous a way as they face history: it seems that they take over all the functions of the earlier idea of God.[11] The theology of creation as a 'framework of thought in which the involvement of God and human beings in the world can be thought of together'[12] then becomes illusory. The 'Great Chain of Being'[13] is broken by all this; the connection between things becomes a problem. From then on 'nature' is no more than contingent matter in which the forms of life emerge and into which they flow back again. It is this changed, instrumental and utilitarian view of nature which has made belief in creation difficult.

A second problem seems to me more the reflection of the first. From the beginning, from the 1960s onwards, when the ecological problem was consciously put on the agenda for the first time, historians of culture and ecologists made the Jewish-Christian view of creation in particular responsible for the unbridled impulse towards exploitation on the part of Westerners. Following Max Weber, who had coupled Christianity (and especially Protestant-ism) and capitalism together, and F. Gogarten, who had attributed to Judaism and Christianity the role of desacralizing forces through which science and technology were first able to unfold, some read the text of Gen. 1.26–8, in which human beings are entrusted with dominion over the earth and life, as the cause of the misery. It was said to have given *carte blanche* to unlimited domination: the impetus towards exploitation, anthropocentrism and over-popula-tion. Have not we Westerners, with a divine mandate, bearers of God's image, God's representatives, God's stewards, ploughed up the earth, consumed its mineral resources, poisoned the air, made holes in the ozone layer, cut down the forests, made the maternity hospitals bulge and thus sawn off the branch on which we were sitting? We have spat in the spring from which we drink, destroyed the very ecosystem that supports us. In 1972 Carl Améry spoke of 'the inexorable consequences of Christianity' and in 1981 Eugen Drewermann spoke of 'deadly progress'.[14] If in the nineteenth century Christians were told that the church and theology were falling behind scientific progress and technical developments, now it is said that they wrongly gave these developments the necessary legitimation. However paradoxical that may be, at all events it has made belief in creation ambivalent.

A third aporia of belief in creation is a consequence of the obsessive attempts of the seventeenth and eighteenth centuries to preserve a place for God, despite all the scientific discoveries about the logical and causal connections between natural phenomena (Galileo, Kepler and Newton). God was seen by the physico-theologians as the first cause of all movement; now, however, he was no longer the chief cause (*arche*) of all that happens, as in Aristotle, but the initiating cause of all that happens and has still to happen. He was a God at a distance, at the beginning of time, who set in motion the wheel of the natural laws and the course of history. Or he was a God who, as with others, was regarded as the deepest driving force of history, who directed all fields of force to himself. In both cases we have an all-determining determinism, a logic of the universe in which God in the long run simply serves as a metaphysical stop-gap. He was a distant and inactive God, this God of deism, to whom one could no longer pray and who left people lukewarm.[15] This robbed real belief in creation of its force.

However theologians are inventive people. When it became clear that the cosmos, the earth and human beings came into being over a period of millions of years and on the basis of an undiscoverably large number of contingent factors, and that they even keep coming into being at each moment, theologians also cut through the theoretical bond between God and nature. They said that God's activity does not relate to nature but to history. What is really interesting is not that matter and all kinds of forms of life exist, but what God intends and plans with matter and life.[16] Indeed, the book of Genesis is not about the beginning of the world but about its course; it is not about the first human beings but about all human beings. It was written only late in the history of Israel and is a compilation from different contexts. It is about the fact that the faith of Moses is the same as that of Abraham, the same as that of the original Adam and the righteous Abel. It sets out to say that God is there, not only for Israel but for all peoples, and that Israel must also disseminate that faith among all peoples. God is concerned to have a covenant with human beings, not with the creation as such: God is concerned with salvation and grace, not with nature as such.[17] Nature is only the chill and cold scene for the polarization of electrons. History, however, is the history of what God wills with and for human beings to the glory of God. This withdrawal from the field of the cosmos has brought theology closer to ethics, to social philosophy, to political responsibility, to culture. But at the same time God is alienated from nature, the

168

environment, the biosphere, the individual experience of birth and death, the bodily passions and emotions of human beings. It has made God a super-governor, a world conscience, a model for rulers, a judge of the nations. Then we no longer know what to make of the first article of the creed of the early church: 'I believe in God, the Father almighty, maker of heaven and earth, of all things visible and invisible.'[18]

And there is a fifth aporia. In a struggle between polytheism and pantheism lasting for centuries we had kept God at a safe distance from the earth. The finite and earthly cannot contain the infinite and eternal: *finitum non capax infiniti*. God himself is sovereign Power and Will, pure Transcendence, the unchangeable, untouchable and incomprehensible Absolute. But such a remote and hidden God cannot be served and worshipped well. Therefore now and then we had to allow God to be immanent: we located God's special presence in holy, i.e. demarcated, places and times and in holy, i.e. special, figures. Thus God could be everywhere and nowhere at the same time. In reaction, nature then became the profane, but particular pieces of nature (the church, the sacramental elements, Jesus Christ, the saints) became places of God's presence.[19] As we saw, the process of secularization swept away this solution to the problem of transcendence and immanence: everything is profane; nothing is still holy except what we ourselves declare to be holy. The last traces of God can be wiped out. All that is left is the tangle of fragments which we bring together under the term 'nature'. We hardly know what we mean by that: there are around 140 meanings in circulation. But could we still say that by it we mean none other than this system of factors which surrounds us, from which we ourselves emerge and into which we ourselves sink back; which partly and at least for a time seems to be self-supporting as long as its equilibrium and harmony are not destroyed by too many interventions? Many eco-philosophies seem to want to take this line. They like to write 'Environment' with a capital E, as if this were a last support, a last remnant of 'The Great Chain of Being'. Here the old genies come out of the old bottles and the herbals of the alchemists. Anyone who wants to make a chest must first ask the tree for forgiveness; those about to eat must not thank God for the food but remind themselves of the injustice that has been done to other life in producing it.

It seems to me that an authentic theology of creation needs to take up these five aporias: they form the actual context of our Western attitude to nature. Does the idea of a creator God as this shines out from the Jewish-Christian tradition offer us a way out here?

THE HYMN TO THE CREATION: CREATION AS PRAISE

The hymn by Francis of Assisi which I quoted above makes clear what is first needed in theology – the confession of creaturely humility towards the creating God. But at the same time it makes clear what this theological approach from a confession of God's creation means and what it does not mean.

It is meant to be praise, a doxology of the creating God, as offered by the Psalms of Israel and the suffering Job, the author of Genesis and the creed of the church, East and West. It does not aim to offer an explanation of the existence, the origin or the passing away of the reality into which we are woven, nor is it a human 'opinion' which God wants to complement with his powerful beginning or wants to resound at the final good outcome. It is a configuration of reality which gives it a quite distinctive tone: the tone of gratitude for the unique opportunity of living, the tone of gratuitousness.

I take the term 'configuration' from P. Ricoeur, who uses it in his analysis of the threefold mimesis of knowledge and of culture.[20] All knowledge and representation, all culture, is based on a concrete reciprocal interaction or mimesis with reality, which is given but cannot be seen through (*mimesis* I). Knowledge and imagination are certainly aware of this prefigurative reality of the course of things (e.g. in bodily experiences), but it can be seen through and communicated only by a poetical configuration. Our scheme of the body – as we have learned it – is a first primitive content given to this, as too is the geocentric or heliocentric picture of the world. However, most configurations, the more complicated ones, come into being through staging: through stories, feasts, the theatre (tragedies and comedies), supportive fields of symbols, epic compositions. It is this world of texts and symbols which leads us to think, but we ourselves also weave new scenarios into it (*mimesis* II). Ultimately it is a matter of appropriating these, a matter of refiguration, as this takes place in a third mimetic movement, that of reading and interpreting texts and symbols (*mimesis* III). So nothing of what is comes to us as 'brute fact', but always as material 'to read', as an element of possible configuration and refiguration in the process of reading. Reading therefore means 'collecting':

recueillir, ré-collection, gathering meaning and connection. The creation story is therefore essentially a story of connection and meaning. It reorganizes reality as the work of God and configures human beings as the image of God. It is also constantly configured differently in the course of history: Atrahasis, Gilgamesh, Genesis, Plato's *Timaeus*, etc.: these are different configurations of the one reality.

Ilya Prigogine and others have shown that at the level of what Ricoeur calls prefiguration – the interplay of natural forces – what at the level of reflection is called configuration and what Ricoeur calls 'poetic activity', which is the privilege of human beings, already leads to 'dramatic' patterns. The laws of nature and of history are then less distant from each other than the sciences of the last hundred years (since Dilthey and Windelband split them into nomothetic natural sciences and idiographic humane sciences) thought that they had to assume. For this argument this is the occasion to relate the process side (the course of things) and the stage side (the narrated story or argument) as much as possible to each other. In that case there can be no excessive opposition between metaphysics and hermeneutics, or between ontology and narrativity: 'If the soul listens, everything that lives has something to say' (Gezelle).

So anyone who configures nature as creation at the same time baptizes dramatic and blind fate into a personal vocation and destiny. Thus reality is robbed of its character as tragedy, fate or doom: nothing happens to us with the infallible precision of a Supreme Being who guides all things, who 'with predetermined counsel' dominates the course of all natural processes, as Spinoza imagined. Nowhere is the course of things the consequence of the outcome of a scenario established beforehand or the automatic aftermath of a mysterious and paralysing guilt which happened previously ('if only we had ...'). There is an enormous scope for freedom and chance between what happens, what could have happened and what could happen. But that does not make what happens to us, even suffering or death, absurd or meaningless. Praying to the creator God, human beings are freed from what happens to them and elevated above the course of things. They continue to share in all matter, in all pain and mourning, but at the same time, by virtue of their relation to God, they remain above it. So the relationship with the creator God reorganizes all other relationships and associations.[21]

171

CREATION FAITH: BELIEF IN THE POSSIBILITY OF GOOD

Over the last twenty years theology has not played much in the register of creation. There have been a number of wrong tones: remnants of the geocentric and anthropocentric picture of the world, fragments of creationism (a rejection of the theory of evolution or of more recent cosmological hypotheses), an undertone of a historicized story of paradise, too good to be true, but time and again good for the utopia of a 'whole world' and especially the remnants of a metaphysics which was above all interested in cause and effect. However, with Matthew Fox[22] and Henry Santmire[23] I think that this register of creation theology and the spirituality that goes with it is indispensable, and that at this moment it is even better to play on than the theology of salvation and redemption, soteriology. Only when it is possible to play again on the register of creation can the register of redemption also begin to sound convincing.[24]

Over recent decades – as the result of a better hermeneutic, i.e. a better sense of the aim of theological language, and purged by the critique of natural scientists and philosophers of religion – we have returned from a way of thinking which wants to add up or subtract the confession of the creating God – *Pater*, *Pantocrator* and *Poietes* of all that is – in the way in which we count, measure and weigh up natural processes. Newton, Darwin and Einstein cannot rob of its force the story of God's creative light or the story of Adam and Eve in their garden – with all its misery – or the story of God's time and eternity. Feuerbach, Marx and Freud may have raised our self-awareness and sharpened our critical gaze and sense of responsibility to the injustice that happens among human beings, and made us sensitive to the false gods of our life of infantile passion, but in doing so they have not swept away the principle of God's creation, or wiped away Adam's and Cain's responsibility before the face of God; nor can they sublimate the healing power of God's fatherly and motherly mercy (cf. Ps. 84) in the unmasking of our dreams.

What remains is the narrative structure of salvation history from the beginning, which gives us direction, which configures our existence in days good and bad, and frees us from our 'God complex': we are not the ones who control the course of things, and it is not the experience of our own freedom that spurs us towards liberation. Rather, our striving both for freedom and for the liberation of others comes from the call of God and its norm is God's good purpose for creation. Anyone who supposes, as does L.

White, that Jewish-Christian creation faith is the root of the end of the world that we are now causing has failed to understand anything about that creation faith and the responsibility 'in the image of God' which is intended in Gen. 1.26–28. By way of an excuse for such a person, it has to be said that part of theology has itself produced the misunderstanding, through a perverse notion of God's almighty rule. Those who in reaction want to find God only in the call for liberation in the historical praxis of the poor, in the soteriology of the struggle for liberation, run the risk of continuing that misunderstanding and threaten to add new ones to it. The project of the historical call for liberation by and through the poor, however legitimate it may be, is imprisoned in the same kind of thought in terms of domination as the project of the technological civilization of prosperous peoples. Only a good theology of creation which humbles everyone, which challenges the power of violence at the root, out of respect for the possible good, and which summons people to think and act in this direction, can really be wholesome for all.

THE PRIMACY OF BELIEF IN THE CREATING GOD

Thus theology needs to begin at the beginning, as do the scriptures and the creeds of the church, i.e. with the confession of God's creative power. The credibility of the Jewish-Christian tradition depends on the way in which reality as it can be experienced (nature, world, *saeculum*) can be connected with God (and that is the basic meaning of *religio*).[25]

It seems that there are a number of objections to this position. What does it really add if at the same time we give the name 'creation', *creatura*, to the reality which we denote as nature, history, cosmos, matter, environment or universe? Don't the pagans also do that? Isn't this an outdated remnant of metaphysics, unnecessary and vague pictorial language which at best is a metaphor for the aporia of our imprisonment in space and time, from which our thought cannot escape? Is the thesis of God's creative primal beginning from nothing any more than such a vain escape clause? Doesn't this clause of a creative beginning put God outside space and time – because the finite can never contain the infinite – thus detaching, isolating, everything that happens in space and time from any relationship with God? Hasn't belief in this 'God factor' down the ages become the butt of criticism, and as the demiurge at a distance, the unmoved mover, the *deus otiosus*, the eternal monad, the primal cause, the eternal mind, the absolute spirit, the fine tuner and driving force of the universe, hasn't God become the metaphysical stop-gap which only strengthens the powerful in their status quo, so that for the poor he must be like a red rag to a bull?

Over against that, it is a fundamental element of Jewish-Christian theology – though here that theology is already an heir of previous metaphysical ways of thinking[26] – to speak of the creation not just as a mechanical product or as a spontaneous emanation, but as an original work of art in which God's own being is expressed. Moreover it is not even a finished work of art but an ongoing performance, in which God himself is fully present as creative artist, constantly also in new ways as Father, Son and Spirit. In the Psalms (Pss. 8; 19; 44; 74; 77; 78; 89; 104; 135; 136; 139; 150), in Deutero-Isaiah (Isa. 40.3–6; 42.15–16; 43.16–21; 48.3–7; 51.9–11), in Genesis and in the wisdom literature God is the one who orders the cosmos and life and to whose care everything has been entrusted. God's protective care is confessed as the principle of all that is. The story of this care from the beginning is thus also far more than a story of origins; it is certainly not a chronology or a natural history. In Augustine's *Confessions*, in which doubt in God's care already colours the thought of the believer (Mani, Epicurus, the Stoics and Plotinus had already raised their tormenting questions for the author), God's care is also already spoken of in terms of being, in other words of being real:

> Lord my God, light of the blind and strength of the weak – and constantly also light of those who can see and strength of the mighty: Listen to my soul and hear it crying from the depth. For if your ears are not present also in the depth, where shall we go? To whom shall we cry? 'The day is yours and the night is yours.' At your nod the moments fly by ... Let me confess to you what I find in your books. 'Let me hear the voice of praise' and drink you, and let me consider 'wonderful things out of your law' – from the beginning in which you made heaven and earth until the perpetual reign with you in your heavenly city ...
>
> See, heaven and earth exist, they cry aloud that they are made, for they suffer change and variation. But in anything which is not made and yet is, there is nothing which previously was not present. To be what once was not the case is to be subject to change and variation. They also cry aloud that they have not

made themselves: 'The manner of our existence shows that we are made. For before we came to be, we did not exist to be able to make ourselves.' And the voice with which they speak is self-evidence. You, Lord, who are beautiful, made them for they are beautiful. You are good, for they are good. You are, for they are. Yet they are not beautiful or good or possessed of being in the sense that you their Maker are. In comparison with you they are deficient in beauty and goodness and being.[27]

Thus nothing can be said about the being of reality itself except in relation to the divine creation. Personal fortunes (the suffering of the blind and weak, but also the light of those who see and the power of the strong: Augustine not only wagers on the so-called contrast experience of sufferers but also connects God with all that is positive, good and beautiful), both the course of history and the evident existence of things, are all connected with God's creative action. All that is, is good, as building material for the glory of God, but as far as God is concerned it is not perfect; it is not good enough and in this sense it is really not yet being. The link between reality and the creator God thus colours the very being of all that is and the way all things are. It is not otherwise, as though a general idea of being (or of the good and the beautiful and the true) were to be able to determine the nature of God and his creative action.

Thomas Aquinas, too, speaks of creation only in the framework of *divina potentia* and God's will.[28] Without involving God himself in thought it is impossible to think about reality as 'created'. There is no such thing as a creation which has been thought of or can be thought of apart from God, as the modern terminology would have it. Reality as a whole is thought of as 'in God'. This being 'in God' must then naturally be qualified further in all kinds of ways, and Augustine and Thomas go on to do this; however, at all events there can be no question of a *deus otiosus*, a God at rest, a God outside history: all that is goes to the heart of God. Theology would lose all its meaning if any correlation between nature and God – and thus any theology of nature or natural theology – were excluded or simply grounded in particular historical (and then exceptional) events, like the exodus of Israel under the leadership of Moses, the appearance of Jesus, or the flight of the Prophet from Mecca. As if God's good will for reality (expressed in terms of grace: *hanan, hesed, eudokia*) were to begin somewhere half-way through human history and at a different moment for each religious tradition!

Therefore the reference to God's guidance from the beginning, God's care for all peoples and the whole cosmos, as the book of Genesis bears witness, is an extremely important starting point, especially also for the Jewish-Christian tradition. The Jewish decision to regard the Book of Genesis as the first book of the Torah and of the whole of the Tenach was a prophetic one:[29] as Deutero-Isaiah in particular demonstrates, the story of Genesis is written as consolation for the exiles of Israel,[30] for even the gardens of Babylon are God's own terrain. And the story is also written as a summons to rulers not to overestimate their autonomy or to abuse it: like everyone else they are taken from the earth, their stars and fortunes have been established long in advance; their judgement on good and evil is always premature, since judgement is reserved for God; and deadly violence – with which they kill the righteous like Cain to please their gods – is a blot on their escutcheons which brands their ongoing existence as a reprieve. Finally, the story also summons Israel and Christianity itself to show humility in the midst of the peoples and to constant conversion. Adam is led astray time and again; Abel is killed time and again; Noah must be saved time and again; and time and again Babel falls.

The way in which the old myths of Mesopotamia – Gilgamesh and Atrahasis – are revived in this story serves the same purpose. Paul Ricoeur in particular,[31] and recently again Ellen van Wolde,[32] have shown that Israel's creation epic is an explicit critique of the tenor of the creation epic of Assyria and Babylon; human beings do not do the foul work of arrogant feudal gods. Nor are they there to provide for the needs of the gods, as in Atrahasis. Far less are they merely in search of immortal fame or the herb of life, trapped in life-and-death rivalry between hunters and townsmen, like the hero Gilgamesh. The work that we human beings do, with all the burden of sweat and pain that goes with it, is certainly a task from God, but it does not leave God cold or looking on inactively. And the cycle of seasons and of the ages does not revolve in an eternal circle, but leads people to the promised land. Although being like God is denied to us, we have a share in God's own work and in God's own governance. Mortal life bears fruits which abide. Genesis does not know another message. This is the blessing which holds for the children of Abraham, but it is not denied other people, although they are advised to go by the covenant with Noah, Abraham and Moses.

Although Christians are convinced that it is concentrated in the events surrounding Jesus and an essential supplement to the soteriological perspective of the promise of blessing to Israel, the story of Christ also begins 'before all times'; it takes place in time, but leads beyond space and time. As the Christ, Jesus shares in the creative wisdom of God,[33] and for that reason alone he can be confessed as the Son of God who sits at the right hand of God. Therefore he also appears as the ambassador of God's care for the disfigured and handicapped and chooses to share their fate; he is put through the mill by human rulers and by the dictatorship of citizens of substance. Those who pass over the confession of God's creative wisdom resting upon him, by definition arrive at 'Jesuology', and finally at the idea of a Gnostic self-redemption on the part of human beings, on the basis of the wisdom of a guru. However important Jesus is as a historical figure, however important his message may be, in that case he is a tragic figure, or rather the umpteenth victim of virtue and justice. Perhaps he is greater than Socrates or Buddha and certainly different from them: indeed an optimal human being but no more than that. However, anyone who confesses him as the Christ, that is, as the one who is finally sent and anointed by God, the one in whom God himself has dwelt among us, cannot avoid seeing this contingent historical and tragic life as part of God's own work in creation, a chapter in God's own biography. This embedding of Jesus' liberating life and death in God's own work of creation also corrects all kinds of risky metaphors and expedients in soteriology, like the thought of Jesus as the vicarious scapegoat who through his suffering bears people's sins into the wilderness and assuages God's anger. What was meant in Paul and John as confessional imagery about the paradox of cross and resurrection, created after the event, has over the centuries become the myth of God who needed the execution of Jesus to assuage his wrath.

But the gospel says clearly that God saves Jesus and those who follow him *from* the dead, not *by* death. God's liberating action is life-giving, despite death, and precisely that is the core of the New Testament confession of the resurrection from the dead, beyond space and time.

On the other hand, what we call 'salvation history' and also what we call – statically – 'salvation' is inconceivable and unattainable without bringing in the concrete, material world in which we live: our ideas of God's good will cannot be abstracted from the concrete, always ambiguous, human experiences of the good. The incarnation of the *Logos*, in the power of God's *Pneuma*, fits in with the confession of God's creative faithfulness and covenant, with God's bond with home and hearth, field and harvest, city and culture, as this forms the core of belief in Abraham. Here Moltmann refers to God's dwelling in his *shekinah* and in his *zimzum* which cannot be located anywhere.[34] Without this primitive confession, belief in God's gracious action in Christ is vain.

Finally, it must be stated that the significance of belief in Jesus as redeemer and liberator cannot consist in an improvement of creation (however great this task may be for human beings), but only in its fulfilment and glorification, in its re-creation. This *nova creatio* or 'integrity of creation' (including belief in resurrection and eternal life or the definitive breakthrough of God's *basileia*) is inconceivable in historical categories and certainly does not coincide with them. And it certainly does not coincide with a historical project of rebellion (resurrection = uprising) of the poor and the marginalized, or with a reckoning with or retribution for past injustice related to historical conditions. In that case Jesus would be a historical hero, the initiator of a just revolution of the oppressed, but not the Christ of the New Testament, the Son of Man who comes on the clouds to judge both the righteous and the unrighteous. Only a good theology of creation can make belief in the resurrection plausible, as I Corinthians 15 shows.

Thus 'soteriology' must be broader than a correlate of christology: it presupposes belief in God's creative involvement in goodness 'from the beginning' and 'for ever and ever'.

In fact belief in creation seems above all to emphasize the primal beginning: *creatio ex nihilo*. The statements of the church's magisterium have in fact always been opposed to any attempt to assume any other matter or forces outside the reality that we know, by means of which or through which these were created by God. The Christian theology of creation has opposed any dualism and any middle term between God and the cosmos, and also any identification or mixture of a pantheistic or panentheistic kind.[35]

However, the focal point of the creation story is not the transition from not-being to being but the ordering of chaos and void into a cosmos and an environment to live in and the attribution of all that is, not to blind fate but to divine wisdom and providence. Nothingness cannot be conceived of except as the negation of all that is. God's creation preserves us from this negation. What we confess is not a formal beginning but God's permanent initiative and guidance through history. Anyone who reads the creation story in Genesis only as a beginning which is intended chronologically runs the risk of watering creation down to a vague cosmogony, to a cosmological myth, with no meaning for salvation, or to an onto-theological metaphysics which does no justice to the brokenness of creation.

Thus to confess God's creativity is to put the emphasis on the divine governance in the face of 'annihilation',[36] more eschatological than protological, not chronological but 'kairological', i.e. from moment to moment.[37]

GOD'S CONSTANT CARE: PROVIDENCE?

The great question of how God governs the world remains. Is there, above and behind human creativity and the natural course of things, a reality which determines and supports all things, 'given with' reality by God himself, as Küng and Pannenberg argue, which could then be worshipped and invoked as creator God even by natural scientists who want to keep any *deus ex machina* out of their calculating thought? Or must we assume with the process theologians, in the footsteps of Whitehead and Hartshorne, that in analogy with the natural behaviour of the smallest particles, such a thing is like a God in two phases: a primordial nature of God which is the model and blueprint of all that is, and a consequent nature of God which lives with all that comes into being? Would God thus constantly oscillate in all the processes of nature in a stochastic way, that is through laws of statistical probability, between plan and actual realization, between potency and sympathy, omnipotence and mercy? Or is God, as political theology and liberation theology assert, the one who constantly opts for the poor, the oppressed, and those who need his special care, a God who is a constant positive force against all that is negative, so that in this way the vicious circles of evil – the struggle for life, the survival of the fittest, the law of competition and rivalry, the ongoing polarization of all that is – can be overcome? Or must we, going beyond all models of process or political cybernetics in terms of which we think of God, express God's creative care in yet another way?

We have to concede that traditional faith in the providence of the creating God is not easy, even if we have got rid of the deistic ideas of a God as Author and First Cause or as the driving force and Final Goal, while still wanting to see God's care as more than a general metaphor for human responsibility and sympathy. But belief in God's constant care for the world, for individuals and peoples, is one of the basic data of the Jewish, Christian and Muslim tradition. In connection with the confession of God's creative power, it is expressed in terms of grace and faithfulness, covenant and salvation, love and guidance. At an early stage in this tradition the facts of nature and events in history were also seen as determined by God,[38] and as we saw, precisely that is the core of belief in creation. But this determination by God is seldom expressed in terms of planning or advance guidance, and never in terms of the precise analysis of a causal course. That applies to the six-days work of Genesis, to the story of the flood, the settlement of the patriarchs in Canaan, the exodus from Egypt and the entry into the promised land. Even in Job 38, the great hymn to God's rule over natural phenomena, there is no speculation about the how and the what: human beings must avoid such speculations! The New Testament expresses similar thoughts, for example in the Sermon on the Mount. Indeed it is also very striking, and often has been noted, that the Greek terms for the constant guidance and government of the gods – *pronoia, pronoein, heimarmene* – appear extremely sporadically in the Hellenistic writings of the Old Testament and in the New Testament and are never used of God.[39] Nowhere are the later associations with providence, which associate this with predetermination and foreknowledge, connected with this term. The texts to which one can refer for this are in fact very scarce, although they have had a powerful historical influence, above all in the theology of the sixteenth and seventeenth centuries (within both the Reformation and in the Counter-Reformation centring on the exegesis of Augustine's views of grace), and in the polemic with the natural sciences from the Enlightenment on. So we must concede that the notion of God's constant care took on the meaning of rule of the world only in Hellenism and under the influence of the Stoics. In this view everything leads to the good goal, just as a father governs his household or an artist makes a work of art. The specific idea of God's providence, which as a doctrine of predetermination later came into conflict with the experiences of human freedom and with the moral call to use these well, is therefore a marginal line of thought in the scriptures and more of Greek and pagan than of Christian origin. It is worked out above all by the early Christian apologists in order to express their belief in God's capacity for creation, which is effective everywhere and cannot be prevented by any opposing power. The notion of God's constant care and supervision is a protest against any determinism or fatalism and against the notion of the apathy of the gods. But it is God's universal care (*katholike pronoia*, as Clement of Alexandria puts it) and part of his manner of housekeeping (*oikonomia* is the term used by John Chrysostom) that he hands on his own potencies to what is created, so that it is appropriate to desire things as they are intended by God's *oikonomia*. Thus this subtle tension between God's intentions and their realization by human beings and between the good that God wills and the actual experience of evil is not argued away by the theological tradition. It creates the space for trusting prayer to God, that we may encounter the good and that the evil will pass us by. The people of the Middle Ages also read in this way the texts of the Sermon on the Mount about relativizing human cares about all kinds of matters: the texts in Luke 12.6–7 about the hairs on our heads which are all counted and about the loving care of God who does not forget even the sparrow, far less those who follow Christ. Any form of metaphysical, let alone causal and mechanistic, speculation is alien to this tradition of thought. It is only a fascination with the Aristotelian theory of movement in high scholasticism and the laws of gravity as a universal principle to explain 'everything that is the case' that have made the vision of a caring God the oppressive strait-jacket against which writers like Graham Greene and Evelyn Waugh have fired their poisoned arrows.

In this way, over the course of the centuries *providentia* has undergone a development in meaning analogous to the problem of theodicy. That is only logical, because each is the opposite side to the other. From an attitude of unconditional fundamental trust in God or gods (as is depicted, for example, in Gen. 22, in the story of Abraham and Isaac, *Deus providebit*), the idea of providence becomes a theory about the consistency of God's action, parallel to the Stoic idea of the invisible but firm hand of the gods (*heimarmene*). Moreover the consistency – which does not match experience – is itself theorized until it becomes the distinctive world of the divine *logica*, so-called supernature. *Pronoia* came to stand for God's universal foreknowledge or eternal counsel. This is worked out in particular in the doctrine of predestination. Within the doctrine of predestination one can note a further accentuation: from a doctrine which expresses trust in God's good will towards human beings, worked out in terms of covenant, of God's support and trust in the persecuted ('the little flock', to use the term which Theodore Beza in particular applied to the church),[40] to a doctrine of punishment and exclusion of the godless, i.e. the opponents. In the long run, in combination with the doctrine of the universal guilt of human beings and the dogma of God's sovereign righteousness, it also becomes a source of fear and uncertainty for believers.

According to A. Geense[41] there is also a second development. From a more historical approach which was focused on what happens to people, on events and people's fortunes, attention shifted to a more cosmological approach: the order of the universe, the natural laws and the exceptions to these in miracles. It became the function of the doctrine of providence to offer comfort in a tragic fate, to provide the basis for a belief in progress which governed everything. This belief in progress finds its culmination in Adam Smith's economic theory, which begins from the fact that God's invisible hand will automatically distribute the wealth of the rich among the poor. As belief in providence it was to become the theological basis of the *laissez-faire*, *laissez-aller* capitalism of belief in the free market. Christian theology in the twentieth century reacted against this on the one hand by means of a strong emphasis on eschatology: no progress is to be found here below, but God still has something up his sleeve. The outcome will make all things good. Providence then becomes the conclusion to belief in the hereafter (as with K. H. Ratschow). On the other hand, it led to a great emphasis on the freedom and sovereignty of God, who rules not only through the laws of nature but also through faith and prayer: as Pascal remarked, 'God governs the world by prayer.' This is pre-eminently the case with Karl Barth.

It seems to me that it is not this transition from a historical to a cosmic providence which has caused problems for belief in God, as Geense thought. From the beginning the doctrine of *pronoia* had as marked cosmic overtones as theodicy. Rather, the problem is that God's care both in nature and in history is thought of in terms of causality: God is the super-cause behind all causes or the super-goal of all efforts.[42]

It is part of the tragedy of the Reformed and particularly the Calvinist theological tradition that for fear of infringing God's absolute sovereignty and in opposition to the triumphalist appeal to the humanist idea of freedom, for a long time it succumbed to the temptation of causal determination and in this way broke with both the freedom of the creator God and the glorious freedom of the children of God.

In fact it was the historicizing reading of God's creative activity, fixated on the causality of the course of the cosmos, which generated the deistic, physico-theological and Spinozistic temptation that in its turn led to the modern critique of religion.[43] In my opinion, the improved expositions of this, for example in the evolutionary theology of Teilhard de Chardin or in process theology in the footsteps of Whitehead and Hartshorne, do not avoid this deism. Here God remains synonymous with the logic of the universe.[44] Why should that not be a needless duplication of the experience of the human *logos* or human self-awareness (Feuerbach), the will to power (Nietzsche), our restless freedom (Sartre) and care (Heidegger), or, in less anthropocentric terms, the contingency of the whole process of nature (Whitehead)?

For this reason, too, it is of the utmost importance to follow Thomas Aquinas in de-historicizing the confession of the creator God:

- by again reading it first of all as a qualification (= doxology) of God, not as an explanation of existing reality (cf. the Psalms, Deutero-Isaiah, Wisdom and Genesis);
- by keeping it remote from the imagery of production, movement or change;[45]
- by avoiding any kind of concordism with scientific hypotheses to explain the cosmic system, based on the type of instrumental or mechanical causality.

GOD'S GOOD CREATION AS '*REDEMPTIO CONTINUA*': THE BASIS FOR ANOTHER METAPHYSICS

The classical theological scheme, grafted on to the structure of the 'articles of faith' of the church's creed, made 'creation' a kind of 'condition' for God's real work of salvation. The emphasis was placed on the qualitative difference between the old and the new dispensations of salvation. It was noted that the story of Genesis 1–3 really does not know any redemption, except that the immediate punishment for sin is mitigated (Adam and Eve do not die immediately, as is announced, Gen. 2.17); despite his crime Cain is given a divine safe-conduct (Gen. 4.15); because God repents of it, the criminal action of human beings (Gen. 6.7) which makes God decide to destroy his creation (and not just human beings) does not exclude a new beginning (Gen. 9.8–17). But whether or not we call this 'redemption', this pattern of a merciful God, who demands a great deal but continually also spares and forgives, continues throughout scripture. The creator God is at the same time the gracious God 'who does not allow the work of his hands to drop'.

This far more present and dynamic view of the grace of God is not a fortuitous one, but is a matter of trustworthiness, *emunah*.

What has been created is not immediately destroyed again. There is coherence despite all contingency. There is a metaphysical trustworthiness and irreversibility in contingent facts. What takes place – running quite contrary to what perishes with it – discloses not only irreversibility and the process of a course, but also a mechanism of choice and selection: all that happens represents a 'choice' from existing possibilities. There are these existing, given possibilities (fields of energy, particles, atoms, molecules, cells, organisms, stems, particular plans and purposes, desires and passions); there is the moment of choice, in other words, the connection to cores, frequencies, systems, pairs, associations, alliances; and there is the moment of fulfilment, enjoyment, joy, equilibrium. Stability and continuity entail the maintaining of the same variables as a consequence of our limited possibilities of choice or particular capacities for choice, or a great longing for constantly the same equilibrium.

We can call these properties of nature 'gratuitous': every moment offers opportunities for choice and desire, hesitation and opposition, re-examination and resumption, enjoyment and perception. This gratuituousness is reflected in the (human) consciousness as conscience, as freedom and as criticism. It is experienced physically as fear or passion, as resistance and tension, as loathing and intoxication, pain and pleasure. Creation is the 'concentration', the narrative form, of this fact of gratuitousness. It is a specific 'configuration' of 'prefigurative' reality which modern physics shows us, with an eye to the recognition of God's gracious *kairos* for human beings (according to Ricoeur, the moment of refiguration in the threefold movement of mimesis). The origin of reality in this idea or 'figure' of creation is its constant realization 'from nothing', because other possibilities could also have been realized. It adds to the sense of contingency the experience of the new and the unique, God's *kairos* as the moment of blessing. Indeed it is what Matthew Fox calls 'original blessing'.

Anyone who wants to be faithful to the Jewish-Christian view of the relationship between God and the reality in which we share – but which as human beings we also know critically – does not need to express the notion of 'creation' and 'createdness' only in the terms of instrumental reason, in which cause and effect form the only heuristic key. The notions of 'covenant', 'blessing', 'grace', 'joy', 'salvation' and 'glory' are essentially bound up with this. Creating and preserving, creating and liberating, creating and fulfilling/renewing/re-creating are one. Chrysostom remarked that the creation is part of God's own *oikonomia*.

The metaphysics argued for here can avoid the problems of the Aristotelian and scholastic onto-theology. The narrative structure of God's creation does not destroy this ontology of causality and teleology, but elevates it to the *redemptio continua* of God's gracious *kairos*. The prayers of the Roman Missal,[46] Francis's Hymn of the Sun, Hildegard of Bingen's cosmic poetry or Luther's sober respect for everyday life are indication of this.

Hildegard of Bingen, the medieval abbess, biologist, preacher and herbalist (1098–1179), as yet had no difficulty with the idea of a creator God, far less with the traditional metaphysics. Yet she gives it a striking narrative force. In her book on the divine activities (*Liber Divinorum Operum*), long before Henri Bergson began to speak of an '*élan vital*' which moves nature forwards, she writes:

> God is life, from which all life breathes ...
> fire, by which all fire is kindled ...
> It cannot be that this Life does not give life,
> that this Fire does not give warmth and light.[47]

For Hildegard, the whole vitality of all the natural processes is the direct reflection or mirror of a divine dynamic. That also applies to human beings, who share in the divine, creative light and fire:

> Then human beings began to be active creatively with creation ... for just as the light kindles and perfects all the rest, so too human beings are occupied with the rest of creation. God is the living light, through him all light shines, so human beings too prove through Him to be life-giving light, even essential fire. How could human beings remain dark and immovable, if they light by light and live by fire? Without working and dwelling the human being remains an empty thing.[48]

> Such is the human being, existing as the work of God with all creation.[49]

For centuries this experience of a bond with a divine spark of light and fire and of the mutual bond between things in this light was part of the symbolic universe of both Persians and Greeks, Jews and Christians. The scriptures of the Old and New Testament are full of it, as are the prayers of the church and the synagogue.

Luther could still begin his day like this – and also advise his followers to do the same:

> I believe that God has created me, together with all creatures,

that he has given me body and soul, eyes, ears and all members, mind and all senses, and that he keeps everything going; and moreover clothes and shoes, eating and drinking, house and home, wife and child, fields, cattle and all possessions, together with all that I need, and every day has provided me richly with food for the body and sustenance for life.[50]

Such a hermeneutical structure is thus more than a distinctive 'language game' for the religious imagination; it is a gift of God which is rooted in reality itself and gives it a foundation. It had a metaphysical influence on the tradition as *logos tou theou*. The condition for such a view of creation is a realistic awareness of the fundamental dialectic (which is therefore not a dualism) of good and evil, life and death, evolution and entropy, coherence and dissipation. The experience of contingency and the irreversibility of all that happens and in this sense the characterization of all being as becoming (process) and passing away is coupled in this dialectic with the experience of a fundamental respect for the given, gratuitous character of all conditions for life which have been offered people and for the primacy of the given reality 'which resists becoming just a fable' (as H. Berger puts it). This experience of contingency as gratuitousness, or rather of the 'configuration' of reality as gratuitousness, does not destroy contingency, nor does it make it controllable, but elevates it to a calling and opportunity for grace.

Such a configuration implies opposition to fatalism; it calls for courage (= responsibility and hope); it represents opposition to deadly violence and threat and calls for respect for fragile nature and the defenceless other; it also represents a protest against flat empiricism and the trivial determinism of instrumental reason.

CREATION AND THE ROLE OF THE HUMAN BEING

All this certainly presupposes a central role for the human being. Only the human being can arrive at the idea of a creation understood in this way. Indeed it is impossible to think of nature as creation other than anthropologically and anthropocentrically. That is of course a provocative statement which goes against the grain when there is so much vigorous criticism of anthropocentricity. Are not human beings far too arrogant, the minimal and late facet of the biosphere of the cosmos that we are? Is it not time to abandon the primacy of human beings within their environment? That may be true, but creation faith is not about the eternal sustainability of the cosmos or living nature. And of course it does not arise there. Stones, plants and animals do not think up metaphysics. It is impossible to think the creative wisdom of God, or to experience it, outside the human configuration. Animals and plants, mountains and forests, heaven and earth will pass away. The concept of creation does not denote a utilitarian steady-state project, an idealistic programme of permanent recycling. Apart from the fact that such a *perpetuum mobile* is quite improbable, there is of course nothing against looking for it, and given the acute crisis of the ecosystem, the pleas for sustainability and survival cannot be powerful enough. But creation faith, of which the eschatological expectation of God's new creation is a part, implies that God sees ways of saving human beings from the inescapable entropy which the believer knows as 'eternal death'. In principle there is no difference between *creatio ex nihilo* and belief in eternal life. Without belief in the eternal destiny of human beings, the configuration of nature as natality (to use Hannah Arendt's term) and from contingency to gratuitousness is meaningless and vain (I Cor. 15 and Rom. 8). Without belief in creation and belief in resurrection as an aspect of God's liberating covenant with human beings, ecological theology is reduced to an utilitarian ethic of a better diachronous and synchronous distribution of production and consumption of the finite goods of the earth.

SYNTHESIS

The relation of God to the world in which we live – cosmos, nature environment – is not so easily and directly thought of as we have sometimes supposed. We can stroke little seals or produce cod liver oil with or without belief in God; we can decipher genes or grow biodynamic food with or without belief in God; we can argue for one and against the other with or without belief in God. The three great religions of the Abrahamic covenant have always thought of God as being at a distance from all the rest of life and yet have confessed his nearness. Any divinization of the elements is forbidden to us: the sun, the moon, the stars, the plants and the trees, the animals and human beings. None of that is God, and we do not encounter God in any of it; God is not submerged in the cycle of matter and life, and yet God began with it and is concerned for it. He wants to use the clouds and the wind as his messengers; to use balking asses and screaming madmen as his voice; to make thunder and lightning heard as signs of his majesty. We can therefore satisfy our religious needs very well in the forest, recognize the creator in baby seals, experience the hand of God in birth and death, prove the passion of God's spirit in love and pleasure. For the core of God's own being we have no other metaphor than such natural words as father and son, mother and child, breath and wind, life and love, source and home; and if need be, and with all fragility, also those of cause and goal. And although God cannot be captured in temples or signs, in rites or series, in priests or prophets, we still say that God dwells among humankind.

Nature represents a process of sharing and ordering to produce cohesion and synthesis. God is the master and the guardian of this cohesion and in this respect he is a creator God. Nature is the marvellous riddle of synthesis of which God is the source: *creatio continua*. According to Genesis, God brings about a division and difference between light and darkness, earth and air, water and land, sun and moon, birds and fishes, plants and animals, men and women, and in this very way forges their connection. The scriptures have a key word for this connection: covenant. We have a rather flatter word: solidarity. But that word contains the word *solidus*, solidity. That is: support, adhesion, connection, steadfastness. There is the notion of faithfulness and mutual trust. Our perspective is not determined by progress and cycles but by the reciprocal gaze, the respect that comes from recognition of the other, the unique, the different. Of course nature also has its cycles, but anyone who divinizes the cycles as such does not arrive at the God of the covenant. We then eternally experience the same things. Death and life slide into each other. In the ills of creation, everything repeatedly becomes the same matter and is ground down into similar cells. As in D. C. Escher's famous etching 'Metamorphosis', fish become birds and birds become fish. There is room for God in this cyclical way of thinking only as the axis of the wheel: everything turns around God, but there is nothing that is directed to God. Those who think in linear terms and divinize process gaze straight ahead and do not think beyond that. Such a perspective does not arrive at the God of the covenant. For those who think in terms of progress, God comes to light only if the process is successful in their eyes. Everything that goes wrong on the way does not count. Everything serves something else, is useful, gives comfort, is for the convenience of human beings or the glory of

God. Thus the human eye is blinded by the splendour of what human beings make; they do not see behind or around themselves, and the glory of God seems to show off the whole tragedy of progress. But those who think in terms of solidarity look at their friends, look at fish and birds, human beings and animals, and inhale and exhale trust.

The Christian faith in the creating God thus invites us to circumspection. The Second Letter of Peter says: 'You must live lives of holiness and godliness, waiting for and hastening the coming of the day of God' (3.11), which transcends the hustle and bustle of the cosmic processes. Belief in God entails a receptive attitude which relativizes gathering and planning, free as the birds and the fish, free as the flowers in the field. But it is not without cares. It is concerned simply for what is happening now, so that there will be a tomorrow; it is also concerned about the suffering that is now taking place and that is worth all our concern. Thus scripture calls for attention in the present to relevance and connection, to solidarity and covenant: 'to value the earthly as is its due and to be concerned for the heavenly' (Roman Missal, post-communion prayer). God saw that it was good: not only then, in the fresh beginning; not only later, at the very end; but now, in so far as there is reciprocity and connection, mutuality and solidarity.

Creator God and created nature: here is no simple connection with the being of beings, no product of power and will, cause and effect, no progress or cycle, but a question of connection, participation and involvement, freedom and responsibility, expectation and receptiveness. As creator and Father, God is to be experienced only in life itself, as the one who acts:

> God of God and light of light, guardian of all things, has a human face, is the brother of all men and women. Everywhere he is near, human in every way, but no human beings recognize him. They are usually silent about him. Be joyful, free from care: God whom we worship is very close to us, dwelling in our midst.[51]

8

The God of the Living: Jesus of Nazareth as God's Messenger

WHO IS JESUS OF NAZARETH?

Is Jesus of Nazareth a place where God can be found? Christians certainly think so, and more than that: they confess him to be the decisive messenger of God and guide to God, the final judge of the living and the dead, the one who is all things a faithful servant of God, his heir, indeed among all the sons of God the only – begotten and oldest son of God. With many other titles, an attempt is made in the account and the epic of his life to say who he was, what he wanted and what he means for those who seek to follow him. The question of who he was is the leading question in this account. It is put by those who stand by his cradle. It continues to be put by those who stand by his cross and watch by his grave. Over the centuries the question has not fallen silent, nor has the mystery of his existence been solved. In the nineteenth century, the heyday of historical investigation of the old texts and ruins of Mediterranean culture, people thought that they had found a reasonable solution to the many puzzles surrounding the appearance of Jesus. A number of biographies of him were published and the details of the history of the dissemination of the Jesus movement also seemed to have been filled in. A reaction set in in the twentieth century. The historical basis became uncertain at many points. The sources that we have are not meant as an account or as reports. We have learned that there is a good deal of interpretation, a good deal of credit that his disciples gave Jesus after the event. And above all there is a great faith that with him new times have dawned. Thus on the authority of exegetes like Bultmann, the conclusion was reached that the important thing is not the historical Jesus but the Jesus of faith, the Christ of proclamation. There was yet another change from the 1960s onwards. Again under the instigation of exegetes – Käsemann, Hahn, Blank – theologians like Schillebeeckx,[1] Kasper,[2] and Küng[3] composed the story of Jesus again, now above all as the story of a Jewish reform movement which achieved a decisive breakthrough in Jesus of Nazareth. For all kinds of cultural and sociological reasons[4] this movement achieved a wide-ranging success within the Roman Empire and even reached its extreme frontiers on the trade routes to the Nile, the Ganges, the Danube and the Rhine. Many philosophical systems[5] within Hellenism wanted to master the movement or were used to attach it to the culture of the time: the theory of God's descent to human beings – incarnation; the theory of human beings' rise to God – deification; the theory of the ongoing battle between God and the powers of evil – dualism; the theory of the gradual decay of the cosmos and the hope of a miraculous deliverance by God of the one who trusted in him – eschatology; the theory of the divine upholding or revelation of the mystery of God and the true happiness of human beings in history – salvation history or *oikonomia tou theou*; and finally the trendy views of life held by the Stoics and Gnosticism, which promised higher virtue and wisdom for a cultural élite by following a practical source of insight into themselves. In this way christologies and soteriologies developed right from the very beginning. They divided Christianity into many streams of tradition and continue to do so to the present day. At the same time, however, again and again there was a concentration within Christianity of new and urgent cultural questions. Thus in a way the God who was sought through the life and message of Jesus remains an open question, if only as a result of the interpretations and the dialogue with the other guides to salvation: Moses, Muhammad and Buddha. Above all, however, this is because Jesus' life and death raise the question of God, his God, whom he called 'Abba' and through whose *Pneuma* he felt himself to be supported. Who is this Jesus, and who is his God?[6]

A PREVIEW

In our agnostic culture the answer cannot be given without a preview. The question who Jesus is and what God he confesses cannot be detached from the tradition in which he stands: Israel's belief in the one God, YHWH.[7] Jesus does not establish that belief, he confirms it. In the previous chapter we saw that Israel's belief in the creative care of God arms us against the fatalism of nature and against the harshness of human reality. All that is, is not a matter of course; it does not happen automatically. It is fragile, transitory, contingent, an opportunity given to human beings. And all those who are our living companions between cradle and grave deserve respect; they reflect the image of God. To 'read' nature and history as God's creation offers a counterbalance to the ordinary course of things and directs the human gaze to the good, to what God wills. It accepts the world as an opportunity which has been given to overcome suffering and evil, and it arouses compassion for all those who suffer and are the victims of abuse and violence. Anyone who thinks this belief dishonest or impossible has a problem: whence the unequal opportunities of blind fate? Whence the war of all against all which keeps breaking out? Why compassion on those who are left behind and why a new chance for those who perpetrate injustice? And above all, how can these unequal opportunities, all this injustice and violence against people, ever be justified? If there is a God who cares in a creative way as Father, Mother, Shepherd and Guardian of all that lives, then those who say to others in their misery, 'Tough luck, it's your own fault', are speaking out of turn, for the last judgement, the last qualification of anyone's life, is reserved for God. The same goes for those who say '*sauve qui peut*' and '*après moi le déluge*', for God can never have made a beginning only for the sake of the strongest or with this one generation of human beings; God is concerned with all generations and also with the least of human beings. Those who are great in their own eyes can still be shown up in God's eyes. Those who have suffered a great deal have not yet been written off. Those who think that they can win by injustice and violence have not yet prospered. Therefore belief in God lays a great burden on our existence and our estimation of values. Those who believe in God must take their life more seriously than others and yet constantly set aside their supposed gains in the light of higher options.

Is there such a God? Is there something like an ultimate justice which happens to human beings, a last test of purification which is meant to purge the vicissitudes and the conflicts? Even those who want to believe this are confronted with a problem. All talk about God remains a comparison with two unknowns, the invisible God and life after death, and the two unknowns are connected. There can only be such a God if there is also life after death. Belief in this one God can ultimately be made plausible only through belief in the resurrection of human beings. There is no proof of that, nor are there blueprints for such a risen person. At most we have signs, indications, symbols. The story of Jesus is such an indication: a crucified man, the victim of human rivalry and religious conflict, of whom his disciples bore witness, 'Behold, he lives.' And Jesus himself bears witness that he comes from God, is one with God, one in spirit with the holy *Pneuma* of God, which he hands on to those who follow him and in the power of which all will be freed from death. According to E. Jüngel, both atheism and theism can be overcome in him: atheism, because his life and death cannot be explained without belief in God and without a commission from God; theism, because in his life and activity it becomes evident whether at the least it proves acceptable that 'God is not far from each one of us' and will personally save us from the aporias of finitude and death. This can hardly be said more evocatively than in the words which Luke makes Paul speak on the Areopagus in Athens (Acts 17.22–31):

Men of Athens, I perceive that in every way you are very religious. For as I passed along, and observed the objects of your worship, I found also an altar with this inscription, 'To an unknown god.' What therefore you worship as unknown, this I proclaim to you. The God who made the world and everything in it, being Lord of heaven and earth, does not live in shrines made by man, nor is he served by human hands, as though he needed anything, since he himself gives to all men life and breath and everything. And he made from one every nation of men to live on all the face of the earth, having determined allotted periods and the boundaries of their habitation, that they should seek God, in the hope that they might feel after him and find him. Yet he is not far from each one of us, for 'in him we live and move and have our being'; as even some of your poets have said, 'For we are indeed his offspring.' Being then God's offspring, we ought not to think that the deity is like gold, or silver, or stone, a representation by the art and imagination of man. The times of ignorance God overlooked, but now he commands all men everywhere to repent, because he has fixed a day on which he will judge the world in righteousness by a man whom he has appointed, and of this he has given assurance to all men by raising him from the dead.

JESUS, THE OLDEST SON OF GOD?

Thus with his belief in Jesus Paul puts himself in the existing religious thought-pattern of his days. In principle we have the same task. However, the calling of Christians to the gospel of Jesus now has to do with quite different religious aporias and experiences, of the kind that I have sketched out in the first six chapters. We Westerners are no longer as religious as the people of Athens; we no longer have much to do with gods and spirits.[8]

According to the Polish philosopher Leszek Kolakowski, we can no longer believe in God because we no longer believe in angels. In antiquity, in Roman culture and even still in medieval culture, angels are the messengers, the media of God or gods. For Babylonians and Egyptians, for Jews and Greeks, for Romans and Germans and to the present day for Africans and Latin Americans, the firmament is full of powers and spirits which can bring about salvation or doom.

Not so long ago, fourteen angels stood even around our Western beds, and every day at noon the angelus rang out in our cities and villages. Catholics could then dream: 'The angel of the Lord appeared to Mary and she conceived by the Holy Spirit.' There were guardian angels for all perils, and on its last journey the soul was accompanied by angels to paradise, as portrayed so splendidly by Hieronymus Bosch. Our cultural history is full of angels. It seems that all these angels reached their ceiling and died of obesity. Perhaps we still want an angel in bed, but otherwise our firmament is filled with other codes of communication. There is no trace of God in them, hardly a message to God, and all lines to God are dead.

In fact Kolakowski is right: if God no longer has any messengers, communication between God and human beings becomes impossible. God cannot even show himself to human beings: whoever sees me must die, God says to Moses in Ex. 33.20. Moses must go and sit in a cleft with his eyes closed if he is to be in a position to see God. Only when God has gone past may Moses look and see God from behind, as the one who goes before us (Ex. 33.20). God is always there before we are; with human beings and things God goes before us as a sower who has sowed while we were still asleep, as one who created us when we were as yet no one. God is not the being of things, nor the other side of our existence, but the foreland of being, the possibility of our existence. God goes before us, says scripture; we look towards him. We can never catch up with

194

God or pass God, with our thinking, our action or our prayer. However, fortunately God leaves traces, and in olden times angels, God's heavenly following, were part of those traces. As Hebrews 1.14 says, what are they but serving spirits, sent out at the need of those for whom salvation is in store? Angels could assume all kinds of forms, or rather, all kinds of phenomena could become the medium of divine communication: dreams, visions, appearances, the storm wind, a blazing fire, a voice from heaven, a dove flapping its wings, a star in the firmament. As Psalm 104 – misquoted in Heb. 1.7 – puts it: 'Bless the Lord, O my soul ... who makes the clouds your chariot, who rides on the wings of the wind, who makes the winds your messengers, fire and flame your ministers.' We Westerners have banished this world of spirits and demons and we pride ourselves in finally having no more to fear. Anyone who still hears voices has to go to the doctor, and anyone who sees angels is seeing ghosts. How then is it possible to communicate with God?

But Kolakowski is also wrong, as the Letter to the Hebrews already shows. For God is not dependent on spirits and angels. God, who is always ahead of us, has proved able to send us a mark of his being, an imprint and likeness of who he is, a messenger or delegate, an angel of flesh and blood, with Word and Spirit. The story of Jesus of Nazareth is a witness to such an angel of God who is exalted above all angels, God's last and abiding messenger, one who is God's messenger himself, who indeed is God's oldest son and the apple of God's eye, who takes us along as guide, after God, who is ahead of us, and who finally as the judge of history will test us all by the criteria of God's kingdom.

The story is well known. An angel of God announces his procreation, an angel of God informs us after his death that he has left the tomb and has gone ahead of us into the wide world, that he has returned to God's world to look out for us there as spokesman and advocate, and as Son of Man on God's clouds to be the standard for all peoples. And between the two angels, those of Christmas and Easter, there is his life, full of surprising changes, full of human tragedy and crimes committed on a righteous person, an innocent advocate of the oppressed. Thus Jesus, himself surrounded by the angels of God, is the messenger of God *par excellence* and at the same time more than an angel: he is also God's representative, God with us bodily, God dwelling among us, God sharing our fate: 'In many and various ways God spoke of old to our fathers by the prophets; but in these last days he has spoken to us by a Son ... the image of his being' (Heb. 1.1). Not just a storm wind or a glowing fire, not just a voice or a flash of lightning, but a living, speaking human being of flesh and blood has become God's messenger, his lawful and only representative and heir (Heb. 1.2). From now on, those seeking God can no longer pass over Jesus as messenger and guide. Any reference to magical powers, any fear of terrifying demons, melts like snow before the sun, now that he has come into our midst (Heb. 2.5–9, 14). The Letter to the Hebrews[9] is a document which seeks to dispel the crisis of faith in the second generation. Those who follow Jesus have very little to show externally: no more temples, priests or sacrifices. They have no spectacular signs; only the testimony to their life and death and the hope of the resurrection. And in the meantime they have much persecution, social marginalization, and little credit from fellow human beings. Christians have to wager on their faith, no longer supported by the Jewish religion of old, and looked on with suspicion with the Greek wisdom of the time. They have no more support than Abraham and Sarah; they have to run as much risk as Noah and Moses and all the martyrs, 'stoned, sawn in two, killed by the sword. They were too good for this world' (Heb. 11.37–38). In the midst of this crisis the appeal to Jesus, who has withstood suffering, is the only support (Heb. 2.18; 3.1).

But isn't that one bridge too far? Isn't it theological talk after the event? Who then is Jesus? On what do we base his authority as a messenger of God? Why is he more than Moses and the prophets? Isn't Israel also called the Son of God? Why isn't Muhammad just as much a prophet of God? Can't just anyone be proclaimed pope and ayatollah who wants to be the leader of one human ideal or another? Who can we say that he is?

WHO HE IS: A QUESTION WHICH REMAINS

The New Testament bears witness that this is not a superfluous question. The New Testament is one long testimony – by the mouth of Jesus' disciples; by Paul, the converted persecutor; by Peter, the converted liar; and by Thomas, the converted sceptic – of the truth of Jesus' claim to speak and act in the name of God. They think that it was this claim which led to his death, to his execution as one accursed. Anyone who says that he is doing the work of God already finds little faith. Anyone who says that the work of God is rather different from human success or power or honour, and that God shows himself in the weak, the children, the lepers, the prostitutes and the strangers, only comes up against contradiction. Anyone who says that God is not enthroned in royal palaces or in the adjacent temples; that sacrifices and rites, priests and levites, scribes and lawyers are superfluous, has for ever alienated whole sections of the populace. The rich will find it difficult to convert when they are told that God can be found only in sharing possessions with the poor. Employees and employers will find it difficult to accept that those who have worked all day should be paid the same as those who have worked only for one hour. Good citizens will find it difficult to tolerate degenerate dropouts being fêted as lost sons when they return to society. Jesus relates all this in his parables; this is how he sketches out God's judgement; this is how he must have come over to his disciples. Anyone who says that this Jesus is the Son of God, is like God, robs all rulers of their divine claims: that is the bizarre irony and paradox of the New Testament account of Jesus. So in the third and fourth centuries he was still being talked about in the barbers' shops, as Athanasius reports: it is not the emperor who is *homoousios*, like God, God's right hand, as his title was, but the crucified one, Jesus. And down to our days it is the case that whether we do the good is not determined by speeches from the throne or golden cushions, but by the question of how many people have no bread to eat or whether we are then willing to give it daily – in the name of Jesus' God.

JESUS THE CHRIST, BUT HOW?

So it is not easy to accept that Jesus is the only trustworthy messenger of God. Anyone who confesses him as the Christ takes leave of all kinds of messiahs: of the kingdom of David and the emperor Augustus, of Constantine and Charlemagne, of Napoleon and a One Power World.

Anyone who confesses Jesus as God's only Son stands apart from all sons of God. Such a person knows, like Peter, that this means contradiction, risk, a danger to life. Such a person has understood little of all the views of Jesus which make him a harmless Christ. Much so-called christology[10] does not meet this criterion. That has happened in church history above all for two reasons.

Some people have wanted to explain Jesus so much as a child of his time that there is hardly any reason to see him as a special messenger of God. That he and no one else is called God's messiah then becomes improbable. There were more heroes and saints who planned good for people. Why should he and he in particular then be able to be called the sole judge from God: the Son of Man from the vision of Daniel (Dan. 7.14; Matt. 25; Matt. 28.19–20) who will judge all peoples, coming on God's clouds? Soon people often did not want to have anything to do with such a judgement. The title Son of Man was levelled down to human son, human child. And he was then a special child. An excellent teacher of wisdom, certainly, who sadly came to a tragic end. Such a levelled-down Jesus is still good for shared humanity, for a general sense of justice, perhaps, for honour and virtue and civic qualities. He is also good for lovers of film, music and the graphic arts, who can comfort themselves with the epic of his life and death: the Jesus of Rembrandt, Bach and Pasolini. Then there is no longer any question of christology, but at most of Jesuology. We have then lost sight of Jesus as God's messenger, as God's Christ.

Others have lost sight of Jesus in the Christ figure. They stared up so much, their head in the clouds, looking so far away, that they lost sight of the one who was in their midst. His coming in the flesh then becomes a manoeuvre of God, a masquerade. Those who saw it in this way suffered from the sickness of docetism. In that case Jesus was no more than a shining angelic figure, who came and went away again, leaving behind only his Word, God's Word. In that case his birth and death are only a phase in an eternal existence with God. He was already there long before he showed himself in Jesus, the Son of God, from eternity at God's right hand, God's Wisdom and Word (*Sophia* and *Logos*). For a while God lent us his arm in the figure of Jesus, proclaiming God's eternal logic to us. In him there suffered not a human being like ourselves, but rather God himself underwent death. Jesus is the crucified God, and in his execution we have put God to death, wanting to remove God's Word and Wisdom from our lives. We are still active in doing that, they say, if we do not recognize that Jesus was like God, was truly God. But this christology also levels Jesus down. Who would have us believe that God, the God who gives life to everything in the first place, who escapes all death, has to die as a human being, as an animal, to enlighten us on how far he wants to go? Anyone who thinks that God, to be our God, must also kill himself, has once again not found God, but has devised a theory about God which dies of a lack of credibility. Of course it is to God, the living God, that Jesus offers his life, gives up his spirit. It is to God that Jesus turns in prayer. It is in the power of God that he heals the sick, drives out demons, defies the elements. And it is God who makes him rise: he does not himself step out of the tomb; he does not himself roll the stone from the tomb; it is God's angel, God's self who does that. In the power of God's holy, life-giving breath and breeze – the holy *Pneuma* of God – he is raised from the dead. Anyone who loses sight of the dialectic between God and Jesus may perhaps seem pious, but such a person puts Jesus outside our tragic existence, outside the cradle and outside the grave.

The New Testament already opposes both oversimplifications. Two main lines can be recognized in the story, as Schoonenberg in particular has demonstrated.[11]

In the one line people look to Jesus, his cradle, his baptism in the Jordan, his pilgrimage to Jerusalem, his death on the cross, and see how the Spirit of God masters him: 'This shall be for the fall and rising of many'; 'the child that you bear shall be the saviour of his people'; 'this is my well-beloved, hear him'; 'God has made this Jesus whom you crucified judge of living and dead.' God adopts this human child as witness, as faithful servant and messenger; God makes demands on him through his Spirit. He is more than the other messengers, more than a storm wind or a pillar of fire, more than the word and the signs of the prophets. He has entered God himself, entered the very life of God. Like all human beings he arises from the history of his people, but unlike others he rises as the blessed one, above history, taking all who believe in him with him to a life with God, through the power of God's Spirit which was in him and which is now being realized in all kinds of gifts and talents in the church.

Along the other line people think about Jesus and come to the conclusion that here God himself must be at work. Kings and wise men come to his star; where he appears the sick are healed and the dead rise again. All words of God are fulfilled in him, from creation to the end of time; he is the divine logic himself, which takes form in a human being: God himself in the form of a bodily human being. In Jesus, God is incarnate reality, i.e. reality made flesh, descended from on high. For a time Jesus is the dwelling of God himself among human beings: Emmanuel, God among us. What remains is more than memory. What remains is the word of God and the sign of the covenant, the community of his disciples, where he is at the centre, as the head of a body, a mystical body dispersed in time, dispersed over the earth.

JESUS: AN OPEN QUESTION TO GOD

Whether we begin below, with the historical account about Jesus, or above, with the purposes of the creator God – more technically, whether we follow a Spirit or adoption christology or a Word or incarnation christology – in both cases Jesus remains a mystery. He continues to pose questions to us. We can be his disciples only by asking questions and seeking. The classical doctrine of God's trinity and of Jesus as the eternal second person of the threefold God does not solve that mystery; it is another image for it. It keeps taking us back to the time that he spent among us. It is impossible to speak about Jesus as the Son of God apart from his human biography and vice versa. The old dogma of Chalcedon wanted to say precisely that. Therefore no single abstract speculation about God is appropriate which does not at the same time do justice to the parables of Jesus, to his miraculous signs in the name of God, to his liberating way of dealing with all the victims of religious conventions and intuitions, and above all to his concrete choice of 'worship in spirit and in truth' which leads him to a martyr's death. Who Jesus is in his uttermost depths escapes us, but we come upon the track of God only through who he was for human beings and through the witness that human beings bore to him.

'The greatest obstacle to humanity is not ignorance but the illusion of knowledge,' remarks the American historian Daniel Boorstin.[12] And in an interview with Stan van Houcke, Frans Kellendonk once said: 'The horrible thing is that as soon as you put something in words, as soon as you write something down, it hardens. The danger is that you then in fact begin to believe that things are as you say that they are. What you must keep is a scepticism, a freedom, the feeling of the incomprehensibility of everything.'[13] That also applies to theology and certainly to Christian theology, when it comes to the person of Jesus: for Jews a scandal, for Greeks folly, for Christians all too often a stereotype. Jesus is another word for God or an easy mantra: 'Jesus says, Jesus says.' Those who know for certain who Jesus is have certainly not understood him. 'Who do men say that I am?' is not a rhetorical question on the part of Jesus but a real question with which he himself also wrestled. Jesus himself replies to Peter's answer – which is given in different forms in the Synoptic Gospels – that he cannot know that on the basis of human insight: it is not flesh and blood that have revealed to him who Jesus is. Only God can make the answer true. That Jesus is the Son of God is not the achievement of Joseph's seed or of Mary's womb, but only a consequence of God's own Spirit: we human beings cannot produce sons of God; God himself does not need to produce the Son, because what God shows in Jesus is equal in origin with the being of God. It is so dedicated, so responsible, so completely filled with hope and yet is not without questions. Precisely in his questions to men and women, Jesus is someone who opens up ways where others have already nailed down God's cause with their dogmas. Nowhere does it emerge that Jesus himself knew the infallible answer. He was someone whose origin was not known, the Synoptics say, and so do his contemporaries. And the people of Jerusalem say in John 7.27: even if we know where Jesus comes from, we do not know where the Messiah comes from. Jesus' role is not that of an instrument without a will which points to God automatically, or a monument which points to God statically. His role is that of a living, seeking, suffering human being who has shared our hurt and our aporias. The only-begotten Son of God is not a robot who like a satellite dish receives and transmits the divine vibrations that are sent out and registered, but as a human being he has 'learned obedience'; as a Jew he has listened to what the creed of Israel from Deuteronomy 6 meant for him: 'Hear, O Israel ...'

In the Apostles' Creed, which in its present version comes from the fifth century but which goes back to old texts from the second century after Christ, the title 'only-begotten Son' clearly refers to the unique character of the messenger of God which Jesus is. However, the Letter to the Hebrews does not have *monogenes*, only-begotten, but *prototokos*, the firstborn. Jesus is already there before creation, and for God nothing was conceivable without him. For Christians, God cannot be thought of apart from him. Both together, the only-begotten and the firstborn, indicate Jesus' own relationship to God. He is so to speak the first edition of God; he gives the true impression of God. He is God's original, not a copy (Heb. 9.23); not a phantom form, not a second-rate God, but the Son of God. But he is at the same time the original of a human being, a new type of human being, the last Adam, a new creation who calls all men and women to be his disciples.

THE MYSTERY OF HIS LIFE: THE KINGDOM OF GOD

The passage about Peter's confession at Caesarea Philippi in Luke is followed by this text (9.23ff.):

If any man would come after me, let him deny himself and take up his cross daily and follow me. For whoever would save his life will lose it; and whoever loses his life for my sake, he will save it ... I tell you truly there are some standing here who will not taste death before they see the kingdom of God.

So his secret consists in hope for the kingdom of God, to which he invites everyone. Who he is as a person cannot be detached from his task and calling to be the messenger of what God wills and who God is, and to back it to the death with his life. What can be meant by that kingdom of God?

The reference to the kingdom of God (*basileia tou theou, basileia tōn ouranōn*) occupies a prominent place in the message of Jesus. The expression occurs 122 times in the New Testament, 90 of these on the lips of Jesus himself, and in a large number of cases their authenticity as historical sayings of Jesus may be assumed.[14] Of course it is a Jewish notion: the vision of God's guidance and sovereignty (*malkut YHWH*) over his people (Ex. 15.18), which relativizes (Judg. 8.23; I Sam. 8.7; 12.12–13) and is the norm for (I Chron. 28.5; 29.23; II Chron. 9.8) all forms of leadership and power, but which will also save his people from distress (Isa. 6.5; 33.22; Obad. 21; Zeph. 3.15) and will finally be victorious for ever (Isa. 24.23; Jer. 10.7; Micah 4.7; Pss. 72; 103.19; 145.13; 146.10). In the course of Jewish history this vision takes on three concrete forms or colourings. The most concrete is the dream of a restoration of the kingdom of David which we find in the Jewish apocrypha (Psalms of Solomon 5.18; 17.21–32; IV Ezra 13.35). In order to realize this dream some people were not afraid to use revolution or violence to hasten in the day of YHWH. In Jesus' day, after some tragic failures, this romantic-political theocratic dream was again revived in the opposition to Roman domination, and even among his followers there were those who thought in this way (Mark 11.10; Matt. 20.21; Lev. 19.11; 24.21; Acts 1.6; cf., Matt. 11.12). In reaction to this and perhaps also in frustration at its failure, Jewish apocalyptic gave the vision an eschatological colouring: a day of YHWH is coming – within history or at the end of history, that is still under discussion – on which God himself will judge the peoples and establish for the faithful a thousand-year kingdom or paradise after the annihilation of all those who have turned against God. However, that is an extremely uncertain outcome for the individual: who will be found faithful? Therefore there is a third colouring of the *malkut YHWH*: God's sovereignty comes about through the power of his Torah and Halakhah, law and traditions. It depends on the faithful fulfilment of the Law, through conversion of the heart and through penitence for sin. That is the Pharisaic view of a moral rule of God. By their exemplary behaviour Jews, too, will hasten the universal rule of God over all peoples: these will adopt faith in YHWH out of admiration for their good conduct and thus take upon themselves the yoke of his rule (Matt. 11.29–30).

In the New Testament Jesus gives the notion a quite distinctive colouring. The varying terminology alone indicates that he wants to leave the precise content of God's sovereignty far more open. He speaks of the kingdom of God which comes (Matt. 7.10; Luke 17.20), which is near (Mark 1.15; Luke 10.9–11) or which will come (Mark 9.1; Luke 11.10). That recalls the visions in apocalyptic of the day of YHWH which is to come. But he also speaks of the task of seeking, of striving for the kingdom of God (Matt. 6.33; 13.44–5). That suggests the moral task which it entails. But in most cases Jesus says that people may and can enter the kingdom of God (Matt. 5.20; 7.21; 18.3; 19.23–4; 21.31; Mark 9.47; 10.15, 23–5; Luke 18.24–5; John 3.5; Acts 14.22), that they will see it (Mark 9.1; Luke 9.27; 23.51; John 3.3), inherit it (Matt. 25.34; cf. I Cor. 6.9–10; 15.50; Eph. 5.5; James 2.5) or gain it (Matt. 5.3, 10; 19.14; 21.43; Mark 10.14; Luke 6.20; cf. Heb. 12.18). The mysteries of the kingdom of God are revealed to the disciples (Mark 4.11; Matt. 13.11) and the keys of the kingdom of God are given to Peter (Matt. 16.19). Others are excluded (Matt. 15) or exclude themselves (Matt. 23.13).

Jesus was thus clearly concerned with something that human beings are given in this life, in this history, on the basis of clear choices and tasks. However, these are not structures of violence or power, and in this sense God's kingdom, which Jesus sometimes also calls his kingdom, is not of this world (John 18.36). What people who follow him are to expect is also indicated with other images: gospel or good news, year of grace (Luke 4.18–22), fulfilled time, day of the Lord, eternal life (John 6). The Sermon on the Mount (Matt. 5–7) and the parables of Jesus show most clearly what Jesus has in view: a way of living in which God is the standard, the criterion and the guideline for action. The kingdom of God, the will of God and God's cause are synonymous: for those who invoke God as 'Father', 'Thy kingdom come' and 'Thy will be done' run in parallel. Jesus' own appearance and that of his disciples is a service of mediation (*diakonia*)[15] to God's governance of creation. The distinctive nature of this service is that it again puts people on the trail of God, that it brings about the connection with God and that it sheds light on the true nature of God as the challenging, surprising and merciful God who loves human beings. Sinners, tax collectors and prostitutes will enter the kingdom of God before religious hypocrites; only those who are as open as children have access to it: the unclean, the sick and lepers are not excluded. Time-honoured values are stood on their head: the first shall be the last, and the one who has the highest rank must become like the least. Thus God again takes possession of his domain and forces back the power of evil.[16]

Here Jesus corrects the usual views about the rule of God held in his day. God's government cannot be established with violence or political theocracy: there is no violence in God. There is only defencelessness and compassion, self-denial and faithfulness to the point of a martyr's death, which will disarm the world. That is difficult to take, even for his disciples, as is evident from their impatient questions about power and certainty: 'Lord, will you restore the kingdom of Israel at this time?' (Acts 1.6). The uncertainty remains: 'It is not for you to know the day and the hour that the Father has appointed in his sovereignty' (Acts 1.7). Therefore there is no chiliastic vision either, as if we had to wait for a thousand-year kingdom which comes on the day of the Lord and from which 'the signs of the time' are to be predicted. Rather, it is said that there is a change and reversal which happens now (Mark 9.1; Luke 11.20; cf. Luke 17.20–21; 22.18–20). The coming of the kingdom of God is not characterized by fire from heaven and abominations of desolation, but by conversion, healing, liberation, a new opportunity for those who have none (Matt. 12.38–9; 16.1–4; 24.3; Mark 8.11–12; 16.17; Luke 11.29). That entails a moral appeal: giving bread to the hungry, water to the thirsty, clothes to the naked; visiting the prisoners, comforting the sick (Matt. 25), but no obsessive legalism, no ritualism, no moral division of society into good and bad, perfect and imperfect.

Thus within God's government there can be no party dictatorship or class struggle; people may not be sacrificed for God's good cause. Freedom of religious conviction and only persuasive instruments of conversion characterize the mission which Jesus hands on to his disciples: 'Make disciples of all nations, baptizing them in the name of the Father and of the Son and of the Holy Spirit, teaching them to observe all that I have commanded you' (Matt. 28.19–20). As Schillebeeckx puts it, Jesus 'proclaims a kingdom of God without forming a remnant'.[17] So there is no obsessive quest for signs of God's imminent intervention, or entry into a sect of the pure who turn away from the world and wait for supernatural events. There is no identification of national or international political ideals with the will of God, no moralistic strait-jacket of doing one's duty, fulfilling the law and sanctifying oneself. There is no escapism that makes all hope long-term and says 'It is not here below', but a sober and watchful attempt at ways to the good. So the kingdom of God is a principle of action, a starting point for thinking and doing, through which one begins to look across the course of things in life and society and to choose and act in a different way. How God will succeed here in getting stubborn human beings with all the baggage of their cultural past and all 'the structures of evil' to the point which the scriptures promise us in the vision of a new heaven and a new earth (Rev. 21), and in the announcement of a kingdom of peace, joy and justice (Rom. 14.17), so that we again correspond to the aims of the first day, remains God's secret, and it will be decided in God's time and in God's way.[18]

Time and again Christianity has broken with this eschatological proviso which refuses to fix God to concrete human results and successes. There is a quest for a realized eschatology, in other words for clearly visible, concrete forms of the kingdom of God. Some point to this in the church, others in secular and political ideals, and yet others in personal perfection, inner relationships with God or a spirituality of commitment to all sufferers and to philanthropy. Or people opt for forms of millenarianism, where the eschatological proviso is transformed into a concrete expectation of the future: one day, and usually very soon, God will intervene in history in order to usher in a thousand-year kingdom of peace for the faithful. During the twentieth century the view generally became established that Jesus himself, or at least his disciples, expected such a speedy intervention by God, bound up with the return of Jesus Christ and judgement on the nations, and that the failure of this to materialize – spoken of in terms of the 'delay of the parousia' – caused the early church a good many headaches. Some have even said that the actual forms of the church are the result of this great disappointment about the vision of God's kingdom. Time and again the great historical conflicts and breaks arose precisely over what Jesus meant by his talk of and dedication to the kingdom of God, God's cause. The question of God itself became entangled with the complications around the interpretation of the kingdom of God;

here the plausibility of the idea of God comes to be involved, now that the notion of an eschaton as divine intervention and the end of history, associated with the second coming of Christ, itself has been deconstructed as a theological myth. Now that in particular the end of history as a result of the constant threats to the ecosystem and the insights into the inevitable entropy or heat-death of the cosmos seem more than plausible, the message of an eschaton or end-time seems incredible. So we are simply left with the dissociation from time of all ideas of God's kingdom and of an end-time. God's kingdom will not perish even in the last days of history and at the climax of the cosmic entropy: 'Heaven and earth will pass away, but my words will not pass away.' So as a reading of what Jesus envisaged with his quest for God we are left simply with present eschatology or axiology: an estimation which can make a good distinction between the 'ultimate and penultimate things' and which watches for and is constantly aware of any moment of choice or decision, in accordance with the motto: it is always time and soon will be too late. Jesus' life and work calls us precisely to this watchfulness and urgency, constant attentiveness and zeal for what God wants, and it is also the form of this. To believe in God means to graft our lives on to this attentiveness to the kingdom of God. That entails more than a moral appeal: it calls for a metamorphosis of our existence, for another culture, another view of the meaning of life, another way to take part in society.

The classic christology and soteriology did not see through that sufficiently, because they devoted all their attention to the figure and the person of Jesus and his role as the ontological mediator between God and human beings, God and the world. That his work consisted in being a sign for the peoples in their history, which at the same time is a summons to choice and conversion, which indicates a direction and makes a statement about the will and governance of God, faded into the background here. In the long run that resulted in the notion of a divine theodrama, God's wrestling to restore the contact with God which had been broken by human beings, indeed even a dispute within the deity between divine omnipotence and mercy, wrath and reconciliation: a dispute between the Father who wants satisfaction and the Son who sacrifices himself, a dialectic which through Word and Sacraments in the church of Christ constantly needs to be remembered and reconfessed 'for complete atonement for all our sins'. If there is anything that has made the Christian faith a faith which is generally doubted, then it is the excesses of this so-called doctrine of satisfaction. A christology and soteriology of God's *basileia* which has a beginning in Christ and which takes up into the authentic perspective of God's creation everything that attaches itself to him, pointing this in the direction of God's will and governance, avoids a whole series of problems posed by the theology of history and prevents the face of the Eternal One being perpetually set on punishment.

JESUS, THE RISEN ONE?

But even then we have still not unravelled the mystery of God in Jesus Christ. For he himself said that not only was he among us but that he remains with us; he indeed died, but we confess that he lives. It would not do justice to the disciples' account of what happened around his execution to assert something as vague as 'the cause of Jesus goes on'. Something like that can be heard in any crematorium in the world and in every funeral oration. The scriptures of the New Testament and the creed of the church state that he himself goes on and is present among his followers. But how?

It cannot be a matter of bodily, physical, local presence: we no longer encounter him. He really is dead and buried and did not escape death as by a miracle; he did not come back among us by reincarnation, as an angel or a spirit. Only in prayer and discipleship can we know that he is in our midst, in the bread and the cup, in friendship and solidarity, in opposition to injustice and in longing for the peace of God's sabbath rest: 'Thy kingdom come.' Just as during his lifetime he was present among us as God with us by doing the will of God, so his presence among us is not continued otherwise than by doing the will of God who sent him. Anyone who with Jesus says 'Abba, Father', confesses him as the Son of God and shares his longing to come home to God and acts 'in the Spirit of God' (I Cor. 12.3) which also overshadowed him. But even this language remains too vague, too much a variant of the metaphor of acting in someone's spirit. The Christian life is 'filled with Christ', not because we respect his last testament and 'do as he did' or live 'in memory of him'; rather, we invoke him, and through him, via him, we address ourselves to God. Christians confess him and honour him as the Living One, as our advocate with God and as the one who lives and reigns for ever and ever.

THE LIVING FROM THE DEAD

In the Nicene Creed the resurrection of Jesus is confessed as the enthronement of the crucified one. Here Jesus' resurrection is a phase – transition, *pascha* – from humiliation and curse (crucifixion) to elevation to the status of the Son of Man of Dan. 7.14: '... to judge the living and the dead and his kingdom shall have no end.' This confession is taken up in a scheme of descent and ascent, starting from God and returning to God again (*katabasis-anabasis, exitus-reditus*), which first of all has a christological function: the resurrection of Jesus has everything to do with his origin in God and future in God. Here the Nicene Creed corresponds to a number of confessional formulae in the New Testament (Phil. 2.1–11; Rom. 1.3–4; Acts 2.22–36; 3.13–19; 5.30–2; 10.37–43; 10.26–41; I Tim. 3.16). Although executed at human hands, he was snatched away from the kingdom of the dead by God. Although he shared our mortal fate and was murdered as a criminal by mortals, he shares without interruption in the glory of God.

The resurrection of the crucified Jesus and his exaltation to Kyrios and Son of Man breaks through both the Jewish apocalyptic and the Greek anthropological frameworks of thought. Jesus is not a martyr for the cause of Israel alone but for the kingdom of God for all peoples. He earns his eternal life not on the basis of heroic human acts (like those of the heroes in Elysium) but as a result of surrender ('unless a grain of wheat falls into the earth ...'). Thus the cross is a stumbling block for Jews and folly for Greeks. The Synoptic Gospels and the Acts of the Apostles are primarily concerned with the first, and Paul (Rom. 8.9–11; I Cor. 15), John and I Peter (especially I Peter 1.13–25; 3.18–22) with the second. I Cor. 15 is an exemplary catechesis which documents the transition from the Jewish-apocalyptic iconography of the resurrection (raising up as a sign of rehabilitation) to a Greek anthropological axiology (*pneuma-sarx* dialectic: that the body of human beings is simply the temporal form of a spirit supported by God and directed towards God).

That needs some explanation. In the Jewish tradition there is no mention of a fundamental dualism of the body and the soul. The body is itself the seat of life which, as experience teaches, is dependent on blood and breath. People die as a result of loss of blood or a lack of breath, which is what one had to suppose in a culture which as yet had no sense of the circulation of the blood and physiological metabolism. The difference between human beings and animals then lies in the nature of the blood. With human beings the blood is filled with a special life-force, the *nephesh*. However, in Greek anthropology from Pythagoras on a third factor is introduced: the spirit or the *Nous*. Of course even then blood and breath are important, but they do not indicate what is specifically human as opposed to animal. Apart from living by breath and blood, human beings also share in the divine *Nous*. At death, blood and breath lose their force, but the *Nous* remains intact and returns to its divine source, there in a process of purification to be prepared for a further cycle of the bodily life of flesh and blood. For Jewish anthropology a life without the body, without breath and blood, is quite unimaginable. If there is to be any question of a life after death, that can only be in the form of a new bodily life. Something like an independent *Nous*, or, as will later be assumed, a soul which is split off (*anima separata*), is inconceivable. As soon as apocalyptic begins to develop ideas about a kind of restoration of the righteous who have died unjustly and prematurely, the thought automatically occurs of a resurrection of the dead from their tombs. That is also the picture in Ezek. 37: skeletons are again clothed with flesh and filled with breath and blood. We must read the stories of the raisings of the dead by Jesus in this same framework: the young man of Nain and Jairus' daughter, and also the young Lazarus, rise from their bier or emerge from their graves so that, having died prematurely, they may be restored to their parents or friends.

For Greek ears this language was incomprehensible, as emerges from e.g. Acts 17. Therefore in I Cor. 15 Paul works with the Greek notion of the different cosmic forms – the heavenly bodies, plants, animals, human beings – who differ by virtue of the different share that they have in the divine *Nous*. He presents the resurrection of the dead as a new creation and a new form of life which is unknown to us, a *soma pneumatikon*: a being supported by God's breath that no longer experiences any bodily decay, any death and corruption. The risen Christ is the prototype and pioneer of this: another Adam, but a better one.

Thus (and this has often been neglected), solely on the basis of the structure of the creed (both the Niceno-Constantinopolitan and the Apostles' Creed) a sharp distinction has to be made between the resurrection of Jesus from the dead and the resurrection of the dead to eternal life. The first stands in a christological perspective, the second in a pneumatological perspective. The resurrection of Jesus from the dead is more than a particular case, let alone a proof, of the general resurrection of the dead or an immortality which is intrinsically human. It is the sign above all of God's rule over the world and the underworld. It orders every possible world by the criteria of the kingdom of God. The expectation of a future for the dead with God is a pneumatological confession which is bound up with the experience of the Spirit in word and sacrament, baptism and the forgiveness of sins, as this is foreshadowed in Rom. 6. and 8 (especially Rom. 8.3–11 and 17) and also in the Synoptic Gospels and in Acts.

The christological and pneumatological dimensions of the kerygma of the resurrection already flow together in Acts 2.22–36, as they do in the Gospel of John: Easter and Pentecost fall on the same day. The consequence of Paul's 'in Christ' texts and his thinking in terms of the 'firstborn from the dead' (Col. 1.18; I Cor. 15.23; Acts 26.23) who has gone ahead of us as leader (Acts 3.15) is a direct coupling of the kerygma about the resurrection of Jesus with the promise of eternal life to those who have been faithful to him.

The New Testament Easter stories are not verification stories, but rather legitimation stories about the rehabilitation of a crucified man and the mission to Israel and beyond which are based on that. In contrast to the raising of Lazarus or the young man of Nain from the dead, and in contrast to the apocalyptic visions of the opened graves, Jesus was not restored to his parents and did not return to the land of the living but returned to God his Father. At all events that is true of the appearance stories, in which especially the encounters of Paul with the Kyrios must be understood as stories of a prophetic mission and calling. The mission of initially doubting disciples (Luke 24, the disciples on the Emmaus Road; John 21, unbelieving Thomas; Acts 9, the conversion of Paul) is legitimated.

The stories of the empty tomb are secondary to these appearance stories (in other words they are at their service, though that does not make them less important) and are above all meant as a correction of the apocalyptic belief in the resurrection: 'Why do you seek the living among the dead?' '*Ouk estin hode*': he is not here, but goes before you ... In contrast to the apocalyptic notion of the open tombs, Easter and the Kyrios evade any form of historical perception (cf. Luke 16.31). And indeed nowhere is there any mention of verification of the resurrection, but rather of the conscious witness that there can have been no question of human fraud in the burial or a miraculous escape from death by a pseudo-death. Biologically speaking Jesus is no longer alive. The story about the forty days between Easter and the Ascension is not confirmed in the other Gospels. Even for Luke it is the stylistic composition of Jesus' Pasch: his transition from the cross and grave to the glory of the Father.

Our present-day concern about the historical character of the Easter event, like the speculation about the historical moment of the dawning of the Lord's Day, thus bears witness more to curiosity than to faith. That also applies to attempts like those of Pannenberg to root the hypothesis of 'God' in the historical resurrection. The only thing that is confessed in scripture and creed is the identity of the pre-existent Word and the eternal Wisdom of God with the human being who is born from Mary as the only-begotten and firstborn Son of God on the one hand, and the identity of the human being who under Pontius Pilate was crucified, suffered death and was buried with the Kyrios who is enthroned at the right hand of God, or as the Son of Man who will come to judge the living and the dead, on the other. This identity was later (at Chalcedon) carefully nuanced as far as the katabatic aspect (the incarnation) is concerned in the scheme of the doctrine of two natures. According to the ancient councils of Ephesus (431) and Chalcedon (451), who the Jesus is who comes into the world from Mary can be stated only in two movements of thought: in his whole being he is wholly from God and at the same time in his whole being he has crossed the threshold to a human existence like ours, but without any damage to his soul. This nuance must not be lost in the anabasis: the Jesus who rises from this life to God was like human beings to the very death; he remained so faithful to his divine self that beyond the frontier of death with all his humanity he was allowed to enter into the very life of God (but neither Nicaea nor Chalcedon says anything about how this happened). Christmas and Easter are thus both about a mysterious event, a twofold natality of the Christ from God, about which it is impossible to engage in biological speculations. Just as we were not witnesses to his conception, so too we are not witnesses to his resurrection, except by the word of the angel of God. Anyone who wants to engage in more investigations into Mary's womb or Abraham's bosom infringes the mystery of God's contact. Just as the wise men from the East were sent away from the manger to proclaim the praise of God to Herod and the peoples, so the disciples were sent away from the tomb to proclaim that the risen Christ will point all peoples – Jews, Samaritans, Greeks and Romans – towards God.

What the disciples – at that time – saw and experienced remains

211

at this level of the sign: it cannot and may not be objectified historically. What we are to expect – in due course – remains at the level of God's promises: it cannot and may not be extrapolated from anthropological frameworks of thought (immortality, the body-soul scheme). In this sense both the resurrection of Jesus and the resurrection of the dead to eternal life are meta-historical realities. They can be verified only *coram deo* and precisely in this way are the object of faith.

Of course belief in human immortality is not specifically Jewish or Christian, but the expression of a religious sense which has grown up about the unique and abiding value of the human person. This belief in immortality is now in crisis: it has been either firmly abandoned or replaced by esoteric forms of escapism (reincarnation, spiritualism). At first sight here Asian wisdom seems to be being imported into Western thought. Others even see a certain affinity and influence of African ancestor belief. Isn't the desire for a subsequent life with possibly better opportunities and the awe at the spiritual influence of all those who have lived before us a legitimate extension and extrapolation of the experience that we human beings are more than the body which enfolds us? Little objection could be made to that were it not that Asians and Africans themselves are rather less romantic, and think more with fear and trembling about the cycles of successive life and the sphere of influence of forefathers. We are open to the charge from our forefathers that we are profiting from their difficulties, and that imposes great obligations on us. Or the indigenous African traditions think that we are suffering to the fourth generation from their misdeeds and are inheriting the scars of their failures. In both cases they limit our freedom. And for Asians the succession of incarnations is an overwhelming matter, in which we shall find no rest unless we have already in some life stilled the unrest of our desires. That too puts a heavy burden on our freedom. Within the traditions of Judaism, Christianity and Islam there is only one opportunity to direct our biography towards the truth and truthfulness of being human in accordance with God's purposes. Thus there is only one evaluation, one judgement, one reward: of rest in Abraham's bosom, sitting at the banquet of paradise, eternal life before God's throne, or eternal rejection and forgetfulness in the shadow realm of death. When it comes to the outcome of our life and the last judgement we face a gaping aporia, however much mourning and funeral culture we engage in, and however much courage we also want to show.[19]

Christian faith in eternal life on the basis of the resurrection of Jesus need not suffer in the present-day crisis of the Western belief in immortality, because it does not coincide with it. It can be proclaimed with a complete acceptance of the biological and philosophical finitude of human corporeality. That also proved possible in a Jewish apocalyptic framework of thought and in the atmosphere of the Greek dialectic between *sarx* and *pneuma*, of which the doctrine of the immortal soul was the result. The proclamation of Jesus the Christ as the firstfruits from the dead, the advocate (intercessor) for his faithful, the instigator and guide of those who seek the kingdom of God, in fact primarily relates to the current axiology of the communion of saints in the *Pneuma* and only as an extension of that to the promises for those who have gone to sleep. They will be saved from the wrath to come (I Thess. 1.9–10). But on the other hand, it is true that belief in the one God spans the times and the generations, so that anyone who believes in this God cannot at the same time say, 'When you're dead, you're dead.' For anyone who accepts that the life which is given is given for the glory of God, that life which has once been given has a sequel which will at least be just as creative. We know no blueprint for the nature of this sequel, but only the genetic pattern: we shall be like God's own messenger, wholly taken up by God, if we have looked for God in this life; we shall be wholly alienated from God if we have lived only for ourselves: 'None of us lives to himself, and none of us dies to himself ... whether we live or whether we die, we are the Lord's' (Rom. 14.7–8).

CONCLUSION

'Since people no longer believe in God, they do not believe in nothing, but in whatever you like,' said Chesterton. Because resurrection faith and faith in the creative power of God essentially belong together, the preaching and catechesis of cross and resurrection, of death and eternal life, need to dissociate themselves clearly both from apocalyptic speculations and esoteric images, and also from empiricist reductions ('When you're dead, you're dead'). All three dissociate themselves from belief in the goodness of God's creation and in God's creative attitude to each unique individual; all three dishonour the icon of the resurrection. It is the Father and the Son who have mercy on human beings, crowning the Servant as Son of Man, putting all human beings in his care. It is extremely important for the creed of the church to hold in check our human curiosity about the outcome of life, emphasizing its seriousness *coram Deo*. Eternal life remains a subject of promise, as the liturgical tradition and the theology of baptism and eucharist have it. But in contrast to the Celestine promise of easy enlightenment, human beings are not directed to their own glory, possessions or success but to the glory of God and the service of the other. That does not do away with the aporias of finitude and death, but it does entrust people to one another in their aporias and in their quest for themselves and for the meaning of their lives. Christians go one step further than this appeal to human solidarity in the prospect of death. The core of belief in Jesus consists in the open question whether he was a human being from God who entered into God himself and may therefore ask others to follow him with authority (*exousia*). For each fragile bodily life this question opens up a similar perspective: whether we keep open for ourselves on his authority the possibility that at the end of the journey of our souls we will be greeted by God himself and clad in the mantle of eternal light. As we sing in the Roman liturgy at the departure of any human child of man, despite Kolakowski, '*In paradisum deducant te angeli* ...': may angels guide you to the house of God.[20] Or, with Nijhoff, to put it in a more ordinary but stronger way:

I think that we live eternally,
for what is once given remains given.

9

The Holy *Pneuma* of God
God's life-giving power

Is it necessary to speak not only about God and Jesus Christ but also about the *Pneuma* (literally wind, breath, breeze, sigh) of God which we in the Western tradition of Christianity (except in the Scandinavian languages) usually call the Holy Spirit (*Spiritus Sanctus*)? Does this denote anything or anyone other than God himself, or Jesus Christ as the one sent by God and leading us to God? Haven't I already said everything about the life-giving *Pneuma* of God in connection with the creator God and the risen Christ? Isn't it the case that wherever scripture speaks about the *Pneuma* of God it means none other than the God of Abraham, Isaac and Jacob, the God of Israel, who makes children of God all who confess Jesus as the Christ? In technical theological language, isn't it better to think about God in binitarian – God and Jesus, the Father and the Son[1] – rather than in trinitarian terms? Or does it have to be precisely the other way round, in the order of the scriptures: first speak about the Spirit of God, then about Jesus as the Servant, the one who is sent, the Son of God, who has taught us to call upon God as 'Father'?

The Christian tradition of God wants things to be otherwise. From the Apostles' Creed through the Niceno-Constantinopolitan Creed, up to and including the basis of the World Council of Churches, God is spoken about in the Trinity of Father, Son and Spirit, in that order. That has also been used over the centuries, with many variants, in liturgy and iconography. Prompted by the texts of the creeds, theological reflection has unfolded along the same scheme: attention to the creator God and Father of Israel, the account of Jesus of Nazareth who came or was appointed as the Son, and a separate presentation of the Spirit of God who binds the two together in love, who awakens Jesus to life again and raises him from the dead, and who from the beginning of the world to the end of time is active with his gifts in equipping all the children of God for communion with God and gathering them together into God's fatherly house. We have become so accustomed to this system of faith which concludes with the Spirit of God, the Spirit of sanctification, union with God and the gift of life that we risk overlooking or forgetting its problems and the hesitations there have been about it down the centuries.[2] Paradoxically that also means that we fail to take sufficiently to heart the positive eloquence of a life from God's Spirit, which for us is best expressed in the wordless language of its sighs and makes us, stammering children of God, cry 'Abba, Father' (Rom. 8.26; Rom. 8.15; Gal. 4.16).

In this connection it is worth knowing that it took until the end of the fourth century for the place of the Holy Spirit to be definitively settled in the creed. The Western theological tradition in particular constantly had difficulty with it and thus from the sixth and seventh centuries on added further specifications with the intention of saying that the *Pneuma*, which is the power and the driving force and the support which come from YHWH, the Father of Israel, is none other than the influence and the call that goes forth from Jesus who, called from Israel, is confessed as being at God's right hand and being God's firstborn. But the Latin formula which intended to say this (... *qui ex Patre* Filioque *procedit* ...) suggested that the Spirit of God emanates from a kind of double source, and for all kinds of reasons this was unacceptable to the tradition of the East.[3] Religious movements which especially appeal to God as Spirit have always been looked on in the West with a degree of suspicion. Often in such movements there has been criticism of the power and the historical forms of the church. Or people have complained that the approaches of religion were too intellectual and argued for more feeling, emotion and spiritual depth. The established churches then spoke of 'enthusiasts' and 'fanatics' and tried to restrain such movements – as happened with the Cathars and Albigensians in the twelfth century and with the Anabaptists in the sixteenth – or to incorporate them, as happened with the spiritual movements of the Mendicants, who as an organized monastic movement of the Franciscans were able to make a valued spiritual contribution to the Catholic Church. Thus for centuries talk about the Spirit of God was swept under the carpet, or at any rate put under the guardianship of the official church, official doctrine, the text of the Bible. If the Holy Spirit was spoken of, it was within the framework of confession and magisterium. In the Orthodox churches of the East the Western suspicion of the Spirit as an independent hypostasis of God was always seen as one of the most important points of difference. A quite complicated theological argument developed simply around these points of dispute within Christianity; in an agnostic culture this inevitably comes over as remarkable pedantry and 'super-natural' learning. But the argument is about something: murder and burnings over statements of the church's faith did not just happen by chance. Many Christians had to pay for their attempts to bring some theological simplicity to this area with banishment or even the stake.

The theme is topical once again, now that so many Christian movements and even movements outside Christianity are presenting themselves as 'Spirit churches', as Pentecostals, or as 'charismatic groups', again in opposition to fossilized forms of the church which no longer exercise any attractions. These are proving immensely popular in many regions. Others, above all in Western culture, are said to want through the idea of God as Spirit to restore the connection between Christianity and wisdom, Gnosticism and esotericism: do we not know with the knowledge of the Spirit of God, and do we not breathe with the breath of the living God? Finally, in the ecumenical movement, above all in connection with the dialogue between the religions, there is an argument for reflection on the idea of God from the *Pneuma* tradition. Starting from the notion of God as Wind, Breath, Spirit of Life, is there not far more of a family affinity with the heritage of the Asian and African religions than we have thought of so far in our European clique of Judaism, Christianity and Islam?[4]

We must begin with some more technical clarifications. To start with, this relates to the notion of the Spirit of God as the 'third person' in the trinitarian scheme of the creeds of the early church. Because the Spirit of God comes only in third place there, the most important thing already seems to be being said automatically. But in the epic of Israel and also in the words of Jesus, talk about God as Spirit and as Father comes first. Moreover the trinitarian scheme seems to be too rigid, let alone the binitarian scheme: or rather, it forms only an extract from a far more colourful palette of approaches to God. We clearly find several times in the New Testament the threefold naming of God as the Father, the Son and the (Holy) Spirit (Matt. 28.19; II Cor. 13.13; I Peter 1.2); but this happens so to speak in passing and in an apparently arbitrary order, and these are certainly not the only names for God. God is also called Shepherd, Most High, the Eternal One, Lord and Judge. Alongside this he is also called Light, Strength, Fire, Love. If it were merely a matter of the most important names for God today we might well choose another three. But the issue is clearly about more than the names of God, as is evident, for example, from the Gospel of John: Jesus addresses the Father, whose will and work he does, and he promises the support of the divine Spirit, who will continue his work in the disciples and the church. So this is a threefold articulation of what God does and how human beings have to do with God. It is a matter of three different relations to God and reality which arise from the self-understanding of Jesus and which are connected with the specific epoch-making significance which has been given to his person and work.

At a very early stage in the history of theology, points of comparison were sought for precisely these three, this triad or Trinity.[5] They were found in the Old Testament, which speaks of the Word (e.g. Pss. 119 and 147; Isa. 55.10–11), Wisdom (Prov. 1.20–3; 9.1–6; Job 28; Sirach 24), and the Wind or Breath of God[6] Gen. 1.2; 3.8; 8.1; Ex. 14.21 (the wind of God which opens the Red Sea for the passage through it); Num. 11.25; Judg. 14.6 (Samson); I Sam. 10.6–11; Ezek. 1.12; 37.1–14; Isa. 11.2; 32.15; 40.7 (the wind of God which determines rain and drought, death and life; cf. Hos. 6.3); Isa. 61.1; Joel 2.28). This is presented as more or less active, by way of personification of the divine presence and energy. In a number of passages this *ruach* of God is also called holy *ruach*: *ruach-ha-kodesh* (e.g. Ps. 51.11; Isa. 63.10–11), literally, the wind of the sanctuary, the temple wind. Then we have God's invisible but tangible presence in the cool breeze of the temple complex. Anyone who has ever visited Indian temples knows what that means.

It is sometimes said of these three personifications that they emanate from God, that they have been sent by God, that they are messengers, as e.g. in the hymn of praise to creation in Ps. 104.3–4: 'You make the clouds your chariot, you ride on the wings of the wind, you make the winds your messengers, fire and flame your ministers', and Ps. 104.29–30: 'When you hide your face they are dismayed; when you take away their breath, they die and return to the dust. When you send forth your spirit, they are created; and you

renew the face of the ground.' Here it seems very artificial to forget
the other personifications of God (light, fire, lightning, the voice of
the thunder) which often appear in the same connection (e.g. in
Gen. 3.8 or Job 28). And it seems even more artificial to begin to
read Wisdom, Word and Spirit as Father, Son and Holy Spirit
respectively, as people began to do from the second century on.
Here the New Testament already had connected both Word and
Wisdom with the Son of God, whereas the Old Testament sees
Wisdom as a gift of the Spirit of God (Gen. 41.38–39; Ex. 28.3;
35.31; Deut. 34.9).

The fundamental conviction behind all these images is the direct
involvement of YHWH in all that happens, especially in all that
lives, and quite especially in the wisdom that characterizes human
beings, the well-being that is given them (cooling by the sea breeze),
that can threaten them as disaster (the heat of the wilderness wind),
and that gives them direction (one of the most important functions
of the wind, especially in the desert).

This much is clear: when God is spoken of in the Bible, it is often
in terms of noise, storm and breeze, breath and sigh, cloud and
storm, the seduction of the spirit and ecstasy, the seething and
bubbling of God's creative *Pneuma*. That is already the case in Gen.
1.2, where the Spirit of God blows over the primal sea. It continues
to be the case in the tumult of history, when God puts his Spirit on
Joseph (Gen. 41.38), on Moses, on the elders of Israel (Num. 24.2–
3), on Samson (Judg. 13.25; 14.6, 19; 15.14–16), on Elijah (II Kings
2.15), on Samuel (I Sam. 19.19–24) (and in reaction on Saul, but
then in order to unbalance him: I Sam. 11.6 is positive), on David
(II Sam. 23.2) and on Israel as the Servant of YHWH (Isa. 11.2;
42.1; 61.1). Typically it comes from outside.[7] Thus Jesus also speaks
about the *Pneuma* of God as something that comes upon him. And
if there is talk about the Son of God and the children of God, this is
also always in terms of the *Pneuma* of God, fluttering like a dove or
flickering like a flame of fire, which descends on the prophets, on
Jesus himself and afterwards also on the disciples.

Before, during and after the historical appearance of Jesus, the
effect of God's *Pneuma* is the all-determining constant of belief in
the one God of both Jews and non-Jews. Thus the Spirit of God
first of all binds together belief in YHWH, the God of Israel, and
belief in Jesus as the Christ, who called the same God 'Our Father'.
It then also binds together the belief of Jews and Christians with the
belief in God of all other religions, certainly also the so-called
natural religions.

219

This talk about God's *Pneuma* as an indeterminate force and energy working on people from outside, surprising them, links the Old and New Testaments. Before Jesus' appearance, Christians and Jews share the covenant with YHWH, the caring guardian of Israel, the God of Abraham, Isaac and Jacob, whose *Ruach* brings live-giving force, the word of the prophet and Wisdom, often by means of a storm and then again in a gentle breeze. Jesus himself is the fruit of this same life force from God, born of Mary (Matt. 1.18, 20; Luke 1.35), revealed as God's anointed (Matt. 3.16; Mark 1.10; Luke 3.22; John 1.32–33), coming forth in the power of God's Spirit (Matt. 12.28; Luke 4.14, 18; 10.21; John 3.34; Acts 2.33; 10.38). After his death Christians know that they are led and driven by the same Spirit that Jesus handed down to them or breathed over them (Mark 13.11; Luke 11.13; 12.12; John 3.8, 34; 7.39; 14.17, 26; 15.26; 16.13; 20.22; Acts 1.5, 8; 2.4, 17–18; I John 3.24; 4.13) and which they also hand on in their mission among the peoples (Matt. 28.19; Acts 2.38; 4.8, 31; 5.32; 6.3, 5; 8.15, 17; 9.17; 10.44–7; 11.16; 13.4, 52; 15.8; 19.6; Rom. 5.5; 8.9, 11, 23; 15.16; Col. 1.12; 3.16; 6.11; II Cor. 5.5; Gal. 3.14; 4.6; 5.25; Eph. 1.13; 2.22; 3.16; I Thess. 4.8; II Thess. 2.13; II Tim. 1.14; Titus 3.5; Heb. 2.4; 6.4; I Peter 1.2; 4.14). It is the Spirit of God – the *Pneuma*, i.e. the Breath, the Wind of the Holy God – which according to the witness of the New Testament raised Jesus from the dead and thus makes him Son of God (Rom. 1.4; 8.11; I Peter 3.18). In the same way, through the same *Pneuma* of God those who follow Christ from the first Pentecost are also made sons of God who may say 'Abba, Father' (Rom. 8.14–17), and who are comforted and strengthened to give a world-wide witness and to mutual unity and peace, solidarity and joy (the gifts of the Spirit, I Cor. 12.4ff.; Gal. 5.22ff.).

Very soon people began to compare this articulation of history, determined by the Christ event, as three 'phases' or 'roles' of God, with the *dramatis personae*, the characters of the stage.[8] Tertullian already did that around AD 180. Above all, the theology of baptism in the name of the Father, the Son and the Holy Spirit and the threefold articulation of the content of faith in the creed became the occasion in the fourth century for Basil and Athanasius and later for Hilary of Poitiers and Augustine to speak of three persons in one divine essence or substance. In the East people then spoke of three hypostases which share one substance (*ousia*). This term suggests above all that distinctive initiatives can be attributed to the Father as the God of Israel, to Jesus as the Son of God, and to the Spirit of God who by virtue of Jesus' promise supports the church as Helper and Advocate, and that they can also be invoked and worshipped separately. As far as the divine *Pneuma* was concerned, the theologians of the fourth and fifth centuries emphasized, above all on the basis of the Gospel and the Letters of John, the purifying, renewing and above all sanctifying effect which proceeds from the Spirit of God; through this, in a divine pedagogy, human beings can gradually become like God.

But there continued to be hesitations about calling the Spirit of God just God: the creed of Constantinople chose the cautious formulation: 'Lord and Giver of Life, who proceeds from the Father, and who with the Father and the Son together is worshipped'. It was only on the basis of this decision that people began, still hesitantly at first, to write prayers and hymns in which the Spirit of God was invoked directly. For example, Marius Victorinus, Augustine's teacher, invokes the Spirit as the bond of love between the Father and the Son, who alternately with the Father rests and then becomes active in the Son. Thus the Holy Spirit is the to-and-fro of the relationship between God and Christ; he brings about the community of love between God and human beings.

Through his psychological analogy in doctrine Augustine determined the development of pneumatology (the doctrine of the Holy Spirit) in the West; this led to the Spirit of God being interpreted increasingly strongly as an inner motive force and illumination of human beings, and no longer as a cosmic energy of life, which it is in the Old Testament and in the early church fathers. Augustine sought the comparison in human functions or capabilities: *mens – notitia – amor* or *memoria, intelligentia, voluntas* (self-) awareness, capacity for knowledge, will and desire or love. This analogy derived from his conviction that God has put the imprint of God's own being on human beings, created in the image of God (Gen. 1.26). We find the imprint – *vestigia trinitatis*, traces of the triune God – in the human psyche. The collaboration of the three capacities in the human mind is then the image both of the collaboration and unity of God and of the difference in persons or effects. In later centuries further different threes were added: the trio of past, present and future, the division of world history into three periods (Joachim of Fiore, Bonaventure) or the dichotomy between subject and object which is transcended in the consciousness or relationship, and even – the most artificial picture of all – the geometric figure of the triangle, where the one universal existence consists of the emanation of three overlapping circles.

However, in the Niceno-Constantinopolitan creed what is said about the Holy Spirit is much more restrained and at the same time more concrete, more physical, as in the scriptures themselves. There it is linked with the birth of life, with the words of the prophets which give direction, with the church, with baptism, with the forgiveness of sins, with the communion of saints and with eternal life. In the theological tradition the Spirit of God is mentioned in the debate about the divine inspiration of the books of the Bible, the authority of the preceding tradition and its official guardians. Moreover it appears in the questions about the church's ministry and its alternating forms and in the effect of the sacraments, in which the Spirit is invoked on the celebration of the community (*epiclesis*). In addition it is also traditional to refer to the work of God's Spirit in connection with the significance of the other religions, in which sparks of the fire of the Spirit are disseminated. Finally, from the Middle Ages on, as I have already remarked, there is a separate argument within the doctrine of the Trinity about the relationship of the Spirit to the Father and the Son, which has been a fixed point of discussion in the ecumenical dialogue with the churches of the East.

Granted, philosophically at first sight there is not much potential in this argument about the Holy Spirit. To a large degree it seems to be a discussion for initiates, a system-immanent debate which leads away from the questions of fundamental theology that I want to deal with here, rather than resolving them. Of course there is a long tradition of a philosophy of the Spirit, of reason and consciousness. Certainly in the West, God's Holy *Pneuma* has been bound up with reflection on the human capacity for knowledge. Already in the Qumran community, and then also in Philo of Alexandria and the Christian tradition which flourished there (Clement of Alexandria, Tertullian and Origen), both the holy *Ruach* and the *Pneuma* of God are identified with God's Wisdom and Word (*Hokhmah, Logos*) and thus are coupled with human knowledge and language. In the West Augustine's psychological analogies join up with this, except that he links the *Pneuma* of God to the human capacity for love. Throughout the scholastic tradition the Spirit of God is therefore bound up with the human capacities of mind and will, with the 'seven gifts of the Holy Spirit', as they are celebrated for example in the hymn *Veni Creator*. In the long run the *Pneuma* of God then coincides with the human charisma, what distinguishes human beings from the rest of creation: their mind, their will, their feelings, their human *habitus* and *virtus*. A problem arises here

222

simply in terms of terminology. The classical Greek philosophers said a great deal about what we would now call the human spirit, but they did so in terms of the psyche, the seat of the emotions and the intellect, or at most in terms of the human share in the *Nous* or the *Logos*, the principle of cosmic order and the logic of the universe. However, *Pneuma* has to do with the spirit, not as an intellectual capacity but as the breath of life itself, with bodily living life. Anyone who gives up the spirit does not just lose consciousness, but ceases to live. That is also said of Jesus himself (Luke 23.46: *exepneusen*: he blew out his breath of life), although in the Gospel of Luke this is given a theological interpretation: he gives back the spirit of life to God the Father ('Into your hands, Father, I commend my spirit') (Luke 23.46, cf. also Acts 7.59, Stephen: 'Lord Jesus, receive my spirit'). We also find in Paul and among the church fathers a *pneuma-sarx* dialectic which also comes out of Platonism, in which the experience of our bodily nature and the bond with matter stand in tension with the experience of human consciousness and freedom. Talk of God's Spirit or the Spirit of the Holy One seems indirectly to be connected with this whole debate. Indeed the same thing is true of the age-old tradition of the philosophy of the spirit or consciousness, which first of all regarded reason and the intellect as the point of contact for the divine presence: God as the giver of thought, which culminates in the possibility of thinking of God, as John Scotus Eriugena already argued. This coupling of the Spirit of God and the human capacity for thought found its climax in Hegel's *Philosophy of Spirit* and all its offshoots down to our time, and with that its downfall. This coupling has obscured biblical and Christian theological talk about the *Pneuma* of God all too much and has cast the idea of God itself in a rational mould: 'God' as consciousness, self-consciousness, the absolute, the totality, the universe. This idea of God has gone out like a candle in the night wind of secularization. If the Spirit of God means no more than human understanding, human freedom and human love, then there is 'no need of God'; we can declare God dead.

How then are we to illuminate the question of God as an open question to the tradition of pneumatology? The question of the Spirit of God – and indeed also of pneumatology, i.e. theological reflection on the Spirit of God – can then start better with the experience of life itself, with which the Spirit, from the creation to eternal life, is bound up. As I have remarked, *pneuma* means something tangible and concrete: wind, breath, sigh; *pneo* = blow, snort, rustle, sniff, puff, roar, sigh, breathe. Where there is life, where there is movement, there is *pneuma*. It is as much in the elements of the cosmos as in the dwelling of our soul and in the seedbed of our living cells. This *pneuma* is the Septuagint translation of the Hebrew *ruach*, which also means blowing/wind, sometimes in the more elemental sense, sometimes in the more personal meaning of the breath of life, but also applied to the feelings as anger, care, doubt, fear; as that with which people let off steam or get steamed up (cf. Ex. 15.8: God's warmth is evident from the snorting of the nostrils). *Ruach* is often used together with *nesema*, the breath of life; *leb*, the heart, the human disposition. Thus *pneuma*, through the human emotions, is bound up with all human activity, hope and expectation. It stands for the dynamic of all that lives, and at the same time for God's moving wisdom and power which lurk behind it – without ever being graspable. Indeed there are more than 100 passages which speak about the breath of God which broods on the seas of the primal beginning (Gen. 1.2), which is present everywhere (Ps. 139.7), which prompts people to actions (Isa. 11.2; Judg. 3.10; 6.34; Num. 27.18; 11.25–7), which enlists them as messengers and prophets (Isa. 32.15–20; 11.1–8; 29; 63.11–14), and which will clothe the dead with new flesh and blood (Ezek. 37).

Only in the Hellenistic period and under Persian and Hellenistic influence is *pneuma* also used for the Wisdom of God, for all that is spiritual as compared with the purely corporeal, for all that is lasting by comparison with the transitory. This idea of 'spirit' as the 'absolute' which escapes all the limitations of matter is too clearly an abstraction from our ordinary experience, a combination of factors and a contrast term or at best a vague echo of the refined 'ether' which the Greek natural philosophers presupposed as the filler and bond between the separate atoms. Like the Latin *spiritus*, the chemical term 'spirit' (spirit of salt, spirit of wine, the spirit which escapes from the bottle), which has now become obsolete, still has echoes of the onomatopoeia of the escaping vapours and gases that emerge in processes of fermentation: in this sense yeast and spirit are related. Hence the meaning 'fleeting', 'invisible', is the derived meaning of ghost and spirit. It is above all in the world of esotericism, of theosophy and anthroposophy and all the holistic, bioenergetic and astrological wisdoms derived from it, that this alchemistic notion still lives on. In New Age circles this thought still lives on in the legacy of Asian philosophy (Zen, Dao) and medieval mysticism. But old Greek roots can also be indicated. It is also used for evil or unclean spirits as opposed to good or clean spirits. Here we have a glimmering of the later 'spiritualization' which is brought about when the Latin *spiritus* (English spirit, French *esprit*) is used synonymously with *mens* and *animus* as a translation of the Aristotelian and Stoic *Nous*. Thus the driving and mobile *pneuma*, which is bodily and can be experienced, becomes an invisible, spiritualized, almost ethereal and later above all rational reality: consciousness, self-awareness, God as 'spirit'; of the genre of 'spirits' (= 'Ghost'). As long as God had a home in this world of 'spirit' as the 'refined' and 'fleeting', the 'spiritual' could also be experienced as a divine spirit in the midst of all that is earthly, all that as 'inexplicable chance' and 'fate' could ensure the actual course and coherence of things (*fatum, heimarmene*), their 'interior' (Teilhard de Chardin called it *le de-dans*) and all the 'spiritual surplus' that springs from the material processes of life and escapes objectification: art, love, freedom, happiness, civilization, science, thought, the imagination, the experience of the sublime as that is worked out in Hegel's philosophy.

Another track leads via the Spirit as Wisdom of God, but then as a criterion of truth and truthfulness, to the many views of inwardness, the disposition, the heart or the conscience of human beings. In place of the rumour of God which rustles in the Word of God and in the call to the good, and which appears to us in the question of love and mercy, the Western tradition in particular began to identify the Spirit of God with the inner divine urge which moves us towards God, with the love that we give one another, with the conscience that guides us, with virtue and talents, as gifts of grace from the Spirit and as fruits of sanctification. In the long run the Spirit of God is identified with human capacities for judgement, with a striving for (ethical) perfection and church harmony. The Spirit of God becomes a permanent, habitual function of human beings and a quality of the church, as is the case with the well-known hymn *Veni Creator Spiritus*.

All this is alien to biblical talk about the Spirit of God. As we saw, the metaphor of the *Ruach YHWH* comes from another language field. Moreover Jewish anthropology does not know any dualism of body and soul, body and spirit.

Especially the prophetic texts about *Ruach/Pneuma* have influenced the messianic sense within Judaism and the New Testament: Ezek. 11.9; 18.3; 32.6. God speaks through the prophets. So too Jesus is conceived by the Holy Spirit (Luke 1.35), anointed with the Spirit which rests on him (Mark 1.10) and which drives him to his mission (Luke 4.18–22). Through this Spirit he resists the Evil One and drives out the evil spirits (Mark 1.27; 6.7). This Spirit is handed on to the disciples to do the same thing. It is this spirit of prophecy (Joel 3; Acts 2.17) which from Pentecost onwards inspires the church: it leads to the reassembling of the people. It adds Samaria to Jerusalem (Acts 8) for the worship in spirit and truth (John 4); it gathers God's people to Zion from the diaspora of the peoples.

This Spirit constitutes the church, on the basis of Jesus' birth, preaching, death and resurrection. As in Ezek. 37, this resurrection, too, is the work of God's *Pneuma*: the new creation once and for all, a clothing with a *soma pneumatikon* (I Cor. 15). Thus it is fundamental to the gospel of Jesus that the Spirit of God which was breathed into Adam, which gave Abraham direction, which rested on Moses, on the judges and the prophets of Israel, has become completely manifest in Jesus by the conquest of all demons and by the dissemination on a broad scale of the gifts of the kingdom of God which Jesus hands on to his followers and through which men and women become like prophets. This Spirit of God is among us 'in Christ' and 'through Christ'. So it is the Spirit of Christ, but Christ himself is filled with the Spirit of God.

This rallying force of God also drives Paul out on his missionary work from Jerusalem to Antioch. And it inspires the apostles in their resolution on the renewal of the Torah (Acts 15: 'It seemed good to the Spirit and to us'). A share in this mission, through the laying on of hands and the gift of the Spirit, is given to all the baptized, wherever in the world they allow themselves to be inserted into this movement of God's Spirit.

The word-field surrounding God's restless *Pneuma* which drives men and women towards the kingdom of God thus says something about the energetic character of God's immanence. We saw that we cannot imagine God's nearness as spatial presence. But we cannot imagine it as a kind of inside or other side of things either. We have to imagine it as a constant stream of energy and driving force which is also expressed in human beings and makes them share in the wisdom of God. This culminates in the appearance, the word and the wisdom of Jesus. There – and there alone, as Schoonenberg rightly states – it reveals itself as a power or support with which we can turn to God and towards God. Thus the Spirit itself comes to speak in us as a sigh and a longing for God. The Word and the Spirit of God both emanate from the Father, as the 'Source of Deity', by way of a divine extension which is perceptible to us as the divine energy of *Logos* and *Sophia* that flow together in Jesus and then emanate from him again.

Paul has to proclaim this dynamic gospel to Greeks. He demarcates the *Pneuma* from all that strives against it, all the *sarx*. The consequence of that was that in the long run the Spirit, the Holy Spirit, was spiritualized: it became abstract, remote from reality.

But in fact the question is not just that of this tension within the word-field *Pneuma*, which already takes on these Greek meanings within Hellenistic Judaism. Rather it is a matter of the additional definition of this *Pneuma*: the *Pneuma hagion* and *hagiosunes* which settles on Jesus. It is not the fact that a divine *Pneuma* is at work that is new to the Jews, but that the holy Spirit is effective precisely in the person and movement of Jesus and can be worshipped there: this is what is exciting, new and offensive. It is this *Pneuma* which makes holy, which settles on the disciples and afterwards on the Samaritans, and subsequently on those who are baptized from the peoples, blowing where it wills (John 3), taking all those who are baptized whither it wills. It replaces the presence of YHWH in the temple, is stronger than death, and makes possible the service of the one God among all peoples. The fruit of the Spirit is depicted in Gal. 5: love, joy, peace, mercy, patience. Paul sums up the gifts of the Spirit, the charismata, in I Cor. 12. Clearly Paul presents the indwelling of God's Spirit as a rise in the quality of human relations, as an elevation of their *koinonia*. It is the Holy Spirit of God which brings peace among individuals and among the peoples and which makes God's universal will for salvation known. As *Ruach* and *Pneuma* YHWH is not bound to any place, to any people, to any temple or religion. Thus the analogy of the breath of God on the one hand means the life-giving power of God and on the other the universal and constantly surprising radius of action of the divine inspiration and influence. Alongside this the Spirit is also the most direct channel of God's indwelling in human beings, of the *testimonium internum Spiritus sancti*: the sense of calling, of sanctification and of being able to look towards God. The Spirit speaks in us with sighs unutterable and in its workings within the community of faith is already a sign and a foretaste of life in God (*arrabon*) (II Cor. 1.22; 5.5; Eph. 1.14; cf. Rom. 8.23: first fruit).

We now need to rethink everything that I said about this in Chapter 5: God as *Pneuma* shows himself where the inviolable fragility of life is cherished, overshadowed by God himself; where human dignity is honoured, through tenderness and stimulation;

where violence is expelled and vengeance is tamed, and where love and righteousness dwell; where chaos is turned into peace and harmony.

Put this way, all this is probably terminology which is too alien to our culture. What is it then that this Spirit of the holy brings about among us, and how can we note something of it there?

THE SPIRIT OF GOD AND OUR LONGING FOR SPIRITUAL GROWTH

In our culture, which is orientated on achievement, production and reputation, with its complex demands on people in the public domain – we must not lose our concentration even for a moment – the call for inwardness, silence and repose is a strong one. It seems as if our 'self' comes into its own only when we have closed all the doors behind us, shut all the windows of our soul, closed our eyes, or at least submerged ourselves in the light intoxication of music, film, drink and eroticism. The label 'spirituality' is attached to this desire.[9] Spirituality, too, is on sale, in a separate circuit of therapies and techniques: here we can find ourselves, arrive at our own feelings, take off our masks, let go of our compulsive actions, and be purified and purged at the depth of our souls.

This colouring of spirituality is a remarkable extract from all kinds of currents which over the ages have sought peace with an often harsh existence and the assimilation of finite life at the level of an inner contact with the divine and with God. On the one hand there are all kinds of Gnostic currents in search of a secret key of wisdom and illumination, and on the other there are mystic and ascetical movements which saw the whole of life as a gradual rise to a union with God by various stages of purification and enlightenment. If the classical spiritual movements within Christianity all aimed at contact between human beings and God, the present-day movements which sail under the flag of the spiritual are concerned with the human self, though some like to identify the experience of the highest self with attaining the greatest loss of self in the Buddhist nirvana.

It is very tempting for theology to connect this call for spirituality with the Spirit of God. Isn't the story of Pentecost all about 'enthusiasm', 'daring' and 'courage'? Isn't it about the overcoming of barriers in communication and in relations with strangers? Isn't it about conversion and turning from our existence to the one thing that is needful and truthful and finding a new mission statement for our work and our relationships? Certainly, but it is also part of the core of the story that this enthusiasm does not well up from within, but has its effect from outside, as by a storm wind, as by a glowing fire and above all by the story of Jesus, proclaimed to the peoples. The mission statement of the Spirit of God has an extravert direction, towards God's good will for the peoples; not an introvert direction, towards the satisfaction of the human ego.

I am not saying anything here against the human need for inner rest and peace. But I am saying that it is a distortion of the workings and gifts of God's Spirit first of all to seek these within, and in the human heart. For apart from the fact that the Spirit of God comes from outside, from the Word of the prophets and Jesus, God's *Ruach* usually first of all creates unrest. Those who link the Spirit too closely with people's inner life more easily incur the charge of religious projection. What do we really perceive when we exclude all impressions from outside except for the murmur of our own blood, the delta waves of our brain, the enzymes of contentment? The reference to the creator God can still be made plausibly through the gratuitous, given, character of all that is. The reference to Jesus of Nazareth as God's messenger and the guide to God can be backed up by the special position that his figure occupies in the history of the religions. But with a reference to the Spirit of God we are moving on very thin ice, if the Spirit is connected with the inner experience of the self. The Holy Spirit as the God of introspection, of the ecstatic self, does not seem to be a very trustworthy form of God in an agnostic culture. Of course in terms of cultural history, in God and religion we have championed this 'self' too much as an autonomous psychological or rather psychosomatic reality for us to have to seek for God there, of all places: Darwin, Freud and Maslow would turn in their graves. Nor do psychology and pedagogy, in which the human self has become the subject of the discipline, make it easy to link spirituality with the Spirit of God. Moreover, those who seek God in himself keep coming up against the experience of death and semblance. Who am I? At the least a 'polyphonic self'[10] which is affected by the impressions, incentives, moods, challenges of others. I am a 'self' which cannot exist without a network of relationships and which therefore, if I am honest, knows that it can never completely coincide with itself. There is an evasive I, a will that time and again is caught up in a passion to transcend myself. Must God be sought in this lasting and restless desire to become someone other than I am? Does God come up from or does God loom up behind all human projects as the universal source of all eros, of all needs? And is that then the Spirit of God?

I do not think so. I would want to claim that if the call for more attention to pneumatology, to spirituality, means above all concentration on inner experience, it takes us away from what for centuries has been meant by the divine blowing of the Holy *Pneuma*. The image of wind and breath points to the active grasp of God which leads human beings to themselves, brings them to life, raises them from the dead, surrounds them with energy and fertility, stimulates them to speak about the glory of God and doing the will of God. Religions are not there for the culture of the 'deep self' of human beings, but to give an answer to the gift of life which withstands even death, and which also takes the human self beyond the depth of death. The rest is sentiment, ecstasy, imagination and dread. Thus God is not a God of our need for self-fulfilment, but the fulfilment itself of what we long for most deeply: to see ourselves saved beyond death. Those who kill that longing can dispense with God and be self-sufficient. They may then wager on the unbearable lightness of being and enjoy it as long as possible or devote themselves wholly to pleasure or to diminishing the suffering of others, especially those of the next generation, and so understand themselves as an offer of meaning in the existence of others who have no prospects. In both cases we are imprisoned in our cell mechanisms and the environments in which we live, with no perspective outside, no perspective beyond its demolition. The great entropy is then the only thing which remains for us to combat: to hold it off by living as long as possible. A long life and the durability of life on earth are the highest moral motives.

But if we fit in with the urge of God which comes to us from the call of others, which emanates from Jesus' mission statement about the governance of God and the *kairos* of the creating God, which time and again is new, which confronts us with the choice of the possible good, then belief in God's Spirit represents a permanent stimulus, a wind in the back, a pushing power: being carried forward on the breath of the Eternal One. This is precisely the way in which the Jewish and the Christian tradition understood and experienced the *Pneuma* of God as *dynamis* and *energeia*: as God who moves towards us, through the call of the truly holy.

It will become clear that the nature of this movement is of a different order from that of the analogy with the Aristotelian,

230

physical *motus* from which scholastic theology and also that of the Renaissance derived its imagery for God. Nor is the movement that is meant here that of the *appetitus* or *libido* which impels us in our passions and in our urge for survival. It is an impetus which works on us from the language and signs of the religious tradition: a call which prompts us to set a course for the possible good, to direct our motives and forces to the inviolable holy, a life that leads to God. Believers pray for this impetus. So it is not an automatism which goes along with the ontological *conatus essendi* (the striving for the appropriate form to which each being is directed), with the cosmic *élan vital* or with the dynamic of evolution, but an orientation which is woven into all that and thus also into our bodily existence. This is found in the fellowship of believers, through spiritual counsel, through a prophetic call, through forgiveness of sins and through the recollection of the wisdom of former days. The criterion and standard for all this is the *memoria Christi*, the messenger of God and guide to God which is governed by God's *Pneuma*. Indeed there can be no contradiction between Jesus' gospel and the call of the Spirit. Those who follow the course determined by Jesus have the wind at their backs. Those who take the way of Jesus come to spiritual growth and flourishing as they learn.

Here we do not need to leave thought at home or to exclude it. The guidance of the Spirit is not evident from what we call 'ecstasy of the spirit', from ecstatic song or speaking in tongues. There is no objection to exuberant singing or the infectious enthusiasm of believers, but this is not as such a sign of God's guidance. Paul already points to the need for interpretation, for joining up with – reflecting on – what has been handed down earlier and elsewhere. Belief in the Spirit of God does not, as I said, coincide with our capacity for thought, but it is not of course the irrational counterpart to it either. That God is also connected with human thought, and that thinking-God implies not a lesser but a sublime form of thinking, is the tenor of the whole of this book. But the tradition which speaks about the Holy Pneuma of God gives this thinking a perspective of its own, which also criticizes our own capacity for thinking. The *Pneuma* of God now and then makes the established images of thought – dogma, law, rites, institutions – fluid; it now and then opens up the windows of the church to let in a breath of fresh air (Pope John XXIII), and above all it frees us from a false estimation of the subject that thinks itself. The postmodern criticism of the autonomous subject, and the psychological

231

reference to the ecological network of relations in which each individual becomes himself or herself, form the fertile contemporary cultural soil for renewed speaking about the *Pneuma* of God. Criticism of the subject and the ecology of the self are the unknown gods of our days, where the mission of the gospel of Christians must link up with our Western culture.

Opening up the windows of the church also always includes opening up the windows of theology: to the living traditions of the other churches in ecumenical dialogue. Windows need to be open to the religious experience and reflection in other religions and to the content of an amorphous sense of aporia which is present even in an agnostic culture. We know the limits of knowledge, the indeterminacy of the self, the provisionality of the laws of nature and of justice. As Bloch remarked, we constantly move in the hollow space of the possible, in the useless passion for freedom which becomes useful precisely where it transcends the orientation of freedom on utility and concentrates on human dignity and human rights. In all these experiences of indeterminacy the urge of God's life-giving Spirit shows itself, guiding our thought beyond all possible limits, beyond the fear of the unexpected and new, beyond the fear of the other, and even beyond the lifelong fear of death. Isn't this disposition of humility and courage a quite distinctive foundation for the thought of believers, as we find it in the epic of Israel and of Jesus of Nazareth? And is it perhaps an appropriate answer to scepticism and fundamentalism, both of which kill thought in a mixture of arrogance and indecision? By humility we transcend the will to power, listening to the impetus which stems from what others and the other have to say, in an essential pattern of self-unfolding in intersubjectivity. By courage we transcend the bewitchment of the moment with which insight into our limitations and the limit of death confronts us and which makes us reach out for ecstasy and for the magic of every possible moment of pleasure. If nothing were to guide us but our will to domination and the use of pleasure, then the implosion of our culture would await us. If we allow ourselves to be guided by the impetus of God's *Pneuma*, the life of the age to come awaits us.

232

10

The One God and the Many Religions
The truth that enlightens all human beings[1]

An old story from Muslim theology – prompted by Surah 43.61 (old numbering) where it is said that Isa (Jesus) will be a 'knowledge', i.e. an advocate in the Hour (of God's judgement) – relates that at the last judgement God will allow three prophets to plead for humankind. Moses goes first. He pleads for all the Israelites, even for the sinners among them, and asks God for mercy on his people. God finds his plea credible and gives the Israelites salvation. Then comes Jesus. He pleads for all those who have followed him, from whatever country. God listens to him and all Christians receive salvation. Finally Muhammad has his say. He pleads for all human beings who accept the greatness of Allah and pray to him, who have listened to the holy words of the Qur'an and have not sullied themselves with unbelievers. All Muslims enter paradise and there embrace the Christians and the Jews.

The story shows that religions are ways[2] which finally end up with the same God. And the great figures around which the religious traditions are enfolded – Moses, Jesus, Muhammad and so many other teachers of wisdom – are not the examiners but the advocates of human beings before God. They plead, each for himself, for those who tried to follow their way.

There are many such stories in circulation, also in the Jewish and

233

Christian tradition, like Lessing's story of the three rings in *Nathan the Wise* or that of the famous Nestor chronicle from Kiev which tells the story of Vladimir's comparative investigation of the religions then known, from which he finally chose the Byzantine form of Christianity. This Muslim story also contains implicit elements of comparison. It is clear that Muhammad makes the most developed plea. On the one hand it is the most universal: it is not so much for his followers as for all human beings who have prayed to God and listened to the Qur'an; on the other hand it is the most clearly defined and clear: the only ground for exclusion is pollution from unbelievers. That sounds very strict, but here it is not a matter of doubt, agnosis or atheism. By unbelievers the Qur'an means the Arab polytheists, people with their household gods of utility and pleasure, success and prediction of the future, all those who live for the gods that determine fate and do not recognize Allah's power. So there is also polemic in the story – by comparison with present-day Western culture this is very topical. To serve God is anything but voluntary. But its most typical feature, which transcends the level of a comparative investigation, is that it presents Moses, Jesus and Muhammad as advocates of human beings before God.

Theology, which wants to maintain its narrative competence in a climate of religious pluralism that in the meantime has become radicalized, will do better to train itself in pleading for human beings rather than putting on the garb of the prosecutor. The Ecumenical Movement (especially in the form of the World Council of Churches since 1948) and the Second Vatican Council (1959–65) have adopted this attitude of pleading for human beings within Christianity after a history of intolerance: from Constantine to the Edict of Nantes in connection with those who think otherwise – with forced conversions, crusades, the Inquisition and the Holocaust as cruel consequences; from 1054 to the present day also in connection with the internal balance of power in the churches of the West through the strict regulation of the confession of faith, liturgy, morality and church order. This intolerance towards outsiders and mania for internal organization go together. Respect for many religious forms outside Christianity is coupled with an insight into the pluriformity of Christianity itself and of religions generally. This pluriformity is a consequence of different contexts, languages and cultures and of processes of assimilation and change over the centuries. Religions know not only fixed patterns and institutions which defy the centuries but also changing forms of expression and above all, time and again, new generations of narrators and those who hand down belief in God. Belief in God stands for a religious attitude which combines religious tolerance towards outsiders and more respect for the pluriformity of faith within each religious tradition, specifically out of respect for the living vehicles of the religious tradition; with a sense of the inadequacy of all human approaches to the mystery of God; and, as time goes on, also out of curiosity about and interest in the belief of others. The modern critique of religion thought that such respect and sense within the religions was barely possible. Wasn't taking leave of God and shaking off religion a better way of creating tolerance and peace? It must be said that the humanistic and civil currents did more than the religious institutions and theology to tame religious obscurantism and the wars of religion. First, the humanism of Erasmus and Hugo Grotius, the peace of Münster in 1648 and the secular ideas of the French Revolution, have created a *modus vivendi* which has become the basic law and constitutional starting point in the constitutions of the modern democratic states and in the United Nations Charter of Human Rights. But believers and churches too have taken part in this process, and we can see the humanism of Erasmus and Grotius as the best that the Abrahamic religions have brought forth.

PLURALISM AS A PATTERN OF LIFE

However, the present debate is about more than tolerance. A fundamental flexibility is required of men and women at the beginning of the twenty-first century, coupled with a great capacity for discernment. We have become aware of the constant metamorphosis of systems for giving meaning and of our own polyphonic self. According to Foucault, the second half of the twentieth century was marked by the increasing 'openness of things to criticism'.[3] Texts, laws, customs, relations between individuals, political parties and regimes follow one another at an increasingly rapid pace. Masses of people move every day from pillar to post and often play many roles at the same time. Men and women are involved in a subtle process of exchanging roles through reciprocal emancipation. Our pattern of life and the culture which surrounds us have become intercultural almost all over the world as the result of daily dealings with migrants and foreigners, of making the acquaintance of the cultural heritage and the sacred texts of Judaism, Islam, Hinduism and Buddhism and reflecting on them. In all the great European cities mosques and temples are rising alongside cathedrals, and on the sites of Christian churches which have been closed because of a lack of interest. This gives rise to a cultural and religious pluralism which not only calls for tolerance and respect for those who think otherwise, but also puts pressure on the certainty of its own experience and calls for a constant reorientation. Karl Rahner spoke of an epistemological tolerance,[4] though he was speaking in connection with the pluralism within Christianity: as a result of the complexity of things, our knowledge never attains a degree of absolute certainty. It comes into being only through conversation and dialogue from different perspectives: it is impossible for believers to be expected to agree with all aspects of the truth of faith. One can even speak of the 'essentially dialogical character of thought'.[5]

But this phenomenon is by no means a recent one. In both the Old and the New Testaments, Jews and Christians were aware of the other religions in their environment. Even before Vatican II the Christian tradition knew a theology of the religions which left space for the salvation of non-Christians: on the basis of the 'scattered seed of the Logos', 'sparks from the fire of the Spirit', on the basis of the 'universal revelation of God' to which all human beings 'of good will' have access on the basis of the doctrine of 'innocently erroneous conscience'. Even then it was known that 'there are more of other beliefs than there are Christians in the world. And these others are not dumb or blind.'[6] People boldly asked one another difficult questions: all the great religions are combinations of age-old images and rites, texts and symbols from the history of religion which have borrowed from one another in a constant osmosis. Perhaps 'borrowing' is not quite the right word; what we have are related symbols and forms of expression which transcend cultures and which are rooted in the universal experience of our contingent corporeality. In this sense the specific and distinctive features of the different religions can be terribly exaggerated. They lie more in the field of meanings and intentions than at the level of forms.[7] They have also corrected one another and there has been some evolution: for example, from polytheism to monotheism and from rivalry to dialogue.

However, that insight has often been obscured in Christian circles by a bad exegesis of the adage 'extra ecclesiam nulla salus': outside the church (my church) no salvation. This saying, which comes from the church father Cyprian, called on church members not to go and seek their salvation elsewhere, in order to preserve church unity and avoid schisms. Initially it did not refer to the opportunities for non-Christians to be saved. Moreover Cyprian's standpoint was soon challenged: when groups of Christians depart, they take with them 'elements of salvation' and 'traces of truth', and when they return from schism they bring these back again. So from the third century onwards the validity of baptism and other sacraments in schismatic groups was recognized. But along the lines of the medieval theocratic ideology of a *societas Christiana*, Cyprian's saying was nevertheless for a long time interpreted very literally and bore a trace of violence against those who thought otherwise.[8] On the basis of a return to the Christian and scholastic sources, Vatican II was able to renounce this ideal picture of the human pilgrimage, and from then on argue for a healthy competition of religions (e.g. with a view to liberation, solidarity and human rights); for extending circles of friendship; for the truth of God which enlightens all men and women. In the development of a new 'theology of religions', theologians have added yet other models to this: those of 'anonymous Christians' (Rahner), the 'eschatological' (Pannenberg, Dalferth) or 'provisional' (Duquoc) truth; the syncretism of the religions orientated on the cosmic Christ (Samartha, Panikkar: a synthesis in which the Jordan, the Tiber and the Ganges flow together, not by leaving their own beds but because the clouds of heaven draw from all these waters and make them descend on everything); the reciprocal process of teaching and the permanent interaction of the religions on the way to a 'global ethic' (Küng) and a liberating praxis (Pieris). I shall be returning to some of these models later.

Any talk of the election of Israel or the uniqueness of the church is the outcome of an argument after the event which in faith affirms the special character of the way of Israel or of Jesus, more out of wonderment and perseverance than as a result of the notion that this must be the usual or the only way to salvation. The question of responsibility for one's own choice of YHWH Elohim or of following Jesus in fact went along with the faith of nomads, exiles, diaspora Jews and persecuted Christians as an existential task. Sometimes this led to disapproval, but often it was more a matter of troubled belief in one's own cause and a legal contest with the God of Israel: the people grumbles about its God. In particular, belief in the one God for all human beings must time and again be defended with arguments against the seductions of dualism, because of the phenomenon of evil: belief in one good God does not square with the experience of evil, suffering and catastrophe. And belief in

237

God's universal presence and activity also seems time and again to have to be set aside in the face of all kinds of polytheism: in the face of the experience of the complexity of the factors which determine us as powers and forces. Thus the choice of YHWH, the One, remains a risk, a matter of expectation which can be confirmed only by God himself in the eschaton.

Indeed it is also part of the heart of Jesus' preaching as this is reconstructed by Matthew (Matt. 5–7) and Luke (Luke 6.17–49) in the great speech by Jesus – the Sermon on the Mount or the Sermon in the Plain – that the final judgement on good and evil is reserved for God: do not judge, so that you will not be judged (Matt. 7.1); hypocrite, first take the log out of your own eye, then you will see sharply enough to be able to take the splinter out of your brother's eye (Matt. 7.5; Luke 6.42); wheat and tares must grow up together until the harvest, so that expensive wheat will not be taken for tares (Matt. 13.24–30).

The Inquisitors, and already Innocent III and Gregory IX, interpreted this advice from Jesus in their own way: the church has to prevent the tares from choking the wheat and the enemy, the devil, from sowing tares among the wheat (Mark 13.25–40). They also applied literally the prophetic words of John the Baptist (Luke 3.9) and Jesus (Matt. 7.19; cf. John 15.6) about cutting down and burning the trees which do not bear good fruit. Here, and with all the religious persecutions which have emanated from Christianity, they not only overplayed their hand – conversions cannot be forced; schisms cannot be healed with violence; martyrs strengthen the self-confidence of opposition groups – but also forfeited the credibility of the gospel of Jesus. The antipathy to this violent orthodoxy is now universal, and the confessions of guilt about this dramatic past have not in fact cleared the air in the churches.

There is something else in our situation. We are not confronted simply with the existence side by side of the different religions and the problem of how they relate to one another. As a result of all kinds of factors, within each religion we have far greater flexibility of action and a certain relativization of our own tradition. We no longer have a more or less academic comparative investigation of the religions, as was the case at the beginning of religious studies in the nineteenth century, but an intensive process of osmosis and relativization, which no one escapes.

Historical criticism has made us familiar with the gradual growth of all kinds of dogmatic insights and has exposed the changes of paradigm: within Judaism and within Christianity, as in other religions, there have been successive but also contemporaneous currents, trends, accents and wings which are the echo of changing contexts and also of a growth in critical reflection and of specific reform movements. Really it is better not to want to capture people's specific convictions and modes of action in great schemes. Is perhaps the terminology which speaks of the great religions of humankind itself a dangerous construct, which pays all its attention to texts, attitudes and religious leaders, but loses sight of the faith of believers?[9]

Finally, new hermeneutical methods have drawn attention to the context in which everything is written. Structuralist insights into the interaction of text and reader, and postmodern ideas about the way in which all knowledge is constructed, have taught us a hermeneutics of suspicion: often what we read is just not there. All these insights require theological reflection to be far more flexible. It is a matter of dealing with pluralism as an ongoing ecumenical learning process which works its way through in catechesis and liturgy and which does not fail to have an effect on the way in which people shape their faith in prayer, behaviour and the giving of meaning. Those who exclaim all too quickly that nowadays people collect their own package of faith in accordance with their own insights forget that down the ages people have always been able to make only a limited number of configurations from the rich arsenal of religious experience and religious imagery.

Thus pluralism has many faces, which vary from a happy tolerance and curiosity about the strange other, through the excesses of a global market culture which gets entangled in fatal strategies of differentiation (Baudrillard),[10] to reactionary phenomena like relativism and fundamentalism.

THE INTENTIONS OF VATICAN II

At a crucial moment of church history the Second Vatican Council sought to give direction to Catholic Christianity in a variegated process of teaching which we have witnessed. Especially in the Declaration on the Relation of the Church to the Non-Christian Religions, *Nostra Aetate* (combined with paragraphs 14–16 of *Lumen Gentium*); the Decree on Ecumenism, *Unitatis Redintegratio*; the Declaration on Religious Liberty, *Dignitatis Humanae*; and the Decree on the Church's Missionary Activity, *Ad Gentes*, there were new and creative definitions of the position of the church on those with other views: believers of other churches, people who have adopted other religions and views of life, and even atheists. These documents must be read together, but also in connection with the options of *Gaudium et Spes*. Together they form a unique charter of respect and tolerance starting from the central thought that the truth which people seek and with which some associate the name of God is a truth that enlightens: in other words, it is a truth which is wholesome, brings joy and makes peace. Anything that robs people of their joy, quenches their light; anything that brings war and despair, is in conflict with the truth with which God's name can be associated. This is embodied in the person of Jesus himself, the unique messenger of God, who was murdered at human hands but is a living being who speaks as well as possible for us, who has entered the very life of God. So the important thing is not for the truth of the gospel to glitter or shine or get applause but for it to orientate us and help us. The shining truth of Jesus Christ illuminates the true and the good, and all human beings who seek, and thus can never compete with it. Here is a characteristic quotation:

> All men form but one community. This is so because all stem from the one stock which God created to people the entire earth (cf. Acts 17.26), and also because all share a common destiny, namely God. His providence, evident goodness, and saving designs extend to all men (cf. Wisd. 8.1; Acts 14.17; Rom. 2.6–7; I Tim. 2.4) against the day when the elect are gathered together in the holy city which is illumined by the glory of God, and in whose splendour all peoples will walk (cf. Rev. 21.23ff.). Men look to their different religions for an answer to the unsolved riddles of human existence. The problems that weigh heavily on the hearts of men are the same today as in the ages past. What is man? What is the meaning and purpose of life? What is upright behaviour, and what is sinful? Where does suffering originate, and what end does it serve? How can genuine happiness be found? What happens at death? What is judgement? What reward follows death? Finally, what is the ultimate mystery, beyond human explanation, which embraces our entire existence, from which we take our origin and towards which we tend? (*Nostra Aetate* 1)

As long as these are real questions, and not rhetorical or catechism questions; as long as Christianity also allows these questions without establishing the definitive answer, there can be no question of triumphalism, secularism and intolerance. On the contrary, there is a competitive quest for the mystery of God in Hinduism, Buddhism, Islam and last but not least in Judaism (*Nostra Aetate* 2–4). In particular from Jewish theologians since Vatican II we have learned that God cannot be fixed to our images and definitions of God. There is more: intolerance does not fit with the key data of belief in God, the Father of all:

> We cannot truly pray to God the Father of all if we treat any people in other than brotherly fashion, for all men are created in God's image. Man's relation to God the Father and man's relation to his fellow-men are so dependent on each other that the scripture says 'he who does not love, does not know God' (I John 4.8).

Here it is not just a matter of love for fellow human beings regardless of their views, but also of the particular forms and cultures which other religions can offer to the glory of God and which, according to *Nostra Aetate* 2, must be recognized, valued and encouraged:

> The effect of her [the Church's] work is that whatever good is found sown in the minds and hearts of men or in the rites and customs of peoples, these are not only preserved from destruction, but are purified, raised up, and perfected for the glory of God, the confusion of the devil, and the happiness of man. (*Lumen Gentium* 17)

This attitude of respect is first of all a simple human duty, resting on the freedom of religion as a human right.

> The Vatican Council declares that the human person has a right to religious freedom. Freedom of this kind means that all men should be immune from coercion on the part of individuals, social groups and every human power so that, within due limits, nobody is forced to act against his convictions nor is anyone to be restrained from acting in accordance with his convictions in religious matters in private or in public, alone or in associations with others. (*Dignitatis Humanae* 2)

The only appropriate limit or restriction that the text mentions is the condition that the just public order may not be attacked (ibid. 2 end, 3 end and 4 beginning). No one may be compelled to act against his or her conscience; no one may be hindered from acting in accordance with his or her conscience, precisely because the nature of the act of faith involves an inner and free act of the will which cannot be imposed or forbidden by human authority

(*Dignitatis Humanae* 3 and 10–11). That also entails freedom of religious upbringing, and free choice of school, assembly and gathering in accordance with religious convictions. In keeping with the principle of love the principle of fundamental human freedom is invoked here: 'According to this principle man's freedom should be given the fullest possible recognition and should not be curtailed except when and in so far as is necessary' (*Dignitatis Humanae* 7).

This general principle of tolerance and responsible freedom is made concrete in the example of Jesus' own activity. With a reference to the parable of the wheat and the tares it is stated:

> He [Jesus] did not wish to be a political Messiah who would dominate by force (cf. Matt. 4.8–10; John 6.15), but preferred to call himself the Son of Man who came to serve, and 'to give his life as a ransom for many' (Mark 10.45). He showed himself as the perfect Servant of God (cf. Isa. 42.1–4) who 'will not break a bruised reed or quench a smouldering wick' (Matt. 12.20) ... He bore witness to the truth (cf. John 18.37), but refused to use force to impose it on those who spoke out against it. His kingdom does not make its claims by blows (cf. Matt. 26.51–3; John 18.36), but is established by bearing witness to and hearing the truth and grows by the love with which Christ, lifted up on the cross, draws men to himself (cf. John 12.32). (*Dignitatis Humanae* 11)

Bold proclamation must therefore be coupled with respect for those who cannot or cannot yet believe (ibid. 11). The unique character of Jesus' message, person and fate is not in conflict with this universal and positive character of the truth: his gospel brings together disciples from all peoples and breaks down the dividing wall between Israel and the nations. That could only happen in the name of God himself, and it also determines the content of the name of God as Abba and Pantocrator in a purged universalism. Jesus is the unique witness and messenger of God's universal loving kindness and of the criteria of God's governance and kingdom, according to which he will judge all men and women as the Son of Man. Love for the weak, patience, mercy and forgiveness, are among the most important criteria of this gospel, which is unique precisely in the fact that Jesus' fate is bound up with the realization of these criteria: it is precisely here that he shows himself to be the beloved and anointed Son of God, the servant of YHWH. The universalism purged by the Christ event makes no reference to cosmic and ontological concepts of unity and truth, but calls specific men and women in particular circumstances to join together in freedom in a historical movement which is personally addressed to all individuals among all peoples with a specific call about behaviour and relationships to God (Matt. 28.18–20). All that is true and holy which has been discovered by religions and cultures can be used for the 'inculturation' of the Christian call, but it also has its own value for the 'competitive quest for the mystery of God'. In particular the three 'Abrahamic traditions' supplement one another and correct one another at many points. In the Decree on the Church's Missionary Activity we read:

> Finally, by this missionary activity God is fully glorified when men fully and consciously accept the work of salvation which he accomplished in Christ. By means of it God's plan is realized, a plan to which Christ lovingly and obediently submitted for the glory of the Father who sent him in order that the whole human race might become one people of God, form one body of Christ, and be built up into one temple of the Holy Spirit; all of which, as an expression of brotherly concord, answers to a profound longing in all men. And thus, finally, the intention of the creator in creating man in his own image and likeness will be truly realized, when all who possess human nature, and have been regenerated in Christ through the Holy Spirit, gazing together upon the glory of God, will able to say 'Our Father' [there are references to texts by Irenaeus, Hippolytus, Origen, Augustine and Cyril of Alexandria]. (*Ad Gentes* 7)

What the church of Christ intends with its mission can thus only be that what all human beings long for most deeply and for that reason alone is universal, common to all of them:

> Both Christ and the Church which bears witness to him transcend the distinctions of race and nationality and so cannot be considered strangers to anyone or in any place. (*Ad Gentes* 8)

But this discovery implies a history of critical reading of all kinds of expectations of salvation and is consummated only in God's time and way:

> It purges of evil associations those elements of truth and grace which are found among peoples, and which are, as it were, a secret presence of God; and it restores them to Christ their source ... (*Ad Gentes* 9)

Specifically that means testimony in dialogue and solidarity with the human quest (*Ad Gentes* 11–12), without which evangelization and conversion remain barren and lack credibility. All forms of proselytism, of malicious propaganda and impure motives for conversion are rejected (*Ad Gentes* 13).

SEEKING TRUTH: THE UNIQUE TASK OF JESUS

Between the false certainties of fundamentalism and the apparently non-committal attitude of scepticism lies the sure and certain way of those who seek the truth. 'Christian theology does not just interpret texts; it asks about truth itself and it sees man (and woman) as capable of truth ... If it is functioning correctly, Christian theology is to be seen as a force of enlightenment.'[11] The only question is that of the nature of this truth which is to be attained. An old scholastic adage defines belief as an adhesion to the truth in bearing witness, a desire to strive for it: *adhaesio veritatis tendens in ipsam*. Vatican II again brought the Christian churches into dialogue about this truth to be sought, and thus freed the church from its absolute claims to truth. The readiness for ecumenical dialogue and conciliar discussion with all sister churches is a sign of growing *koinonia* and even a characteristic of the true church. As exegesis of the New Testament shows us, the church of Christ consists of a plurality of churches which together bear witness to him who is the way, the truth and the life and which are thus themselves on the way to the full truth to which the Spirit of God will lead them: the revelation of the glory of God.

The truth which is spoken of here is not an abstract rule or law, not a solution to the riddle of the world, but a way which is taken in the footsteps of one man who as messenger of and witness to God consistently took this way at the risk of his life. The bizarre good news of the Christian gospel consists in the proclamation of the fact that a crucified man, the victim of the truth-claims of others, was made by God the light of the nations. It is not his insights into the riddle of the world, his exalted morality or his heroic martyr death which make him unique: many gurus of wisdom, many sceptics, a whole calendar of martyrs for the good cause of God accompany him on his way. Not even the confession of his divine origin or his enthronement at the right hand of God makes him unique: many religions know such figures.

He is unique in that God has made this seed of Abraham, this son of David, this teacher of Israel, the definitive spokesman and loyal executor of his eschatological governance. Simply because of the message and the praxis of the kingdom of God, heard concretely by his disciples as the fulfilment of Israel's call among all the people, Jesus is unique: the first and only one, of whom it can be said that as a human being he has fulfilled the whole of God's will, has acted to the death entirely in accordance with God's standards. To confess that remains a risk, a choice which does not exclude contradictions, but rather provokes them. The uniqueness of Jesus is a uniqueness and once-for-allness which is confessed and believed and which, paradoxically enough, can be seen only in following him.

Over recent decades, in the light of the pluralism which has been sketched out above, a good deal has again been said and written about the uniqueness of Jesus as the Christ.[12] How can the conviction that in him the governance of God has been revealed and that in him all can experience redemption and salvation from God be compatible with respect for other ways to salvation? How must Christians in Asia or Africa explain their choice of the way of this messiah to their fellow countrymen and women?

EXCLUSIVISM, INCLUSIVISM, PARALLELISM?

In a sweeping way the different positions have been set out on a scale which ranges from exclusivism to inclusivism. In the first instance the strong conviction is cherished that the ultimate salvation of human beings and the world, the true aims of God's creative action, are guaranteed only by access to the community of Christ's church: *extra ecclesiam nulla salus*. God saves only those who have been converted to Christ, or, more specifically, the members of the community who adhere to this faith. Where that is interpreted in strict terms we can speak of Christian fundamentalism.

We use the term inclusivism when there is an approach to the figure of Christ as a universal or cosmic point of orientation for all those who seek God. Then all religions realize in an implicit, anonymous, hidden, partial or even unconscious manner what God has revealed explicitly in Christ as a way to salvation. Teilhard de Chardin[13] already sketched an image of Christ as the outcome and prophetic fulfilment of the evolutionary process of life in accordance with which all religions will finally converge in the omega point. After Vatican II, above all Karl Rahner[14] worked out this notion: without knowing it, the non-Christian ways to salvation gradually fit in with what God intended in Christ. Rahner's imagery, initially welcomed as an encouraging basis for dialogue, was later criticized as a disguised Christian imperialism or as saying little, because all religions in practice could claim the same thing. Raymundo Panikkar[15] has improved Rahner's model by not speaking of anonymous Christianity but of the reciprocal interpenetration or perichoresis of the notions of salvation or images of Christ in all living religions. In a 1986 survey article he uses the image of the flowing together of religious source experiences or streams of tradition for this. Thus the Christian tradition springs from the faith of Israel – symbolized by the river Jordan – and then allows itself to be shaped by the culture of Greece and Rome – the water of the Tiber – after which it tries to drink in the Asian experiences of the transcendent – the water of the Ganges. This is not an attempt to add the these three currents together in one tradition, far less to dam one stream or the other, but to make the water that they carry to the sea descend on all men and women as purified rain. Thus according to M. M. Thomas[16] and S. J. Samartha[17] one can speak of a 'Christ-centred syncretism'.

One objection to all these models is that Jesus' title Christ is almost reduced to an abstract function of God's universal will for salvation, a quasi-metaphysical, sometimes almost Gnostic, dynamic, a universal human myth. The concrete history of Jesus, the fact that his career ended up with his execution, that his followers also encountered strong opposition and that time and again Christians could not accept particular religious notions and rites (the discontinuity of gospel culture), all too easily disappears over the horizon. Moreover, Jesus' unique relation to God, expounded in the doctrine of the incarnation and in the dogma of Chalcedon, as the only basis for his decisive authority (*exousia*), on the basis of which he may and will gather all around himself, is in practice put in brackets, as A. Denaux[18] argued.

All attempts which begin from a kind of competition of the religions on an equal footing, finally to be judged by God, must be seen as lying between the two extremes, or as an attempt to escape this dilemma. I have already mentioned the stories from the tradition which take such a parallelism as their starting point, like Lessing's parable of the three rings. But Wolfhart Pannenberg's theology of religions[19] seems to start from a similar eschatological, theocentric approach, though he now thinks that he can subject the religions, on the basis of the criteria of the kingdom of God revealed in Christ, to a provisional historical critical judgement. Hans Küng,[20] too, argues in a similar way: for him Christianity is intended by God to be a catalyst of the best religious ideas which have been brought to birth in a centuries-long tradition of experience. Indeed the concrete form which Christianity will still assume in dialogue with other religions on the way to God's kingdom also shares in this process of purging. The religious dialogue carried on by the World Conference of Religions for Peace (WCRP) also starts from this model.

This parallelism can degenerate into religious relativism in the sense of a fundamental pluralism of an epistemological kind, as this is defended by John Hick[21] and his followers. They argue that to suppose Jesus of Nazareth, Buddha, Muhammad or whoever to be unique is meaningless. Uniqueness is the result of a particular choice and attribution of meaning by believers; it is not a quality or category of judgement to be established in an objective and unpartisan way. Such preferences are culturally defined and reflect the distinctive religious experiences of a particular group. However, all religions give answers in their own way to the same question about the Infinite, the Real, which transcends cultures. All are also to be characterized as doctrines of salvation or soteriology which in the situation of finite human beings are in search of some form of improvement. Their worth can be measured only by this 'soteriological effect'. According to Paul Knitter,[22] this soteriological effect lies in the contribution of the different religions to social, economic and political liberation and solidarity between people. He thinks that none of the great religions can bring about such liberation by itself. Therefore those religions and those elements in the different religions are most valuable which are an incitement to shared commitment to justice, peace and freedom. Theologians like Aloysius Pieris[23] from Sri Lanka and Michael Amaladoss[24] from India think in this direction.

The question is whether we can escape from this 'trilemma' of exclusivism, inclusivism or parallelism by a more historical and concrete approach to the religions at the moment in which they actually come into being. I would want to call that a kairological approach.

God and history, God and nature, can encounter each other only in the contingent historical event from which the epic of a concrete tradition of faith derives. Only with this approach does it make sense to speak of God's revelation. Here Christianity speaks about incarnation, but also about the descent of the Spirit on Jesus, the indwelling of God, about epiphany and transfiguration and finally about the enthronement and parousia of Jesus as the Son of Man.

Other religions speak of the overshadowing of the prophet, of illumination, of the descent of wisdom. The notion of incarnation within Christianity thus does not stand by itself, and is not without parallels in other religions; however, it does have specifically Jewish and Hellenistic traits, like the connection with the Servant of YHWH songs (Jesus as the representative of the suffering people) and the *Logos* doctrine which expresses the supra-temporal and universal dimension of Jesus' appearance. In the course of the centuries the doctrine of the incarnation has been focused too much on one point: the relationship of the divine to the human nature in Jesus Christ as an ontological paradox (Council of Chalcedon 451). In fact it is about the much wider question of the way in which God can relate to the reality which we experience and know, in which God cannot be seen, touched or located, yet is near to us and bound up with us, as we are with God. The Japanese theologian Katsumi Takizawa calls this the Immanuel principle: that we cannot think of our self and God's self independently of each other, and cannot affirm the independence of the cosmos without confessing the reality of God which supports everything.[25] It is part of the narrative competence of the religions that they can have ideas about this relationship to God which could contribute towards forming a hermeneutical or narrative community. Concrete figures, *dramatis personae*, are the actors in such a configuration. Just as the fortunes and visions of Abraham and Lot, Moses and the Pharaoh, Saul and David, Isaiah and Jeremiah, Ezra and Nehemiah determined the configuration of Israel's community of faith, so too the path of Siddartha Gautama and his companions in their rise to Enlightenment determined Buddhism, and later Muhammad and his family determined Islam. The scriptures which recorded and interpreted their fortunes and which furnished the structures for the later faith communities of Israel, Buddhism and Islam are not just historical or legal protocols or a series of sketches for sermons and wisdom sayings. According e.g. to W. Cantwell Smith[26] and K. Schori,[27] they form a library of scenarios and episodes which, though culturally conditioned, are still a drama of the human quest for the overcoming of the aporias that life itself presents to us which can be communicated between cultures. They are about the scarcities, the dangers, the joys, the needs, the longings, the relations, the happiness and suffering; about conflicts, violence and death. Behind all that, and in the midst of the aporias, people call on their God for redemption from their lives or an extension of them, for recognition and acceptance, for direction and meaning.

Thus the Jesus movement, too, can be seen as an epic woven around his life and death,[28] as a cycle of configurations and scenarios about what happened to him and his disciples in their quest for reformation within the Jewish pluralism of their days, as an invitation by God which goes beyond frontiers, a God who brings together from all nations what has been dispersed and divided 'that all might attain salvation' (*Nostra Aetate* 4). This is the intuition in faith which the great religions share from the start and which has put them in a position to unite people from many tribes and languages: it is what Paul Knitter calls the 'unitive pluralism of the religions'.[29] It is precisely here that in human terms the uniqueness of the way of Jesus lies: in his concrete encounters with John the Baptist, the Galilean fishermen, the Samaritan woman, the tax collectors Levi and Zacchaeus, the Pharisees and Sadducees, the Roman occupying forces, Herod and Pilate, Mary of Magdala, Peter and John, Thomas and Paul. Precisely as the one who is merciful, patient and tolerant, in these encounters he is the Ebed YHWH, God's servant and anointed, the Christ. His way is unique because his concrete biography is unique, differing from the epic of the other religions of humankind. Of course he is also the Son of Man, who sits at the right hand of God and who will judge with divine authority at the eschaton, but wholly along the lines of his earthly encounters. The criteria of God's judgement are announced in his gospel and expounded in parables. The direction of God's governance is clear from the whole history of Israel and the life and fate of Jesus. But the ways towards God's kingdom differ; which one is to be followed depends on the circumstances, along the many scenarios of his encounters and parables. These form an open texture for this encounter, in which we see God's true face, though still veiled. These ways for encountering God cannot be taken without constant reorientation and conversion. Thus God is incarnated in the history of humankind, and thus we encounter God in Jesus in a way which is unique yet different in every age.

Nowhere is the unique, i.e. definite and universal, way of Jesus, in which God reveals himself in his own way as his God, thought of as being exclusive, nor is it thought to be able to remove all the problems in the world. Far less is it thought that the way that people take with other expectations of salvation are meaningless detours or dead-ends. Outside Israel, too, Jesus finds great faith – sometimes greater faith than in Israel. Buddha and Muhammad, Lao-tse and Socrates, also offer us a maieutics of the divine purposes with humankind. Like Buddha, Muhammad, and many

Asian and African gurus and prophets, but unlike Moses, Socrates or Lao-tse, Jesus forms his own community of disciples and invites them to distinguish between what is true and good, between what leads to life and what to death, and between those of whom it can be said 'Blessed are they ...' and those of whom it can be said, 'Woe to them ...' Thus pluralism is indeed the starting point of the Jesus movement, but it is not its end, and the same is true of Buddha and Muhammad. If things were different, the Jesus movement would be robbed of its *ekklesia* character, just as Buddha would lack his vehicle and Muhammad his mission or jihad. It would fritter away its narrative competence, which is based on the kerygma of God's salvation laid up for all. That has consequences for the ecumenical movement, for dialogue between Christians and dialogue between the religions generally.

The pluralism of the religions is a given fact. But no single great religion which understands itself as the way to salvation can abandon the claim to be the true way. Belief in God which abandons any claim to universal truth would be a contradiction in terms, as if the truth about God applied only to this particular group or as if by definition 'a better God' could be found. The idea of God itself is compatible with an epistemological or methodological pluralism, but not an ontological or eschatological pluralism of the truth.

RELIGIOUS FREEDOM FOR THE SAKE OF THE TRUTH

That belief in God can be authentic only out of conviction and in full freedom and thus has to be based on freedom of conscience is a U-turn which had still to be fought for vigorously at Vatican II.[30] This freedom of religion and emphasis on the persuasive character of faith in God is deeply based on a hermeneutical insight: that all religious traditions are the result of witness, interpretation and communication. What we call 'religious traditions' or 'religions' in fact always comprise a multiplicity of views, notions and forms of behaviour which change depending on time and place. The challenge of fear, compulsion and violence in matters of faith is a healthy outcome of this insight. At the same time this freedom of religion is interpreted by some – especially Christians engaged in the study of religions (Hick, Knitter, Swidler, Cantwell Smith) – as the abandonment of any truth-claim whatever. The epistemological insights of postmodernism reinforce this tendency, as does the osmosis of views of life in the communications culture of the media. What remains of universal truth – and thus of universal rights and responsibilities – if history does not have an objective *telos*, if the bearers of ideas and values (the subjects of history) are simply the constantly changing product of so many ideological constructs: imprisoned souls (Plato), thinking things (Descartes), self-creating workers (Marx), travellers in the here and now (Nietzsche), brokers in intoxication (Bataille), heroes to the death (Heidegger), players in a truth game (Gadamer), links in the micro-mechanics of power (Foucault), subjects of the kingdom of appearance (Oosterling)? What has happened to human beings themselves, that they experience their own autonomy and freedom as illusion and deception, their subjectivity as slavery to the meta-stories? Is it true that we are left with only the experience of displacement, movement, change, *différance*? That we live for the kick of the different, the alien, the surprise? And does fundamentalism arise as nostalgia for the fleshpots of securism, physico-theology, occasionalism: the clear idea of God as the author of all that is the case? Or must we let ourselves be lulled by the Gnostic sounds of New Age, the journey within, the gentle powers of alchemy and the alternative therapies: the sweet herb of stupefaction, because no other herb works any longer against our despair?

It is clear that the call for religious pluralism is more than a plea for toleration and dialogue. It is the echo of a deep scepticism about the course of modern culture which is based on the will to know and the use of pleasure (Foucault). Science and technology come up against the limits of the circulation of matter and energy and cause the entropy that they sought to overcome. The mechanisms of economic and social guidance for the free movement of persons and goods in a limitless market come up against all kinds of congestion. The psychoanalysis that was sought to release the self from obsessions leads to an industry of happiness which is itself proving traumatic. The international politics of peace and security for nation states still gives rise to cruel wars and has not been able to exterminate by constitution and respect, even in Europe, the ethnocentricity that it sought to challenge. Everywhere in the theology of the last thirty years there has been a cry for contextuality, for polycentricity, for local theologies, but the ecumenical movement is stagnating because of shameless proselytism and undisguised theocratic nationalism.

Is there a way between fundamentalism and scepticism? Is freedom of religion for the sake of the truth possible? The question is, rather: What is religion about? In the face of absolute scepticism on the one hand and a dangerous fundamentalism on the other, in the face of both naïve scientism and just as naïve esotericism, Descartes and Derrida in particular can teach us that a creative age, true concern with questions, longing, despair and aporia bear more traces of the infinite and holy than the sceptics or the fundamentalists, the technologists and the therapists, are willing to concede. Shouldn't that also help to open up our view of actual religious pluralism? Isn't the aporia into which our comparison of the religions is leading us itself a signal, a trace of the *Deus semper maior*, the God ever greater? I shall sketch out some aspects of an answer to the question.

The Jewish-Christian tradition from Genesis to the Book of Revelation has a far more aporetic character than Western systematic theology has generally wanted to concede. It lives more by the desire for truth than the possession of it. Thus already within Israel there is a long tradition of the theology of religions, of a sense of religious pluralism. This tradition goes back to Genesis (the stories of the second blessing on Ishmael, on Esau; the story of Abraham, Lot and Abimelech; the story about Abraham's role in the community of the nations); to the prophets who are not afraid to attribute a messianic role to non-Israelites like Cyrus. In the New Testament there is the appearance of Jesus, who says that he finds great faith also outside Israel; and there is Paul's Areopagus speech, which uses non-Christian religious feeling as a step towards the gospel of Jesus (Acts 17). In the footsteps of the church fathers and medieval theology, Vatican II used the image of the human pilgrimage, of a healthy rivalry of religions, of extending circles of affinity, of the truth of God which illuminates all men and women.

The scenario and episodic structure sketched out above, in which the great religions, including Christianity, present their way towards God's purposes, leaves plenty of room for aporia. However, the questions of bystanders are given with the narrative as real questions. Nor are the questions of the protagonists, for example of Jesus himself, disguised in it. Amazement and wonderment about the way in which he deals with the tradition, the quest for what he had to do, the confrontation with the expectations of salvation which were alive at the time, the protest against current religious patterns, the search for new forms of prayer, doubt about the course of things: all this forms part of what we have come to call 'gospel', *bissorah* – the bizarre story of someone who was condemned to death, who dies with only a few despairing supporters and who nevertheless seems to issue a call in the name of God himself and with the authority of the Son of Man.

Indeed inter-church and inter-religious dialogue is about real problems and not about rhetorical questions, about authentic choices and not just about supposed misunderstandings. It is about 'the unsolved riddles of human existence' and 'the ultimate mystery which embraces our entire existence' (*Nostra Aetate* 1). It is about searching together for rules of behaviour which 'reflect that truth which enlightens all men', 'rejecting nothing of what is true and holy in (other) religions' (*Nostra Aetate* 2). That is a never-ending process in which Jews, Muslims and Asian religions each contribute valuable answers. With them, 'the Church awaits the day known to God alone, when all peoples will call on God with one voice and "serve him shoulder to shoulder" (Zeph. 3.9)' (*Nostra Aetate* 4).

The way of a healthy pluralism is therefore found in the experience of conciliar dialogue in the ecumenical movement, in the interaction of convictions in a pluralist society which amounts to a sharing of orientations and laws based on democracy: that of the configuration of new heuristic purposes like those of peace, justice, concern for the environment, equality in human relations, tenderness, inwardness and a sense of vocation and destiny. Tolerance cannot be built on negative forces like demythologization, secularization or indifferentism, but only on respect for the sovereign other, on wonderment and curiosity about what has not yet been conceived and still is unknown; on awe at the inviolable holy, gratitude for the gratuitous gift of life, mercy for those who do not attain the norm, patience with those who have not yet found their way. All this together forms part of a culture of pacificism and opposition to violence which is finally grounded in the very being of God: for in God there is no violence. According to Vatican II, truly to be children of the Father who is in heaven presupposes 'that Christians "conduct themselves well among the Gentiles" (I Peter 2.12) and if possible, so far as depends on them, are at peace with all men (cf. Rom. 12.18)' (*Nostra Aetate* 5).

The *de facto* pluralism and increasing exchange of ideas and values in the culture of communication which surrounds us and into which we are woven, as into a world-wide web of ideas, offer unique opportunities for such a culture of pacifism and tolerance. The colourful nature of the world discussion does not get in the way of the competition over the truth. But the truth loses its shine where it is not found in freedom, just as freedom loses its significance if any quest for the truth is denied.

As so often, this whole argument already seems to be summed up much more succinctly in God's Holy Scripture, in the words of the prophet Zephaniah (3.9–13):

> Yes, at that time I will change the speech of the peoples to a pure speech,
> that all of them may call on the name of the Lord, and serve him shoulder to shoulder.
> From beyond the rivers of Ethiopia
> my suppliants, the daughters of my dispersed ones,
> shall bring my offering.
> On that day you shall not be put to shame
> because of the deeds by which you have rebelled against me;
> for then I will remove from your midst your proudly exultant ones,
> and you shall no longer be haughty in my holy mountain.
> For I will leave in the midst of you
> a people humble and lowly.
> They shall seek refuge in the name of the Lord,
> those who are left in Israel; they shall do no wrong
> and utter no lies,
> nor shall there be found in their mouth
> a deceitful tongue.
> For they shall pasture and lie down,
> and no one shall make them afraid.

11

Infinite God: Towards a God who Allows Himself to be Thought

> Theologians must go from the present context to the sources of faith; otherwise they speak in a wilderness.[1]

> Faith and reason fulfil a reciprocal critical function from which we cannot but benefit.[2]

The public audience of the theologian no longer consists of believers who seek better insight, but rather of people who do not believe, no longer believe or do not yet believe, for whom the question of God is an annoying one, or at best a matter of curiosity. Curiosity makes all kinds of religious ideas from different religions interesting to people. However, the Christian theologian needs to demonstrate the plausibility of faith in God by way of Jesus Christ and not to presuppose it. More than before, all theology has taken on the character of fundamental theology. Theology plays on the language of the plea in the human lawsuit about God. Moreover that is none other than the duty to give an account of the hope that lives in us which the New Testament (I Peter 3.15) imposes on Christians.

THREE POSITIONS IN A RECENT DEBATE

After Immanuel Kant had stated that it was in principle impossible to know God except for practical purposes as the bearer of the moral imperative, first Feuerbach and then Bauer, Jean Paul and

Nietzsche had proclaimed the 'death of God' for theology. Where Feuerbach still saw an alternative in the identification of God with the immortal consciousness, the infinite will and the inexhaustible discourse of human beings, with the disappearance of the idea of God Nietzsche also saw the cohesion of things in metaphysics and the coherence of human nature in anthropology disappearing over the horizon. What remains is only the pure will to power and the appropriation of every moment. What remains is the will to know and the use of pleasure (M. Foucault). Since that time philosophers – with some exceptions (like Blondel, the Neo-Thomists, Buber, Jaspers, Tillich, Marcel and Levinas) – have only spoken of God with slight embarrassment or have occupied themselves with arguments about the end of religion (as have Sartre, Merleau-Ponty, Adorno and Habermas). In 1957 Heidegger wrote in his programmatic article about the eclipse of classical metaphysics as onto-theology:

> Anyone who has experienced theology – both that of Christian faith and that of philosophy – from an adult source [Heidegger had a Catholic upbringing behind him] today prefers to be silent about God in the realm of thought.[3]

As van Veghel[4] has shown, that was more than a call for a provisional moratorium in philosophy or fundamental theology. Perhaps one can read the text as taking note of a respectful silence in the expectation of a God who must show himself. But in any case it was an authentic call to break with the onto-theological argument of classical metaphysics,[5] which has to be replaced with an analysis of *Dasein*. From now on the concrete, bodily, finite and historical existence of human beings in nature and history needs to be the only starting point for at least philosophy: the domain of pure thought in search of the truth of being which is disclosing itself.

The few philosophers of the transcendent who were not content with Heidegger's horizontal transcendence of *essents* in search of shining Being sought God in the utopian content of history or the evolution of humankind, like the 'death of God' theologians of the 1960s. Others, like Rahner, tried to show that Heidegger's moratorium on thought about God in his analysis of *Dasein* was extremely inconsistent because Christian anthropology intended precisely the same thing as Heidegger, namely to lead people into shining Being. The name of God had to do with precisely that.[6] So Heidegger's philosophy could be quickly reforged into fundamental theology, even though philosophy thought it to be false coinage. I grew up with this theological re-reading of Heidegger. It had its effect. At all events I have retained the conviction that God does not diminish human beings and that true religion can never be in conflict with the ideals of authentic humanity.

In current philosophical discussion of the image of God – of the necessity and the possibility of speaking about God in the realm of thought – a certain confessional pattern can be recognized:

- There is the plea for a metaphysics and anthropology 'from below' which begins with human experience and then indicates the 'open places' (through parables and paradoxes, through analogy and aporia, through wonderment and bewilderment) which are interpreted as traces of God or questions to God. Theologians and philosophers who adopt this position want to go along with one another as long as possible in what is called philosophical or fundamental theology, out of respect for the questions of human beings, the mystery of things, or as a counterbalance to dogmatic fundamentalism or a positivism of revelation which posits God and proclaims belief in God as an incredible task and leap towards the light. In this position, which is adopted above all by Catholic thinkers, there is a refusal to oppose faith and reason, faith and knowledge. But methodologically the Reformed defenders of the 'philosophy of the idea of the Law' – the pupils of Dooyeweerd – take the same line, though they do not draw the same conclusions about God and the world.

- There is the plea for involvement in the contrary character of the Jewish-Christian tradition as an independent religious phenomenon which criticizes and corrects the Western philosophical tradition that has emerged from Hellenism as a whole, and within it especially the metaphysical framework and the theistic idea of God. The 'Supreme Being' characterized by omnipotence, omniscience and omnipresence, the first cause of all that is, is both a moral and an intellectual failure: it offers no solace for human misery; it adds nothing to the scientific explanations of the cause of things. Of course supports are sought in the criticism of metaphysics in modern theology (e.g. Bataille, Heidegger, Levinas and postmodernism).

- Finally, there is the more detached and analytical approach, verging on a methodological agnosticism, to talk of 'God' (God in quotation marks which cannot be removed), its logic and the consistency of religious language. These philosophers of religion are concerned to expose truth and untruth in talk about God, to distinguish between faith and superstition, by conceptual and semantic analysis of the argument. The dialogue with those of other views is one of the specific approaches to the possibility of discovering common criteria or true or tenable (plausible) images of God. The quest for usable models for the relationship of and to God and for the consequences which flow from them is another. This line is inspired by German and Anglo-Saxon philosophy of religion, often of an orthodox Calvinist stamp.

TAKING LEAVE OF METAPHYSICS?

The two last approaches are dominated by a certain antipathy to the classical approach through the metaphysic of being. The question *'An Deus sit?'* is no longer answered in terms of a relationship to beings, being and the ground of being, but in terms of the action of God, the consequences of the idea of God, the traces of God in the category of reality itself, the narrative counterpoints of the conceptual system, the open and loose ends of the contingent. God does not lie so much along the line of expectations, and therefore does not belong in the sphere of the causal, the systematic and the necessary, but is associated with the experience of the unexpected, the unthought, the future (but not the utopian). So God does not belong in instrumental reason but is found in hermeneutical (Ricoeur) or substantial reason (Adorno).

De Boer[7] demonstrates this possibility by means of Levinas. Levinas disqualifies the notion of 'being' by speaking about it as the anonymous, lugubrious *'il y a'*, the chaotic background noise against which my existence takes place; the phantom pain which I can feel in sleepless nights or if I am sick. Being is something like the packaging of the *essent*, the placenta which is left behind, from which things and human beings emerge, become independent and strive for the good and the divine 'beyond being'. God has nothing to do with the dark world of *'il y a'*, apart from illuminating beings and leading them to the good. Such a disqualification of being so that it becomes a hedge for beings has marked dualistic traits, and labours under anthropological predeterminations which do not fail to have an effect on the image of God. All beings come into being through a divine call, by being called out of the indeterminacy of being and illuminated. The rest is left behind unused and apparently rejected. So it is no longer the case, as it is for Boethius, that 'All things are good in so far as they are.' Rather, 'All things are beings in so far as they are good.' For Levinas, God clearly stands on the side of the good, especially on the side of victims and those who suffer under the evil of the wicked. For him and also for de Boer God is clearly a God of retribution and anger. We hear little of a vague metaphysical Supreme Being for whom all cats are grey or whom we would have to praise because righteous and unrighteous alike are cared for and spared. In their eyes such a God is the God of the powerful and of criminals who do not admit the notion of retribution into their consciousness. But how this divine retribution can be thought of is not said. As in Kant, the angry God is the postulate of practical reason.

Over a number of years Adriaanse[8] has tried to analyse the idea of God by a purely phenomenological method on the basis of human talk about 'God', while at the same time keeping open the possibility of an ontologically referential object of that talk. Anyone who answers the question of an ontological object of that talk is going beyond the sphere of knowledge and moving along the way of religious belief. However, that form of thinking which becomes conscious of the boundaries and limits of thought and of where the movement of transcendence begins is right at the limit of knowledge and belief. 'God' is at least the name for the utopian margin of the world, the limit of the ego, the call which proceeds from the other and which limits my unjustified freedom. Adriaanse himself speaks of a post-theistic, post-ontological philosophy which on the one hand wants to do full justice to the narrative quality of the religious traditions – in which the unspeakable resounds in the story without ever being swallowed up in it – and which on the other hand will never abandon the critical norms of philosophical reflection. He follows Habermas, Ricoeur and Levinas.

Brümmer,[9] who for a long time has devoted himself to the philosophical conceptual analysis of talk about God – among other things through a series of investigations into the traditional 'properties' of God – finally wants to demonstrate the plausibility of the idea of God by means of the model of love. In that model God is alternately the lover and the beloved. The ambivalences of existence – suffering and evil – are interpreted as relational phenomena of distance and remoteness. In this model the metaphysic of being plays no role because everything is thought of in the dynamic terms of relationship and association.

Vroom[10] investigates, from a comparative perspective, the connection between Asian and Western conceptual thinking about

God and transcendence, the self and its determinations. Religions are not static, but constantly borrow from one another and together build on that part of the full truth which is not yet seen. Here there can be no question of a predetermined metaphysical nucleus; all the different ontologies of Europe and Asia are too diverse for this. Ontological talk in terms of abstract and universal properties of God leads to a kind of higher arithmetic and a detached God, shut in on himself, who no longer troubles with anything or anyone. This abstraction is brought about by an abandonment of the narrative frameworks into which the religions have put thought about God. However, unlike de Boer, Vroom is also critical of these narrative traditions: there are good and bad stories. Therefore theology and the philosophy of religion cannot avoid the question of truth: 'If one gives up rational and critical talk about the "narrative tradition", one is trivializing the choice between them. If there are no criteria for a good view of life, all may think as they will: the neo-Nazi, the defender of the caste system, the liberal capitalist, the feminist, the patriarch, and those who fight for the environment.'[11] It is specifically in critical dialogue about religious ideas, rites and narratives that in the long run the truth about God will shine out.

TRUTH AS CONSTRUCT: THE WORDPERFECT LOGISTICS

Perhaps these three forms of philosophical thought about God are still too optimistic. The postmodern pronouncement of the death of the *humanum* and the subject and even the farewell to the last straw of being, Heidegger's ontology of *Dasein*, have thus at first sight made the chances for the philosophical question of God very small, if they have not destroyed them altogether. Now that the subject as collector of being and meaning is dead, everything has become pure construct and predicate, and all that we are left with is the endless sifting of what is said. Being has again become a copula, a meaningless way of linking statements, leaving behind Aristotle's conviction that the metaphysical content of the copula 'be' changes with the nature of the subject and the predicate and their mutual relationship. Laws, instruments, language and finally logic are based on agreements that we can construct, deconstruct and reconstruct: there is the status of philosophy which has staked everything on its power of judgement.[12] Of course there are still the antinomies and aporias, there are the last remnants of existential anxiety in what remains of the once so glorious adventure of Being towards Death. But truth is no longer thought, cannot be thought any longer (Gadamer). What remains is the need for consensus over procedures (Habermas), protocols of preaching, agreements about naming. In a culture dominated by WordPerfect every sentence (= *sententia* = judgement) becomes a question of text processing and the logistics of parts of sentences: open, delete, rename, move, print, restore, view, new directory, copy, search. 'Find' becomes the all-defining and meaningless search-pattern of the humanities. But the key question remains: are there objects which we can view but not edit? Are there objects which offer themselves to us, give themselves to us? Isn't there a referential object (Schori) which defines the direction of our statements, however variable, partial and pluriform they may be, which regulates our power of judgement and distinguishes the true witness from a false witness (Betti versus Gadamer, Havel versus Habermas)? Must we after all reckon with traces of a liberating God, as E. Borgman argues, even within the domain of thought?

DOES GOD ADD ANYTHING TO THOUGHT?

According to Wilhelm Dilthey (1833–1911), following Immanuel Kant, at all events it is not the case that religion provides some kind of knowledge which could not be got in another way, without religion. Religion is not meant to satisfy our concern for knowledge.[13] By this Kant meant first of all that faith and knowledge are each of a different order and that knowledge has to be autonomous, independent of the statements of the church and with no reference to divine revelation. He did not mean to say that religion is therefore irrational, or has nothing to do with knowledge or thought. Nor does Dilthey say that religion lies outside the sphere of thought; he says that religion does not provide sufficient new knowledge, that it therefore leaves him unsatisfied, and that in the end he also wants to test religious experiences scientifically. That is the echo of the nineteenth-century argument from religious studies which sought to map out God and religion historically, philosophically, and afterwards also psychologically and sociologically: comparative religion, the critique of religion and the psychology of religion have left their traces here, one after the other. Dilthey's programme for religious studies is aimed at exposing the distinctive scholarly status of the study of aesthetic, ethical, historical and religious experience in competition with the natural sciences, which have been so successful. Here he wants to do a service both to scholarship and to life itself, which is full of these experiences – at all events fuller than of the abstract principles of mathematics and the natural sciences, with which the so-called exact disciplines work. With his hermeneutics of life Dilthey opened people's eyes to the importance of the everyday course of things in life and society and thus prepared for the phenomenological method, the philosophy of language and existentialism. His approach is still important for the status of academic theology. If Schleiermacher – who died in 1834 – tried to make room for belief in God in the sphere of religious feeling – thus contributing to the view of religion as a private matter and as 'beyond reason' (thus Locke) – Dilthey brought religious experience back into the public domain of the humane sciences. Neither Schleiermacher nor Dilthey could find favour in the eyes of the church's dogmatic theologians. Both were rejected by Barth because neither of them seemed to do justice to the fact that God can make himself known only by revealing himself and because both begin from an anthropological foundation, and so do not find an origin in religious experience and the idea of God. But Dilthey offers far more points of contact for theology than Schleiermacher. For him there is no reason 'to keep silent about God in the realm of thought' or to 'banish God to the realm of the disposition and the feelings'. We should not be surprised that when Catholic hermeneutical theology could deploy itself fully after Vatican II, it sought to make contact more with the hermeneutics of Dilthey than with those of Schleiermacher: especially in the Catholic tradition from the early apologists through Augustine and scholasticism, the starting point had always been the link between faith or knowledge or the assumption that they were not contradictory.

What Dilthey says about faith and knowledge is important in yet another way. Faith – also in its public form as religion – will not and cannot add anything to the realm of knowledge. Our need to know is not satisfied by faith, but that is not at all necessary. The will to know is autonomous and innate in human beings. Belief in God is not: that remains a free choice which does not replace knowledge and is not in conflict with it, but is subject to it in so far as this choice needs to be accounted for to others. Where faith becomes irrational and boasts of its own access to the realm of knowledge with a reference to the unveiling of divine mysteries, Dilthey has to protest. However unique religious experience is, it is not to be reduced to an ethical, aesthetic, historical or psychological experience, though it cannot be had apart from such experiences – it does not differ from the others by wanting to or being able to escape reflection.

In fact, in my view those who try to take refuge in the irrational as the sphere of religion and as a 'dwelling place for God' adopt a more dangerous course than those who want to make belief in God plausible for thought. Even the classical proofs of God can do less damage than a flight into the phantasms of the imaginary and the occult, the self-constructed God of inner light and mystical experience – which is always uncontrollable. It already leads to the most dangerous superstition there has ever been: the thought that I myself am an angel, a God at the depths of my thought, a super-ego, the ultimate goal of all that exists.[14] It is this 'gospel according to Maslow' that has for a time replaced the religious culture of shame and fear (*la religion de la peur*) – and with good results. However, having degenerated into a new religion it is now emanating its therapeutic radiations over us lonely postmoderns as New Age thinking: Seek yourself, brother! Know yourself, sister!

To seek God on the way of thought, in utter respect for the autonomy of all human knowledge, is a weapon against caprice and superstition. Those who submit to this do not submit to a power hostile to God, provided that their thinking continues to remain aware of its open and dynamic character. The idea of God is the most powerful epistemological key for opening up thought in the direction of the possible, of freedom, the good and the infinite. I want to demonstrate, in three stages, that the tradition of the God of Abraham, Isaac and Jacob is healthier and more salutary than the widespread narcissism of our culture, and that God can indeed be thought about, albeit in a different way from that of classical theism.

- I shall first go rather deeper into the concept of modernity and sketch out the background to the postmodern critique of it.
- Then I shall try to rehabilitate Descartes, who in my view has wrongly been declared the scapegoat of Western culture, both by postmodernists and by Pope John Paul II.
- Finally I shall sketch out four ways of thinking – along the lines of Descartes' concept of God – in modern theology and philosophy which perhaps could bring about a certain change of imagery in relation to God in our thought.

MODERNITY: FROM THE 'FOUR IN HARNESS' TO THE 'THREE IN HARNESS'

The concept of modernity is based on the autonomy of instrumental reason, in other words the capacity to weigh, measure and count the sphere of human life; on principles of fair distribution – as much happiness as possible for as many people as possible, as little suffering as possible for as few people as possible; and on the fundamental equality of all men and women in politics: in other words, government with reference to the historical course of things. Technology/science, rational ethics and political democracy form the three most important pillars of the modern system, the three horses in harness with which according to positivism the work has to be done. The fourth horse that had pulled the carriage of culture up to the Enlightenment – the philosophical order of being, coupled with the theological infinite origin and determination of human beings in God (what Heidegger called the four in harness) – is written off here. It has died a gentle death (Feuerbach); unfortunately it has slipped away (Nietzsche); we have to detach ourselves from it because it put too much of a brake on progress (Comte, Marx, Freud, Habermas).

For a long time we overlooked the fact that the three which remained in harness – technology, ethics and politics – still fed on the oats of religion and followed just as ideological a course, i.e. a course determined by particular desires and ideals. The postmodern critique of technology, ethics and politics as a play of interests and as a construct of reason has made a serious attack on the illusion of an objective, universal and therefore authoritative modernity.

Thus believers and non-believers, Christians and those of other faiths, have together landed up at a truly critical point in human history in which we finally want to recognize our own role in the construction of ideals and ideas, values and norms. I want to make it clear that here there are just as many reasons to maintain the ideals of a critical modernity as there are to maintain a critical faith in God after the manner of Abraham and Jesus.

From the Renaissance on we have supplemented our knowledge of God and even the idea of God with the paradigm of causality, more specifically in accordance with the model of mechanical causality, in other words the force of gravity. God formed the conclusion of all the laws of nature, and the laws of nature formed the starting point for our thought. Thus we thought the creation to be a product of God: as cosmos which turns in his hand, as history the course of which is already determined. We found certainty in what is naturally the case. In reaction God became the Great Force and Power in nature and history. God was 'the Absolute', the First Cause, the Governor of All, the One who is Necessary and Immutable. For those for whom the reference to God's mechanics was too foolish – and after Newton, the more time went on the more difficult that became, although Newton still maintained that there was a *deus ex machina*, a fine tuner of the universe – there was still an organicistic approach. For Spinoza, for example, God coincided with the one great Substance of nature in which everything connects with everything else, everything takes place according to fixed laws which go beyond human understanding and on which we try to exercise historical influence in vain and only to our detriment. We also know in our time the descendants of this mechanistic or organicistic view: Whitehead and the process theologians who maintain a refined mechanism of divine 'occasions'. Or there is the esoteric tradition of 'holism', which we meet in all kinds of forms of New Age. And there are all the views, especially the Asian views, of nature or life as the 'body of God'. Scientists who want to continue to believe in God can no longer be at ease with a God who fills the gaps in their knowledge. But they experience a 'God' as a codeword for the mystical cohesion in nature as a romantic duplication or at best as poetry. 'God' remains within quotation marks as the expression of a particular type of feeling and emotion which can quite well be understood and experienced without the codeword 'God'.

The whole of this system of thought, which as a system of world history (Hegel) or consciousness (Kant) aimed at the unity of our fragmented experience of life and which had to form a framework of comfort and hope in the midst of all suffering and distress, has been shaken by the postmodern critique of history and subjectivity. There are only players in a game, only phantom movements of history, only fragmentary decisions in the midst of the excessive aporia, only little biographies and no 'great story'. Responsibility for any hope no longer seems possible.

For many people this critique is liberating because it rescues us from the pressure of systems, from totalitarianism and dogma, and because in making it we get an eye for the special and the peculiar aspects of everyone's views and modes of behaviour, of separate cultures and contexts. But perhaps it also leads to what Alain Finkielkraut[15] has called the decline of thought, and in any case to an absurd individualism, relativism and tribalism in which the strangest characters can again unload their mythical stories about individual and national 'salvation'. The German political theorist Otto Kallscheuer[16] has pointed out that in the postmodern critique of modernity the devil is being driven out by Beelzebub. So we must go back to a point in our history of European culture which lies before the so-called dialectic of the Enlightenment. It seems to me that this is to be found in the much-maligned Descartes.

DESCARTES: ANOTHER WAY OF THINKING

It was Spinoza's contemporary and opponent Descartes who in his *Meditationes Metaphysicae*[17] showed another way. He did not deny the laws of nature; he was himself a great mathematician and natural scientist. He is rightly regarded as the pioneer of modern scientific thinking, which seeks to test everything and lives by a fundamental methodological doubt. But at the same time – and this is often forgotten – he saw that another type of knowledge was possible in which God did not coincide with all of natural necessity but could be thought of in terms of what was surprisingly possible within it: a knowledge of the ever more perfect and the infinite. Here was a God not of power and might, but of infinite freedom and love. Descartes associated that firmly with the concept of the Infinite and the restless questioning and searching of human beings. Here is a quotation from the third meditation (*Of God; That He Exists*):

I shall now close my eyes, stop up my ears, turn away all my senses, even efface from my thought all images of corporeal things, or at least, because this can hardly be done, I shall consider them as being vain and false; and thus communing only with myself, and examining my inner self, I shall try to make myself, little by little, better known and more familiar to myself. I am a thing which thinks, that is to say, which doubts, affirms, denies, knows a few things, is ignorant of many, which loves, hates, wills, does not will, which also imagines, and which perceives ... [I]f I look at these ideas more closely, and if I examine them [all] ... I find very few things there that I perceive clearly and distinctly: viz. magnitude or extension in length, width and depth; figure, which is formed by the limits and boundaries of extension; position, which bodies of different figure maintain among themselves, and movement or the change of position; to which can be added substance, duration and number. As for the other things, such as light, colour, sound, smell, taste, heat, cold, and the other tactile qualities, they are to be found in my thought with such obscurity and confusion that I do not know even whether they are true, or false and only apparent, that is to say, whether the ideas I form of these qualities are truly the ideas of real things, or whether they represent to me only chimera which cannot exist.[18]

Thus it already emerges from the analysis of our ordinary perception that we make only 'cuts' of reality and that much remains vague and unnamed. In the 'journey within' which Descartes describes in his *Meditations*, he does not stop at the *'expérience interieure'*, that I am the one who thinks and thus exists, but at the same time embarks on a confrontation between this inner experience and the outside world, the *res extensa*. The dualistic reading of the tension between inner and outer and the objectivizing exposition of the 'thinking thing' (*res cogitans*) as the source of the rationalism of the Enlightenment do not do justice to what Descartes intended. Even while it is thinking, the I is always situated, but that also applies to thought.[19] In fact all that is finite is simply a human limitation of infinite possibilities. Anyone who sees that can say:

> ... that I have in me in some way the notion of the infinite, before that of the finite, that is to say the notion of God, before that of myself.[20]

As soon as I 'detach' myself from the things that seem to dominate me, I also experience myself as a limited 'case', a 'framework', and thus also a 'limit case', a *chora* at the intersection of infinite possibilities and longings (and in this sense Descartes is a postmodern *avant la lettre*):

> [H]ow would it be possible for me to know that I doubt and desire, that is to say, that I lack something and am not all perfect, if I did not have in me any idea of a more perfect being than myself, by comparison with which I know the deficiencies of my nature? ... [T]his idea [of God], being very clear and distinct, and containing in itself more objective reality than any other, there is no other which can be of itself so true, or which may be less suspected of error and falsity. This idea, I say, of this supremely perfect and infinite being is entirely true; for although perhaps one may pretend that such a being does not exist, one

cannot nevertheless pretend that the idea of him represents nothing real ... And this does not cease to be true, although I do not understand the infinite, or although there be in God an infinity of things that I cannot understand, nor perhaps even reach in any way by thought; for it is in the nature of the infinite that it should not be understood by my nature, which is finite and restricted ...[21]

It is not the understanding, far less the failure to understand, but the awareness of the question, of the doubt and desire, which then leads to the acceptance of God and the rejection of the notion that human life and thought are closed in on themselves, as in a kind of *perpetuum mobile*. As Descartes puts it:

Now, if I were independent of all other existence, and were myself the author of my being, I should certainly doubt nothing, I should conceive no desires, and finally I would lack no perfection; for I should have given myself all those perfections of which I have in me some idea, and thus I should be God.[22]

Descartes then knows that every day human beings project their existence on the morrow, without having any real reasons for doing so or without being able to control the causes. Then he refers to the fact that every day we are put in a context, 'woven' into it, and that the human spirit is 'moulded' like wax by its bodily circumstances, as a result of which materially very transitory but culturally immortal phenomena come into being which are infinite in the sense that they can never be as if they had never been: their influence extends unfathomably deep into the depths of history. Our actual finitude, all our questions and quests and desires, are thus the signal, the trace, of an infinity of possibilities that embraces us. That is God, or rather: that has always put human beings on the track of God.

It is this movement of thought which has become difficult for many people, because they are caught up in what Horkheimer and Adorno call 'instrumental rationality': how with the help of the things that surround us we build up our lives in order to live in them, as in an enclosed house. How we allow ourselves to be regulated by the facts under the cloak of the here and now, the wealth of differences, the chances of fate, the rules of the game. And how in the long run we begin to experience our bodily nature – our fragile existence between cradle and grave – in a 'manipulating existence' as an instrument of such a controllable rationality. The ease with which in their messages the media include eugenics and euthanasia alongside therapies for sex and relationships and all kinds of advertisements for health and the good life bears witness to this 'instrumentalization' of thought.

The more time goes on, the less space there is for the other kind of thinking, seeking and interpreting, meditative and – in this sense – inner thought, for what I call hermeneutical rationality. And thus God too becomes obscured from our sight because the thick cloud of our fixations on the bite-sized chunks of our manipulable life and viable society gets in the way of our infinite longing and the infinite God, as a kind of cosmic grit which obscures all the light of heaven (Buber called it 'the darkness of God').

The reaction of those who want to remain at this meditative moment, who turn away from thought, close their eyes and begin to burrow into the archetypes of their inner experience, or try to invoke the dark night of the senses in imitation of the mystics, is indeed understandable, but it is just as alienating from the Jewish and Christian tradition. Christian faith will have a future only if we again get an eye for this view of the infinite and the infinity of God which Descartes meant. Four contemporary thinkers can help us here.

IDOL OR ICON: JEAN-LUC MARION'S PICTURE OF GOD

In 1982, Jean-Luc Marion, professor in Paris and specialist in the philosophy of Descartes, wrote his first major collection of articles with systematic reflections on the question of God, *Dieu sans l'être*.[23] He followed Heidegger in the latter's critique of classical metaphysics and what Marion called the *discourse theiologique* about God which took place in it. Here God is made the conclusion, sum, outcome and limit of thought, Anselm's *id quod maius cogitari nequit*, Leibniz's foundation of the universe, the thinking subject itself, which coincides with the whole of reality as it takes place (Spinoza), or at least the creator and first mover of the consciousness (this is the way in which Descartes is often interpreted), or the conscience (Kant).

Now of course it would be attractive if we could prove that the God whom we have killed was none other than this theological deity, so that there was room for a better God, for the true God. It would be attractive if we had then rejected none other than the God of causality, consciousness and morality, so that there was room for the God of love, relationship and inner light. The liberation of God from the sphere of thought of Being would again bring more room for beings and for God. Nietzsche himself already kept this possibility open and Heine spoke of the Enlightenment as a gift of God in which God had freed humanity from its false religion.

But it is not so simple to liberate God from Being as long as we are not in a position to liberate Being itself from its embedding in factors and its identification with beings. It is even more difficult to liberate thinking of God from the notion of a pre-existent Being which is there before anything comes into being. Such Being of God 'before all ages' stamps God as a timeless Supreme Being and time as an episode in a heavenly existence which is otherwise undisturbed and calm.

The alternative is not an irrational idea of God outside the domain of thought. A God who could not be thought of in one way or another could have no meaning, no relationship, because our thought lives by making connections and recognizing meanings. What Jean-Luc Marion aims at is to bring God within the domain of thought without making a reference to the ontological difference; in other words, without referring to Being as something 'behind', 'above' or 'among' beings. He too opts for the movement of love here: God can be conceived of as love. Love is nowhere separate from beings who love; God cannot be abstracted from them as a form of Being and can never be materialized as an object.

Marion is concerned above all with this last, when it is a matter of reassessing the idea of God. God needs to be removed from all notions as one independent being, as a hypostasis. But God also needs to be removed from the notion that God could coincide with Being pure and simple. Marion calls both idolatry. Referring to the Greek church father John of Damascus and the Second Council of Nicaea in 787, he then works out the difference between *idolon* and *eikon*. The former is the three-dimensional statue, the latter a depiction on a flat surface. The Council of Nicaea in 787 prohibited the depiction of God, Jesus or the saints as statues, but allowed a depiction on a flat surface. Seven years later, at the Council of Frankfurt in 794, Charlemagne decreed that statues in relief were also legitimate. In the West, this concession led to statues being detached from the wall and leaving their pedestals, to be set up in churchyards and market places and on the tops of high hills. For Marion this difference, which also underlies the alienation between the churches of East and West, is the metaphor which gives him a view of a God-who-is-not, who precedes being and opens up being to constantly new possibilities. The free-standing statue attracts attention, is the focus of attention. The icon gives the viewer attentiveness and points to something else, a higher quality of being. It discloses and at the same time conceals the mystery to which it points, while the plastic statue 'is what it is'. But this difference becomes even clearer when we look at the metaphor behind it. Thus Paul, too, calls Jesus the icon of the invisible God: God never makes an appearance in Jesus. However, Jesus constantly invites those who encounter him to the world of God. The icon invites those who look at it to direct their view to something beyond the representation. The idea is that of a symbol which constantly transmits. According to the Catholic theological tradition, that applies to the sacramental signs which bring about what they depict without the elements of which the sign consists forming part of the result. Bread and wine are the elements which together with the narrative of Jesus' Passover meal bring about the link between believers and God and the presence of the risen Christ among his followers without this being the consequence of eating and drinking them as a vegetative process. They function as an icon, a transfer point for the encounter with God. Something of the same thing also applies to some concepts, as Descartes shows in connection with the concept of the infinite: it does not carry along the one who imagines it to something that is rounded off, but to an open intention: the concern not to limit. In this connection Marion speaks of a hermeneutics of the icon.[24]

Thus the concept of God is also a transitional concept: it produces distance and proximity at the same time; it transfigures thought, it identifies nothing or no one: the image is not God, God is not the image. The name 'God' is not God, but brings us to the thought of God; more, it takes our thought to God; it brings us, depending on our intention, to God, or rather it adds our intention to the intentions of God. A loving relationship does the same thing between two human beings. Their bodies, their loving looks, their kisses, their intercourse, are not their love, but point constantly to their love; or rather, they drive them further on the way of their love. Now God is something like love: a movement to and fro between creator and created, with an eye to further love.

What has happened in the development of Western thought is not so much the distortion of God to the degree that God becomes a factor in nature and history or the moral guarantor of law and virtue, as the forming of an image of God which requires a distinctive standpoint, a distinctive space that claims a time of its

271

own and requires a cult of its own. God as effect and as verb – as in the name YHWH – has been replaced by God as a hypostasis and independent noun (*ho theos*) which – to use Jaspers' term – is the reification of what was meant as an icon, as a transitional concept.

So what we must rediscover are the 'windows', the moments, domains, symbols or configurations in which this passage to the divine and the holy can take place without God being localized in them, where entities become transparent to being, where words, concepts, dreams, experiences, become vehicles of the more-than-ordinary. They are not part of *la pensée calculatrice*; together they form *la pensée méditante*. In the imagery of my word-processor, we must seek circumstances which can be viewed but not edited.

Only if we may interpret the concept of God as icon can we liberate 'God' from his quotation marks. If 'God' is only a code, a function for evoking the conditions to be worked on – 'God' as the supreme value, or as the Fine-tuner of the universe – then the positivists are right who think that theologians deceive all true believers because they use 'God' only as a duplication of their historical and moral projects. If 'God' has to go on standing between quotation marks in the sphere of thought, then any other code which cannot suggest an iconographical meaning is better. On the other hand, the quotation marks would have to remain if by them we meant the deconstruction of the idol god: the quotation marks then say something like 'whom we call God', knowing that God himself cannot be named. But even then we occupy a standpoint in respect of God; we remain on the outside and do not allow ourselves to be taken up by God as an icon; we do not really think with God in the direction of God but think only about God, so that once again God can be understood as a hypostasis. But God is not a hypostasis; God is not an entity among entities or the sum total of all that is. Only by omitting the quotation marks and allowing ourselves to be taken along the distinctive way in which God associates with us; only by thinking that all will to power and self-preservation, on the basis of which we think of beings as hypostases, is alien to God, can we prevent the hypothesis God from becoming meaningless.

SYMBOL AND SACRAMENT: LOUIS-MARIE CHAUVET

The French theologian Louis-Marie Chauvet[25] points to another trace of God: not so much in the nature of our thinking as in language. In the midst of all that is, language – and the symbol in general, for language is not limited to spoken or written texts – has a special function: it contributes something, it mediates something, which cannot be derived from its material substratum (loudness, signs, stimuli). Significance, experience of meaning, emotion, summons and orientation are offered to us as a kind of surplus (Paul Ricoeur calls it *surcroît de sens*) over and above what we register with our senses. The symbolic interaction among human beings, and between human beings and things, which leads to culture is thus itself already an unexpected, gratuitous gift which is not contained in the physical nature of things and does not coincide with it anywhere: its products – for example in art, politics or play, but also in religion – surround us as a universe of symbols which clothes us like a second skin. In the sacraments of the Jewish-Christian tradition this symbolic universe is concentrated on the core moments of life. The water of baptism may be ordinary H_2O, but it does not just wash the body; it cleanses the whole person for a new life. The bread and wine of the eucharist contain virtually no calories, but they mediate the connection with the risen Christ who sits at the right hand of God and make his presence tangible in a transfigured metabolism. We eat and drink a *pharmakon athanasias*, a medicine for eternal life. The oil with which people are anointed at baptism and confirmation, in sickness and dying, massages them to become supple people who allow themselves to be kneaded into the image of God. And the laying on of hands connects people with the circle of witnesses of all places and all times who share in the same mission and blessing from God. Through these sacraments we become aware that we may rejoice in God's favour. But that does not happen by way of causality, as if there were a direct, quasi-mechanical 'outpouring' or 'infusion' of divine power, a magical working 'from on high'. Here we have 'another epistemological terrain of the activity of thought'.[26] This is the domain not of causality – which indicates a chain of events through which things are determined and fixed, where we have more of the same thing – but of the symbolic, which indicates a direction and an intention 'forwards', in which time and again new perspectives open up: 'the symbolic is ... a process of happening which is never finished, so that there is always further to go.'[27] Thus love is never a finished product, but is a lasting orientation on love which at the same time 'takes up' the lover and the loved into its affects. It is ahead of us who love, just as the symbol with its meanings is ahead: it makes us think. We do not possess language but are possessed by it; we are led along by it. Now for Chauvet this phenomenon of being constantly orientated by the symbol, being taken along in the direction of new meanings, is the parable *par excellence* of the idea of God: God goes before us in the power of the sign, in which we are taken along in the direction of God. Thus Abraham went on his way; Moses and the people of Israel saw God going before them; the children of Israel gathered the manna which never ran out. Thus Jesus followed the call of the Father, shared bread and fish with the multitude, surrendered to death, and goes before us to the ends of the earth; he will go before us on the clouds in power and majesty. The sacraments carry us along in this movement. Thus God can be present and absent at the same time: God nowhere becomes one object among others; things can remain as they are, without getting stuck in their physical determinacy, and we can taste and test God to the deepest vessels of our existence.

EMMANUEL LEVINAS: TOTALITY AND INFINITY

Just as Heidegger was the guide for the theological thought of the 1960s, so Levinas is the guide for the 1970s. What was valued in his thinking was the emphasis on ethics, on the call that goes out from the face of the suffering other and his attentiveness to the Other which is expressed speechlessly, but tellingly enough in concern for the other. In Chapter 5 I have already referred to Levinas' thoughts about the holy, which expose a distinctive trace of God.

Levinas has opened up our thought of God as the Infinite along quite another line. He begins from the Jewish tradition of God's hiddenness. God cannot be seen, cannot be depicted; God goes before us in time, escaping all our definitions. That also applies to the definitions of God's being:

> Philosophical discourse should be able to indicate God, of whom the Bible speaks – if this God does have a meaning. But as soon as he is conceived, this God is situated within 'being's move'. He is situated there as the entity *par excellence*. If the intellectual understanding of the biblical God, theology, does not reach to the level of philosophical thought, this is not necessarily because it thinks of God as a *being* without first explicating the 'being of this being', but because in thematizing God it brings theology into the course of being. While in the most unlikely way – that is, not analogous with an idea subject to criteria, or subject to the

demand that it show itself to be true or false – the god of the Bible signifies the beyond being, transcencence ...

In the idea of the Infinite there is described a passivity, more passive still than any passivity befalling consciousness: there is the surprise or susception of the unassimilable, more open still than any openness – wakefulness – but suggesting the passivity of something created ... As if the idea of the Infinite, the Infinite in us, awakened a consciousness which is not awakened enough? As if the idea of the Infinite in us were a demand, and a sign in the sense that an order is signified in a demand.[28]

Thus the idea of God provokes a thought which is destined more to thinking than it thinks;[29] not, however, of necessity; not on the basis of intentionality which proceeds from human beings, but on the basis of invitation and receptiveness: 'This endless desire for what is beyond being is dis-interestedness, transcendence – desire for the Good.'[30] Thus the abstract idea of the Infinite and the Transcendent takes on a prophetic significance: we are raised up by it; like the prophet Habakkuk we are taken from our place and put at the service of God, who raises our desires to a higher plane, that of God himself. But that too can be traced only by the traces of the finite, where the finite is open to the Infinite. The trace of God that lights up in the trace of the suffering other is also such an undetermined and completely open trace. It does not get any materiality yet nevertheless moves us in a sovereign way: those who pass it by suffer damage to their souls. Where human beings are addressed and summoned to rise above themselves and to go into the question of the other, they enter into a relation with themselves, put themselves at risk. One's own I adds itself to the other's question and thus overcomes being imprisoned in its own ego. Levinas accuses Western culture and Western philosophy of suffering from 'egology'. In his view the leave-taking of God and this egology are connected. But not all belief in God can be cured of this egology. As long as the religions take their course from a 'God of need', a God for one's own use, they reinforce egology. As long as we think only of God, for the sake of our own salvation or benefit or out of fear and loss, we are not following the 'trace' of the Most High. That happens only where our thought extends to God in pure longing, the '*Dieu du désir*'. In this extension of thought, which takes place above all in conscientious human action and in the doing of justice, we 'find' God on our way: simply acting in this way, in passing: inserting ourselves into the movement of God himself which is compassion, respect, care and mercy for all that arises from the dark night of the undetermined. Here God shows himself as the Infinite, because this respect for beings knows no limits, but time and again is an invitation to free acts of justice. Any totalitarian occupation of spheres of being to which an absolute value is attached, any idolatry of partial areas, any glorification of dictatorship, dogma and power, thus become atheism. This atheism threatens believers and unbelievers, Jews and non-Jews, Christians and all others who seek God.[31]

GOD AS MORE THAN NECESSARY: EBERHARD JÜNGEL

Theology has taken leave of the idea of God which was denied in nineteenth-century atheism and twentieth-century agnosis by following yet another line of thought. It is expressed by Patriarch Maximus IV Zaigh, who at the Second Vatican Council remarked, 'I too cannot believe in this God in whom the atheists do not want to believe': God in dispute with autonomy (Kant), freedom (Schelling), responsibility (Marx) and human self-deployment (Freud and Maslow); God as a limitation of democracy, tolerance, pluralism and free investigation; God as the secret agent of power, social privileges and the status quo. All these images of God have contributed to the darkness of God in which many people are now moving. Attempts have been made in the theology of the past thirty years to expose the causes of this darkness of God which has been caused by European theology itself and to overcome them. Here three emphases must be distinguished:

- God is not a rival of human beings, a God of the gaps in nature or history; religion is not an added value to existence or a separate sector of culture; it is possible to live the whole of human life *etsi Deus non daretur*; the 'death of God' is not a disaster but a challenge and a blessing. 'The unloosing' of the 'totalitarian idea of God' (to use Pohier's phrase)[32] is a necessary condition for spiritual health and for a possible new quest for God.
- God after the death of God and religion as purified religion are bound up with the whole struggle for liberation on the part of enslaved human beings, the sufferers, the victims. Religion is not the opium but the cocaine of the people (i.e. the poor, the women, the minorities). God is a partisan, critical God, selectively present, and can be experienced through the contrast

276

experience of the suffering of the innocent other. God as the liberator God himself offers the antidote to religious escalation and the arrogance of power.

- God is the symbol given to human beings, the most comprehensive basic metaphor for the horizon of being, the 'all-embracing', the wholeness and unity of all the contingent and particular, the primal source and goal of the whole process of physics and metaphysics. God is the most comprehensive hypothesis about reality as filled with meaning (as W. Pannenberg argued).

Eberhard Jüngel[33] goes along with this argument of purging the idea of God, but does so more radically than the three currents that I have mentioned. For him, God is the 'more than necessary' mystery of the world, the very manifestation of love as the supporting foundation of the cosmos. God is not necessary, in the causal sense of the word, either for the liberation of the suffering other or for the understanding of the meaning of the cosmic process as a whole. It proves possible to live a wholly human life without God. A God who had to be would again be a factor in a system that we had devised.

However it is thought of, necessity is always a relational concept: what is necessary for a particular use, what cannot be avoided within a particular course or process; what determines the validity of an argument or the knowability of a part in the connection of the whole; what is essential for a particular phenomenon, albeit with a causal significance – what is the condition for its coming into being – or in a hermeneutical sense that which is a condition for its understanding.

God is not said to be necessary in any of these meanings: God is neither the first in a chain of cause nor the last as the result of the course of things, nor is God the context of our reality or of knowledge of it. All these things, however important they may be for the theory and praxis of human life, can just as well be named without the hypothesis of 'God'. God cannot belong to the order of utility, the ground or purpose of all that is. God does not fit into the order of causality.

But in the phenomenon of religion itself we note the use of the metaphor 'God', at the same time with the sense that it is more than a metaphor. Time and again there are people who bow or kneel before God, who seek God or who perhaps can find God in a tentative way. This search does not relate to something that can be 'objectified', in the sense of something that we could encounter. Those who seek God are not so naïve as to think that they can come across God somewhere. And yet this search is more than just a 'mood', 'feeling' or 'emotion' of the seeking subject, although this basic religious mood is sharply felt in seeking. As we saw in Chapter 4, the name of God is closely bound up with specific experiences which have to do with human emotions: with cradle and grave, field and harvest, house and home, suffering and guilt, fear and hope, mourning and desire. Or rather, the name of God is not bound up directly with these experiences themselves but with 'experience of these experiences' which is had over the course of time. It has become the collective awareness of a group and has been stylized and represented in ritual.

According to Jüngel, what is sought here belongs to the order of the 'more than necessary'. It belongs to the order of gratuitousness, the experience of coming to and taking part in, the experience of the constant victory of being over nothingness which does not exclude the experience of the constant threat to existence but includes it. This often disorganized quest for God, which is experienced in faith and religion and which there takes shape in a specific universe of symbols, does not exclude other universes (for example of causality and science), but colours and relativizes these; it makes us aware that they are distinctive and thus relative universes. Theology is therefore about the universe of religious symbols which gives form to clarifying and thinking through the 'experience with experience', time and again reassessing its historical articulations, so that the vision of God can be kept bright and the rumour of God audible for all those who seek God.

Christians seek God in a particular way. They derive their 'experience with experience' from the pattern of the life and reading of Abraham's family and especially that of Jesus of Nazareth and his followers. They experience their trust, longing, opposition and forgiveness as a way of God which is marked out for them: as Amen to God's *emunah*, as life in accordance with the will and the governance of God. They can never impose their reading pattern on others, because there is no violence in God – the God of their trust, longing, resistance and forgiveness. Only in a radically secularized world and in a church which offers its symbolic universe to free seekers of God without violent sanctions can the universal significance of God as the more than necessary flourish. If the loss of a metaphysical sense and the erosion of the church which have accompanied the process of secularization in the West are answered

278

too early with verbal homiletic force and bureaucratic sanctions (centralism, forced confession, disciplinary regulations), the fresh sense of God's gratuitousness, of God's loving coming and dwelling with people who seek God, is nipped in the bud.

Must God be? No, for a God who is necessary, a God with all violence, is the very cause of the darkness of God.

Must God be? Yes, for if God is more than necessary, as is experienced by those who seek God in experience with their experiences, they cannot prevent themselves from saying, 'How could we keep silent about what we have seen and heard?' (Acts 4.20).

CONCLUSION

In this light, in other words with this orientation of our thought at the back of our minds, we can also read the scriptures with new eyes: Genesis, for example, as the story of God who makes people go in search of God in the midst of the ambivalence of creation; who makes then familiar with their limitations and their hubris, as if we could ourselves make the last judgement on good and evil; who directs them to the need for respect for the other; who thinks differently even about sacrifice and religion; who restrains them from vengeance, even against Cain; who promises them that the destruction of the world and the great flood will not take place, and who shows them that a new beginning is possible even after catastrophe; who allows them to find peace and joy in the diversity of peoples and languages; and who prevents them from coming together in a one-power-world of Babel; who teaches them that God is not enthroned in temples and holy places but that any place is suitable for seeking a link with God, because God's messengers now and then travel with our prayers, desires and dreams and with God's promises, gifts of grace and blessings. We shall also pray and sing the Psalms differently, as the songs of those on whom God is enthroned: the expressions of praise of the creation as in Psalms 8 and 150; the prospect of the good and just king as in Psalm 72; the lament over our finitude, our shortcomings, our despair and our failings as in Psalm 50; and the wonderment at our fragile existence, though every vessel can nevertheless be regarded as a nerve along which God comes to an understanding with us (Ps. 139).

And finally the story of Jesus will also become more credible, though it will be no less demanding and no less unique. Jesus is God's messenger and guide, in whom the logic of God has become manifest among us, has become God's epiphany: in the way in which he goes out to tax collectors and sinners, lepers and the possessed; in his calls to the leaders of the temple and the city; in his journey to the true worship in spirit and in truth; in his invitation to opt for the criteria of God's government, the values of the kingdom of God, and finally in his surrender to the Infinite, the Eternal, his and our Abba, God, who brings him, a human being, in, brings him home as the firstfruit to the very life of God. He, God with us, leads us to share in that perspective of 'We with God'.

For those who dare to read through the scriptures in the perspective of our thought as hermeneutical discourse, *pensée méditante, trace du vrai saint*, God becomes pure freedom and love, gratuitous future in which we may live, move and have our being for ever and ever. Here God becomes a challenge, an encouragement to faith and hope, to a human adventure which does not leave thought behind but transforms it into an operation of life itself, precisely in its infinite dimensions. That is a healing and wholesome way of thinking – and thus of living – which is far from irrational: it grounds the personal dignity of all human beings in the very breath of God, the Spirit of the Holy, from whom God's *Logos* is born, from whom Jesus lived, through whom he was raised from the dead and who has settled on all those who want to move in his footsteps.

12

Revelation and Experience, Hypothesis and Apotheosis

The unnecessary opposition between revelation and experience and the place and task of theology in academic work

> The faith of Christians is a praxis in history and society which understands itself as hope in solidarity for the God of Jesus as the God of the living and the dead, who calls us all into becoming subjects before his face.[1]

> We cannot avoid taking personal responsibility for the tale that we tell, even while acknowledging that the truth of the tale ultimately depends on a fulfilment of conditions the manner of which is beyond our observation and understanding.[2]

After all that I have said about our culture and the possible question of God, the question of God continues to be an open question. Our emotions, the experience of the holy, the open end of history, the sense of gratuitousness, happiness and blessing in creation, the striving for justice and the call to the way of Jesus of Nazareth; the offer of orientation and fulfilment which constantly comes to us; the quest for truth and the space for thought which the infinite opens up for us: all these are possible traces of God, ways of thinking about God, but not proof of God's existence. They are not conclusive truths like those of mathematics or mechanics. The prospect of God is a hypothesis, not a thesis. It remains an adventure, but after all we have seen it is not a foolish risk, a wager: those who do not want to embark on it are not rejected by God, and those who join in gain space for living and thinking.[3]

The statement 'God is a hypothesis' will not be a reassuring one for either theologians or philosophers. For theologians it is perhaps a painful understatement, patiently borne by way of a '*disciplina arcani*';[4] for philosophers it is perhaps a bridge too far, because they first want to be shown the relationship between subject and predicate in this statement, and then more! In fact few theologians will be satisfied immediately as a matter of course with the way in which the former queen of the sciences has been forced on to the epistemological defensive by the modern critique of religion and the effect of secularization.[5] Must theologians capitulate to the notion that the whole symbolic universe in which religion lives and which is the real object of theological reflection simply lends itself to hypotheses in the same way as other objects of scholarship? Is there nowhere firmer ground for the 'holding' of the believing heart or the 'dependence' on 'feeling', as the nineteenth century still wanted to maintain,[6] let alone for the *perceptio divinae veritatis tendens in ipsam* on which scholastic theology lived,[7] or the 'I am the way, the truth and the life' of the Gospel of John (14.6)? Is there only the chill loneliness of the self-devised plan of freedom which on closer inspection is no freedom but the chance interplay of factors in the style of Umberto Eco?[8] And must philosophers again undergo a metaphysical theogony of the 'God of the philosophers' after the 'reassuring firmness' that they found in the human 'project'; after the 'departure of human beings from their self-imposed tutelage'; after the announcement of the death of God in Nietzsche's *The Joyful Science* and the pedantic insights into linguistic functions and processes of perception? The abundant attention to 'God the problem' in Anglo-Saxon philosophy of religion by notorious agnostics like Kaufman[9] and the late Mackie[10] in any case show that even in the philosophy of the 'announcement of the death of God' philosophers have not succeeded in killing 'God' off.

Down the centuries the love/hate relationship of theologians and philosophers has been governed more by the 'God' of the philosophers than by belief in the living God or its opposite. Even when, and as long as, they were still believers, there were skirmishes and questions of competence, fought out over the themes of faith and knowledge, nature and grace. The debate about revelation and/ or experience is a relatively recent form of this love/hate relationship, but that does not make it less comprehensive and important.

Here the chances of the 'God' hypothesis are weighed and often – on both sides – found too light. In this chapter I propose to expose the meaning or meaninglessness of this debate. But I do not want to do so simply with a view to the relationship between philosophy and theology, but also and preferably with an eye to internal theological contradictions, sometimes euphemistically denoted 'pluralism'. At least since the end of the eighteenth century the current oppositions in theology, both inter-confessional and intra-confessional, have seemed to derive from different models of thinking about revelation and experience. This works its way through, down to extremely practical matters like catechetical methods, theological training and the role in it of philosophy and the behavioural sciences, liturgical forms of expression and ecumenical collaborations. At the same time, although here I am looking through the spectacles of a theologian, I am doing so out of a certain discontent at the leave-taking of metaphysics which I trace and regret in the land of the philosophers. Moreover, I am all too well aware that this discontent arises out of a theological self-interest: the disappearance of the metaphysical framework of thought has also led theology astray into a 'grammatology' which threatens to get stuck in an ever more detailed analysis of its own argument, its texts and signs.[11]

Now both 'revelation' and 'experience' are sometimes used as portmanteau terms which, in a mutually exclusive way, are interpreted as 'knowing more' and 'knowing better'; as the end or as the conclusion of all hypotheses about God and thus as the end or the replacement of all metaphysics. In the case of theology this is the end of doubt, and in the case of philosophy the end of illusion. But wouldn't this 'securism'[12] in the theological sphere be a distortion of the basic elements in the theological concept of revelation in scripture and tradition? And couldn't a particular reductionist model of 'experience' which has become the basic dogma of our Western culture have ensured that any traces in spheres of thought outside those of pleasure and utility were dismissed a priori as meaningless? Simply because of these suppositions, which also take the form of accusations, in my view philosophers and theologians cannot avoid testing and putting to the proof 'God' as a hypothesis, conjecture, search pattern, at least if they want to retain some relevance for culture alongside the other producers of 'chatter' (the media, politics, sport, technology, health care, art). If theologians refuse to enter into dialogue with the experiential sciences (and that has become a pleonasm) by referring to 'revelation', they are in fact condemning the religious existence of human beings (including philosophers) to obscurantism, to irrational behaviour. If philosophers think that conversations with theologians about questions of 'ultimate meaning' and 'being towards death' are meaningless, making a reference to 'revelation', they condemn themselves to passing by important sectors of the production of ideology in society by the institutions of religion and the church, on the right wing or on the left, to the detriment of both society and the relevance of philosophy in this society.

So I do not want simply to treat the theme of 'revelation and experience' as a formal, lexicographical exposition of two key terms from philosophy and theology. From the start, of course, a comparison of these two concepts would be difficult because the philosophical argument has had little to do with 'revelation', but the theological argument has been quite intensively concerned with 'experience'.[13]

The comparison of comprehensive key words of thought which form the sigla and the 'ciphers' of both our current methods of reflection and access to the archives of our knowledge is a comparison with too many unknowns. Just a quick look at lexicons shows how much and how many different 'interests' are invested in the terms 'revelation' and 'experience', how many 'clouds of witnesses' from philosophy and theology have brought clarifications or confusion. However, to help us to understand better I have to indicate some important historical variants of both key terms. I shall do that first diachronically, and then show by which 'models' twentieth-century theology has to be mapped out.

REVELATION

There is quite widespread unanimity among theologians of different confessions that the Christian use of the term 'revelation' as a comprehensive key term for belief and as a formal theological principle is only a few centuries old. Peter Eicher[14] calls revelation 'a principle of modern theology', thus indicating that it is a term from modern times which moreover in his view has become indispensable. The latter point remains to be seen.

Revelation as a principle of theology after the Enlightenment has become the designation both for the content of faith and for the event by which this content of faith is communicated by God as reliable and authoritative. The official church use of 'revelation' with this meaning is certainly not older than the first half of the nineteenth century.[15] Vatican I[16] found a place for this meaning in the pronouncements of the Catholic magisterium, as a result of which revelation has often also been hypostatized: revelation teaches, offers us, and the like. In this way the pronouncements of the magisterium are themselves also legitimated as language 'from God'.[17]

In the Reformation tradition the reaction against the Enlightenment, which in many cases initially found a far more positive response there, has in the long run likewise led to a similar formula which legitimates the authority of scripture and the proclamation of the Word as the dialectical 'counterpart' of natural human thought and actions. The boundaries between such a concept of revelation and fundamentalism then become fluid.[18] In the wake of Bonhoeffer the structure of this thinking is then often branded as a 'positivism of revelation'.[19] Here believing is seen as a distinctive form of *episteme*, added to and elevated above the critique of reason, with a supernatural foundation, extra-territorial in origin.[20] It is precisely this concept of 'revelation' that has also found its way into the comparative study of religion, where this began to speak of 'religions of revelation' (in the cases of Judaism, Christianity and Islam), by comparison, for example, with nature religions. However, in general terminology revelation became *the* qualification of religion.[21]

As such a formal theological principle, revelation is a polemical term directed against any foundation of religion in experience or reason, focused on the superiority of the truth of faith to all other human truth. Belief on the basis of the authority of the revealing God becomes a form of knowing better, even about God.[22]

In the beginning this was not the case. The biblical language field which was later claimed for this formal concept of revelation relates to what later was to be called religious experience, as a number of studies have demonstrated.[23] We encounter the word-field 'revelation' (*apokalyptein*, *phaneroun* and *deloun* with their derivatives) in views and visions, dreams and oracular signs, encounters and directions, prophecies and the interpretation of history in which the Word, the Spirit, the Wisdom of God is seen, the Hand of God which guides life and frees peoples and individuals from the distress of death. The description of these revelations – the plural here is essential – is limited to the categories of experience (I saw, I heard, I felt) and remains within phenomenal reality: what is perceived is light, wind, noise and fire. Great care is taken – particularly in the face of the surrounding non-Jewish cultures – not to divinize phenomenal reality itself. There is seldom mention of theophanies: God allows himself to be seen only through messengers and human forms, in phenomena of light and fire and wind. We can see God only from behind. To see God means death; his dwelling place – which is not a dwelling place but empty space above the ark – brings destruction on those who enter without precautionary measures and with other intentions than showing awe of the Unnameable and the Invisible. Touching the ark cost Uzzah his life (II Sam. 6.6–7). God's name is a mystery,[24] a mystery like that of life itself.

In apocalyptic, too – in which so often heaven seems open and without veils – there are indirect perceptions, pseudepigraphically presented in the name of seers who are already long dead: Adam, Enoch, the Twelve Patriarchs, Moses, Solomon and Daniel. But even then these visions are mediated through messengers and spirits of God. Moreover the Jewish-Christian tradition has kept the majority of this apocalyptic outside its canonical heritage.[25]

What is true of the Jewish scriptures is also true of the Christian-Jewish scriptures which later came to be called the New Testament. The signs and wonders, dreams and visions are just as present as in the Jewish scriptures, while here too angels and demons are messengers of God. Elements from the 'open heaven' of apocalyptic play a role, like the resurrection from the dead, the signs of the final crisis, the accusation of the ruling powers. But what predominates is the appeal to the faith tradition itself and to the exegesis of texts, especially from what came to be called the Old Testament. With a somewhat anachronistic term one could say that certainly in the New Testament hermeneutic wins out over apocalyptic and that the witnesses even more than their testimonies are forms of the epiphany of God. In the appearance and fate of Jesus and his followers God now appears as word, as light, as is demonstrated by the fulfilment of the vision of Joel at Pentecost according to Acts 2 and the fulfilment of the Isaiah visions in Jesus according to the account of his baptism and anointing with the Spirit in the Jordan. This is he, these are those from whom the ways of God, the governance and the will of God will from now on be read off in mutual counsel (Acts 15) and in loyal memory (I Cor. 11; 15). There is nowhere any mention of theophany, even if the heaven is sometimes seen to open (Acts 7: Stephen, and the Apocalypse of John). Jesus himself remains godforsaken (Mark 15.34). Even now it is a matter of keeping the encounter with God within the categories of phenomenal reality. The Johannine corpus in particular wrestles with the dialectic of God's transcendent unseen holiness and the human desire to see God. What can be seen is only the *logos tou theou*, the form of the invisible God, the human being Jesus of Nazareth 'whom we have seen, heard and touched with our hands' (I John 1.1). The whole theological dispute of the third, fourth and fifth centuries is about the correct terminology for using this dialectic.

Thus what later would be called 'anthropomorphism', i.e. talk in human terms about the mystery of God wherever 'God' has himself spoken of (Malebranche would call that 'anthropologies', but Aquinas uses the term *analogiae* for it and Alain of Lille 'metamorphoses'),[26] is not a stumbling block for faith, as it was for the Gnostics, nor just a primitive myth which has to be 'demythologized' in the name of enlightened reason or with a view to a rational account of faith. On the contrary, it is protection for the mystery of God which must prevent it from being unveiled and profaned, and which at the same time makes the experience of God possible. It becomes the task of theology in its earliest forms,[27] both among the Jewish rabbis and among the Christian 'apostolic fathers' and apologists, to make that clear in the Greek and Hellenistic world with all kinds of hermeneutical methods. That different emphases were placed on it in Antioch (Ignatius, Theophilus and Irenaeus, who is strongly dependent on him) and in Alexandria (Clement, Origen) – in Antioch more with reference to the historical witnesses and in Alexandria more with reference to the transhistorical significance of the signs and texts and the divine *paideia* afterwards – certainly caused abiding differences of emphasis in Christianity East and West, but need not endanger this mutual consensus about the Mystery of God in history, as is evident from the history of the church and theology in the first millennium, despite all the conflicts.

What is true for the period of the New Testament also continues in the subsequent period. As is evident, for example, from the Shepherd of Hermas, the period of visionary revelations is anything but ended. Apocalypses were still being written in the fourth century. *Revelare* and *inspirare* were used side by side as synonyms. There was no question of a 'closed revelation'; that proves to be a twentieth-century invention.[28] Nowhere is revelation a specific noetic category which is thought to procure a greater knowledge of salvation history or the mystery of God; at most it is an expressive indication of the mystery, which moreover proves to be far less important and frequent than for example *paradosis*, *oikonomia*, *paideia* and *soteria*. Over against Gnosticism, the character of the revealing action of God as knowledge is toned down, in favour of its character as fulfilment. For example, Origen writes: 'We must not understand the term "revealed" (*apokalyptomenon*) in two ways: as that which we can learn but also as that which is promised, which becomes present in such a way that it is realized and brought to fulfilment. For revelation takes place when something comes to completion through fulfilment.'[29]

In the light of the later concept of history the conclusion that e.g. Peter Stockmeier comes to after a detailed study of the use of the term *revelatio* and the like in patristics is in fact bewildering: '. . . that the church fathers did not either subsume the biblical message under the perspective of revelation or investigate the possibility of revelation generally'.[30] If the early church already knew the usage, as for example in the case of Tertullian, it was in quite a different meaning from later times. One of the explanations can be that in the Hellenistic pattern of culture the quest for higher knowledge by means of direct revelations and oracle texts called for a more critical attitude, as already in the Jewish environment of the time of the prophets. But that is not a sufficient explanation, because on the other hand points of contact were also sought in this *Zeitgeist*, as in the apologetic usage of the Sibylline oracles. Rather, in the Graeco-Roman world, too, the quest for 'traces of God' was admired: the Jewish-Christian concept of revelation was full of them, and to avoid too subjective a reference to divine illuminations the certainty and the criterion of the exegesis of the apostolic tradition was set alongside them as *regula fidei*.[31]

Indeed it should not surprise us that in the Middle Ages, as time went on, revelation increasingly became synonymous with the scriptures of the Old and New Testaments, although people continued to see the salvation-historical background to them, and in this sense also did not understand the text of scripture as being dictated by the Spirit or as 'objective revelation', which would be the case in neo-scholasticism. The real *revelatum* is not the word of scripture as such, but what is brought about by it as fulfilment of what is attested in it. Thomas Aquinas' basic hermeneutical rule is: *Actus credentis non terminatur ad enuntiabile sed ad rem* (faith does not relate to the formulation but to the matter); here he also wanted to prevent the *articuli fidei* of the *symbolum* from being fixed as dogma.[32]

At the same time, along the lines of the apologetic of the early church but also in direct confrontation with Islam, a theological treatise began to be outlined which tried to derive the truth of the faith that is grounded in scripture also from outside scripture, from the 'book of nature'. In the face of Islam with its own 'source of revelation' it was no longer possible to appeal to the common Jewish-Christian foundation to which reference had hitherto been made in polemic with the Jews and, together with them, against Graeco-Roman literature. Alain of Lille in the twelfth century, Raimundus Lull in the thirteenth, Raimundus of Sabunde in the fourteenth century and, as their remote successors, Herbert of Cherbury and Hugo Grotius in the sixteenth and seventeenth centuries, were representatives of a theological tradition which tried to bring the content of religion under universal anthropological headings.[33] Moreover the reception of Aristotle from the twelfth century on led to the revival of a distinctive circuit of knowledge among philosophers, and – from Anselm onwards – thinkers began to formulate proofs of God on the basis of philosophical premises. Albert the Great already stated that it was without doubt a human possibility to prove the existence of God from created reality.[34] However, that cannot yet be called theology in the real sense. Where it is a question of the being, the properties and the action of God, the *lumen divinum* which is given with revelation must come about.

Thus gradually two schools of thought came into being, or at any rate two ways of giving an account of the faith: one was to issue in the Reformation and the other in deism and the Enlightenment. One sought traces of God in the witness of the scripture and the *articuli fidei* of the *symbolum* which were derived from that or associated with it; the other tried to read traces of God in the book of nature in order also to be able to legitimate the *nova scientia* that was developing in it. A desire to combine these two approaches has remained a characteristic of the Catholic tradition. That led to the Counter-Reformation criticism of the scriptural principle and to the disastrous effort in the sphere of the 'book of nature', which with the development of the new experiential sciences and epistemological approaches was increasingly being disclosed to the human eye and ear, not only to keep a finger on the pulse but also to keep a firm finger in the pie.

Be this as it may, the first more systematic treatises about the concept of revelation from the end of the seventeenth and the beginning of the eighteenth century were explicitly directed against the deists, Islam and the Protestants, who were amazed to find themselves lumped together![35] In every case the treatises are directed against the appeal to 'experience': against the appeal of Islam to its own 'experience of revelation'; against the Reformation appeal to its 'own experience of faith', presented in the reading of scripture; and against the deistic reference to the universality and the uniformity of the knowledge of experience. For Locke (1632–1704), Collins (1675–1729) and Tindal (1657–1733) revelation means the removal of all veils, the end of any religious mystery: *Christianity not Mysterious.*[36] Direct lines run from these thinkers to Voltaire, Diderot, Comte and Rousseau in France and to Christian Wolff, Reimarus and Lessing in Germany, the authentic fathers of the Enlightenment. While their rationalism was rejected by the *Syllabus errorum* of 1864[37] and by the constitution *Dei Filius* of Vatican I in 1870 with a reference to the specific concept of revelation and the distinctive character of the act of faith on the authority of the God who reveals, at the same time people felt compelled to reject the 'fideism' of authors like Bautain and Bonnetty and to maintain the possibility of natural knowledge of God.[38] But the gulf between 'revelation' and 'experience' had by then already become so great and the appeal to the authority of the church as the hermeneutical principle which determined all interpretations so strong that any appeal to subjective religious experience or reference to the salvation-historical, dynamic view of the event of revelation which had characterized the whole of the first millennium could be declared the cause of all heresies. Here for almost a century neo-scholastic thinking prevailed over, for example, the more historical-dynamic thinking of the scholars of Tübingen.[39] Their conversation with Kant and Hegel was renewed in Catholic modernism at the end of the nineteenth century, but again resulted in sharp condemnations. The developments before, during and after Vatican II show that this dispute is far from being settled.[40] Revelation and church teaching are not only constantly identified as *doctrina revelata*, as a fixed whole of truths of faith, but are also legitimated and 'proved' from outside.[41] That the Word of God has authority by virtue of its content and witness and deserves faith is something that keeps being lost sight of.[42]

Fortunately there are other 'models of revelation' in twentieth-century theology, including important Catholic options. Before I sketch them out, however, it is necessary to see what lines of development the term 'experience' underwent before it could be so sharply contrasted with 'revelation'.

EXPERIENCE

'It is from memory that men gain experience (*empeiria*), because the numerous memories of the same thing eventually produce the effect (*dynamis*) of a single experience (*empeiria*).' Thus Aristotle in his *Metaphysics*.[43] His concern is with a condition for *techne* and *episteme*: insight into specific facts and situations on the basis of the recollection of perceptions. This concept of experience gained from transient experiences was adopted by the Middle Ages and was still influential in a later period, among others with Hobbes and Christian Wolff.[44] Especially for the discussion with theology, it seems important to recall this Aristotelian coupling of experience with concrete perception and the (cumulative) recollection of it; here the later and indeed the current colouring of the concept of experience has come to be bound up so much with the induction of predictable future events on the basis of general regularities. That began the very moment that the book of nature could be better deciphered. Usually Francis Bacon[45] is cited as the founder of this new concept of experience: out of discontent over an *experientia vaga* he wanted to aim at *experientia ordinata*, a methodical approach to reality (*interpretatio naturae*) in accordance with precise descriptions and calculations (*experientia literata*). Meanwhile the word *experientia* also took on a new content in another sphere of knowledge: that of *experimentum* in the sense of 'voyage of discovery' and 'adventure'. Here it was a matter of gaining experience through travel. Here we have not only etymologically a basic meaning of the term 'experience' but also the notion of the future-orientated acquisition of experiences through travel. Lorenzo Valla and Pico della Mirandola gave this meaning content,[46] but the notion was also fruitful in the Reformation: the act of faith rests on an event which has to be experienced, and according to Luther[47] and Gottfried Arnold[48] theology, too, has to rely more on such an experience – which must be sought in life and death – than on speculative thought. It needs to develop the conscience rather than to expound dogma.

Like the later empiricists, Bacon thought this *experientia vaga* which has to do with chance events far too uncertain for science and technology. John Locke, Berkeley and David Hume[49] then developed experience into a universal theory of perception which Kant[50] built up into the transcendental epistemological system of the categories, in polemic with Hume. If for Hume 'experience' is based above all on the habits of our mind, and on the basis of perceptions is to be given universal validity, for Kant transcendental categories are involved here. Knowledge arises out of the synthesis of perceptions and universal rules of perception. As a result of this, while our knowledge is preserved from scepticism, on the other hand it is resolutely bound to the world of phenomena, as perceived by the perceiving subject. Sensual perception, intellectual synthesis and rational interpretation from now on come together in the concept of 'experience'.

Is there still room here for the religious, for those experiences which in the Christian tradition down to the Middle Ages were known as 'revelations'? Here the development which had meanwhile taken place in theology and which had wanted to remove these 'religious experiences' from the universal human circuit of perception and knowledge took its revenge. Individuals like Schleiermacher[51] on the Reformed side and Hermes[52] on the Catholic side, who wanted to regard Christian revelation as a universal category of the religious consciousness, were suspected of delivering 'God' over to the subject: 'God' then becomes another word for a particular way of perceiving reality, another word for human self-awareness, the awareness of infinity; another word for the infinity of the consciousness, as Feuerbach was to formulate it.

Does Hegel's philosophy of history offer more of a way out here? Hegel again drew attention to the object of perception that itself remains a critical authority for the consciousness and referred to the 'historicity' of perception, at least in the 'philosophical consciousness' of the 'concept'. We have experience of our experiences.[53] Theology made grateful use of this notion by paying new attention to the idea of salvation history, in which God reveals himself by revealing human beings to themselves in history.[54]

But the question is, as we saw in Chapter 6: where and how does that happen? In the movements of history itself? But who then passes judgement on good and evil? Or in the theories of history, ideology? But who then decides whether or not they have value, including all kinds of religious ideologies?

The double question of the 'who', the subject of the interpretation of all experiences, leads back to those views of 'experience' in which the concrete subject disappears less into the background than in the empiricistic, Kantian and Hegelian views. We find them above all from psychology, where desire is the real form of perception, and in existential philosophy, on which part of 'awareness' psychology is dependent. Religious experience is here understood as 'disclosure' and '*blik*' (van Buren), and these 'disclosures', experiences of opening up and losing limits, are the vehicle of God's revelatory action with human beings in their history. Every moment of this history is a unique chance to encounter God, open-ended, focused on the truthfulness and authenticity of the subject that becomes 'itself'.[55]

MODELS OF REVELATION IN THE TWENTIETH CENTURY

Against the background of these various colourings, models or emphases of revelation and experience, which at least have associations with the comparison or contrast of the two, I can now sketch out five current synchronous models of revelation which characterize present-day pluralism.[56]

The first model is the continuation of the rationalistic, 'securistic' concept of revelation which was developed in the nineteenth century as a reaction against the Enlightenment. This is about the communication of truths which are unattainable by reason or at all events would have been more difficult to attain in that way. This report of truths about God, about Jesus as the Christ and about the church can be made authoritative only if it can be 'proved' that here there really is a revelation of God. Theology provides that proof by means of signs of verification brought about by God himself: miracle and prophecy are the strongest of these signs of verification, most of all the resurrection of Jesus, which is the greatest of all miracles. This model of revelation, which a part of the great Christian tradition now shares with more fundamentalist groups, churches and movements, offers the advantage of certainty, clarity and unity. The power of this thought to grow and gain adherents in a world full of experiences of fear, division and complexity is obvious. Moreover this tradition on the one hand protects the historical archive – texts are of the utmost importance – and on the other emphasizes the unity and the identity of Christianity as a given, as an initiative of God, which is not dependent on some ideology or *philosophicum inventum*. So it is also a critical force. However, the disadvantages are just as evident: there is inevitably a certain incompatibility; a notarial hermeneutics of the texts from the archive is obvious, and this leaves little scope for new ways of seeing and speaking. The character of the verification of faith, which comes from outside, stands directly opposed to 'experience' in all the meanings that we have seen. What is argued against it in fact time and again rests on the 'experiences' of those who maintain another concept of revelation, whereas from the perspective of this thought in terms of revelation in which 'propositional truth' has a central place, this reference to the truth of experience as 'subjectivism' is rejected out of hand.

The second model is diametrically opposed to this and is best described with the title of a pioneering collection of articles by Pannenberg and others, *Revelation as History*.[57] A return to the historical sources which exposed the genesis of the modern concept of revelation sketched out above and brought to light the priority of thought in terms of salvation history in the patristic period formed the beginning of the '*nouvelle théologie*'[58] after 1945 on the Catholic side and comparable currents in Reformation theology.[59] It became possible to see that historical events and experiences underlie the written traditions and that what is attributed to God is also the result of the historical experience of God. The rise of philosophical and theological hermeneutics makes it clear that there are as few brute facts within the religious language field as there are within the profane language field. Fact and interpretation, event and text, are far more closely linked than has often been assumed in rationalistic thinking in theology and philosophy. Moreover – in the footsteps of Kant and Hegel – it is recognized that salvation history is not a closed compartment of a secular history, and religious reality is not a reality outside phenomenal reality. There is the one reality and the one history, but from the perspective of eschatological fulfilment, consummation. God is the goal of history; Jesus, the Risen One, the proleptic culminating point of total history; the church the sacrament of this universal salvation. Vatican II[60] offered every opportunity to this way of thinking about 'revelation', though there were hesitations about leaving aside the first model completely. Revelation, Gospel and Word of God were said to be synonyms. God is concerned through both words and actions with the salvation of men and women who have a share in God's community of life and love. The church is on the way to the eschatological vision of God (I John 3.2), but lives now, in the meantime, by the tradition of the scriptures, 'the mirror of God'.[61] This tradition relates to the whole of religious life, thought, speaking and action by the church community. So a permanent colloquium takes place between God and the church through which believers come to the full truth, and the gospel thus also rings out for all men and women.

The advantages of this model of thought are likewise evident: it speaks of God's present action in history, which wants to do justice to transcendence and immanence, to autonomy and heteronomy of

God and the world, God and human beings. There is every opportunity for a rational account of faith through openness to historical criticism and for a historical approach, for example, to the Jesus event. Full benefit is taken of critical hermeneutics in re-reading texts and events, and that also makes it possible to put the reductions of empiricism under the microscope with a good conscience. But there are also disadvantages: can the most important content of the Christian kerygma (like the creation, original sin, the exodus, the incarnation, the resurrection and God's judgement at the end of history) be understood as historical events? Is the criticism which Bultmann made of this, and which made him opt for a reading of the kerygma as a direct summons to the 'decision' of the believing subject, really warded off in this way of thinking? Isn't 'history' too recent and too Western a category, alien to biblical thought and to many non-Western cultures, and therefore hardly suitable as a universal paradigm of 'revelation'?

A third model – also on the basis of this criticism, but taking up the nineteenth-century choice of the subject as the real *locus de Deo* – opts for revelation as inner experience and a personal encounter with God. Schleiermacher, Ritschl and Herrmann, Tyrrell and von Hügel, up to and including John Hick, are the representatives of this current. God is always concerned to be directly present in the consciousness and conscience of human beings, with their life of grace. Dogma is simply the protective garb of the apostolic experience of the Spirit which has to be activated time and again. The natural and the supernatural still come from God, but cannot be separated from human beings: *revelatio* and *religio* coincide. In this model we find a positive connection with the – predominantly Reformation – mystical colouring of the concept of experience (compare Gottfried Arnold, but above all also Schleiermacher and Herrmann) and in the field of religious studies the insights of Rudolf Otto and others. This concept of revelation can easily be reconciled with the more empirical aspects of the concept of experience, because there is another language field or language game. But the difficulties are also clear: only religious geniuses qualify for this; the community of the church no longer makes an appearance; and the difference between religious and other 'peak experiences' is then in the long run unclear. And above all, the historical component of the concept of experience – the cumulative remembrance, the experience, the seeking – is absent. The facts of salvation themselves are really hardly interpreted, except as stimuli and as an occasion for the momentary experience of disclosure.

This thinking does not itself again call for a liberating praxis from which the original experiences of *apokalypsis* seem to have arisen, so that the critical force of the tradition also disappears.

We find a fourth model where, on the basis of the models already sketched out, the question is whether God can and will allow himself to be caught within dogma, within church history or universal history, or in religious experience. The school of dialectical theology emphasizes the sovereignty of God which remains hidden, even if it discloses our heart to itself in the 'word of God' so that we can hear him better. We do not reach God – *finitum non capax infiniti* – either with our dogmatic knowledge or with our ecclesiastical or religious experiences, but only God can reach us with his word, namely as the Christ who is proclaimed in preaching, who brings about reconciliation with God.

The advantage here is that 'God' remains God, not tailored to human measure, a priori guaranteed against Feuerbach's criticism that God himself remains the subject of his revealing Word – not the church or the believing subject – which avoids any false claims to authority on the part of church preachers. The disadvantage is that this way of thinking a priori excludes any dialogue with philosophical outlooks and insights into reality; that dialogue with non-Christians becomes virtually impossible; and that human experience itself is declared unsuitable for an encounter with God. What kind of communication is it that comes entirely from one side? It is no more than the command 'Take it or leave it!'

A fifth model is the model of revelation as the Way. God's revelation relates to 'orthogenesis', the establishment of human beings in all their potencies, the fulfilment of history in hominiza-tion and self-transcendence of the person-in-community. Here we find the names of Karl Rahner, Paul Tillich, Pierre Teilhard de Chardin, Gregory Baum, and earlier also that of M. Blondel. Here the issue is what God wills: his kingdom in human history – not, though, understood in terms of universal history, where the fulfilment comes at the end and all who contribute towards it are used as fertilizer on the field of history, but in terms of concrete history, as a praxis of the liberation of men and women. It should not be difficult – Dulles does not do this – to put political theology and liberation theology in this same scheme of thought, and there is nothing against doing that, because the concrete practices of the critique of society and the harsh fight for justice do not fit well with any of the other models, although some spokesmen perhaps used to come from the sphere of the second model.

The attractive side of this way of thinking about 'revelation' is that it is open-ended, as the second model also is, but related in a far more concrete way to the personal history of human beings in diverse contexts. It emanates hope and encouragement, as do the biblical dreams, visions and prophecies. Jesus himself characterized himself as the Way, the Truth and the Life, and the earliest Christian communities also saw themselves as a community of 'the Way'. A disadvantage could be that the terms of growth, progress and liberation can better or just as easily be given content from the human 'project' itself, so that 'revelation' comes to coincide with the human desire for improvement and progress.

This diachronous development and the twentieth-century pluralism that I have sketched out disclose – reveal – the truth of two connected structures of the Christian confession and thus of the identity of the Jesus movement (and *mutatis mutandis* also of Judaism and Islam): first there is the growing importance of the system of religious language, the embedding of the communication of faith within which 'God' reveals himself as *Logos*, i.e. gives himself to be known, to be approached. Here 'revelation' is a different word for the evocative force of the symbolic universe in which and from which religion lives. It was Locke's great mistake – but he could already appeal to later scholasticism – to think that within this symbolic universe he had to distinguish between what can be known by reason and what can be known only through 'revelation': 'beyond reason'.[62] Here we have to say that nothing in that symbolic universe lies outside the order of what can be experienced, although it all remains symbolic in so far as it points to a more comprehensive sense. This second structure, the abiding reference of the system of religious language to the reality of the *auctoritas Dei revelantis*, is a reference to God himself, who can not only be known and traced within this language system as 'God', who not only leaves a trace in history as 'God', but who also guides history itself and directs it towards fulfilment. That is the '*logos*' of the historical event in which the Word of God incarnates itself 'in the midst of time', in the event of Jesus the Christ.

The first structure determines the importance of the theological theory of language and hermeneutics. A defective hermeneutic is the cause of many unnecessary contrasts between 'belief in revelation' and the 'reference to experience'. The second determines the importance of theological metaphysics as an ontological hermeneutic: who, what, where and how gives meaning and direction to our personal and collective, historical existence? All statements within the symbolic universe of the believer ultimately stand or fall with the reality of a history supported and guided by God and with the epiphany of this guidance in the Way of Jesus the Christ. We must now turn our attention to these two structures of the confession to show that thinking in terms of 'revelation' and 'experience' is not finally an opposition, but the disclosure and unfolding of the truth: the *aletheia* of the *logos tou theou*.

THE SYMBOLIC UNIVERSE OF REVELATION-IN-TRADITION. SOME THOUGHTS FROM THEOLOGICAL LANGUAGE THEORY[63]

The first thing that is striking in a re-reading of the concept of revelation in relation to the concept of experience is that religious experiences are collected and interpreted in the very concept of 'revelation'. It functions as a 'search pattern' for a diversity of religious phenomena: the death struggle of individuals and peoples; the desire for the fulfilment and improvement of human fortunes; the need for wisdom, knowledge and insight into the meaning of history; the handing on of a particular interpretation of history as salvation history, and so on. If we make this search pattern for the religious with its many possible interpretations and the many different 'interests' that have been invested in it over the course of time itself the criterion for authentic belief – belief as obedience to the authority of the God who reveals – then we immediately come up against the charge of Feuerbach and others that religion rests on self-deception and is the result of thought-processes which start from the wrong places, a diversionary manoeuvre from the real historical problems of humankind.

Rather than making this way of thinking the normative principle of theology, as Eicher wants to continue to do after all his reinterpretations, we need to recognize the relative historical function of the concept of revelation. It is this function which demonstrates that the experience of faith is the history of experiences of faith. The concept of revelation takes our present-day thought and action back to the thought and action of witnesses of former times, who have handed down particular religious experiences as normative for us. Revelation is therefore above all tradition.[64] We cannot escape from this history of the experience of faith in order – with a reference to a formal concept of revelation – to remove all the veils from faith and thus demonstrate it as

298

evidenced ('... put it on the bier').[65] Pannenberg formulates this insight as follows:

> Now it is important that we can know of divine revelation only through the mediation of the religious figures in which human beings receive this revelation. From this follows the far-reaching conclusion that human beings do not know the divine revelation a priori, before they can survey all human religion and compare it. So in all their many statements about the divine reality and about divine activity, the religious traditions must be regarded first of all as forms of religion, as expressions of human experience and its assimilation, which first must be tested for their reliability and truth.[66]

The tradition itself – in confrontation with the changing context which is actually present – forms the process of testing of these experiences, and thus only in this living tradition does it become clear what revelation is.[67]   That is a long-drawn-out process. Schillebeeckx remarks on it:

> God's revelation follows the course of human experiences. Of course revelation – the sheer initiative of God's loving freedom – transcends any human experience; in other words, it does not emerge from subjective human experience and thinking; it can, however, only be perceived in and through human experiences. There is no revelation without experience. God's revelation is the opposite of our achievements or plans, but this contrast in no way excludes the fact that revelation also includes human plans and experiences and thus in no way suggests that revelation should fall outside our experience. Revelation is communicated through a long process of events, experiences and interpretations ... and not in a supernatural 'intervention', as it were by magic, though at the same time it is by no means a human creation: it comes 'from above'. The self-revelation of God does not manifest itself from our experiences but in them, as an inner pointer to what this experience and the interpretative language of faith have called into life.[68]

There is more. Only in the form of language and sign do we know the experience of faith in the past, which we perceive through tradition and through which we allow ourselves to be taken up into it, in order to begin to share in it. To quote Schillebeeckx again:

> The very fact that revelation comes to us in human language – as in the Old and New Testaments – shows that revelation is

essentially concerned with human experience. However, language is the deposit of common experience. Revelation is experience expressed in the word: it is God's saving action as experienced and communicated by human beings.[69]

In that case it becomes crucially important to show that this language is more than simply wasting one's breath in communicating facts to an anonymous mass. The theological theory of language tries to expose the process of tradition in all its anthropological breadth. Only within that is 'God' mentioned, can God be addressed and does God have a say. Here are some aspects which seem to me important for a contemporary justification of faith in the forum of the 'experiential sciences'.

The first principle of faith seems to be a truism, but it risks being forgotten in all the theological statements which present themselves as 'God-talk': human beings know no other language than human language. Even God can make himself understandable only in human language. And the transmission of any experience of God whatever can take place only in expressions of human language: hymns, prayers, visions, precepts, blessing or curse, wisdom or prophecy, ecstasy or mourning. In fact all this is the content of the collection of texts which forms the heart of the Jewish-Christian tradition. They are regarded as the interpretation of God's own life-giving *Pneuma*, which also bestows on human beings the 'gift of tongues'. Heidegger's statement 'To be human means to be a sayer'[70] has been translated in the Jewish-Christian tradition of experience into a theological statement: 'To be human means to be a hearer of the word.'[71] This theological statement does not do away with the anthropological presuppositions of the first statement, but presupposes them. That is also taken up as an explicit reflection in the Jewish-Christian collection of texts (compare e.g. Heb. 1.1; I John 1.2–3).

A second fundamental rule is that language is first of all language spoken by human beings. That means that any text which has been handed down in writing continues to presuppose the speaker or writer. Within the religious tradition we do not have anonymous oracles but the communication of faith rooted in autobiography: the names of the witnesses and their fortunes continue to be remembered. Therefore the hearers, too, are taken up into the context of the text: the hearers of then and the hearers today. Author, herald and bystanders, redactor, narrator and hearers together form the context of the religious language-act. This context functions well only in the religious community. The texts mean what they are going to mean in current preaching. Here they echo the history of their meaning. Even when being used, texts are taken out of the original context, they do not lose their meaning but add meaning to the reading history of the text. Only reading and re-reading make the use of the texts meaningful as an instrument for the tradition of faith. Only within this process of reception is it possible to speak of God's self-revelation.[72] The Jewish-Christian tradition is therefore least of all a 'religion of the book', as is often said. Christians are not Mormons, though it must be recognized that the structure of the concept of revelation in Mormonism in the nineteenth century could play a full part in the Christian views of revelation at that time.[73]

Expressions of religious language by definition have a 'narrative' structure; they have the character of 'story'.[74] They do not contain descriptive information as on notice boards or on notices saying 'no entry', nor are they 'recipe language', as for cooking or prescriptions. Nor are they timetables for the future or telephone numbers for heaven, but directions for life and criteria for God's governance of this world. It is bewildering how this now universal theological insight is not recognized in accounts of the concept of revelation in the philosophy of religion, where the latest theological wisdom still seems to come from John Locke.[75]

Of course religious texts like those from the Jewish-Christian tradition also lend themselves to linguistic analysis, archaeological research or literary and aesthetic assessment. They do not escape the general rules of semiotics and hermeneutics, but give up their secrets only where they are read as stories of people who are in search of God: in the 'listening tradition'[76] in which they came into being. Their revelatory character, their effect and efficacy, their authority and meaning, stand or fall with the readiness to listen to them, which is the theological form of the hermeneutical circle. Thus revelation is not a formal guarantee of quality which has been woven into the texts – for example in the 'thus says the Lord' – detached from their functioning as story. Far less is it the indication of a surplus of knowledge that would eliminate faith and hope and take away all despair and doubt. That does not prove to be the case even in the stories of scripture themselves. The greatest witnesses who had 'revelations' as 'guidance' for their lives, which according to the biblical narrative fundamentally changed their lives – Abraham, Moses, Jeremiah, Jonah, Peter, Paul, the two disciples in Emmaus, Thomas and also Jesus himself – were not freed from doubt, impatience or fear. Belief in authority and in the guidance of God does not do away with the categories of experience, however gripping the mystical feelings which can master believers may be. And on the other hand, not a single attempt to create a separate milieu for religious experiences – and thus to mark off the sacred from the profane – provides a safer and a faster access to God, though some people can experience the 'numinous' better. What makes God speak and makes religion infectious is simply the living story of the witnesses who took responsibility for the story that they told.[77]

But in this way doesn't 'God' become another word for the power of the self-constructed story, a superfluous predicate of the human project? Within the story itself there are two critical elements which prevent it from being a *philosophicum inventum*. The first critical element is that the story is a dangerous memory. The witnesses have bought it with their lives; the narrators, prophets and apostles have given their lives for it; and the story cannot be told or listened to as a matter of indifference. Now that is also true of Socrates and many radical righteous after him, and it would be arrogant to assert that the Jewish-Christian tradition in particular, with its preaching of surrender and cross, has contributed only good to the human project. Far from it! But along with Socrates and many righteous, the Jewish-Christian story does stand on the side of the victims and not on the side of their executioners. The Christian story, however, has a second and in my view unique criterion, which in many cases lifts the story above any human project whatever: the preaching of the overcoming of killing and death in a new creation to eternal life, in 'becoming a subject' *coram Deo*, or whatever metaphor we may wish to choose from the rich arsenal of tradition. We are not simply telling the story of the noble courage of the sufferer who was crucified – Jesus of Nazareth – but also the story of the nerve of those who say, 'Look, he is alive' – Christ, the Lord. This kerygma of the resurrection is not a miracle-story-at-its-strongest which has to legitimate the authority of the noble courage of Jesus as a man of God or demonstrate that he was a man after God's heart, although those were also functions of the story in the tradition. At its deepest it is a proclamation of God's guidance of our existence, a proclamation that chaos, violence and death do not have the last word in it, and that 'God' is a God of the living and not of the dead. If this heart of the story is an empty dream, as Paul already pointed out in I Corinthians 15, then the choice of the story of Jesus as *logos tou theou* is a threatening ideology. Of course that does not mean that it is worthless – there are worse ideologies than the humanism of Socrates or Jesus – but in the end it is joyless and hopeless.

That must lead us to a last reflection: does the 'God' hypothesis, which fills the story and has given form to the symbolic universe of the tradition, have a *fundamentum in re*, and if so, do we have any knowledge or experience of it? Or does the hypothesis that 'God' – the one whom we call 'God' – in fact and in word is God, in whom everything happens, after all rest on revelation, 'beyond reason', 'beyond all experience'? That is the crucial question for theology, and if we do not want to get stuck in 'grammatology' or declare our semiotics and hermeneutics themselves to be metaphysics, we cannot avoid it.[78]

HYPOTHESIS OR APOTHEOSIS?

For those prone to agnosis and scepticism, the reference to the religious language system as the given framework for the interpretation of reality, through which for those who stand in the tradition of this system 'revelation' lights up in experience, is not yet a principle which provides sufficient basis for the plausibility of the 'God' hypothesis. Experiences which some call 'religious' are not so for others. They will then use the rule of Occam's razor and say, 'Let us not presuppose any superfluous entities' (*entia non sunt multiplicanda praeter necessitatem*). And indeed it does not matter whether here thought begins 'from above' or 'from below'. Even if, like Kuitert, as a theologian one wants to creep through the material and say 'All statements about "above" come from "below"',[79] or 'All statements about "after this life" take place "in this life"', God still remains hidden behind the hypothesis 'God'. Kaufmann calls this shift in thinking 'from above' to 'from below' a neo-orthodox variant of the emperor's new clothes.[80] For Hans Albert, thinking in terms of God as the hypothesis of the 'all-determining reality' produces a metaphysical God of the gaps, with no better foundation than more primitive ideas of a God who intervenes directly in history.[81] Are there other ways – not of proving the existence of God (*An Deus sit?*), for a God who is proved is always only a 'God' who is thought up – of clarifying the meaning of 'God' within the religious language system in the midst of what is often the agnostic and sceptical framework of the interpretation of contemporary experience? I think that there are, but that presupposes a shift of perspective in our thinking about God and thus in the 'God' hypothesis. I would want to describe this as 'from hypothesis to apotheosis'. I must content myself with some broad outlines of this change of perspective, which still needs to be completed.

In the footsteps of Paul Tillich a change has taken place in theology in thinking about 'God' as 'God of the beginning', 'God as First Cause' and 'Author', to the 'God of Hope', of the 'Future', of 'Fulfilment'. Moltmann, Pannenberg and also Rahner, Schillebeeckx and the liberation theologians have brought about this change in perspective. In this way a metaphysic of first principles – the Greek *archai* – has been abandoned in favour of an 'eschatological ontology': God as the Totality of what will be.[82] But the great difficulty is perhaps that this 'universal-historical' hypothesis 'God' cannot be 'experienced', is as 'inaccessible' as the 'God of the beginning' or 'God from on high', and that 'revelation' again becomes a category of thought, an 'end word' without real relevance to history. So it must be recognized that Rudolf Bultmann's concept of revelation is at least partially right: only the present 'address' of the specific person in his or her fate by the living God who gives life deserves the name 'revelation occurrence'.[83]

I see two possibilities of doing justice to the shift of perspective in theology which is intended, while at the same time keeping the relevance to concrete everyday experience. One has been tried by Langdon Gilkey,[84] who, taking up a *cri de coeur* of Bonhoeffer's,[85] has tried to distil a new vocabulary for the religious language-field from current everyday experience. Despite all the emphasis which he notes in people in the second half of the twentieth century (in the West) on facticity and contingency; on the possibility of empirical measurement and the predictability of our existence; and on the autonomous human self-determination in freedom, in people's ordinary life a factor of ultimacy has remained:

- in short-term anxiety about security and assurance against every possible disaster he traces a hidden fear of the void;
- in the vitalistic and hedonistic tendencies and the striving for fulfilment he sees a remnant of joy and the celebration of life;
- in humanistic ethics a powerful ideal of human beings is looming up where nothing in everyday reality or human history thus far seems to give any support, but which still time and again arouses people to try it;

- modern views of society are dominated by an ideal of peace and justice on the basis of which we can put our opponents under scrutiny as public sinners, but on what basis?

Earlier, people like Erikson and Horkheimer, Levinas and Weischedel, had exposed similar aspects of our everyday experience as analogies for the infinite meaning of reality.[86] In Chapters 4, 5, and 6 I developed some of these in greater detail as traces of God. They have helped us to broaden the horizon of our experience and not to limit this to the flat surface of the empiricistic theory of perception. But do they also lead to God-talk, to expressions of religious language, not only about 'God', but to God? Are such symptoms of ultimacy perhaps the rudiments of the religious language system which risks dying out in the West? However this question is answered, there is evidently a basis on which faith, proclamation and theology can make themselves understood to people in their everyday experience and which, as we saw, in any case is of enormous importance within that field of religious language that cannot live without the reception of preaching.[87]

However, I would want to go yet a step further, and show that the quest of ultimacy is an essential component of humanity, which can be filled sufficiently only with the answer 'God'. The shift of perspective from 'God' as hypothesis to God as apotheosis cannot be an event which does not touch human beings themselves in their concrete experience or which they only suspect is there by chance. It is a question of salvation and health, of attaining one's deepest purpose and possibility. Because this soteriological focus is the goal of science, technology, politics and ethics (Heidegger's 'three in harness'), in principle there can be no opposition between faith and science, and the reflection on faith which we call theology fits perfectly within the framework of university disciplines.

THEOLOGY AS A DISCIPLINE SERVING HUMAN SALVATION

The old doctrine of the four senses of scripture, in other words the fourfold way in which the Bible functioned in the Christian culture of the Middle Ages, included wisdom, which even after the loss of the Christian culture seems to have been of the utmost importance for the *universitas artium*. We find this view pregnantly expressed in a poem attributed to Augustine of Denmark (died 1295):

Littera gesta docet,
quod credis allegoria,
moralis quid agas,
quo tendas anagogia.

This text indicates that traditional canonical texts reflect and
make possible a fourfold hermeneusis of human existence: they
teach us what has happened, what makes us believe in it, what we
have to do on the basis of it, and what purpose all this serves. They
teach us the whence and whither, the why and wherefore of life.
This fourfold hermeneusis is not simply a matter of the correct
interpretation of the text as text, but of the correct use of it in life
and society, not so that the interpreter is right but so that the
reader is happy. Like Aristotle's famous four factors or causes, it
indicates the connection of the system of meaning in which we live
and the depth of the text which is the guiding thread for life: the
given text is the matter, faith is the form, ethics is the motive force,
and our ultimate destiny the aim of the text. What has been
handed down is at the service of human beings; accumulated
experience structures knowledge about the past, present and
future. Thus a connection was woven into the labyrinth of reality.
Theology, medical science and law formed the superstructure of
the medieval university (the so-called *trivium*), all three with a
clearly therapeutic aim for life and society. The other sciences
(physics, mathematics, dialectics and philosophy, the so-called
quadrivium) were auxiliary. Just as physicians had to ensure bodily
well-being and combat diseases, and lawyers had to ensure just
forms of society and fight against misdeeds, so theologians needed
to ensure the ultimate salvation of human beings and to combat
anxiety and superstition.

Now it seems that since the secularization of modern times this
connection has finally crumbled away.[88] This fragmentation not
only affects theology but is characteristic of Western culture and
certainly of Western society. Scientific knowledge excludes ideals,
values, visions and therapies from its argument and limits itself to
what can be listed: *res gesta*. It limits itself to the simple literal
meaning: *littera*. The fragmentation of the context, the connection
between words and things, leads to ever more refined, ever more
analytical attention to detail: the lexeme, the particle, the gene. All
synthetic work comes to stand in the shadow of the demands in the
sphere of analysis, measured by its importance. It seems to me that
that applies throughout the sciences, but at all events it is fatal for

the humanities, and the more time goes on, the less obvious the place of theology in the university becomes.

At this point a short excursus on the development of the disciplines is instructive. The designation of part of the sciences as humanities is itself already a symptom of a changed view of science. In the division of disciplines which is current in the Netherlands, for example in the Netherlands Organization for the Advancement of Research (NWO), a distinction is made between the natural sciences (including the technical sciences and medical science), the social or behavioural sciences, and the humanities. They often go by the name of the beta, gamma and alpha sciences, in that order. They are organized under different governing bodies and councils and as such also get their share of funds for teaching and research.

This division is quite recent, and the outcome of many shifts over the past century.[89] Thus according to Dilthey's *Einleitung in die Geisteswissenschaften*, medicine and the rising psychology and sociology still belonged among the humanities. Dilthey knew only a division between the natural sciences and the humanities. That was itself already a shift from the classical division of scholarship, which for a long time followed the tripartite division taken from Aristotle's *Metaphysics*:[90] physics, mathematics and theology. Even on the eve of the Enlightenment the term *Geisteslehre* was a synonym for 'theology'; after that, for example in Schelling, 'pneumatology' is another word for philosophy.

Meanwhile a whole series of branches of science had been added. From the Middle Ages onwards, what for the ancients was *theologia*, the science of the connection of things, had fanned out into separate spheres of knowledge like philosophy and theology, history and literature, aesthetics and ethics. As a result of the dominant force of physics and mathematics, from the sixteenth century onwards these disciplines, based on deeply inventive demonstration, could claim for themselves the title of 'sciences', leaving the rest to fantasy or art, whether pious or not. In Comte's positivism, whatever cannot positively be called a science is denied any scientific character whatsoever. Precisely in order to give the other disciplines a scientific status and not without an anti-scientistic affect, Dilthey, following others (e.g. Calinich), began to speak of a separate sphere of knowledge: that of the humane sciences or humanities. Dilthey tried to indicate that in that sphere distinctive laws and methods applied which are no less scientific than those of the sciences but are scientific in a different way. He was concerned above all to give the phenomena of the spirit a

307

foundation in experience. Supplementing Kant, he wanted a *Critique of Historical Reason*. For Dilthey, it was a matter of differentiating areas of knowledge: the natural sciences cannot describe all the phenomena of life exhaustively. The spheres of art and law, history and human society, largely escape scientific or mathematical description and explanation. They call for understanding and interpretation. Windelband reduced the difference between the disciplines of the natural sciences and the humanities to a difference in method. The humanities do not seek the general and universal, the nomothetic, as the natural sciences do. They seek the idiographic, the special and unique. They do not analyse, but produce a synthesis. Logic and psychology, both of which study the laws of knowledge and thus in a certain sense are also nomothetic disciplines, form the bridge or the link between the two spheres of knowledge, although they were still classified by Dilthey and his contemporaries among the humanities.

After that there were again great shifts within the humanities. The study of human life and society – *quid agas* – in the behavioural sciences, sociology and psychology, broke out of the sphere of the humanities and formed a distinct domain which eyed the precise results of the natural sciences. Life and society were ordered according to laws involving measuring and counting, statistics and scores, experiment and prognosis. They were read as *res gesta*, as data to be registered literally. The knowledge of human behaviour is knowledge of the registers of our behaviour; we have a mouthful of labels and models at our disposal.

That caused a brain drain in the humanities, because as a result the character of moral sciences, of science for and with a view to human action, which they had had hitherto – compare the division into disciplines by J. S. Mill which still lives on in the English name for the humane sciences (moral sciences or humanities) – was weakened. The humanities forgot that they were there for right, as food for the soul, for the attraction of the beautiful, for the depiction of meaning, for the vision of the divine. They came to be turned in on themselves, on the phenomenon of speculation and reflection.

What then remained of the humanities was trapped again in a 'scientistic affect'. Anything that was prescriptive or normative science sought to offer itself as objective and descriptive. The study of languages and literature was also orientated more on the linguistic and literary rules of the game and did not claim to offer any thematic reflection on what is expressed in literature. They became a doctrine of the codes of language. Empirical study of languages replaced the comparative study of literature. Rhetoric was overtaken by grammatology, stylistic theory by phonetics.

A further reduction of the content of history as a discipline has taken place. It has been reduced to historism on the one hand and to historicism on the other. Historism is fascinated with detail, with each singular event, and refuses to learn lessons from the past, to expound it in broad outline and to attempt constructions from it. It tells the stories as stories, without purpose or connotation. It, too, is no longer moral science. And in historicism history seeks determinism and also leaves the path of the idiographic, to devote itself to the nomothetic: as this ... then that.

Finally, philosophy and theology, too, are succumbing to the scientistic affect. They are limiting the radius of their action to the field of language. Truth is thought to be only linguistic. Spirit cannot work without word and concept. Texts form the web for the philosophical and theological dissecting table. Everything becomes exegesis, or at best a hermeneutics of what has already been said. The space for what has not yet been thought is becoming increasingly small now that what is thought can be set down in signs, listed on an ever greater scale. The hermeneusis of life and the synthesis of lives lose out to the unravelling of the literal text and its codes.

This concentration on the linguistic has different elements. Dilthey had already given philosophy above all the task of being the theoretical discipline of all the other disciplines. In logical positivism that was limited more closely to the analysis of scientific language, to rules of falsification and verification, of rationality and empiricism. Granted, in analytical philosophy it was extended to everyday language, but with the same empirical cutting edge and the same anatomical tables. As I have said, with Ernst Cassirer the *animal rationale* was replaced by the *animal symbolicum*. An important part of modern and postmodern French philosophy has followed this path: Foucault, Derrida, Lyotard. Merleau-Ponty said that the human being is a *sujet parlant*; Heidegger's term was 'an *essent* which speaks'. Now we are going a step further: subject and being are only the illusion of an argument, the construct of language, the phantom of linguistic usage. Everything is text, and the reader is a function of the text.

Thus we have first limited the concern for synthesis, connection and meaning which for a long time was the hallmark of science to the sphere of the humanities, leaving the rest to the natural sciences with their *pensée calculatrice*. But then the humanities, too, in an exemplary self-reduction and self-asceticism, have limited themselves to their product: the text. The fate of the reader, the soteriological and therapeutic aspect of the discipline, seems secondary.

But it is precisely that fate of the reader which forms the real theme of theology, the real object of the prospect of God. It is the task of theology to achieve a coherent image of human beings which explains the place of human beings among the living and offers a healthy insight – i.e. an insight that induces health and furthers peace – into the nature of the human relationship with God.

APOTHEOSIS

Here the thought of a medieval author, Alain of Lille, or Alanus ab Insulis (1120–1202), is interesting.[91] He belongs with Abelard (1079–1142), Gilbert of Poitiers (1076–1154) and Hugo of St Victor (1096–1141) among the founders of scientific theology who began to set the rediscovered work of Aristotle alongside the authorities of Augustine, Dionysius the Areopagite and Boethius, who thought far more in terms of the Platonic tradition. Like the others whom I have mentioned, Alain comes from the time before the great monastic orders (of Franciscans, Dominicans and Augustinian hermits, who were to dominate the sphere of scholasticism); he was a secular clergyman and thus a 'man of the world' with a by no means optimistic view of the world, as might be expected of a Platonist, certainly in his tormented time. Among his works, which were very influential – he already bore the name 'Doctor Universalis' a century before Thomas Aquinas – there is an early form of theological hermeneutics, the *Regulae de sacra theologia*.[92] Alain elsewhere[93] divides theology into a 'hypothetical' and an 'apothetical' part. The first is about life on earth, angels and human beings, everything that underlies our knowledge, what is already at our disposal. The second is about God's own being as Trinity, the mysteries of God, the things that are still hidden, what is laid up for us in light inaccessible. The *Regulae* belong to the *pars apothetica* or, as he calls it here, *supercoelestis*. The treatise is interesting for all kinds of reasons, but above all for the extremely cautious, almost apophatic, approach to the mystery of God. Of the 125 *regulae*, half (I–LXVII) are about theological talk about God; a further quarter are about good and evil, sin and grace (LXVIII–XCIX); and the rest are about the Christ event (incarnation and crucifixion) (C–CVI), the sacraments (CVII–CXV) and the concept of *causa* (CXVI–CXXV). This 'distribution of weight' already indicates what according to Alain are the most important articles in the theological 'pharmacy', which is why I mentioned it: the things of God. He discusses these (and thus also gives instructions, 'recipes', for treating them) in a far from abstract way, taking up and being very conscious of the human, all too human, talk and with constant reference to human existence. If we say something about God, for example that he is just, then we do so on the basis of his just action, which justifies our existence (XIX and CXVIIII). So rather than saying 'God is righteous', we can say 'righteous God': we need not attribute anything to God, as we derive everything from God. Our projections are projections taken from God himself.

But human beings have a real and great responsibility to order their existence by God, since this ultimately determines the quality of that experience. Alain criticizes Boethius' axiom that everything is good in so far as it is (*omnia in quantum sunt, bona sunt*) (LXVIII) and says that it is true only because all that is has a part in the goodness of God, and also in so far as that remains the case. That we can act is a gift of God, but that we can act wrongly is certain and is our responsibility. God is not responsible for the misuse of knowledge or power. From this basic conviction Alain then formulates in *regula* XCIX, the last rule which relates to the difference between good and evil, and the transition to *regula* C, which is about the incarnation, a fundamental anthropological option which in my view is directly connected with our theme. He distinguishes three possible 'states' (*status*) of the human being: thesis, hypothesis and apotheosis. In so far as human beings use their understanding to see what is good and what is evil, what they must do and what they must not do, they are '*in these*': what we might call a normal state of equilibrium. But they teeter on the brink: they can deviate in the direction of evil (*vitia*) and they can be taken up higher by the contemplation of heavenly things, by ecstasy and metamorphosis. The highest metamorphosis is *deificatio*, divinization or *apotheosis*. This apotheosis – which is like (*quasi*) deification, the cautious Alain hastens to add – consists in the understanding of divine things, as the highest step of concepts. Human beings become human through speculative thought (*ratio*), and through the comprehending intellect (*intellectus*) they also 'comprehend' visible things and become spirit (*spiritus*), but through the contemplation of the divine things they come to apotheosis. *Speculatio, comprehensio* and *contemplatio* are thus the powers (*potentiae*) which draw human beings upwards. Over against them is the downward force of sensuality, through which the beast in human beings comes into existence: *per quam homo fit homo pecus* (as opposed to the *secundum quam potentiam homo fit Deus*). Thus the first leads to the 'state' of 'apotheosis', the second to the 'hypothesis'. Human beings teeter on the brink; they must choose between God and beast. But God himself comes from his 'state' of 'apotheosis' to help them and empties himself into the thesis of our nature, indeed even into the hypothesis or our wretchedness, and bears the punishment, if not the guilt, for it.[94]

The notion of human beings on the brink or in the balance is classical from Philo onwards,[95] as is the thought of ecstasy, of opening oneself up to God (Gregory of Nyssa). Of course the notion of God's descent is also part of the vocabulary of the Christian tradition and is worked out in all kinds of ways.

But Alain's *regula* XCIX is perhaps new in being such a compact combination of anthropology and theology, and in any case it is still striking. It once again shows us ourselves and demonstrates that a consistent picture of human nature is the condition for an adequate image of God and vice versa. Evidently human beings are called – as the tradition of humanity confirms to us – to transcend themselves, although time and again they experience the downward pressure of continuing to fall short of the mark. Our existence has a shaky equilibrium in which subtle shifts of force determine our 'metamorphoses'. The over-riding attraction to the good is God, who in Jesus Christ has given himself in our history of suffering and evil in order from below to raise us anew to apotheosis. So we live from God and to God; there is no other truth, whether about human beings or about God, except that the direction of the way is determined and the attraction of the good is given us in the *logos tou theou*.

God – the one whom we call 'God' – remains a hypothesis, because God dwells in light inaccessible. But those who believe need not stop at the 'God' hypothesis. God who calls us by name is the apotheosis, and we would do well to take account of this in our hypothesis. Both terms – the hypothesis 'God' and the apotheosis-in-God – must be established at the same time for those who believe in the way of Jesus Christ. Neither of them conflicts with our cumulative experience if at least we leave room in it for the traditions of religious experiences that we call 'revelation'. Speaking about 'revelation' does not add anything to the 'God' hypothesis, nor does the question of 'experience' prevent the apotheosis of God or human beings. But those who remain stuck in the 'God' hypothesis or are choked by it do not arrive at the thesis of true, righteous humanity and hinder apotheosis. All kinds of religions which do not serve the truth and the exaltation of human beings, but oppress and diminish people, are not the work of God but the diabolical work of human beings. That has been revealed to us, and so we can also experience one another as people of God who are open to God: now still constantly teetering on the brink, but destined for apotheosis. The last belief to be presupposed is the hypothesis of apotheosis, which is the apotheosis of all hypotheses.

Epilogue
God: An Open Question
in Our Aporia

Left to themselves, human beings are no more than examples of their species, and humankind is the result of a collection of interactions, just as one stone piled on another becomes a mountain, trees together form a forest, grains of sand a seashore, and drops of water the sea. Seen in himself or herself, of course every human being is unique in its species, more complex and thus more varied than those drops of water, grains of sand or trees. And so the collection of human beings that we call humankind is less homogeneous than a lake or stretch of sand; not more of the same thing, like a forest or a herd of cows. But every human being is still a recognizable example of a species, i.e. of a more or less fixed combination of natural materials which can handle itself with reasonable success.

We have in common with all living beings that we can maintain ourselves only by procreation, and also that combinations of different germ cells are used for our procreation. That distinguishes all living beings from the rest of matter, in which new structures like crystals, salts, acids, sugars, proteins and polymers come into being simply through splitting or the addition of constantly identical elements. Moreover our procreation and thus the perpetuation of the species does not take place through the wind or the force of gravity or one principle of mechanical transport or another, as is the case with plants, single cells and some fishes. Rather, as with the higher animals, it comes about through forming pairs and thus through an element of choice.

It is this element of choice in which, without ever getting rid of it, we escape the gravity and the connection and the natural equilibrium of things, but at the same time also necessarily take some responsibility for the course of things in nature. Our freedom and responsibility are rooted in this self-determination, which therefore does not apply so much to ourselves as to the life that is handed down, the natality of the other. Every human being decides for himself or herself whether and how he or she will hand on life. This piece of freedom is limited, not only because even then we do not have everything in our hands – even if we were to manipulate this process yet further – but above all because the element of choice is limited by concrete circumstances and because the freedom which makes this choice possible is also in turn handed on to a new example of the species.

This element of choice is not isolated. The gathering of human beings into families, peoples, humankind has a far more mobile character than that of a forest, a natural area, the shore or the sea, and it also differs from that of a herd of cows or a school of fishes. Through exogamy it even breaks through the tribal alliance. On the other hand it is limited by monogamy or by a limited polygamy. Thus our natality is already connected with mobility. Therefore mobility together with natality is the basis of our experience of freedom and uniqueness. I am the only one in my species and I am the only one here. Thus the experience of my bodily nature also holds the experience of my freedom: I am here and no one else can take my place; I am here and no one prevents me from going elsewhere. Similarly, a lack of freedom implies the opposite: being hindered in our movements, not being able to go anywhere, simply being used as the material or instrument for someone else's purposes. Where this lack of freedom holds us in thrall, we experience it as violence and as an attack on our human dignity and position, as if we have been assigned a place which we may not leave; as if we are a given rather than a unique opportunity, simply stones rather than architects.

In this experience of freedom – with all the qualifications of responsibility and relationship to the freedom of others that it involves – is also rooted the religious experience which is given with *Homo sapiens* and which has taken form in the great religious traditions. The primal religious story is thus a birth story and a travel story at the same time, and the original image of all religions is the Way, the Path, the Vehicle, the Journey. On this journey there is a quest, an adventure with opportunities and dangers, flight and hospitality, encounters with rivals and loved ones, fixed rhythms and changing conjunctions. Nomadic cultural patterns give way to settled societies, but the latter cannot take root without mobility and transport, communication and exchange. Therefore the city lives by the toing and froing of goods, services and people, and the market is the point of encounter for settlers and commercial travellers.

Religions have spread along the great trade routes, with prophets going from city to city. Therefore in many religions the most popular god is the god of the ways, the god of travellers and merchants: Hermes, Hecate, Cybele, often sharing first place with the god of fertility and love. Mobility and natality are the highest expressions of our experience of freedom and of our human dignity, and at the same time the greatest challenge, with the most dangers.

Here the Jewish-Christian tradition is no exception. Abraham is a wandering Aramaean. His religious experience circles around natality and mobility. In his faith, Isaac, the son of the promise, and Canaan, the land of promise, are the core of his idea of God: God who goes with people on their way through life, who takes their path through life into the service of the history of creation. Time and again that also implies a history of liberation, a redemption and exodus from violence, and a new quest for a land of milk and honey, as Moses experiences and shows. On the way new promises and guidelines are found for a society in justice and peace. Again the fate of the firstborn is central. Religious men and women are asylum-seekers from the wilderness among alien peoples, returned exiles under foreign government, gathered together by God from the diaspora. Jews feel that this is what they are from the beginning: driven from the safe place of Eden, the land of once upon a time; after Adam and Eve never at home anywhere and therefore living with a desire for nowhere. They live by utopia, the *ou-topos* or no-place of finite and contingent existence, of life that survives only by being handed down, and by encounters on the way, where we may offer hospitality to messengers and ambassadors from eternity in the form of gods visiting us. The temple and the kingdom of David time and again prove to be of short duration: building is followed by demolition. We have a portable dwelling place for God, a portable chest with commandments and traditions, a portable fatherland. So prophets rebuke kings who want to establish peace with violence, and cities are destroyed if they wall themselves in and close the doors to aliens who do not want to dance to their tunes. And Jesus, who is born on the way and lives without a fixed abode, who has left behind neither cradle nor grave and who summons people to leave house and home, family and friends, wife and children, in order to go off in all directions, becomes the Jewish prophet of the end of times, when God's day of visitation will come to draw all people to him. In his footsteps, fishermen leave their nets, tax collectors their money chests, and Pharisees their schools, and go with him from city to city, along caravan routes and sailing routes, as far as their vehicles or vessels will take them. He announces a way to God, like Siddharta Gautama in India before him and Muhammad after him: a summons to let go, to trust in God's purposes, a disposition of respect and love for fellow travellers and mutual solidarity in the community of fate: *koinonia*.

On the way he sharpens the standards of behaviour for the culture of his day. What he aims at is a movement among men and women which goes along with their desire for natality and mobility. But above all he sharpens people's view of God: who God is and what God does; from whom and to whom we are. Unlike Buddha, who seeks the room for freedom in detachment from *karma* (causality and desire) – here followed moreover by some of the later ascetic traditions of Christianity – Jesus puts human beings – with all their desires – and the cosmos with all its laws in the space of God. In contrast to what Muhammad will do later – moreover together with part of the Jewish and Christian tradition – in this space of God, there is a place for all those who seek God and not just for a group of elect or of those who swear by one law, one pattern of religion, one holy book, one code of religious obligations. Jesus wants to unite all under one perspective of the divine: the finite space of the form of God who unites the living, who overcomes death, but who gives the waymarks and pointers for this and who discloses them in a hierarchy of truths summed up in the image of God's *politeia*, God's sovereignty, God's domain of salvation. That is the God of the children playing before his face, of the poor, the widows and orphans, the tax collectors and the prostitutes, the sick and the eunuchs, the reviled soldiers of the occupying forces and the collaborators, the lepers, the possessed and the unclean. For the meaning and sense of human life does not lie in power or potency, in success or health, in national pride or civil honour and respect, and certainly not in the consequences of law and customs, but in the hope and prospect of acceptance by God: having a share in God's purposes, making a beginning in the direction of the hierarchy of values of the kingdom of God and directing one's life along the way of peace.

Jesus' message of liberation from oppression, fear and violence is a bizarre message which gives offence and which also proved fatal for him: violence will always keep killing prophets, and violent men will always want to seize the kingdom of God and lay hands on it. His fate becomes the disclosure of God's deepest purposes: only the one who does the will of the Father may finally dwell with God; no corruption will affect such a person, nor will death strangle them. Those who do the will of God will live for ever: their names will be written in the palm of God's hand.

All gods along the way, all sanctuaries and statues, pale before this one kingdom of God, which spans the cosmos and in which causality and freedom both become the pliable mixture of gratuitousness: the living space given by God. All too soon there was a great temptation to limit this space again. Tribal gods and city gods compete with this broad view of the God and Father of all human beings who oversees all things, as Jesus saw him and showed him. The Jesus movement quickly fell apart into local institutions and particular churches, which had great difficulty in maintaining communion with one another. Natural interests, cultural blocs, rival interests: all this accompanied his gospel. The structures of the Pax Romana were based more on domination than hospitality, more on subjecting the peoples than on their solidarity, and that has remained so until the present day, in all the world empires which have followed.

The realm of science and technology which promised us eternal peace and which we disseminated all over the world as light for the peoples – as Enlightenment – usually accompanied by Christian missionaries, has not brought the kingdom of God to the peoples: it has proved not to guarantee an end of wars, but makes them escalate by ever more devastating firepower and a Promethean accumulation of force. Moreover while it may extend our life span, it does not extend the durability of life on earth. As a result of the greater possibilities of manipulation, natality and mobility do not become better instances of our freedom but escalate to impossible proportions: overpopulation and the restriction of movement, and accelerated exhaustion of the earthly resources for life. And certainly this technological Enlightenment does not overcome finitude and death, however much it may also want to achieve this by a meaningful and a dignified dying. It is not the acceptance of death but the acceptance of the determination of life that marks our freedom.

However, if the determination of life is sought only within the co-ordinates of the time and space that is assigned to us and measured by us, then God is dead. The death of God is the proclamation of the absolute finitude of human life and the ultimate meaninglessness of all that lives: the end of history. History as a story of purpose and meaning can survive only with its prospect of God, its sense of God as the one who embraces space and time, in whom it runs its course, takes place and gains significance. Without such an Omega point the arrangement of the moments from A up to and including Z is always no more than a human sum, an alphabet for the language and grammar of our urge for control, not a coherent *historia*. Even if we configure this collection of moments as the epic of human beings or humankind, it is not yet *historia* but at most the scenario for a play which is performed repeatedly, with human beings as actors in a drama that they have composed themselves, whether we call it Progress or Decline. Only if the drama really reveals something about who we are and to whom we are, if it is called Revelation or Apocalypse, do we have a *historia*. Without God as producer and critic, however, such an Apocalypse is only the receptacle and echoing well of our dreams and illusions, the establishment of an absolute utopia or of a still more subtle agnosis: we never know what it is good for, or at least we do not know how it will turn out.

The Christian picture of the world – the attempt at a total explanation of the phenomena of contingency and its absolute meaningfulness in a comprehensive history of salvation – rests on two pillars which are directly built around the key points of all religious experience: natality and mobility. God as the comprehensive One is interpreted in terms of mover: author, unmoved mover, creator and cause (*dynamis*) of all that moves. God is the cause of all causality, all effort, all freedom. Behind all our effort, manipulation and will there is somewhere in the distance or the depth the primal will and origin of God, initiator, creator out of nothing: in him we live, move and have our being. So he is called Father, Abba: procreator, carer, lawgiver, judge.

But God is also interpreted as the one who has entered human history, as the one who has dwelt among us and who has allowed himself to be woven into the chain of generations as a contingent, unique and historical example of the human species, the Jew Jesus of Nazareth, God with us, Emmanuel. Alongside God, the author of the universe, there is therefore God who shares our history, the one who supports it, who cradles and cherishes us under her wings, who through Jesus Christ bears us as children of God. The Christian tradition says that from both of these springs the force of God, the dynamic of God, the holy *Pneuma* of God (although on this point there is a great difference of opinion between East and West). God's threefold influence thus expresses itself in the cosmos with its laws; in history with all its vicissitudes; and in the heart, reason and will of human beings, who are breathed on, inspired and enspirited by God through all this. The signs of God's presence can indeed be found in these three fields: in the order of the universe with all its creatures; in the plan of history with all its striving for perfection; and in the order of the willing, feeling and thinking of human beings between cradle and grave, in which God's Spirit bears direct witness to us (here the Reformation tradition spoke of the *testimonium internum Spiritus Sancti*, the Roman Catholic tradition of the *lumen fidei*). This threefold articulation of the idea of God has been systematized within Christianity, and in the process it has so to speak comprehensively brought together the experience of other religions. Thus Christianity unites all kinds of forms of nature religions, all kinds of forms of historical and political messianisms, and all kinds of forms of inner experience, especially those which have been developed in the Asian religions. If there is syncretism anywhere – and that need not necessarily be a term of abuse – it is certainly in Christianity. Moreover we also find a similar syncretism already within Judaism and afterwards in Islam, except that in both cases God is kept at a great distance from nature, history and the human heart: the prohibition against images means that no single category of reality can ever in any way be identified with God. Of course that cannot happen in Christianity either, but Christians are much less shy of seeing God himself speaking in the things of nature, history and inner experience. In all things God forms what Christians perceive as the source and the test of their perception. They begin from the analogy between God himself and what God shows of himself in the world as human beings see this. Revelation and experience are more on the same wavelength.

At least that is how it was until recently. Whether it is a matter of the way in which we are conscious of ourselves, our experience of the world or history, any reference to God seems to have become superfluous. That is above all because we have grown up with too sharp an idea of God which has already been filled with content. It is the healthy role of theology to free these rigid images of God from their strait-jackets and again to see the question of God as an open question, i.e. as an adventure, a quest, a journey of the soul. Every premature fixation of the idea of God, any image that has become independent, must therefore be removed by a holy iconoclasm. At the same time we should not hesitate to indicate iconographically traces of God, figures of God in nature and history, as heavenly ladders for the journey of our souls (cf. Gen. 28). I hope that this book has also been an example of this, even if, with a variant of a well-known saying from the 1960s, it still has to be stated that there is no way to God; God himself is the way. For to believe in God means at the end of the soul's journey, purified, to be able to say, and constantly to think on the way: 'O God, I have trusted in you, longed for you; I shall not be put to shame, I shall never be confounded.'[1]

Notes

DS = H. Denzinger and A. Schönmetzer, *Enchiridion Symbolorum, Definitionum et Declarationum*, 23rd edn, Freiburg 1965.
PL = J. P. Migne, *Patrologia Latina*, 221 vols, 1844–64.

INTRODUCTION: A CULTURE WITHOUT GOD?

1   For what follows see A. Felling and J. Peters, *Der Säkularisierungsprozess in den Niederlanden zwischen 1966 und 1985*, Nijmegen 1988.

2   Recently stated powerfully by H. Philipse, *Atheistisch manifest. Drie wijsgerige opstellen over godsdienst en moraal*, Amsterdam: Prometheus 1995. Cf. his short summary in *NRC*, 20 February 1996: '... the unscientific assumption that there is a God ...'.

3   For the different aspects and forms of this agnosis, see Chapter 2, 31ff.

4   Here I follow the broad description of culture in Clifford Geertz, *The Interpretation of Cultures*, New York: Basic Books 1973, 89: 'It denotes an historically transmitted pattern of meanings embodied in symbols, a system of inherited conceptions expressed in symbolic forms by means of which men communicate, perpetuate, and develop their knowledge about and attitudes toward life.'

5   Of course theology has the hermeneutical task of constantly reassessing past forms of belief in the light of culture and, as H. Wiersinga puts it in his *Geloven bij daglicht* (Baarn: Ten Have 1992), also cutting out the dead wood in good time. Theologians have cut out a good deal in past decades. In particular the fossilization of narrative forms into doctrinal propositions and the reduction of the mythical, epic expressiveness of creation stories to historical accounts and reports had obscured the content of faith. Here the work of H. Berkhof, H. Kuitert and E. Schillebeeckx has something of the same tenor: a renewal of notions of belief by relativizing conventions. This is done by making comparisons with other faith traditions (Berkhof); by an analysis of the anthropological presuppositions of the language of faith (Kuitert); and by a

return to the history of theology and the biblical sources (Schillebeeckx). But in my view the crisis of faith has come about not just at the level of a crisis in the articulation of faith – i.e. at the level of language, which could be parried and repaired by philological manoeuvres – but at the level of thought itself and of views of human life.

6   F.-X. Kaufmann, *Kirche begreifen. Analysen und Thesen zur gesellschaftlichen Verfassung des Christentums*, Freiburg 1979; N. Mette, *Kirchlich distanzierte Christenheit*, Munich 1982. Both point to the fact that being a Christian can no longer be identified with being a member of the church. For many people the church is merely the purveyor of a kind of civil religion, the services of which are invoked in the ceremonies surrounding birth, marriage and burial, at public festivals like national festivals and the installation of authorities. Many people seek a deeper level in their life in forms of religion outside the church, in all kinds of movements and groups. Cf H. Zirker, *Ekklesiologie*, Düsseldorf: Patmos Verlag 1984, 56ff.

7   Cf. J. Derrida and G. Vattimo, *La religion*, Paris: du Seuil 1996.

8   Cf. I. Bulhof and L. ten Kate (eds), *Ons ontbreken heilige namen. Negatieve theologie in de hedendaagse cultuurfilosofie*, Kampen: Kok Agora 1992.

9   S. McFague, *Metaphorical Theology. Models of God in Religious Language*, London: SCM Press 1983; id., *Models of God. Theology for an Ecological Nuclear Age*, London: SCM Press 1987. Cf. earlier already Don Cupitt, *Christ and the Hiddenness of God* (1971), London: SCM Press 1985; id., *The Sea of Faith. Christianity in Change*, London: BBC Publications 1984.

10   Cf. E. Jüngel, *God as the Mystery of the World*, Edinburgh: T & T Clark 1983, 154: 'These two tasks, to learn to think both God and thought anew, cannot be separated from one another theologically ... For Christian theology, the decision about what thought means is to be made in relation to the possibility of thinking the God who is an event.' I regard the second part of this sentence as an overestimation of theology by itself. Its critical contribution to thinking does not mean that it should be able to monopolize or define all thinking. It is certainly possible to think without referring to God, as is proved by the Western scientific ideal. But thinking about God or in the direction of God adds dimensions to thought which remain inconceivable without the idea of God. That applies both to the prophetic role of theology, above all represented in the forms of liberation theology and political theology with their criticism of society, and also to the more sapiental forms of theological reflection about the meaning and the destiny of human beings and the world. This last takes form in the cosmological approach of process theology; in holistic and apocalyptic approaches to the ecosystem; in cultural and anthropological reflections on the roots of regional cultures; in the return to the sources of the thought of the mystics in a spiritual theology; in literary methods which take up the philosophy of language, semiotics and the theory of metaphor (above all also in feminist theology); and in new ontological schemes. In all these approaches there are very careful forms of thought in which there is an awareness of the hermeneutical problems caused by the traditional forms and texts of religion and the aporia and scepticism of the hearers and readers presupposed: there is a public audience which looks over the shoulders of theologians and listens in to the theological laboratory. Anyone who wanted to close this laboratory because the results are not sufficiently applicable or resonant – and this temptation is called both fundamentalism and scepticism – would destroy a set of instruments

which keep watch over the humanity of religion, which together with language, the law, art, technology and health care serve towards social cohesion, though their function is not exhausted in that. Cf. D. Tracy, 'The Return of God in Contemporary Theology', *Concilium* 1994/6, 37–46; id., 'Theology and the Many Faces of Postmodernity', *Theology Today* 51, 1994, 104–14.

1. TAKING LEAVE OF GOD: AN INEVITABLE PROCESS?

1   The literature on secularization in this sense is almost too vast to survey. Here I shall mention some important survey works. For the sociological account see H. Lübbe, *Säkularisierung. Geschichte eines Ideenpolitischen Begriffs*, Munich 1965; B. Wilson, *Religion in Sociological Perspective*, Oxford 1982; P. E. Hammond (ed.), *The Sacred in a Secular Age. Towards Revision in the Scientific Study of Religion*, Berkeley 1985. For the historical account see U. Ruh, *Säkularisierung als Interpretationskategorie. Zur Bedeutung des christlichen Erbes in der modernen Geistesgeschichte*, Freiburg, etc.: Herder 1980; O. Chadwick, *The Secularization of the European Mind in the Nineteenth Century*, Cambridge: Cambridge University Press 1975. For the philosophical argument see H. de Lubac, *Le drame de l'humanisme athée*, Paris 1944 (= *Le Monde en 10/18*, nos 103–4); A. J. Nijk, *Secularisatie. Over het gebruik van een woord*, Rotterdam: Lemniscaat 1978.

2   M. Weber, *Wirtschaft und Gesellschaft. Grundriss der verstehenden Soziologie* (1921–2), fifth revised edition ed. J. Wickelmann, Tübingen: Mohr 1972, 44ff. (economic rationality: the primal form of all *ratio*, i.e. calculating reasoning), 468ff. (the rationalization of law), 245ff. (the rational explanation of religions), 815 (the rational state). M. Lemmen, *Max Weber's Sociology of Religion. Its Method and Content in the Light of the Concept of Rationality*, Hilversum: Gooi & Sticht 1990, 104ff., sums up Weber's idea of the progressive rationalization of all spheres of life like this: '... man attempted to make empirical, opaque (irrational) and therefore unpredictable reality ever more intelligible as a "meaningful" cosmos in order to bring his behaviour into greater harmony with it and so to give form to his autonomy, whatever this autonomy might mean (in this case: the goal of salvation)' (132). Taking up Weber, but drawing the line to other cultural spheres (history), M. Gauchet, *La dèsenchantement du monde*, Paris: Gallimard 1985, concludes that rationality consists not so much in calculation in the sense of planning for a better future (thus Weber) as in calculating thought on the basis of insight into the mutability, the constant change of perspective, the possibility of manipulation and adaptation: planning without any last perspective or teleology. However, that is only the postmodern variant of rationality and the background of modern Western cultural agnosis: we no longer want to know any last goal of history or of human destiny. This short-term rationalism lay outside the perspective of Comte and Weber, both of whom certainly envisaged 'salvation' but thought that myth, magic and religion could not offer that. Cf. A. Comte, *Introduction to Positive Philosophy* (1822), Cambridge, Mass: Hackett 1988.

3   Above all after 1950 and in the 1960s the positive theological evaluation of the process of secularization caused a stir, especially under the influence of the work of Bonhoeffer, Gogarten, Kraemer, Tillich and Bultmann on the Protestant side

and Teilhard de Chardin, Chenu, Rahner, Metz and Schillebeeckx on the Catholic side. The American 'theologians of secularization' (Cox, Van Buren, Hamilton, Altizer) even made Nietzsche's proclamation 'God is dead' a message of salvation. Robinson's *Honest to God* formed a provisional climax to the song of praise to modernity. This argument was most deeply about taking leave of false images of God and church claims, in order to recognize in a mature way the social changes and a greater commitment to the problems of secular society in 'the secular city' (the title of a book by Harvey Cox). Vatican II between 1962 and 1965 and the meeting of the World Council of Churches in Uppsala in 1968 were strongly inspired by this positive interpretation. This brought a provisional end to a century of opposition and hesitation, expressed most clearly in the so-called *Syllabus errorum* and the encyclical *Quanta cura* of 1864. But there were also reactions. Within Reformation theology from the 1980s on we heard the warning voices of, for example, Newbigin and Berkhof, and Barth pupils like Moltmann and Link, Liedke and Jüngel, also put question-marks against the project of the Enlightenment. 'Evangelicals' entered the lists against 'ecumenicals'. A renewed fundamentalism reared its head. On the Roman Catholic side Pope John Paul II (Bishop of Rome from 1978) and theologians and bishops in his footsteps again opposed what Cardinal Danneels called the 'poisons of culture' with which Enlightenment thought was infected.

4   A. van Harskamp, 'Revisie van de secularisatiethese?', in id. (ed.), *Verborgen God of lege kerk? Theologen en sociologen over secularisatie*, Kampen: Kok 1991, 9–28. A more fundamental question about the secularization thesis is that offered by A. Wessels, *Europe. Was it Ever Really Christian?*, London: SCM Press 1994; id., *Secularized Europe. Who Will Carry Off Its Soul?*, Geneva: WCC 1996. Wessels states that over the centuries European Christianity has achieved only a limited degree of 'Christianization' and makes mincemeat of the myth of 'Christian Europe'. The socialization of belief is always dependent on the degree to which the cultural images and myths are used as a vehicle for the Christian gospel. He sees the so-called phenomenon of secularization as a consequence of a 'demythologizing' which was carried too far in the twentieth century, out of a fear of and departure from the 'religious', the sacral and the culture of the image which was above all evident at the Reformation, and the general inability of church and theology to enter the media period. In that case secularization is the other side of failed inculturation.

5   Many people have queried the standard questions which sociological surveys use about religious views and church involvement. The mere definition of the term 'religion' within the social sciences is debatable, as social scientists themselves usually recognize. Most begin from a description which is universally valid in the sociology of religion. It defines religion as involvement in another, decisive reality or as the recognition in faith of a supernatural, transcendent reality of God, gods or spirits, into which human beings, too, are taken after their death or in another way. Others, like Luckmann and Yinger, drop the idea of transcendence and take religion in a broader sense: all the cognitive and value systems from which people derive the ultimate meaning of their life (thus Luckmann); the universal sense of the constantly recurring problems of human existence, which confront human beings with their limitations, or, more precisely, the statement that evil (injustice, sickness, death) is a fundamental characteristic of existence and the hope that human beings will finally be saved from this evil (thus Yinger). Cf. the review by J. van

der Lans in T. Andree and P. Steegman (eds), *Religieuze socialisatie. Een uitdaging voor onderzoek*, Utrecht 1987, 55–7. In particular on the Roman Catholic side, the Netherlands has a strong tradition of investigation by sociologists of religion which is favourable towards the church. Here much attention is paid to the concrete forms of expression of Christian faith. In general Reformed sociology is more critical about forms of the church. See e.g. Mady Thung, *The Precarious Organization. Sociological Explorations of the Church's Mission and Structure*, The Hague and Paris: Mouton 1976.

6   J. W. Becker and R. Vink, *Secularisatie in Nederland 1966–1991. De verandering van opvattingen en enkele gedragingen*, Rijswijk: Sociaal en Cultureel Planbureau 1994, 52, 53, 73, and *Sociaal en Cultureel Rapport (SCP) 1994*, Rijswijk 1994.

7   The key figures for 1994/1995 are taken from the church statistics of the Roman Catholic Church in the Netherlands, *Kerkelijke documentatie* 121, 23, 1995, nos 9, 14.

8   Becker and Vink, *Secularisatie in Nederland* (n. 6), 57.

9   Ibid., 172.

10 J. Kerkhofs, 'Young People and Values in Western Europe', *Pro Mundi Vita: Dossiers* 1984/4, 28.

11 *SCP 1994*, 173.

12 Cf. T. Andree, *Gelovig word je niet vanzelf*, Nijmegen 1983, and T. Andree and P. Steegman (eds), *Religieuze socialisatie. Een uitdaging voor onderzoek*, Utrecht 1987. However, the description of the term 'religious socialization' is not itself without problems. What is meant by 'religion'? How do we measure religious growth? What is the indication of religious maturity? What is the relationship between the internal component of religion (giving meaning, a spiritual sense, the forming of the conscience) and the political aspects (the church as a community, a sense of identity, cultural impact)? Mady Thung, *The Precarious Organization* (n. 5), for the first time systematically posed the question of the actual points of contact of religious socialization by means of Etzioni's agogic theory, with reference to the 'operands' of ideological and mental influence on ideal movements. Little use has been made by the church authorities of her work. Cf. A. Houtepen, 'De oecumenische beweging als spirituele doorbraak. Enkele suggesties voor de organisatie van een nieuwe confessionaliteit', in D. Koelega and H. Noordegraaf (eds), *Visie en Volharding (Opstellling voor Mady A. Thung)*, Driebergen: MCKS 1991.

13 D. Hutsebaut, *Een zekere onzekerheid. Jongeren en Geloof*, Leuven: Acco 1995. In a survey among European young people Kerkhofs already found in 1984 that young people in 1966 had far more often given firmly negative answers, for example to the question of the possibility of a life after death, than they did in 1984. The agnosis of young people between seventeen and twenty-four may have increased, but it has become a far more questing and curious agnosis. Apart from the question of sexual relations and participation in the liturgy, young people, too, do not want any break with the tradition and are more interested than before in the questions of life and death (pop culture): J. Kerkhofs, *God in Europe, Pro Mundi Vita Dossier 1984*, Brussels 1984. From this Kerkhofs concludes: 'This requires deep-going rethinking of the whole pastoral strategy (to a much greater extent than in the past, things will have to be done "together with" rather than "for" modern young people). For this reason, the most important task of believing communities ... will be to provide

a space in which hope for meaningful developments will be the principal concern: a space in which people can overcome their alienation, in which their exaggerated individualism can be healed; a space in which new styles of interpersonal relationships and contacts between groups can develop. Within the framework of these possibilities for true human togetherness, the witness of hope in the kingdom of God renewed by the Bible and the liturgy, will be able to develop. It can also be a place where dedication and commitment to the (Second), Third and Fourth World can be nurtured.' Perhaps there is too much wishful thinking here as far as Europe is concerned.

14 Cf. H. Cox, *Religion in the Secular City*, New York: Simon and Schuster 1984.

15 Cf. M. ter Borg, *Een uitgewaaierde eeuwigheid. Het menselijk tekort in de moderne cultuur*, Baarn: Ten Have 1991. There is certainly a quest for meaning, but this is somewhat fragmentary, flexible, in an enormous pluralism which is also defended rationally, but it lacks any systematic character, any form of striving for cultural influence and institutionalization.

16 O. Chadwick, *The Secularization of the European Mind in the Nineteenth Century*, Cambridge: Cambridge University Press 1991, 4: 'We cannot begin our quests for secularization by formulating a dream-society that once upon a time was not secular.' In many church texts, but also in a number of studies by sociologists of religion – certainly if they are well disposed towards the church and are looking for 'mitigating factors' in the loss of credit by religion and the church – there is in fact a romanticism, hidden or open, about the past times of a *societas christiana* or a Christian Europe.

17 S. Sykes, *The Identity of Christianity*, London: SPCK 1984, 251ff. Sykes takes this term from a book by W. B. Gallie, *Philosophy and the Historical Understanding*, London: Chatto and Windus 1964, which refers to a large number of basic concepts of thought, like science, art, religion, justice and democracy. These are similarly marked by ongoing discussions about their content and essence and can be clarified only by the vicissitudes of their usage in history. According to Sykes, that is also the case with Christianity. That explains its changing cultural form and its *de facto* pluralism. It seems to me that here reference must also be made to the critical character of the gospel itself. It is not only historical and contingent and to be found solely in the interpretation of any age, it is also 'contested', because it is full of critical pointers for culture.

18 P. Valadier, *L'Église en procès. Catholicisme et société moderne*, Paris: Calmann-Lévy 1985. Valadier speaks of a lawsuit in which church and culture are intertwined, a reflection or echo of the suit between human beings and their God: 'It [the church] participates in the lawsuit of the world, in that it is affected by its troubles, its hopes and its utopias. It also and above all participates in it because by virtue of its origins and its end it is in a position of maintaining the lawsuit of the world. Now this lawsuit involves arguments, debates, contradictions; it is an unending lawsuit' (233). 'Whether or not it wants to, by its very presence and by its message the church is a challenge to self-sufficiency; thus it breaks the narcissism of those who think it enough to examine themselves to know themselves. It bears witness to a God who is neither an idol that can be manipulated or appropriated nor a pure Otherness protected by its infinite distance, but a divine Trinity characterized by the gratuitousness of the exchange. It proclaims an upside-down Messiah, to use M. Gauchet's phrase, showing that he who serves commands, and that the service of the lowest is consecration to the Most High.'

19 Valadier, *L'Église en procès* (n. 18), 65. Cf. M. Gauchet, *Le dèsenchantement du monde. Une histoire politique de la religion*, Paris: Gallimard 1985, 191: 'The death of God is not a matter of human beings becoming God, reappropriating to themselves the absolute conscious disposition of themselves which they have ascribed to themselves; on the contrary, it is a matter of human beings who are expressively obliged to renounce the dream of their own divinity. It is when the gods are in eclipse that it really proves that human beings are not gods.' For Derrida, too, the discovery of the radical finitude of life and the absolute contingency of death is the most characteristic consequence of 'the death of God'; J. Derrida, *Aporias. Dying – awaiting (one another at) the 'limits of truth'* (= *Mourir – s'attendre aux 'limites de la vérité'*), Stanford: Stanford University Press 1993. The minority position of the church in culture therefore corresponds to a far more modest position of human beings in nature and history.

20 See n. 4.

21 J. Sperna Weiland, *Romeins Schetsboek. Over de metamorfose van het geloven*, Baarn 1980, 36.

22 A. J. Nijk, *Secularisatie. Over het gebruik van een woord*, Rotterdam 1968. W. Pannenberg, *Christianity in a Secularized World*, London: SCM Press 1988, immediately points out that the word has very different meanings, so that both the positive and the negative connotations of the term also each in turn bring with them different phenomena and value judgements. He assesses this ambiguity positively, in contrast to all one-sided interpretations. One of these one-sided interpretations is that of H. Blumenberg, who in his book *Die Legitimität der Neuzeit*, Frankfurt 1966, opposes the use of the term because it wrongly suggests that the ideals of modernity, i.e. of the Enlightenment, must be taken to be derived from Christianity as 'secularity', or even as an illegitimate appropriation. On the other hand that is also the thesis of Friedrich Gogarten, who sees the prelude to the process of secularization in the demythologizing ideals of Christianity and especially in the division between the worldly and the spiritual governments of Luther's Reformation (the doctrine of the two realms): cf. F. Gogarten, *Verhängnis und Hoffnung der Neuzeit*, Stuttgart 1953; from another perspective – the conception of history and belief in progress – K. Löwith, *Weltgeschichte und Heilsgeschichte*, Stuttgart 1953, made the same attempt to interpret the event of secularization in 'Christian' terms (as is well known, Blumenberg's book is a direct refutation of Löwith's theses).

23 David Martin, The *Religious and the Secular*, London: Routledge 1969, 1. He argues for deleting the term from the sociological dictionary (22). He accuses sociologists of giving content to religion from their own beliefs – for example by concentrating on attitudes and doctrines – in order to show that the leave-taking from religion is an irreversible process (16).

24 Charles West, 'Community, Christian and Secular', in E. de Vries (ed.), *Man and Community*, New York and London 1966, 343.

25 Peter Berger, *The Sacred Canopy*, Garden City: Prentice-Hall 1967, 107.

26 W. Hartmann, 'Säkularisierung', in *Evangelisches Kirchenlexikon*, Göttingen 1959, 768.

27 G. Dekker, *De mens en zijn godsdienst*, Bilthoven 1975, 42–3.

28 O. Chadwick, *The Secularization of the European Mind* (n. 16), 17. For the ambivalences of the term 'religion' and the changing theological evaluation of

this concept in the twentieth century see A. Houtepen, 'Ambiguous Religion and the Authentic Holy', *Exchange* 25, 1996, 2–26.

29   J. Lauwers, *Secularisatietheorieën*, Leuven 1974, 2–3.

30   For Weber and Gauchet see n. 2. O. Chadwick sums up Weber's view, which derives this from the influence of the Reformation in Europe, as follows: 'The Reformation made all secular life into a vocation of God. It was like a baptism of the secular world. It refused any longer to regard the specially religious calling of priest or monk as higher in moral scale than the calling of cobbler or of prince. Christian energy was turned away from the still and the contemplative towards action. The man who would leave the world turned into the man who would change it. Religion centred upon ritual veered towards religion centred upon ethic. *Supreme good, which once was Being, now began to be Doing.* Once they had waited for the New Jerusalem which should descend from heaven, now they resolved not to cease from strife till they had built it in this green and pleasant land' (Chadwick, *The Secularization of the European Mind* [n. 16], 8). As early as 1929, however, R. H. Tawney made it clear that the rise of this new spirit of trade and mentality of progress – in Weber's famous *Protestantism and the Rise of Capitalism* – had already begun long before the Reformation, in northern Italy.

31   Sperna Weiland, *Romeins Schetsboek* (n. 21), 46–7.

32   Nijk, *Secularisatie* (n. 22), 18–19. For this historical foundation Nijk refers to J. G. von Meiern, *Acta Pacis Westphalicae*, Hanover 1734, and M. Stallmann, *Was ist Säkularisierung?*, Tübingen 1960. Many saw this dethroning of the church by the law of property as 'the judgement of history, which is exacted on the lies of theocracy', see Lübbe, *Säkularisierung* (n. 1).

33   Du Cange, *Glossarium Mediae et Infimae Latinitatis*, Graz 1954, s.v. 'saeculum'.

34   R. Koper, *Das Weltverständis des Hl. Franziskus von Assisi. Eine Untersuchung über das 'Exivi de Saeculo'*, Werl 1959. According to Koper, however, Francis is also concerned with the theological meaning of *saeculum = aion*: the world which derives from God and not the opposition between monastic life and life outside the monastery as such.

35   *Codex Iuris Canonici* 1917: cc. 640–643. In the *CIC* 1983 these terms are avoided, and where buildings are concerned the term used is *redigere in usum profanum non sordidum* (*CIC* 122), and, in connection with religious and clergy, *amissio status clericalis* (*CIC* 290–293). Certainly there is a section *de institutis saecularibus*, i.e. forms of religious life which are not connected with a monastery (*CIC* 710–730), and also mention of *clerici saeculares* (*CIC* 278), i.e. clergy who are not members of an order.

36   B. Tierney, *The Crisis of Church and State, 1050–1300*, Englewood Cliffs, NJ: Prentice-Hall 1980.

37   Cf. A. Wessels, *Europe. Was it Ever Really Christian?* (n. 4).

38   I. Kant, *Was ist Aufklärung?*, 1784.

39   G. Danneels, 'Het geseculariseerde Europa evangeliseren', *Benedictijns Tijdschrift*, 1985, no. 4.

40   L. Newbigin, *Foolishness to the Greeks. The Gospel and Western Culture*, Geneva: WCC 1986. Cf. id., *The Other Side of 1984. Questions for the Churches*, Geneva: WCC 1983; id., *The Gospel in a Pluralist Society*, Geneva: WCC and Grand Rapids: Eerdmans 1989; id., *The Gospel as Public Truth*, Geneva: WCC and Grand Rapids: Eerdmans 1991.

41   H. Blumenberg, *Die Legitimität der Neuzeit* (n. 22).

42 Augustine, *Confessions* X, 17, 26, edited and translated by Henry Chadwick, Oxford: Oxford University Press 1991, 194.

43 *Confessions* X, 17, 26, edited and translated by F. J. Sheed, London: Sheed and Ward [10]1978, 181.

44 F. Nietzsche, *The Joyful Science* (1882), 125.

45 J. Pottmeyer, *Der Glaube vor dem Anspruch der Wissenschaft*, Freiburg 1968; H. Waldenfels, *Kontextuelle Fundamentaltheologie*, Paderborn, Munich, Vienna and Zurich 1985, 316–35, 464–88. V. Conzemius, 'Die Kritik der Kirche', in W. Kern et al. (eds), *Handbuch der Fundamentaltheologie* 3, Freiburg 1986, 30–48, speaks of the 'repression of criticism' (38–41).

46 J. Hoekendijk, *De kerk binnenstebuiten*, extracts from his work by L. A. Hoedemaker and P. Tijmes, Amsterdam 1964.

47 Cf. A. Houtepen, *Theology of the 'Saeculum'*, Kampen 1976.

48 E. Jüngel, *God as the Mystery of the World*, Edinburgh: T & T Clark 1983.

49 Ibid., 226–98. Cf. Per Lonning, *Der begreiflich Unergreifbare. 'Sein Gottes' und modern-theologische Denkstrukturen*, Göttingen 1986.

50 J. Barr, *Fundamentalism*, London: SCM Press [3]1988; H. Cox, *Religion in the Secular City* (n.14).

51 J. Kerkhofs, 'God in Europe', in *Pro Mundi Vita: Dossiers 1987/2* (Europe-North America Dossier 37).

52 John Paul II, *Adhortatio Familiaris Consortio* 1985 and Synod of Bishops 1985.

53 *Common Witness. A Study Document of the Joint Working Group of the Roman Catholic Church and the World Council of Churches*, Geneva 1980.

54 David Gill (ed.), *Gathered for Life. VIth Assembly World Council of Churches, Vancouver*, Geneva: WCC and Grand Rapids: Eerdmans 1983, 251–2.

55 K. Barth, *Humanismus*, Theologische Studien 28, Zurich 1949; cf. W. Banning et al., *Modern niet-godsdienstig humanisme*, Nijmegen and Utrecht 1960.

56 J. Lochman, *Neue Zürcher Zeitung* 202, 1984, 1 September 1984, 29. Cf. id., *Christ and Prometheus?*, Geneva 1988, 38–40, 41–50. Cf. Vaclav Havel, quoted by Lochman in *Christ and Prometheus?*, 49: 'Only a human being can lead a relatively tolerable life in this world, which is oriented "beyond" this world; a human being, who refers to the infinite, the absolute and the eternal with every one of his or her "heres" and every one of his or her "nows". An unconditional orientation upon "now" and "here" converts every bearable "now" and "here" into desert and wilderness and finally discolours it with blood.'

57 Barth, *Humanismus* (n. 55), 8 and 12: 'The Christian message ... thus protects commitment against Nietzsche, freedom against Marx ... socialist truth against the West and personalistic truth against the East ... inexorable protest against those who dominate and against the masses.'

2. THE MANY COLOURS OF AGNOSIS

1 In the metatheism that J. A. Krüger has described (*Metatheism. Early Buddhism and Traditional Christian Theism*, Pretoria 1989, 118–26), it is not denied that God is personal or that he is impersonal, because God's own character transcends that. This metatheism is meta-personal and meta-impersonal. It points to the mystery that as a source and power is present in everything and at the same time forms the 'great depth' of it.' It seems to me that 'theism' had

another focus, so that by the term 'post-theism' I mean something different from Krüger. This 'metatheism' is still a relatively innocent form of 'post-theism'. *De facto* agnosis implies the denial of all claims of 'theism', or at least implies no longer asking the questions to which these claims tried to give an answer. The term 'theism' was used for the first time by the British physico-theologian Ralph Cudworth in his book *The True Intellectual System of the Universe*, London 1678. By it he understands the specific and shared conviction of Judaism, Christianity and Islam of the existence of an absolute God who transcends the world and is in fact personal, the First Cause and Supreme Goal of all that is, who created the world out of nothing, who keeps it permanently in existence and who through properties of infinity, perfection, providence and omnipotence is the *guideline for human action*. Cf. *The Encyclopedia of Philosophy*, Vol. 6, London: Macmillan 1967, 509: 'Theism is belief in one God who is (a) personal (b) worthy of adoration (c) separate from the world (d) continuously active.' It is the character of the idea of God as *guideline* which is involved in the phenomenon of secularization; all the positive attributes given to God have lost their divine character as predicates: infinity, perfection, providence, omnipotence, eternity, etc. We no longer derive pointers for action from them in our sense of contingency, feasibility, changing values and purposes, ecological vulnerability and mortality. Our concrete projects in life no longer reflect eternal ideas or pre-existing ideals but derive exclusively from our fear of disorder and lawlessness. Ours is a 'fanned out eternity' (M. ter Borg, *Eenuitgewaaierde eeuwigheid. Het menschelijk tekort in de moderne cultuur*, Baarn: Ten Have 1991). But if all former divine characteristics no longer serve as a mirror for human virtue, why then still maintain a subject of whom these characteristics are predicated? If these characteristics themselves are no longer 'of use' within our picture of human beings, then the God who supported them will sooner or later be driven out of our consciousness. That there are *More Things in Heaven and Earth* (the title of a book by A. van den Beukel, London: SCM Press 1991) than we dream of or that *the heart has its reasons that the mind does not know* (Pascal), as young people confess in either a vague pantheism or an esoteric 'holism', can be said just as well or better by art or poetry. But Schleiermacher already knew that to cherish such sentiments is not the same thing as worship. To use the term 'metatheism' for this proves confusing. Cf. in the same direction, but already with rather more understanding of the hermeneutical scope of the language field of 'person' and 'self' in connection with the idea of God, J. van der Ven, 'De structuur van het religieuze bewustzijn. Verkenning van de spanning tussen religiositeit en kerkelijkheid', *Tijdschrift voor Theologie* 36, 1996, 39–60.

2   Cf. H. Waldenfels, *Kontextuelle Fundamentaltheologie*, Paderborn: Schoningh 1984.

3   Ibid.,118ff., speaks of a 'lack' of God: '... the number is increasing of those who in practice live as if God did not exist or even explicitly deny the existence of God. God is removed from human life as it were in two ways: (a) God is no longer spoken of, and thus is kept silent about, so that God is in practice 'lacking' from human life; (b) an attempt is made to exclude the existence of God with rational arguments, so that God is denied.' In both cases, to use Bonhoeffer's phrase, 'God as a working hypothesis' is done away with. However, it is important to see that both the affirmation of belief in God and the denial of God have become exceptions. What we have is a broad middle

ground of those for whom God no longer adds anything. Here Waldenfels speaks of two kinds of 'agnosticism', a term coined by T. H. Huxley in 1869: by this he meant the theoretical basic attitude which thinks that it cannot make statements about God and the divine because on these matters no certainty in the scientific sense can be attained. With H. R. Schlette (*Der moderne Agnostizismus*, Düsseldorf 1979), he distinguishes between an analytical form (Wittgenstein, Ayer, Flew, Albert), which for epistemological reasons puts the idea of God in brackets, and an aporetic enigmatic form which is the modern form of the classical question of theodicy: 'If God exists, why is there so much suffering?' It seems to me that both forms simply represent the intellectual tip of a much larger iceberg of practical agnosis, at the basis of which lie yet other factors. Cf. Chapter 1, n. 1.

4   F. Schleiermacher, *On Religion. Speeches to Its Cultured Despisers*, translated by John Oman, New York: Harper and Brothers 1958, 1f.

5   J. Delumeau, *Sin and Fear. The Emergence of a Western Guilt Culture 13th–18th Centuries*, New York: St Martin's Press 1990.

6   E. Drewermann, *Tiefenpsychologie und Exegese* (2 vols), Munich: DTV 1993, 1997; id., *Das Markusevangelium* I–II, Olten: Walter 1988–9; id., *Das Matthäusevangelium*, Olten: Walter 1992ff. ; id., *Psychoanalyse und Moraltheologie* I–II, Mainz: Grünewald 1992–4; id., *Strukturen des Bösen*, Paderborns etc. 1988 (his 1978 Habilitationsschrift).

7   W. Hanegraaff, *New Age Religion and Western Culture. Esotericism in the Mirror of Secular Thought*, Utrecht dissertation 1995. As Hanegraaff convincingly demonstrates, it is too easy to see the phenomenon of New Age exclusively as a form of longing for a religion of comfort and security, harmony with nature and non-violence. New Age is a conscious ideology for getting rid of guilt. It is always exclusively a matter of responsibility for one's own well-being and equilibrium. Evil consists in all forms of subjection of the self to the will of the other or to the forces of nature. 'Bear one another's burdens' does not appear in New Age ethics.

8   H. Wiersinga, *De verzoening in de theologische discussie*, Kampen: Kok [4]1972; *Doem of daad. Een boek over zonde*, Baarn: Ten Have 1982; *Geloven bij daglicht. Verlies en toekomst van een traditie*, Baarn: Ten Have 1992.

9   Wiersinga, *Doem of daad* (n. 8), 49.

10   Cf. H. Haag, *Teufelsglaube*, Tübingen 1975; E. Schillebeeckx, *Christ*, London: SCM Press 1980, 500–11; E. H. Pagels, *The Origin of Satan*, New York: Random House 1995; G. Messadié, *De Geschiedenis van het Kwaad. Historie, Legenden en beeldvorming van de Duivel*, Baarn: Tirion 1994 (a popular but in many places confused account of exegetical studies and facts from the history of religion); B. McGinn, The *Antichrist*, New York: Crossroad 1994; A. Bernstein, *The Formation of Hell, Death and Retribution in the Ancient and Early Christian Worlds*, London: UCL Press 1993. The present-day scholarly and exegetical consensus about the figure of Satan or the devil is important: Schillebeeckx sums it up like this: 'As "prince of this world", Satan is thus an extra-biblical figure, generally accepted in Palestine from about 150 BC onwards ... The Old Testament and even large parts of the extra-biblical literature have no Satanology at all. This is not a part of traditional Jewish faith: it became a part of popular Palestinian belief and also (though perhaps to a lesser degree) that of Diaspora Judaism in pre-Christian, intertestamental, syncretistic literature on the basis of a number of legends ... The devil or Satan or the

demons are an element of the cultural and religious consciousness of all the New Testament authors ... The New Testament takes it for granted that Satan and all the demons have been conquered by Christ ... For Christians, devils are nothing: they no longer exist ... Whatever ideas there may have been about Satan during the time of the appearance of Jesus in Palestine, Jesus sees his own appearance as God's salvation. He is not interested in Satan, but in man with his weaknesses and sicknesses, his lack of faith and his sinfulness which God seeks to remove – and that emerges from Jesus' ministry' (Schillebeeckx, *Christ*, 506–11).

11 For the influence of this dualism on the reading of Genesis see Drewermann, *Strukturen des Bösen*, Vol. 1 (n. 6). For the historical implications of the doctrine of the Two Kingdoms see A. Houtepen, 'De Twee Rijkenleer is ook niet alles', *Gereformeerd Theologische Tijdschrift* 87, 1987, 47–62.

12 H. Wegman, *De geschiedenis van de christelijke eredienst in het Westen en in het Oosten. Een Wegwijzer*, Hilversum: Gooi & Sticht 1976, mentions Augustine, Ambrose, Cyril of Alexandria, John Chrysostom, Theodore of Mopsuestia and a number of Syriac documents. Probably the rite of forswearing Satan comes from Syria (ibid., 40) and also penetrated the West via Egypt (Alexandria) and Cappadocia. We do not find this element in Hippolytus' description of the baptismal liturgy. Presumably the initial rite also represented only the forswearing of the pagan past with all its dualistic ideas: forsaking Satan meant taking leave of the belief in Satan which had spread everywhere. Hence the Greek term *apotaxis*: putting off, setting aside. Later the significance of a real exorcism began to dominate: here from the time of the service book for the celebration of the sacraments, *Gelasianum Vetus*, onwards, Satan is also addressed directly: *Proinde, damnate, da honorem deo vivo et vero*, with a reference to the healing of the man who was deaf and dumb in Mark 7.34–35: *Effeta, quod est adaperire, in odorem suavitatis. Tu autem effugare, diabole, adpropinquavit enim iudicium dei*. The forsaking of the devil is coupled with an anointing of chest and shoulders, the athlete's massage, which has to be performed when facing a strong opponent (ibid., 137). In the Middle Ages these exorcisms were also practised on babies. The rite was also maintained by the Council of Trent and only dropped from the baptismal liturgy after Vatican II. Precisely because of this baptismal liturgy, for centuries the Christian doctrine of salvation was formulated in terms of escaping the power of the devil. The constitutional sinfulness of human beings – original sin – read out of Genesis 3 is projected back on to the power of evil through Adam and Eve and the serpent.

13 *De Belijdenisgeschriften volgens artikel X van de Kerkorde van de Nederlandse Hervormde Kerk*, The Hague [2]1966, 32.

14 Ibid., 33.

15 Ibid., 34.

16 Ibid., 35.

17 Ibid., 63–4.

18 DS 297, 1567.

19 *Catechism of the Catholic Church*, nos 2850–4.

20 Cf. P. Ricoeur, *Philosophie de la volonté. Finitude et culpabilité II: La Symbolique du mal*, Paris: Aubier 1960; id., *Le mal, un défi à la philosophie et à la théologie*, Geneva: Labor et Fides 1986.

21 Peter Brown, *The Body and Society. Men, Women and Sexual Renunciation in*

Early Christianity, New York: Columbia University Press 1988, shows how much the basically negative attitude towards physical and sexual pleasure which accompanied the Christian ascetic ideal and the view of the human will weakened by Adam's fall is the outcome of a complex inculturation of the Jewish-Christian tradition (which itself is governed by all kinds of cultural views from the ancient Near East) in Hellenistic, Celtic and Germanic culture: there is no isolated negative Christian basic attitude. In their history of sexual views and behaviour Van Ussel and Foucault have demonstrated something of this kind. That does not alter the fact that the church, by virtue of its great share in the culture of the West from the Middle Ages on, contributed to a 'disciplining' of the body as a source of danger, as a gateway and an outlet for evil. Morality came to mean curbing the beast within human beings. Passion and emotion were seen as defeats of the will and a loss of reason. Women were blamed for men giving way to their instincts: they became the seducers *par excellence*, incarnations of the great seducer, daughters of Eve, who allowed herself to be led up the garden path by the serpent.

22 I. Dalferth, *Existenz Gottes und christlicher Glaube. Skizzen zu einer eschatologischen Ontologie*, Munich 1984.

23 R. Burggraeve, *Mens en Medemens. Verantwoordelijkheid en God. De metafysische ethiek van Emmanuel Levinas*, Leuven and Amersfoort: Acco: 1986: 'Any trace [of the divine] is so enigmatic and ambiguous, precisely because of God's *illeité* or transcendent glory, that it may just as well not be a "trace" of God, but only an affective filling in of a projection of me or a collective projection of us' (597).

24 Cf. the sharp analysis by W. Pannenberg, *Metaphysik und Gottesgedanke*, Göttingen: Vandenhoeck & Ruprecht 1988. Pannenberg derives this critique of metaphysics from the positivism of Auguste Comte, who regarded metaphysics as a transitional stage between myth and empirical reason; from the nihilism of Nietzsche, for whom metaphysics is the form of a fundamental heteronomy which takes away our sight, our freedom and our infinity and which restricts us in our will to power; and from the epistemological critique of Kant and his followers, including Dilthey and Heidegger, who thought that the filter of our subjectivity and the equipment of our spirit make us lose sight of being itself, the *Ding an sich* and the Absolute: we cannot leave the categories of our thought system, the hermeneutical circle of our standpoint, the 'thrownness' of our actual existence. In theology since Ritschl and Harnack a certain abhorrence of the Hellenistic origin of Plato's and Aristotle's metaphysics of being, as an aberration from more 'original' Jewish thought, has been associated with this. We also find traces of it in Karl Barth, Tillich and Bonhoeffer. The Catholic tradition opted for another track here and, inspired by Thomas Aquinas, sought new foundations for metaphysics, (see Chapter 11). Pannenberg wants something of the same kind and opts above all for Hegel. The problem here is that Hegel's systematic thought formed the point of contact for the nineteenth-century critique of metaphysics and that postmodern deconstructionism as the critique of subject and system also has a markedly anti-Hegelian character. But I share Pannenberg's basic insight that without metaphysics it is impossible to open up a consistent way of thought towards God, and also that the classical metaphysics of being need not be the only metaphysical method.

25 E. Levinas, 'God and Philosophy', in S. Hand (ed.), *The Levinas Reader*,

Oxford: Blackwell 1989, 166–87. The contrast between 'the God of Abraham, Isaac and Jacob' (after Ex. 3.6 and 14–15, taken up in the New Testament by Jesus according to Luke 20.37, Mark 12.26 and Matt. 22.32, by Peter in Acts 3.13 and by Stephen in Acts 7.31–32) and the 'God of the philosophers' already comes from Philo of Alexandria (*De Vita Moysis* I, 74–76; *De Abrahamo*, 50–52; *De mutatione nominum*, 11–14), but more in the opposite sense: for those for whom the name of God as Being is too exalted, there are – for the weak in understanding – the names of the teacher Abraham, the natural wisdom of Isaac and the practical wisdom of Jacob: in other words, God's own name – *to on*, the One who is, is unfathomable, God has no proper name and can be named only indirectly by substitute names: even Abraham, Isaac and Jacob did not know the proper name of God (Ex. 6.3); see D. T. Runia, 'God of the Philosophers, God of the Patriarchs. Exegetical Backgrounds in Philo of Alexandria', in R. Munk and F. J. Hoogewoud (eds), *Joodse filosofie tussen rede en traditie*, Kampen: Kok 1993, 13–23. Runia (20): 'It would be wrong, however, to overinterpret this distinction and read it as an antithesis. We cannot read into this text the kind of opposition envisaged by Pascal between a God of the philosophers and a God of the Patriarchs, the former (vainly) approached by reason, the latter through belief and prophetic experience. Although distinguishing between the two texts, Philo nevertheless regards them as complementary ... Nowhere in Philo's writings do we find a polemic against the "God of the philosophers", but rather against the "God" of misguided thinkers who fail to recognize the utter uniqueness of the First and only true cause.' Indeed it is hard to brand Philo's work as a critique of metaphysics: quite the contrary. According to Runia, Pascal distorted the distinction between God in himself and 'God in relation to human beings' (viz., Israel), which had been used earlier, into an opposition between philosophy and faith. Neither he nor De Boer are to be followed here. And Levinas, to whom de Boer refers for his opposition to the 'God of the philosophers', rejects this contrast: see Levinas, 'God and Philosophy', 169: 'To ask, as we are trying to do here, if God can be expressed in a rational discourse which would be neither ontology nor faith, is implicitly to doubt the formal opposition, established by Yehouda Halevy and taken up by Pascal, between the God of Abraham, Isaac and Jacob, invoked in faith without philosophy, and the God of the philosophers. It is to doubt that this opposition constitutes an alternative.'

26 J. Habermas, *Theory of Communicative Action* II, Oxford: Polity Press 1989, 77–8.

27 E. Arens, 'Theologie nach Habermas. Eine Einführung', in E. Arens (ed.), *Habermas und die Theologie*, Düsseldorf ²1989, 14.

28 W. Pannenberg, *Wissenschaftstheorie und Theologie*, Frankfurt 1973, 299–348. Cf. Chapter 12.

29 M. Heidegger, *Identität und Differenz*, Pfüllingen 1957, 45: 'Anyone who has experienced theology, both that of Christian faith and that of philosophy, from an adult source today prefers to be silent about God *in the realm of thought*.'

30 A. Dumas, *Nommer Dieu*, Paris 1980.

31 Hans Küng, *Does God Exist? An Answer for Today*, London: Collins 1984, 529–51. For the proofs of the existence of God and especially the ontological proof of God see J. Rohls, *Theologie und Metaphysik. Der ontologische Gottesbeweis und seine Kritiker*, Gütersloh: Mohn 1987; Iris Murdoch, *Hoe bewijs ik het bestaan van God. Enkele bespiegelingen omtrent het ontologisch bewijs*, Van der

Leeuw lecture 1986, Amsterdam and Groningen 1986. Both make a plea for the revival of Anselm's proof of God. But at the same time both show that Anselm's picture of God (*id quo maius cogitari nequit*) fits better with Plato's (or Aristotle's) impersonal deity than with the living God of the Jewish-Christian tradition. The basic error has continued to be influential despite all the nuances and refinements which were introduced by Thomas, Duns Scotus, Leibniz, Descartes and Kant, especially in deism and the natural or positive theology defended by deism. A number of philosophers – Heidegger, Horkheimer and Adorno – have equally criticized the metaphysic coupled with this proof of God: it does not touch on the true being of *essents* (Heidegger); it leads to a view of *ratio* which is characterized by necessity, causality, mechanics and instrumentality (Horkheimer and Adorno). At best such Platonic metaphysics has a healthy effect on today's agnosis, but at the same time this 'deity', from a historical perspective, is also the cause of the rejection of God as a projection of human striving for the true, the good and the beautiful. A return to this deity therefore does not seem to be a solution 'beyond secularization'.

32 E. P. Meijering, 'Het ferment van de Griekse wijsbegeerte', in H. W. van der Dunk et al. (eds), *Europese theologie in mondiaal perspectief*, Utrecht 1985, 47–52. We find a classic example of such a comparative in Augustine's *Confessions*, Book III.

33 Cf. Chapter 1, n. 22.

34 Cf. O. Kallscheuer, *Gottes Wort und Volkes Stimme. Glaube, Macht, Politik*, Frankfurt: Fischer 1994.

35 A. Burms and H. de Dijn, *De rationaliteit en haar grenzen. Kritiek en deconstructie*, Leuven, Assen and Maastricht 1986.

36 W. Goddijn, 'Some Religious Developments in the Netherlands (1947–1979) as Documented by a Few Surveys and Census Data', *Social Compass* 30, 1983, 409–23: 419. According to the survey *God in Nederland 1979* the values of health (52%), happiness (38%), peace (31%) and love (22%) score most highly in a selection of the three most important values from a list of twenty-five. To the question what the highest value is in someone's personal life 23% answered health, 17% happiness and 16% peace. Love and a comfortable life then together scored notably lower: 7%.

37 Cf. M. Horkheimer, *Zur Kritik der instrumentellen Vernunft*, Frankfurt 1967. Cf. M. Jay, *De dialektische verbeelding*, Baarn ²1985, who quotes from T. W. Adorno and M. Horkeimer, *Dialectic of Enlightenment*, London: Allen Lane 1973: 'According to Horkheimer and Adorno the Enlightenment programme of domination was based on a secularized version of the religious conviction that God governed the world. As a result the natural object stood as an inferior, external other over against the human subject. Despite its lack of self-confidence, the primitive animism was at least aware of how the two spheres permeated one another. This had been completely lost in the Enlightenment ideal; there the world is seen as being composed of lifeless, interchangeable atoms: "Animism had ensouled things, industry makes souls things."'

38 Fénelon, *De l'existence de Dieu*, Paris: Garnier 1877, 2.

3. THE DESPAIRING QUESTION: WHERE IS GOD?

1 Cf. Ps. 10.1: 'Why do you stand afar off, O Lord? Why do you hide yourself in time of trouble?'; Ps.13.2: 'How long, O Lord? Will you forget me for ever? How long will you hide your face from me?'; Ps. 22.1: 'My God, my God, why have you forsaken me?' (= Matt. 27.46); Ps. 35.22: 'Do not be silent! O Lord, be not far from me'; Ps. 38.22: 'Do not forsake me, O Lord! O my God, be not far from me'; Ps. 42.10: 'I say to God, my rock, "Why have you forgotten me? Why go I mourning because of the oppression of the enemy?" As with a deadly wound in my body, my adversaries taunt me, while they say to me continually, "Where is your God?" '; Ps. 71.12: 'O God, be not far from me; O my God, make haste to help me'; Ps. 77.10: 'Has God forgotten to be gracious? Has he in anger shut up his compassion?'; Ps. 79.10 (= 115.2): 'Why should the nations say, "Where is their God?" '; Ps. 89.46: 'How long, O Lord? Will you hide yourself for ever? How long will your wrath burn like this?' It is striking how often this experience of God's absence is expressed in the psalms of Israel. The question of God is a real question, not a rhetorical introduction to a dogmatic certainty, as in the old catechism question: 'Where is God?', and the answer: 'God is in heaven, on earth and in all places: He is everywhere' (*Catechism of the Dutch Dioceses*, 1948, question and answer 12).

2 H. Waldenfels, *Kontextuelle Fundamentaltheologie*, 120–1. See Chapter 2, nn. 2, 3.

3 Here the position of L. Wittgenstein (1889–1951) in his *Tractatus logico-philosophicus* has become decisive. The preface states: 'What can be said at all can be said clearly, and whereof one cannot speak thereof one must be silent.' And: 'Whereof one cannot speak thereof one must be silent' (7). Here the most important statement of 6.52 is usually forgotten: 'We feel that even if all possible scientific questions be answered, the problems of life have still not been touched at all. Of course, there is then no question left, and just this is the answer.' Thus Wittgenstein is well aware that there is a sphere of life where no exact questions and answers are appropriate: 6.522: 'There is indeed the inexpressible. This shows itself, it is the mystical.'

4 Thomas Aquinas, *Summa Theologica*, I, q. 2, a. 3 (*Utrum Deus sit?*):

> 1. *'Videtur quod Deus non sit ... intelligitur in hoc nomine:* Deus, scilicet quod sit *quoddam bonum infinitum. Si ergo Deus esset, nullum malum inveniretur. Invenitur autem malum in mundo: ergo Deus non est.*
> 2. *... videtur quod omnia quae apparent in mundo possunt compleri per alia principia, supposito quod Deus non sit:*
> – *quia ea quae sunt naturalia reducuntur in principium quod est natura,*
> – *ea vero quae sunt a proposito reducuntur in principium quod est ratio humana vel voluntas. Nulla igitur necessitas est ponere Deum esse.'*

5 The whole Western theodicy tradition has followed this line: if we knew all factors, then it would become evident that what in our eyes is a disaster ultimately serves some good. We find this notion explicitly, for example, in Spinoza. Whether natural evil, human evil deeds or the aporias of injustice and irreparable suffering, there is always a human judgement on the situation. Evil is therefore not objective but a predicate, a qualification which expresses a particular relationship between human beings and nature. Something is bad,

not because it is bad in itself but because it produces the wrong thing for human beings: *malum est id quod nocet* (Augustine). Konrad Lorenz, *Das sogenannte Böse. Zur Naturgeschichte der Aggression*, Vienna: Bortoha-Scholer 1963, has developed this notion. According to Lorenz, the experience of evil is only the consequence of a wrong interpretation of the fight for existence which is simply built into existence, as the Greek natural philosophers Anaximander and Heraclitus already knew. Characterized by Darwin as 'struggle for life' and by Lorenz himself as 'the pressure of selection', this is in fact the motive force of progress and evolution. Evil is thus the growing pains of the good. One can best arm oneself against it with a certain patience or *ataraxia* and by collaborating as far as possible with the forces of nature: *secundum naturam vivere*. This notion of the old Stoics crops up again in many new religious movements and all kinds of therapies originating from California, which promise their followers a 'whole world'. Evil then becomes a trick of perspective, according to the famous remark by Alexander Pope: 'All partial evil, universal good' and 'whatever is, is right'. For a survey of the main lines of philosophical theodicy see C. F. Geyer, *Leid und Böses in philosophischen Deutungen*, Freiburg and Munich: Alber 1983; for Thomas, Schelling and Kierkegaard see B. Welte, *Über das Böse*, Quaestiones disputatae 6, Freiburg im Breisgau, Basel and Vienna: Herder 1959; for the theological developments see H. Häring, *Das Problem des Bösen in der Theologie*, Darmstadt: Wissenschaftliche Buchgesellschaft 1985; id., *Die Macht des Bösen: Das Erbe Augustins*, Zurich: Benziger Verlag 1979; for the 'modern' theodicy and critique of theodicy since Hegel cf. G. Neuhaus, *Theodizee – Abbruch oder Anstoss des Glaubens*, Freiburg, Basel and Vienna: Herder 1994.

6   H. Häring, *Das Problem des Bösen* (n. 5), 135–6, points out that for Voltaire this also meant a U-turn in his thought; he quotes Voltaire's less well-known didactic poem of 1756, immediately after the Lisbon earthquake: 'Poème sur la désastre de Lisbonne 1755 ou examen de cet axiome: TOUT EST BIEN', in *Oeuvres complètes* XII, Paris 1833, 183–204: 'Deceived philosophers who cry, "All is well". Run, contemplate these fearful ruins, this debris, these torches, these wretched ashes.' It is wiser to look the facts in the face and to concede that God – or the idea of God – is inconsistent than to continue to believe in God's providence which would put all this misery in a higher association with 'the good'.

7   J. Milton Yinger, 'A Structural Examination of Religion' *Journal for the Scientific Study of Religion* 8, 1969/1, 91. German philosophy of religion speaks of coping with contingency as the source of all religion: how to deal with the fate of life and death, of finitude, misery, guilt and human failure. This kind of negative or contrast experience certainly forms a source of questioning about God – it used to be said that necessity teaches prayer – but it is certainly not the only one. As a source of religion there is just as much the positive and vital part of the experience of the power of life, the good, enjoyment and blessing. I shall be discussing that in Chapter 7. There is also the appeal to freedom, solidarity and justice, the utopian dynamic of the social project of life on which the Christian message of the kingdom of God is orientated. I shall be discussing that in Chapter 8. There is finally the power of healing, cure, comfort, a new opportunity and restoration, which in the Christian tradition are bound up with the holy Breath of God, the Spirit, the Paraclete. I shall be discussing that in Chapter 9.

8   According to B. Janowski this is even the scarlet thread which runs right
    through the biblical epic: see his *Rettungsgewissheit und Epiphanie des Heils.
    Das Motif der Hilfe Gottes 'am Morgen' im Alten Orient und im Alten
    Testament*, Neukirchen-Vluyn: Neukirchener Verlag 1993.

9   Thus the title of the best-seller by Harold Kushner, *When Bad Things Happen to
    Good People*, London: Pan Books 1982.

10 H. Häring, *Das Problem des Bösen* (n. 5),1: 'The more resolutely we oppose evil,
    the more we come under the spell of its methods: veiling, disquieting, violence.
    We want the good, but in the context of the world we also create evil: possession
    as disguised theft, justice through unjust violence, security through a readiness
    for unlimited killing, health through creeping poison, perhaps a whole culture
    which is permeated with cynicism and learns to fear nothing so much as other
    human beings ... in short, evil may not be and must not be, *but it is*.' So in
    principle we must leave behind us the solution of Plotinus, Augustine and
    Thomas: they did not want to assign any character of being to the negative, and
    therefore described evil as *privatio boni*. But there is too much evil to
    characterize evil as *privatio boni*.

11 A. van de Beek, *Waarom? Over lijden, schuld en God*, Nijkerk: Callenbach 1984.

12 For an extended commentary on Job, its structure and focus, see A. de Wilde,
    Das Buch Hiob. Eingeleitet, übersetzt und erläutert, Leiden 1981; H. Jagersma
    (ed.), *Job. Studies over en rondom een bijbelboek*, Kampen: Kok 1990; Ellen van
    Wolde, *Mr and Mrs Job*, London: SCM Press 1997; W. Beuken (ed.), *The Book
    of Job*, Leuven: Peeters 1994.

13 According to some exegetes the dialogue with Elihu in Job 32–7 is a later
    insertion, with heightened arguments to support the doctrine of retribution: see
    Dictionnaire de la Bible, 1080; Jagersma, *Job* (n. 12), 10.

14 Cf. G. Schiwy, *Abschied vom allmächtigen Gott*, Munich: Kösel Verlag 1995.

15 K. Koch, 'Gibt es ein Vergeltungsdogma im Alten Testament?', in K. Koch
    (ed.), *Um das Prinzip der Vergeltung in Religion und Recht des Alten Testaments*,
    Darmstadt 1972, 130–80; H. Wiersinga, *Doem of daad. Een boek over zonde*,
    Baarn: Ten Have 1982; N. A. Schuman, *Gelijk om gelijk. Verslag en balans van
    een discussie over goddelijke vergelding in het Oude Testament*, Amsterdam: VU
    Uitgeverij 1993.

16 So I also find it incomprehensible that part of Reformation theology up to the
    recent work by A. van de Beek (*Waarom?* [n. 11], 165ff.) continues above all to
    emphasize the tragic character of sin, its character as mystery: 'For evil we must
    first of all address ourselves. However, we can also describe evil as power. This
    power of evil brings about both sin and suffering in the world. Sin is not
    something over which human beings consciously have control, which they
    choose or reject; sin is a mystery which transcends human beings, which gnaws
    at them, which infects them. Sin corrodes people, and the symptoms become
    visible in the sinful deeds which human beings do ... Evidently there is a power
    which is stronger than they [human beings] themselves are. There is a creeping
    pressure which holds people captive, carries them along to where they do not
    want to be. It is as if they fall into a drunken fit, a strange passion which puts a
    brake on their will, their choices, their sober thinking, and even makes them
    inactive. Guilt follows the sobering up. I have allowed myself to be led where I
    did not want to be ... We are victims of a power which transcends us ... The
    more we are victims, the more we are guilty.'
        Here conditioning and guilt feelings about the failure of human plans are

wrongly confused with a superhuman 'power of evil' – though it is always a matter of human, all-too-human tendencies, desires and passions – and with a concept of guilt which is not bound up with responsibility and a capacity for taking account, but with the experience of impotence. Of course that is a real experience, like that of human failure. But seen against the background of the biblical message as a whole, for this impotence to be called guilt is a serious lapse into mythical thought. One cannot appeal to some isolated texts in Paul (Rom. 1.21–23; Rom. 5; Rom. 7.8), let alone Genesis 3 for this view, despite the confessional writings. There are too many texts in scripture which speak of human responsibility and freedom and which emphasize that sin is personal desecration of 'the holy', i.e. the integrity of creation intended by God. But does not the imagery of sickness, infection, creeping poison, intoxication, an unavoidable tidal wave, the kingdom of darkness and the beast that has been let loose and which will not go back into its cave, equally lead to the end of all ethics as the notion that human beings have to give up all ideals as a way of unburdening themselves of guilt, which Van de Beek rightly criticizes? Can we Christians truly maintain that 'human beings have purchased evil like Faust' (169), and that 'there is nothing left of the freedom for which human beings are created' (169)?

17 E. Bloch, *Das Prinzip Hoffnung*, Gesamtausgabe V, Frankfurt 1977, 1392 (ET *The Principle of Hope*, MIT Press 1995, Vol. 3); id., *Atheismus im Christentum. Zur Religion des Exodus und des Reichs*, Gesamtausgabe XIV, Frankfurt 1977, 345ff. Cf. R. G. van Roon, 'Ernst Bloch over Job', in Jagersma, *Job* (n. 12), 36– 55.

18 Häring, *Die Macht des Bösen* (n. 5); E. Schillebeeckx, 'Mysterie van ongerechtigheid en mysterie van erbarmen; vragen rond het menselijk lijden', *Tijdschrift voor Theologie* 15, 1975, 3–25; W. Sparn, *Leiden – Erfahrung und Denken. Materialien zum Theodizeeproblem*, Munich: Christian Kaiser 1980; C. F. Geyer, *Leid und Böses in philosophischen Deutungen*, Freiburg and Munich 1983.

19 M. Weber, *Wirtschaft und Gesellschaft*, Tübingen 1922, 314–19 (ET *Economy and Society*, University of California Press 1979). Weber describes the types in a rather different order: he begins with the three forms of a 'messianic doctrine of retribution' within Judaism, Christianity and Islam and goes on to mention dualism and the doctrine of karma. Because in my view the Jewish-Christian – and also the Muslim – tradition already forms a reflection on the two last options and rejects these – albeit with fits and starts and not without having been influenced by it – I prefer a more chronological typology. That also makes it clearer that the solution to the question of theodicy in the different types of doctrine of retribution is not *per se* the best possible, whether for a purer image of God (cf. Job 42) or its ethical quality. Weber rates the last – with the exception of belief in predestination – very highly, although he thinks the option of the (Buddhist) doctrine of karma the most rational and radical solution to the question of theodicy: there, at any rate, the insight into suffering becomes the vehicle of liberation which finally consists in a return to absolute tranquillity and the absence of any desire.

20 Schillebeeckx, 'Mysterie van ongerechtigheid en mysterie van erbarmen' (n. 18).

21 Paul Ricoeur says sharply in his introduction to *Le mal*, 23: 'What raises the problem is a way of thinking which is subject to the demand for logical coherence, in other words at the same time the principle of a lack of conflict and

systematic totality. This way of thinking governs the theodicy argument in the technical sense of the word; however different its answers may be, they agree in stating the problem in the following terms: God is almighty, God is absolutely good, nevertheless evil exists. Theodicy appears as a fight for coherence in answer to the objection that only two of these three propositions are compatible, and never the three together. What is presupposed by the way of putting the problem is not discussed: *the propositional form itself in which the terms of the problem are expressed and the rule of coherence to which the solution must correspond*' (my italics).

22   Ricoeur, ibid., 45, calls classical theodicy 'the pearl of ontotheology', in other words the climax of the coupling of the doctrine of God and the metaphysics of being to which Heidegger takes such exception in which all *essents* are thought of sharing in Being, i.e. God, through causality.

23   See Epicurus, *The Extant Remains*, ed. Cyril Bailey, Oxford: Oxford University Press 1926.

24   In Anglo-Saxon philosophy of religion the term 'the argument from evil' has begun to be used in discussions about the foundations of theism. What is meant is the demonstration of the inconsistency of theism (see Chapter 2) because of the necessary conflicts in belief in a good and almighty God on the basis of the experience of evil. In the twentieth century, J. L. Mackie, William Rowe, Bruce Russell and Richard M. Gale have produced important forms of this argument; Alvin Plantinga, Richard Swinburne, Eleonore Stump, Marilyn McCord Adams and John Hick have produced important arguments on the other side. For a survey of this debate see M. McCord Adams and R. Adams (eds), *The Problem of Evil*, Oxford: Oxford University Press 1991; G. van den Brink, 'Natural Evil and Eschatology', in id., L. van den Brom and M. Sarot, *Christian Faith and Philosophical Theology*, Kampen: Kok Pharos 1992; D. Howard-Snyder (ed.), *The Evidential Argument from Evil*, Bloomington, Indiana: Indiana University Press 1996. The exclusive issue throughout this debate is the logical consistency of the theistic view of God. The connection between theodicy, soteriology and eschatology in the Jewish and Christian view of God is mentioned only in passing. The question of the reality of the promised redemption from evil is put well only in existentialism, especially by Albert Camus. But it also resounds in the Psalms, 'When will you redeem Israel?', and also in the remarks of those who pass by the cross of Jesus according to Matt. 27.39 (= Mark 15.29–32; Luke 23.35–37): 'O you who destroy the temple and build it up again in three days, save yourself; if you are the Son of God, come down from the cross!' And the chief priests in Matt. 27.42: 'He saved others, himself he cannot save. He is the king of Israel. Let him now come down from the cross, then we shall believe in him. For he said, "I am the Son of God."' Compare the question of the disciples in Acts 1.6: 'Lord, will you at this time restore the kingdom to Israel?'

25   Cf. Robin Lane Fox, *Pagans and Christians in the Mediterranean World from the Second Century AD to the Conversion of Constantine*, Harmondsworth: Penguin Books 1986, 34ff., 64ff., cf. 38: 'From Britain to Syria, pagan cults aimed to honour the gods and avert the misfortunes which might result from the gods' own anger at their neglect. Like an electric current, the power of the gods had great potential for helping and harming; unlike electricity, it was unpredictable and mortals could do no more than attempt to channel its force in advance.' Cf. A. H. Armstrong, 'Dualism, Platonic, Gnostic and Christian',

in A. P. Bos et al. (eds), *Plotinus and Gnostics and Christians*, Amsterdam: Vrije Universiteit 1984, 29–52. For Paul's doctrine of the cosmic and demonic powers and the history of its reading see A. W. Cramer, *Stoicheia tou kosmou. Interpretatie van een nieuwtestamentische term*, The Hague: Mouton 1961.

26   Plotinus, who in *Enneads*,V,1 [10], 8, 1155, calls himself 'exegete of Plato', lived between 204 and 270 in Naples and Rome, where he died a leper: another Job. After Plato and Aristotle, as the founder of Neoplatonism he is regarded as the third great philosopher of Hellenism. See Plotinus, *The Enneads* (6 vols), translated by A. H. Armstrong, Loeb Classical Library, London: Heinemann 1966ff. Plotinus' influence on Augustine is unmistakable: see J. van Oort, *Jerusalem en Babylon*, The Hague: Boekencentrum 1986; J. O'Meara, *Neo-Platonism and Christian Thought*, Albany, NY 1982. His *magnum opus*, the *Enneads*, is a collection of writings made by his disciple Porphyry (AD 234–304), divided into six 'Enneads' or ninth parts. The section 47–48, 'On Providence' , which deals with the problem of evil, was written late in Plotinus' life, between 268 and 270, when he was already a leper.

27   *The Laws*, X, 903 a–b.

28   Plotinus, *Enneads*, III, 2 [47], 1: 'To attribute the being (*ousia*) and structure (*sustasis*) of this All to accident (*to automaton*) and chance is unreasonable and belongs to a man without intelligence or perception; this is obvious even before demonstration, and many adequate demonstrations have been set down which show it. But the way in which all these individual things here come into being and are made, some of which, on the ground that they have not rightly come into being, produce difficulties about universal providence (and it has occurred to some people to say that it does not exist at all), and to others that the universe has been made by an evil maker), this we ought to consider, starting our discussion from the very beginning. Let us leave out that providence [or foresight] which belongs to the individual, which is a calculation before action how something should happen, or not happen in the case of things which ought not to be done, or how we may have something, or not have it. Let us postulate what we call universal providence and connect up with it what comes after. If, then, we said that after a certain time the universe, which did not previously exist, came into being, we should in our discussion lay down that providence in the All was the same as we said it was in partial things; since we affirm that this universe is everlasting and has never not existed, we should be correct and consistent in saying that providence for the All is its being according to Intellect, and that Intellect is before it, not in the sense that it is prior in time but because the universe comes from Intellect (*Nous*) and Intellect (*Nous*) is prior in nature, and the cause of the universe as a kind of archetype and model, the universe being an image of it and existing by means of it and everlastingly coming into existence in this way; the nature of Intellect (*Nous*) and Being is the true and first universe, which does not stand apart from itself and is not weakened by division and is not incomplete even in its parts, since each part is not cut off from the whole; but the whole life of it and the whole Intellect lives and thinks all together in one, and makes the part the whole and all bound in friendship with itself, since one part is not separated from another and has not become merely other, estranged from the rest; and, therefore, one does not wrong another, even if they are opposites ... But that true All is blessed in such a way that in not making it accomplishes great works and in remaining in itself makes no small things.'

29 Plotinus, *Enneads*, III, 2 [47], 9: 'Providence ought not to exist in such a way as
    to make us nothing. If everything was providence and nothing but providence,
    then providence would not exist; for what would it have to provide for? There
    would be nothing but the divine. But the divine exists also as things are; and has
    come to something other than itself, not to destroy the other but, when a man,
    for instance, comes to it, it stands over him and sees to it that he is man; that is,
    that he lives by the law of providence, which means doing everything that its
    law says. But it says that those who have become good shall have a good life,
    now, and laid up for them hereafter as well, and the wicked the opposite ...
    Since, then, men are not the best of living creatures but the human species
    occupies a middle position, and has chosen it, yet all the same is not allowed by
    providence to perish in the place where it is set but is always being lifted up to
    the higher regions by all sorts of devices which the divine uses to give virtue the
    greater power, mankind has not lost its character of being rational but is a
    participant, even if not to the highest degree, in wisdom and intellect and skill,
    and righteousness – each and all have a share at least in the righteousness that
    governs their dealings with each other; and those whom they wrong, they think
    that they wrong rightly, because they deserve it. In this way man is a noble
    creation, as far as he can be noble, and, being woven into the All, has a part
    which is better than that of other living things, of all, that is, which live on the
    earth. And besides, no one of any intelligence complains of all the other
    creatures, lower than himself, which ornament the earth. It would be ridiculous
    if someone complained of their biting men, as if men ought to pass their lives
    asleep. No, it is necessary that these, too, should exist; and some of the benefits
    which come from them are obvious, and those which are not evident, many of
    them time discovers; so that none of them exist without good purpose, even for
    men. But it is absurd, too, to complain that many of them are savage, when
    there are savage men as well ...'

30 Plotinus, *Enneads*, III, 2 [47], 15: 'The rational principle (*logos*), then, is the
    origin, and all things are reason, both those which are brought into being
    according to the principle and those which, in their coming to birth, are
    altogether ranged in this common order. What, then, is the necessity of the
    undeclared war among animals and among men? It is necessary that animals
    should eat each other; these eatings are transformations into each other of
    animals which could not stay as they are for ever, even if no one killed them.
    And if, at the time when they had to depart, they had to depart in such a way
    that they were useful to others, why do we have to make a grievance out of their
    usefulness? And what does it matter if, when they are eaten, they come alive
    again as different animals? It is like on the stage, when the actor who has been
    murdered changes his costume and comes on again in another character. But [in
    real life, not on the stage,] the man is really dead. If, then, death is a changing of
    body, like changing of clothes on the stage, or, for some of us, a putting off of
    body, like in the theatre the final exit, in that performance, of an actor who will
    on a later occasion come in again to play, what would there be that is terrible in
    a change of this kind, of living beings into each other? It is far better than if they
    had never come into existence at all. For that way there would be a barren
    absence of life and no possibility of a life which exists in something else; but as it
    is a manifold life exists in the All and makes all things, and in its living
    embroiders a rich variety and does not rest from ceaselessly making beautiful
    and shapely living toys. And when men, mortal as they are, direct their weapons

against each other, fighting in orderly ranks, doing what they do in sport in their war-dances, their battles show that all human concerns are children's games, and tell us that deaths are nothing terrible, and that those who die in wars and battles anticipate only a little the death which comes in old age – they go away and come back quicker. But if their property is taken away while they are still alive, they may recognize that it was not theirs before either, and that its possession is a mockery to the robbers themselves when others take it away from them; for even to those who do not have it taken away, to have it is worse than being deprived of it. We should be spectators of murders, and all deaths, and takings and sackings of cities, as if they were on the stages of theatres, all changes of scenery and costume and acted wailings and weepings. For really here in the events of our life it is not the soul within but the outside shadow of man which cries and moans and carries on in every sort of way on a stage which is the whole earth where men have in many places set up their stages. Doings like these belong to a man who knows how to live only the lower and external life and is not aware that he is playing in his tears, even when they are serious tears ... But we must consider this further point, too, that one must not take weeping and lamenting as evidence of the presence of evils, for children, too, weep and wail over things that are not evils.'

These are terrible statements, but alas they have become all too normative, even in Christian circles, blasphemies to those who suffer. Take the case of Srebrenice!

31   Cf. Sparn, *Leiden – Erfahrung und Denken*, (n. 18), 165ff.
32   For Augustine's treatment of the problem of evil see H. Häring, *Die Macht des Bösen* (n. 5).
33   See his *Enchiridion, Concerning Faith, Hope and Charity*, translated and edited by Ernest Evans, London: SPCK 1953, chs 11–13.
34   Häring, *Die Macht des Bösen* (n. 5), 14.
35   Wiersinga, *Doem of Daad* (n. 15).
36   Häring, *Die Macht des Bösen* (n. 5), 16.
37   Thus for example in Alain of Lille:, see Chapter 12 below.
38   Cf. *De Civitate Dei*, V, 11: XX, 21 (against the notion of the eternal cycle of souls); XIX, 4. The true happiness, in which human beings will share at the end of the journey of their souls, is not the product of their lives nor the result of virtue or desire, nor the climax of all pleasure, but a new creation of God. Without belief in this infinite and unique new creation of God – which implies definitive happiness or definitive misery – Augustine thinks that the 'problem of evil' and the apparent reward of transgressions and injustice is inconceivable. His theodicy therefore implies not only a teleology – the search for what God wills – but also an eschatology: an action of God at the end of each person's biography and a consummation by God of the whole creation at the end of the world, the end of time. He rejects the view that all will go well for all human beings (Origen) or that the cycle will begin all over again (Plato).
39   Boethius, *De consolatione philosophiae*, I.4.
40   Thomas Aquinas, *Summa contra Gentiles*, III, 71.
41   Thomas, *Summa Theologica*, I, q. 5, a. 1, 3; q. 11, a. 1, 2; q. 17, a. 1.
42   Geyer, *Leid und Böses*, 58 and 78.
43   *Summa Theologica*, I, II, q. 44, a. 1: '*Cum Deus sit ipsum subsistens esse, quod unum tantum est, necesse est omne ens, quod quocumque modo est, ad Deo esse.*' Therefore the diversity of things, the fragmentary and diverse character of

nature, is not a fall nor the result of two opposing powers. Cf. ibid., 44 responsum: '*Necesse est igitur omnia quae diversificantur secundum diversam participationem essendi, ut sint perfectius vel minus perfecte, causari ab uno primo ente, quod perfectissimus est.*'

44   Ibid., q.48, 1: '*Non existens aliquid, vel natura aliqua, sed ipsa boni absentia malum est.*'

45   Ibid., q. 48, a. 1 and 2: '*Unde malum, inquantum malum, non est differentia constitutiva, sed ratione boni adjuncti.*'

46   Ibid., q. 28, a. 2: '*Ipsum autem totum, quod est universitas creaturum, melius et perfectius est, si in eo sint quaedam, quae a bono deficere possunt, quae interdum deficiunt. Deo hoc non impediente.*' It is this focus on the whole, on the 'totality', which has been criticized in Thomism and in the Catholic tradition of thought generally. People are said to have too little an eye for local differences, the pluriform context, the personal situation, and thus also to fail to see the personal character of suffering and ethics. But Thomas is not thinking in terms of totality here. He is calling attention to the diversity. The reference to the *totum* certainly relativizes the particular, but does not give it up, does not force it away, does not banish it by abstract and universal principles, as happens in totalitarian thought.

47   Ibid., q. 48 a. 2: '*Deus est adeo potens, quod etiam bona potest facere de malis*': there is no fire without the consumption of fuel; the lion would not survive without the death of the ass; neither the justice of the judge nor the patience of the victim could be praised without the crime of the criminal. Indeed there is no such thing as absolute evil (q. 48, a. 4).

48   Ibid., q. 48, a. 2: '*Unde multa bona tollerentur, si Deus nullum malum permitteret esse?*'

49   Ibid., q. 49 a. 1.

50   Ibid., q. 49 a. 2: in God there is no '*causa tendendi ad non esse*'.

51   Ibid., q. 48, a. 5.

52   Thomas Aquinas, *De Veritate* 22.7: '*Nihil enim est aliud peccatum sive in rebus naturalibus sive artificialibus sive voluntariis dicatur, quam defectum vel inordinatio propriae actionis, cum aliquid agitur non secundum quod debitum est agi, ut patet II Physicae*' (199, b 1).

53   Ibid., q. 48, a. 6. Also according to Augustine, fear of punishment is the worst evil. In Thomas, however, there is more a sense of the missed opportunity, of falling short. Perhaps that is also the nature of fear: paralysis, not being able to get back, not daring to act, the desire but no longer the ability to flee, cf. B. Welte, *Über das Böse* (n. 5), 11.

54   Augustine, *De Veritate*, 22.5; Welte, *Über das Böse* (n. 5), 44.

55   Cf. U. Duchrow, *Christenheit und Weltverantwortung. Traditionsgeschichte und systematische Struktur der Zweireichenlehre*, Stuttgart: Klett-Cotta ²1983.

56   Cf. W. Stoker, *De christelijke godsdienst in de filosofie van de Verlichting*, Assen: Van Gorcum 1980, 58ff.

57   G. W. Leibniz, *Theodicy. Essays on the Goodness of God, the Freedom of Man and the Origin of Evil*, London: Routledge and Kegan Paul 1952.

58   Thomas Hobbes: 'Reason is the linking together of truths, but especially (when it is compared with faith) of those where the human mind can attain naturally without being aided by the light of faith ... Reason, pure and simple, as distinct from experience, only has to do with truths independent from the senses.' Thus the background here is not polemic with empiricism but the view of science as

the quest for universally valid insights. Faith lies on the same level as sensory perception, which is contingent and untrustworthy: miracles, the actual tradition, the inner light of the Holy Spirit: none of these can be proved to be generally valid. Indeed, according to Hobbes the only difference between faith and superstition is that in one case we have the fear of invisible powers – either invented or handed down in long traditions – which have been generally accepted, whereas superstition involves such powers as have not been generally accepted. The scholastic view that faith is a mean between pure assertion or assumption (*opinio*) and pure knowledge (*scientia*) is abandoned here: faith is reduced to *opinio*. Leibniz chooses, against Hobbes, the other one-sidedness: he argues for faith as a form of rational knowledge, *scientia*. For the relationship between faith and reason, revelation and experience, philosophy and theology see his *Reflexions on the Work that Mr Hobbes published in English on 'Freedom, Necessity and Chance'* (1656), in Leibniz, *Theodicy. Essays on the Goodness of God, the Freedom of Man and the Origin of Evil* (n. 57), 392, 389–404. Cf. Chapter 12 below.

59 For Leibniz's theodicy see W. Sparn, *Leiden – Erfahrung und Denken*, 19ff.; see also G. W. Leibniz, *Discourse on Metaphysics*, in R. S. Woolhouse and Richard Franks (eds), *Leibniz. Philosophical Texts*, Oxford: Oxford University Press 1998.

60 Leibniz, *Theodicy* (n. 57), 379: '... good can and does go on *ad infinitum*, whereas evil has its bounds.'

61 Ibid., 382: 'So the predetermination of events by their causes is precisely what contributes to morality instead of destroying it, and the causes incline the will without necessitating it. For this reason the determination we are concerned with is not a necessitation. It is certain (to him who knows all) that the effect will follow this inclination; but this effect does not follow thence by a consequence which is necessary, that is, whose contrary implies contradiction; and it is also by such inward inclination that the will is determined, without the presence of necessity.' Although there is never complete indifference over the choice of one or the other – for there must be something that moves me to choose a particular direction – I am not forced to take a particular side.

62 Ibid., 383: 'Likewise one may say that the consequent, or final and total, divine will, tends towards the production of as many goods as can be put together, whose combination thereby becomes determined, and involves also the permission of some evils and the exclusion of some goods, as the best possible plan of the universe demands.'

63 Ibid., 378.

64 Ibid., 383.

65 Leibniz, *Discourse on Metaphysics* (n. 59), 55.

66 Ibid., 56.

67 Ibid.

68 I. Kant, 'Über das Misslingen aller philosophischen Versuche in der Theodizee', in *Schriften zur Anthropologie, Geschichtsphilosophie, Politik und Pädagogik*, Darmstadt: Wissenschaftliche Buchgesellschaft 1975.

69 Cf. A. Peperzak, 'Gaandeweg', in id., *Tussen filosofie en theologie*, Kampen and Kapellen: Kok Agora, DNB and Pelckmans 1991, 168–90: 'The conversion of thought for which the gospel calls requires solidarity with those who try to become wise from the labyrinth of present-day confusion. Groping and stammering, we seek ways of liberation from the fears in which our time is

imprisoned. To endure bewilderment and not evade bitterness, without neurotically clinging on to the dated ideal of round systems, established dogmas and supreme fathers who are never wrong ...' (188). So it is the sufferers themselves who contribute to the pathos for the good, through lament and complaint, but also those who suffer and think with them in solidarity for the sake of the good. This pathos binds victims and helpers together. Both can call on the same God, as the God of the possibly good.

70 Häring, *Das Problem des Bösen* (n. 5), 83.

71 C. Gestrich, *Die Wiederkehr des Glanzes in der Welt. Die christliche Lehre von der Sünde und ihrer Vergebung in gegenwärtiger Verantwortung*, Tübingen: Mohr 1989.

72 M. Brinkman, *God of lot. Over de schepper van dood en leven*, Zoetermeer: Meinema 1993.

73 A. Houtepen, *In God is geen geweld*, Vught: Radboudstichting 1985.

4. TRACES OF GOD: THE HUMAN EMOTIONS

1 M. Lathouwers, 'De Sovjet-mens op zoek naar zijn grond', *Benedictijns Tijdschrift* 43, 1982, 63–73, 111–123.

2 M. Heidegger, *Being and Time*, London: SCM Press 1963, 456–80; Hannah Arendt, *The Life of the Mind: Thinking*, New York: Harcourt Brace Jovanovich 1978, 205ff.

3 R. Girard, *Violence and the Sacred*, London: Athlone Press 1988; id., *Things Hidden Since the Foundation of the World* (research with J. M. Oughourlian and Guy Lefort), London: Athlone Press 1987; *The Scapegoat*, London: Athlone Press 1986; id., *La route antique des hommes pervers*, Grasset: Paris 1985; on Girard: F. Chirpaz, *Enjeux de la Violence. Essai sur René Girard*, Paris: Cerf 1980; A. Lascaris, *Advocaat van de zondebok. Het werk van René Girard en het evangelie van Jezus*, Hilversum: Gooi & Sticht 1987.

4 V. Havel, *Dopisy Olze*, Toronto: Sixty-Eight Publishers 1985, 434ff., quoted by J. M. Lochman, *Christ and Prometheus? A Quest for Theological Identity*, Geneva: WCC 1988, 49.

5 Cf. T. W. Adorno and M. Horkheimer, *Dialectic of Enlightenment* (1944), London: Allen Lane 1973. Cf. H. de Vries, *Theologie im Pianissimo & Zwischen Rationalität und Dekonstruktion*, Kampen: Kok 1989; J. Hoogland, *Autonomie en antonomie. Adorno's ambivalente verhouding tot de metafysica*, Rotterdam: RFS 1992; H. Oosterling, *Door schijn bewogen. Naar een hyperkritiek van de xenofobe rede*, Kampen: Kok Agora 1996.

6 Cf. O. Kallscheuer, *Gottes Wort und Volkes Stimme. Glaube, Macht, Politik*, Frankfurt: Fischer 1994.

7 K. Popper, 'Utopia and Violence', in id., *Conjectures and Refutations. The Growth of Scientific Knowledge*, London: Routledge and Kegan Paul [4]1981, 355–64.

8 H. Küng, *Does God Exist? An Answer for Today*, London: Collins 1984, xxii. Cf. also the criticism by H. Kuitert of this danger of duplication, i.e. that the appeal to God in faith can go wrong when it comes to clearly political, i.e. party-political, standpoints: H. Kuitert, *Everything is Politics, But Politics is Not Everything*, London: SCM Press 1986.

9 Cf. T. Beemer, 'Onze emoties en onze toewijding', in F. Haarsma (ed.), *Tussen aarde en hemel. Naar nieuwe vormen van spiritualiteit*, Baarn: Ten Have 1988, 110–27.

10 N. Frijda, *The Emotions*, Cambridge: Cambridge University Press 1987.

11 E. Schillebeeckx, *Christ*, London: SCM Press and New York: Crossroad Publishing Co. 1980, 83ff.

12 The concept of value intended here differs fundamentally from the term '*Werte*' in German discussions about '*Grundwerte*'. Here the concept of purpose is central, and in reaction also elements like utility and social order. In the collection of essays entitled *Wertlose Wahrheit. Zur Identität und Relevanz des christliche Glaubens*, Theologische Erörterungen III, Munich: Kaiser 1990, 90–109, Jüngel rejects this 'tyranny of values' and wants to keep belief in God far from them, just as Levinas also protests against a 'God of need'.

13 Desire – *le désir* – has again been discussed extensively in present-day philosophy and psychology, no longer as an aspect of the 'philosophy of the will' but also as the driving force of culture, language and communication. See e.g. J. de Mul, *Het romantische verlangen in (post) moderne kunst en filosofie*, Rotterdamse Filosofische Studies, Rotterdam 1991; A. Vergote, *Religie, geloof en ongeloof. Psychologische studie*, Antwerp and Amsterdam: DNB 1984, 40ff.; id., *Bekentenis en begeerte in de religies. Psychoanalytische verkenning*, Antwerp and Amsterdam: DNB 1978. Vergote distinguishes between longings which arise out of impotence or guilt and others which arise out of striving for a higher good or aim. Plato already stated that *eros* is the child of *poros* (prosperity, literally: way out, means of achieving something) and *penia* (poverty, deprivation). This distinction is like that made by Levinas, who in connection with the relationship to God emphasizes the difference between 'religion of need' and 'religion of desire', in *Totality and Infinity*, Pittsburgh: Duquesne University Press 1969, 118ff.; id., 'God and Philosophy', in S. Hand (ed.), *The Levinas Reader*, Oxford: Blackwell 1989, 166–87; cf. R. Burggraeve, *Mens en Medemens. Verantwoordelijkheid en God. De metafysische ethiek van Emmanuel Levinas*, Leuven and Amersfoort: Acco 1986: 'From "need" we arrive at a religion tailored to human standards and needs – albeit the deepest needs. Out of their lack of salvation human beings create for themselves a God in their own image and likeness. The religion that is based on desire is, however, in the literal sense of the term "service of God". I do not enter into relations with God for my own sake but for his sake. The desire issues in worship and praise, despite myself. My service of God does not emerge from the fact that I need God but from the fact that God attracts me. Over against the selfish and "economic" religion of need stands the unselfish religion of desire!' I ask myself whether this distinction, given the actual aporia, the hopelessness, in which human beings find themselves when faced with suffering and death, is so relevant in religious terms. Is there something like a power of attraction from God, detached from human beings, who in their needs look to God? Is any God other than a 'redeeming God' conceivable?

14 K. Waayman, *Betekenis van de naam Jahwe*, Kampen: Kok 1984, 48–59.

15 E. Jüngel, 'Quae supra nos nihil ad nos', in id., *Entsprechungen: Gott – Wahrheit – Mensch*, Munich: Christain Kaiser 1980, 202–51.

16 Gregory of Nyssa, *The Life of Moses*, New York and Toronto 1979, 115 (no. 233).

17 E. Erikson, *Identity and the Life-cycle* (1959), New York: Norton 1994, 56. For this form of life in trust cf. Küng, *Does God Exist?* (n. 8), 453–78.

18 G. Kaufman, 'Nuclear Eschatology and the Study of Religion', *Journal of the American Academy of Religion*, 51, 1983, 3–4.

19 H. Arendt, *The Human Condition*, Chicago: Chicago University Press 1958.

20 Cf. *Baptism, Eucharist, Ministry*, Geneva: WCC 1983 (the Lima Text), Eucharist 7, 13.

21 Arendt, *The Human Condition* (n. 19), 236–41. Cf. id., *Men in Dark Times*, New York: Harcourt Brace Jovanovich 1968, 248 (quoting Brecht): 'Every judgment is open to forgiveness, every act of judging can change into an act of forgiving; to judge and to forgive are but the two sides of the same coin. But the two sides follow different rules. The majesty of the law demands that we be equal – that only our acts count, and not the person who committed them. The act of forgiving, on the contrary, takes the person into account: no pardon pardons murder or theft but only the murderer or thief. We always forgive some*body*, never some*thing*, and this is the reason people think that only love can forgive. But, with or without love, we forgive for the sake of the person, and while justice demands that all be equal, mercy insists on inequality – an inequality implying that every man is, or should be, more than whatever he did or achieved.'

5. THE HOLY THAT MAY NOT BE VIOLATED: A SIGHT OF THE DIVINE

1   J. Habermas, *Theory of Communicative Action* II, Oxford: Polity Press 1989, 77.

2   In *Theory of Communicative Action* I, Oxford: Polity Press 1986, 244ff., Habermas had already accused Weber of being stuck in the critique of religion and paying no attention to the positive consequences of secularization.

3   J. Habermas, *Politik, Kunst, Religion*, Stuttgart 1978, 141.

4   J. Habermas, *Legitimationsprobleme im Spätkapitalismus*, Frankfurt 1974, 167.

5   E. Arens, 'Theologie nach Habermas, Eine Einführung', in E. Arens (ed.), *Habermas und die Theologie*, Düsseldorf ²1989, 14.

6   Cf. Habermas, *Legitimationsprobleme im Spätkapitalismus* (n. 4), 115; Arens, *Habermas und die Theologie* (n. 5), 15, where Habermas himself says: 'In the atheism of the masses the utopian content of tradition also threatens to perish.'

7   E.g. M. Eliade, *The Sacred and the Profane*, New York: Harcourt Brace Jovanovich 1968.

8   R. Otto, *The Idea of the Holy*, Oxford: Oxford University Press ²1950.

9   G. van der Leeuw, *Religion in Essence and Manifestation*, Princeton: Princeton University Press 1958.

10 E. Durkheim, *The Elementary Forms of Religious Life* (1912), New York: Free Press of Glencoe 1995.

11 P. Berger, *The Sacred Canopy*, New York: Anchor Press 1988.

12 R. Girard, *Violence and the Sacred*, London: Athlone Press 1988.

13 M. ter Borg, *Een uitgewaaierde eeuwigheid. Het menselijk tekort in de moderne cultuur*, Baarn 1991.

14 Cf. especially the contribution by C. Geffré to the collection of articles by E. Castelli (ed.), *Le sacré: Études et Recherches*, Paris 1974.

15 For more semantic details see e.g. L. Coenen (ed.), *Theologische Begriffslexikon zum Neuen Testament* I, Wuppertal 1986, s.v. *hagios, hieros, hosios*, and J.

Verheul, *Het heilige in de wereld. Verkenning van de verhouding tussen cultische heiligheid en secularisatie in het Oude Testament*, Utrecht 1976.

16   M. Fox, *Original Blessing*, Santa Fe: Bear & Co. 1983.

17   K. Barth, *Church Dogmatics* II/1, Edinburgh 1957, 351–68.

18   Otto, *The Idea of the Holy* (n. 8), 18ff.

19   Barth, *Church Dogmatics* II/1 (n.17), 359.

20   Quenstedt 1685, quoted by Barth, ibid., 359: God is holy because there is absolute purity in God, which God also requires of his creatures: '... *summa omnino labis aut vicii expers in Deo puritas, munditiem et puritatem debitam exigens a creaturis.*'

21   E. Levinas, *Du sacré au saint, Cinq nouvelles lectures talmudiques*, Paris: Minuit 1977. These are five lectures which Levinas gave at the XXᵉ Colloque des Intellectuels Juifs de langue française on the topic of 'The Jews in a Desacralized Society' on 31 October/1 November 1971.

22   Ibid., 89: here in my view Levinas is describing the work of the illusionist: '... the verso or the other side of the real, Nothingness condensed into Mystery, bubbles of Nothing in things – everyday objects that come out of a "mine of nothingness" or disappear into it.'

23   Ibid., 95–6.

24   In Derrida we find the categories of *indemnité* and *l'indemne* as the real content of the holy and of religion: see J. Derrida and G. Vattimo, *La religion*, Paris: du Seuil 1996, *passim*.

25   A. Vergote, 'Equivoque et articulation du sacré', in E. Castelli (ed.), *Le sacré*, Paris 1974, 471–92. Vergote points to the transition from the reified holy which stands outside human beings to that which is inwardly 'holy' for them. However, that is more than a choice of ethical value. For a reversal takes place in culture in the sphere of the imagination. By this cultural U-turn the experience of the holiness of God – in its height dimension the expression of an unassailable character and sovereignty of God – undergoes a change in which at the same time the depth dimension can be reflected on – God as present in my innermost self. Anyone who calls on the holy God – like the prophet in Isa. 6 – is taken over by him, and arrives at a different basic attitude in life. The metaphysical and the relational pictures of God flow together in religious experience: cf. A. Vergote, 'Het imaginaire en het symbolische in het godsbeeld', *Tijdschrift voor Theologie*, 13, 1973, 310–26.

26   In this connection one can also point to the caution about genetic manipulation which forbids particular experiments – the cloning of human embryos – or at any rate is cautious because of possible unforeseen consequences or perhaps simply because of the anthropological frontier which must not be crossed here. We describe this limit experience as 'Not everything that can be may be.'

27   *Now is the Time. Final Document & Other Texts from the World Convocation on Justice, Peace and the Integrity of Creation, Seoul 5–12 March 1990*, Geneva: WCC 1990, 11ff.

28   For the exegesis, the tradition history and the history of the reading of the Decalogue see K. Merks, N. Poulsen and W. Weren, *Weg of Wet?. Over de tien woorden*, Boxtel: KBS and Bruges: Tabor 1980; F. L. Hossfeld, *Der Dekalog: seine späten Fassungen, die originale Komposition und seine Vorstufe*, Fribourg CH: Universitätsverlag 1982; rather earlier: H. Schängel-Straumann, *Der Dekalog, Gottes Geboten*, Stuttgart: KBW Verlag 1973; J. Stamm and M. Andrew, *The Ten Commandments in Recent Research*, London: SCM Press

1967; H. Reventlow, *Gebot und Predigt im Dekalog*, Gütersloh 1962; there are more systematic and ethical reflections in A. Deissler, *God bevrijdt. De Tien Geboden, een poging tot nieuw verstaan*, Boxtel: KBS 1976; A. Exeler, *In Gottes Freiheit leben. Die Zehn Gebote*, Freiburg, etc.: Herder Verlag 1981; F. Crüsemann, *Bewahrung der Freiheit. Das Thema des Dekalogs in sozial-geschichtlicher Perspektive*, Munich 1983; F. Lefevre, 'De tien geboden. Bijbelse en actuele betekenis', *Collationes* 15, 1985, 161–89; 16, 1986, 5–35, 387–404; Merks et al., *Weg of Wet?* (n. 28), 93; O. H. Pesch, *Die Zehn Gebote*, Mainz: Matthias Grünewald Verlag 1976; 'Dekalog', *Theologische Realenzyklopädie* 8, 408ff.; J. Schreiner, *Die Zehn Gebote im Leben des Gottesvolkes*, Munich ²1988. The scenarios of Kieslowski's masterpiece *Dekalog* are also illuminating: K. Kieslowski and K. Piesewicz, *Dekaloog. Tien scenario 's*, Amsterdam 1990.

6. CAN GOD BE FOUND IN HISTORY?

1   Thus L. J. van den Brom, *God alomtegenwoordig?*, Kampen: Kok 1982: 'the assertion "Yahweh is God" means "Yahweh is worthy of worship everywhere, at every place", and by implication "he *is present everywhere to receive worship*". The confession that in the exclusive sense Yahweh needs to be worshipped thus implies the statement that he is omnipresent.'

2   Per Lonning, *Der begreiflich Unergreifbare. 'Sein Gottes' und moderne theologische Denkstrukturen*, Göttingen 1986.

3   Van den Brom, *God alomtegenwoordig?* (n. 1); id., *Creatieve twijfel. Een studie in de wijsgerige theologie*, Kampen 1990, 77ff. There Van den Brom speaks of 'an infinitely extended homogeneous radius of action or power' (85) as of 'a magnet surrounded by its field', but in such a way that 'God's influence does not diminish in relation to the distance from the place where he is located (which is not the case in a magnetic field)'. Van den Brom rightly points out (*Creatieve twijfel*, 88ff.) that in the question of God's presence the underlying notion of space or the theory of space which one adopts is all-decisive. He himself opts for the relational theory of space (the generalized relationship 'side by side' extended over all things), which can also apply to the idea that he introduces of God's transcendental, higher-dimensional space into which the three-dimensional space that we know is introduced. 'God is present everywhere in space as an extended being in a higher dimensional space which embraces three-dimensional space' (ibid., 100). God voluntarily 'limits' himself to this higher-dimensional space in order to make room for creation, without thus becoming 'spaceless' and without needing to coincide with the space that we know (ibid., 100). H. Berkhof, *Christian Faith*, Grand Rapids: Eerdmans 1986, 155ff., speaks of God's self-limitation, but relates that to God's condescension: 'that God stoops down, that he limits himself, that he provides living and breathing space for the other which as such is imperfect and will even be rebellious' (158). That is quite a different language-field from the question raised by Van den Brom. The question 'Where is God?' can be detached from the idea of 'living space and scope' for human beings in conceptual analysis but not theologically. Rather than being served with an extrapolation of the scientific concept of space in the direction of a 'higher-dimensional space', the theological answer to the question 'Where is God?' seems to be served more with a reflection on the idea of history

as the 'living space and scope' (= *kairos*) for human beings, which is what happens with Berkhof.

4   Jean-Luc Marion, *Dieu sans l'être*, Paris 1982. Cf. Chapter 11.

5   M. Horkheimer, *The Eclipse of Reason*, New York 1967.

6   Thus also A. van den Beukel, *More Things in Heaven and Earth*, London: SCM Press 1991, 57, and many other so-called 'holists'.

7   For some impressive surveys of this experience of fragmentation see H. Oosterling, *Door schijn bewogen. Naar een hyperkritiek van de xenofobe rede*, Kampen: Kok Agora 1996; J. Pohier, *God – in Fragments*, London: SCM Press 1985; E. Schillebeeckx et al. (eds), *Breuklijnen. Grenservaringen en zoektochten*, Baarn: Nelissen 1994; A. Lascaris et al. (eds), *Scherven brengen geluk. Identiteit en geloven in een wereld van verschillen*, Nijmegen: DSTS and Zoetermeer: De Horstink 1996.

8   Cf. A. Houtepen, 'De vrede van God en de oorlogen der mensen', in P. van Dijk, A. Houtepen and H. Zeldenrust et al., *Geloof en Geweld*, Kampen: Kok 1988, 79–124.

9   Cf. Levinas' questions about the modern tendency towards astrology and occultism in *Du sacré au saint*, 97ff. (Chapter 5 above, nn. 21 and 22). According to Levinas, the difference between the way in which the Bible deals with prophetic signs and modern predictions of the future is the difference between caution and curiosity about the future.

10   D. Tracy, *The Analogical Imagination. Christian Theology and the Culture of Pluralism*, London: SCM Press 1981, 429ff.

11   Expressed most evocatively perhaps in the preface to the fifth impression of *Christus, de zin der geschiedenis*, Nijkerk: Callenbach 1981, 18. Chapter V of that book deals explicitly with the problem of secularization.

12   H. Berkhof, 'Om de waarheid en om de kerk. Een theologische autobiografie', in *Bruggen en bruggehoofden*, Nijkerk: Callenbach 1981. 'Really from the time of my dissertation to the present day I have been fascinated by history as a theological concept.'

13   H. Berkhof, *Gegronde Verwachting*, Nijkerk: Callenbach 1967, 100.

14   In the later variant of this poem, entitled 'Deism', Achterberg is even more cynical.

> Man is for a time a place of God.
> When all identifiers cease to fit,
> then he is written off on a stone.
> The agreement seems to run to
> this consummation, this abrupt conclusion.
> For God goes further, turning from him
> in his millions. God is never alone.
> *For this any other could stand in.*
> For him we are a full can of petrol,
> which he leaves empty behind. He has to get rid of it,
> all the rubbish, conflicting with his being ...

Cf. J. Sperna Weiland, *Romeins Schetboek. Over de metamorfose van het geloven*, Baarn 1980, 145–50.

15   Cf. H. Berkhof, *Inleiding tot de studie van de dogmatiek*, Kampen 1982, 79, 89ff.

16   Ibid., 95.

17   Ibid, 98. Cf. 86–7: 'Given all the changes of culture and styles of thought, for centuries there has been relative quiet in the doctrine of God. God was

immutability itself by comparison with a restless world ... By comparison with the Hellenistic pluriform world of religions and of many and often limited and capricious gods, they [the Fathers] (courting the monotheistic philosophy of this time) confessed the one unchangeable God, far exalted above the tumult and suffering of the human world. With Plato it was taught that "God has no properties", and since the Middle Ages people followed the definition which Aristotle gave of the deity: "The first that sets in motion without being set in motion by anything (*to proton kinoun akineton*)." This God is almighty, omnipresent, omniscient, immutable, infinite, incomprehensible. These all- and un-words dominated the doctrine of God for centuries. They express both the exaltation and the fixity that people wanted to find in God ... Only German idealism developed another picture of God: the immanent One, the Spirit of our spirit which dwells and is at work in history ... After the rigidity of the picture of God in the footsteps of Aristotle, God now risked being evaporated in the footsteps of Hegel, or God became a projection of our ethical sense in the footsteps of Kant. Barth then referred back powerfully to the Godness, the sovereignty and the transcendence of God ... For him God is consistently defined through his reconciling incarnation in Christ. From eternity God is a communicative God, to be defined as "the one who loves in freedom ...". In the long run many dogmatic theologians, however, felt compelled to go further along the path indicated by Barth than he himself had done. At any rate, if God is a communicative God who by virtue of his being involves himself in the life and suffering of his human beings, to the point of the incarnation of the Word and the outpouring of the Spirit, must we not then say that God takes part in history, that he shares our suffering, that through his liberation among us he himself is even enriched? And can that be otherwise than by eternally having a history of communication in himself and the possibility of suffering ... And in that case must not the characteristics of omnipotence and immutability be thoroughly revised ...? Bonhoeffer ... his notes about the powerless God become fundamental to the development that now follows ... Jüngel, Pannenberg, Whitehead, etc., Moltmann, Pohier, feminism ... It is always a question of the "humanity of God", an expression which already comes from Barth. A common theological heading and route of march cannot at present be indicated. What holds things together is the negative, the turn away from God as the great Outsider.'

18   Ibid., 53 and 101.

19   Cf. W. Weisse, *Praktisches Christentum und Reich Gottes. Die ökumenische Bewegung Life and Work, 1919–1937*, Göttingen: Vandenhoeck & Ruprecht 1991.

20   H. Kraemer et al. (eds), *On the Meaning of History*, Papers of the Ecumenical Institute No. V, Geneva 1949.

21   W. den Boer, 'Greco-Roman Historiography in its Relation to Biblical and Modern Thinking', in Kraemer et al., *On the Meaning of History* (n. 20), 28–47.

22   Cf. the reflections on the 'end of time' in W. Logister, ' "Hij zal komen in macht en majesteit": De vreemde wereld van de christelijke parousieverwachting', *Tijdschrift voor Theologie*, 35, 1995, 373–95, and H. Häring, ' "Uitschreeuwen wat er gaande is": Over de relevantie van eschatologie en apokalyptiek', *Tijdschrift voor Theologie*, 36, 1996, 246–69. Logister refers to the fulfilled time of which the return of Christ, time and again celebrated in the liturgy, is the crown: Häring draws attention to the seriousness of suffering and human misdeeds, an end to which will come at the end of time.

23   *God in Nature and History*, *Study Encounter* 1, 1965, no. 3. The final report is in

New Directions in Faith and Order. Bristol 1967, Faith and Order Paper 50, Geneva 1968, 7–41 (= *Bristol Report*).

24   *Bristol Report*, 13–14.

25   Ibid., 27–8.

26   For the concept of 'signs of the times' see A. Houtepen, 'Discerning the Signs of the Times: Some Reflections on Justice, Peace and the Integrity of the Church', in T. Best and W. Granberg-Michalson (eds), *Costly Unity. Presentations and Reports from the World Council of Churches' Consultation in Ronde, Denmark*, Geneva: World Council of Churches 1993, 22–41.

27   *Bristol Report*, 131.

28   H. Berkhof, 'Wie A zegt, moet ook B zeggen', in *Bruggen en bruggehoofden* (n. 12), 56.

29   P. Schoonenberg, *God of mens: een vals dilemma*, s' Hertogenbosch: Malmberg 1965: 'God's guidance remains immanent. It appears in created causes and not alongside them. Here too the Creator does not fill up what is lacking in the forces within the world, but ensures that they unfold from within in the best possible way...' (13). God and creature, God and human beings do not compete, but go together in such a way that in our state of being created and given grace we owe everything to God and everything to realities within the world' (28).

30   Berkhof takes this verse as the starting point of his theological anthropology: H. Berkhof, 'Theologische anthropologie', in L. W. Nauta et al. (eds), *De veranderbaarheid van de mens*, Kampen 1973, 106–20: 112, 119.

31   Ibid., 120. Cf. H. Berkhof, *De mens onderweg. Een christlijke mensbeschouwing* (1960), The Hague ⁶1976; id., *Wat dunkt u van de mens?*, Kampen 1970. In the latter book he remarks on the first point that the theme of human 'historicity' has not been sufficiently discussed. That lack is made good in *Christian Faith* (n. 3), sections 57 and 58, but much attention is already paid to 'the glorified man' in *De mens onderweg* (90–102).

32   Berkhof has a special place among the theologians who have reflected on history as the place where God is to be found. In *Christ, the Meaning of History*, London: SCM Press 1966, Berkhof follows Karl Barth in the latter's concentration on the figure of Christ as the key to reading the confession of faith about God, creating Preserver of nature and re-creating Spirit of history. But he does not follow Barth in Barth's actualistic, present exposition of eschaton and kingdom of God, just as he does not expect any solace from Bultmann's concentration on the existence of every human being and of salvation at every 'moment, moment' (Nietzsche). Death takes any moment away, and the death of so many millions in catastrophe and violence, through sickness and ageing, is too serious a counterpart to all glorification of the here and now to stake all one's cards on it. In his *magnum opus*, *Christian Faith*, Berkhof has summed up his thoughts systematically on this point without removing all the ambivalences: he will have nothing to do with Hegel's idolization of systems and he also finds Teilhard de Chardin's or Rahner's belief in the rise of nature and human beings to the kingdom of God Hegelian and Pelagian. Pannenberg's approach in terms of 'universal history' is also too rectilinear for him, as if one could extend the final rise to God's universal rule along an unbroken line of an ever more universal acceptance of the Jewish-Christian idea of God: insufficient account is then taken of the fractures and the suffering. Jürgen Moltmann, who takes suffering, evil and all the ambivalences of the church, religion and culture seriously, too easily makes these part of

God's own suffering and agony, which seems to conflict with a consistent view of God: what is to be expected of a God who is as defenceless as the victims, who is very affected by their suffering but can do nothing about it?

33 H. Berkhof, 'God voorwerp van wetenschap?', in *Bruggen en bruggehoofden* (n. 12), 26.

34 Ibid., 28–9.

35 Such a view of the conflict of the powers also colours Berkhof's thought about history and has thus become popular in catechesis and preaching in the Dutch Reformed churches. He is strongly under the impact of the failure of all optimistic, evolutionist views of history in the twentieth century with its cruel world wars, the Communist dictatorship, the colonial injustice and above all the Holocaust. At the same time he wants to give full weight to the human task and responsibility from God. But perhaps in reaction – so as not to fall victim to pessimism – he arrives at a view of history which sometimes verges on a Gnostic dualism between the forces of light and darkness. For example, in *Gegronde Verwachting* he says: 'Both the crucifixion and the resurrection of Christ find their continuation in history, in order to intensify it to the end ... This last is expressed in the images of the Antichrist and the thousand-year kingdom. History is ambiguous and the future means a further accentuation of this double image until the supremacy of Christ tips the scales towards the resurrection of the renewed world of human beings.'

However, elsewhere he adds that in the power of the resurrection this dualism is in principle overcome: *Christ, the Meaning of History* (n. 32) 22: 'In Israel man is emancipated from nature by the Word, which asks for a definite answer, and then goes before man through time, pointing the way. In this way history is freed from nature much more radically than in Greece. There is no cycle. Nor is there chance, or an inflexible fate. History is the terrain of human freedom and responsibility because it is primarily the terrain of God's calling and leading. Man is delivered from nature, because he is delivered by and for God. Thus he is set upon the road to the great goal, the kingdom of God.'

36 P. Ricoeur, *Time and Narrative*, Chicago: University of Chicago Press 1984–88. Cf. T. Kemp and D. Rasmussen, *The Narrative Path. The Later Works of Paul Ricoeur*, Cambridge, Mass and London: MIT Press 1989.

37 'History and fiction constitute two varieties of passions for the possible', in K. Vanhoozer, *Biblical Narrative in the Philosophy of Paul Ricoeur. A Study in Hermeneutics and Theology*, Cambridge: Cambridge University Press 1990, 92.

38 Cf. J. Verhoeven, *Dynamiek van het verlangen. De godsdienstfilosofische methode van Rahner tegen de achtergrond van Maréchal en Blondel*, Utrecht dissertation 1996.

39 H. Frei, *The Eclipse of Biblical Narrative*, New Haven: Yale University Press 1974. For this debate see Vanhoozer, *Biblical Narrative* (n. 37), 148–89.

40 K. Armstrong, *A History of God*, London: Mandarin Books 1999.

7. GOD WHO CREATES AND CARES: THE FATHER OF ALL HUMAN BEINGS

1 In the catechism texts from the beginning of the nineteenth century, which were strongly coloured by the Enlightenment, the description of God as 'pure spirit'

formed the starting point for the exposition of the doctrine of creation. See e.g. *Explication des premières vérités de la religion, pour en faciliter l'intelligence au jeunes gens, par MPC, docteur de Sorbonne*, Paris: Méguignon 1827, 1:

– 'What is God? God is an eternal Spirit, independent, immovable and infinite, who is present everywhere, who sees everything, can do everything, has created all things and who governs them all.

– Why do you say that God is a Spirit? Because God is a sovereign Intelligence who has neither body, nor shape, nor colour, and who cannot fall under the senses.

– How many kinds of intelligence are there? There are three kinds ... God, the angels and our souls.'

2   Cf. I. Dalferth, *Existenz Gottes und christlicher Glaube. Skizze zu einer eschatologischen Ontologie*, Munich 1984, 175–7: 'God is not an object that we can identify by means of the criterion of space and time and can thus objectify ... God is neither here as opposed to there nor now as opposed to then. Nor is he simply here and there and thus everywhere or now, then and thus always. For in that case God would be an object in space and time who can be characterized as a particular extension of duration or at least would have a position in space or time.' Cf. also L. J. van den Brom, *God alomtegenwoordig?*, Kampen: Kok 1982.

3   Compare the experience of those who have a severe bodily handicap and report what in a sense is an ambivalent attitude to their body, and who as persons do not want to be addressed in terms of their handicap.

4   Lateran IV 1215, cf. *Lexikon für Theologie und Kirche*, 1957, 470–3.

5   Such metaphysical models of God's threefold being, which come to a climax in Hegel (cf. H. Küng, *The Incarnation of God. An Introduction to Hegel's Theological Thought as Prolegomena to a Future Christology*, Edinburgh: T & T Clark 1987), already existed in antiquity. Church fathers like Justin, Theophilus of Antioch and Clement of Alexandria took up the classical doctrine of the *Nous* manifesting itself in *Logos* and *Sophia* as an analogy to the Christian, trinitarian idea of God. In general afterwards, too, people looked in Greek culture for parallels to the Christian doctrine of God and found it for example in the work of Hermes Trismegistos. Cf. A. J. Festugière, *La révélation d'Hermès Trismégiste I–IV*, Paris 1944–54: Dionysius the Areopagite touches on the same theme of unity and multiplicity in God in connection with the Neoplatonism of Proclus: see W. Beierwaltes, *Denken des Einen. Studien zur neuplatonischen Philosophie und ihrer Wirkungsgeschichte*, Frankfurt 1985, 205ff. His approach then influenced Thomas Aquinas and the whole of Western systematic theology, in which the unity of God (*De deo uno*) comes first and the Trinity seems to be a derivative of it. The East has always sought its starting point in the plurality of divine manifestations, all of which flow from the same *fons Trinitatis*, i.e. the Father or YHWH. Cf. F. O'Rourke, *Pseudo-Dionysius and the Metaphysics of Aquinas*, Leiden: Brill 1992. W. Pannenberg, *Systematic Theology* I, Grand Rapids: Eerdmans and Edinburgh: T & T Clark 1992, 259ff., powerfully opposes the whole of this tradition: the doctrine of the Trinity exclusively finds its origin in the twofold relation of Jesus to God as Father and Spirit.

6   *Adversus Haereses*, IV, 20, 1.

7   In particular Karl Rahner in his treatise 'Der dreifaltige Gott als transzendenter Urgrund der Heilgeschichte' (in J. Feiner and M. Löhrer, *Mysterium Salutis* II,

Einsiedeln, etc.: Benziger 1967, 317–97) again emphasizes this, followed by Jürgen Moltmann in his *Trinity and the Kingdom of God*, London: SCM Press and New York: Harper 1981, and by W. Pannenberg in his *Systematic Theology* II, Grand Rapids: Eerdmans and Edinburgh: T & T Clark 1991, and, in a less christocentric but more pneumatocentric way, by P. Schoonenberg in *De Geest, het Woord en de Zoon*, Averbode: Altiora and Kok: Kampen 1991.

8   Schoonenberg, *De Geest, het Woord en de Zoon* (n. 7), 212.

9   E. Jüngel, *God as Mystery of the World*, Edinburgh: T & T Clark 1983, 159: 'God's ways are also his ways to himself. They are different from our ways of life in that his "to himself" is not removed from the divine subject – "God's way is his work" (Luther) – like the man who must seek himself and find his way to himself. But they are like the human ways of life in that the way *is inextricably united with the subject* [my italics]. On the human way of life, a man becomes what he is. On the divine way of life, God makes himself into that which he is. The formulation of this content is this: God's being is in coming.' In this connection Jüngel also speaks of the humanity of God as a story to be told (ibid., 299ff.). See in this connection also K. Armstrong, *A History of God*, London: Mandarin Books 1999; she also couples the 'biography of God' – which by now has become a modern literary theme – with the growing religious images of God. Cf. also Jack Miles, *God. A Biography*, New York: Knopf 1995; Mark S. Smith, *The Early History of God. Yahweh and the Other Deities in Ancient Israel*, San Francisco: Harper 1990.

10   Cf. B. Burrell, *Freedom and Creation in Three Traditions*, Notre Dame: University of Notre Dame Press 1993.

11   Cf. H. Richter, *Der Gotteskomplex*, Frankfurt 1979, in connection with Feuerbach and Nietzsche. It is striking that Thomas Aquinas in his discussion of the question of God (*Utrum Deus sit?*, *Summa Theologica*, I, q. 2, a. 3) discusses not only the so-called theodicy argument (how can God and evil exist at the same time?) but also the far more modern argument of God's superfluity: everything that is can be explained from natural causes and from human purpose (reason and will). His answer to the second argument (ad 2) really amounts to the fact that anyone who takes refuge in the determinism of nature and human planning finds it even more difficult to explain the actual deficiencies and contingency.

12   Cf. M. Brinkman, *Schepping en Sacrament*, Zoetermeer 1991, 29.

13   A. Lovejoy, *The Great Chain of Being*, New York 1936.

14   C. Améry, *Das Ende der Vorsehung. Die gnadenlosen Folgen des Christentums*, Hamburg 1972; E. Drewermann, *Der tödliche Fortschritt. Von der Zerstörung der Erde und des Menschen im Erbe des Christentums*, Regensburg 1981. For the history of the reading of Gen. 1.28: U. Krolzik, 'Die Wirkungsgeschichte von Genesis 1,28', in G. Altner (ed.), *Ökologische Theologie. Perspektiven zur Orientierung*, Stuttgart 1989, 149–63.

15   Thus what must be regarded as an honest attempt to give a reason for the faith ended up as the opposite. Cf. W. Stoker, *De christelijke godsdienst in de filosofie van de Verlichting. Een vergelijkende studie over de geloofsverantwoording in het denken van Locke, de deïsten, Lessing en Kant*, Assen: Van Gorcum 1980.

16   Cf. recently A. van de Beek, *Schepping. De wereld als voorspel voor de eeuwigheid*, Baarn: Callenbach 1996.

17   Thus the biblical theology of von Rad, who puts all the emphasis on the special place of Israel and reads Genesis from Exodus; and Westermann, who prefers

the opposite reading and starts from an original universalism of belief in YHWH.

18 Cf. *God in Nature and History (Bristol 1967)*, Geneva: WCC 1967, and H. Berkhof, *Christian Faith*, Grand Rapids: Eerdmans 1986, 155ff. The World Council of Churches Assembly in Canberra in 1991 called for a restoration of this bond between nature and history; see the report of section I in M. Kinnamon (ed.), *Signs of the Spirit. Official Report of the Seventh Assembly*, Geneva: WCC and Grand Rapids: Eerdmans 1991, 54–72.

19 Cf. H. de Lubac, *Le Surnaturel: Études historiques*, Paris: Aubier 1946, which has set the tone for the criticism of the dualism of nature and supernature, time and eternity in modern Catholic theology after Vatican II.

20 E.g. in *Time and Narrative*, I, Chicago: Chicago University Press 1984, 52–87; cf. also Chapter 6 above, 149ff.

21 V. Brümmer overlooks precisely this anthropological significance of prayer in his *What Are We Doing When We Pray? A Philosophical Enquiry*, London: SCM Press 1984. He mentions only the therapeutic, instrumental and relational effects of prayer.

22 Matthew Fox, *Original Blessing. A Primer in Creation Spirituality*, Santa Fe: Bear & Co. 1983.

23 H. Santmire, *The Travail of Nature*, Philadelphia: Fortress Press 1985.

24 Fox thinks that Western theology since Augustine has replaced a creation theology paradigm with a soteriological paradigm that starts from 'original sin'. The goodness of God's creation is here shifted to the future. All distress and misery is transitory. Thus the positive, dynamic forces are not developed: 'What religion must let go of in the west is an exclusively fall/redemption mode of spirituality – a model that has dominated theology, Bible studies, seminary and novitiate training, hagiography, psychology, for centuries. It is a dualistic model and a patriarchal one; it begins its theology with sin and original sin, and it generally ends with redemption. Fall/redemption spirituality does not teach believers about the New Creation or creativity, about justice-making and social transformation, or about Eros, play, pleasure, and the God of delight. It fails to teach love of the earth or care for the cosmos, and is so frightened of passion that it fails to listen to the impassioned pleas of the *anawim*, the little ones, of human history. This same fear of passion prevents it from helping lovers to celebrate their experiences as spiritual and mystical. This tradition has not proven friendly to artists or prophets or Native American peoples or women' (*Original Blessing* [n. 22], 11).

25 Cf. A. Houtepen, 'Ambiguous Religion and the Authentic Holy', *Exchange* 25, 1996, 2–26.

26 Cf. H. Dörrie, 'Spätantike Metaphysik als Theologie', in H. Fröhnes (ed.), *Kirchengeschichte als Missionsgeschichte* IV, Munich 1974, 261–82.

27 Augustine, *Confessions*, XI, II, 3 and IV, 6, translated by Henry Chadwick, Oxford: Oxford University Press 1991, 222 and 224.

28 Thomas Aquinas, *Summa Theologica*, I, q. 94ff.

29 Cf. W. H. Schmidt, *Theologisches Handwörterbuch zum Alten Testament* I, 337. Systematic reflection on God as creator only arose late in the religion of Israel, in the Babylonian exile, and very probably under the influence of Mesopotamian creation theology. We encounter the specific term 'create' (*bara'*), which occurs exclusively with YHWH as subject, almost only in exilic and post-exilic texts. This fact led G. von Rad as early as 1935 to state that the Old Testament

must be read from the perspective of Exodus, the earliest writing, and not Genesis: G. von Rad, 'The Theological Problem of the Old Testament Doctrine of Creation', in *The Problem of the Hexateuch*, Edinburgh: Oliver and Boyd 1966, 131–43. He later worked out this thesis in his *Genesis*, London: SCM Press ²1972 and *Old Testament Theology* I, London: SCM Press 1975. In 1974 Westermann rejected this thesis in his *Genesis*, ET London: SPCK 1984, and referred to the place of Genesis in the Torah, and also to the affinity of Genesis to the prophetic texts, which are just as much part of the perspective of Israel. Later, on the basis of his study of the wisdom literature, von Rad (partly) retreated from his standpoint. J. Ebach, 'Schöpfung in der hebräischen Bibel', in G. Altner (ed.), *Ökologische Theologie. Perspektiven zur Orientierung*, Stuttgart 1989, 98–129, refers to the time-conditioned and contextual character of von Rad's theses, which were also taken over by Barth: against the 'natural theology' of the Nazis, in which there was no place for a special role for Israel, it was important to emphasize the special history of this people. Westermann thought that a solely soteriological interpretation of Genesis exclusively from the perspective of the history of the liberation of Israel was damaging to belief in God as such. In my view it also subsumes the New Testament soteriology too much under the Exodus motif (and the Exodus or Sinai covenant). Christian salvation picks up just as much from Abraham, father of the peoples, as from Moses, the lawgiver of Israel. Paul's theology can be read as an explicitation of the tension between Adam, Abraham and Moses. For him Jesus is the new Adam, just as for John Jesus is 'before Abraham' (John 8.58).

30 Thus especially R. Rendtorff, 'Die theologische Stellung des Schöpfungsglaubens bei Deuterojesaja', *Zeitschrift für Theologie und Kirche* 51, 1954, 3ff., and id., '"Wo warst du, als ich die Erde gründete?", Schöpfung und Heilsgeschichte', in G. Rau et al. (eds), *Frieden in der Schöpfung*, Gütersloh 1987, 35–57.

31 P. Ricoeur, *La Symbolique du mal*, Paris: Aubier 1960.

32 E. van Wolde, 'Van tekst via tekst naar betekenis', *Tijdschrift voor Theologie* 30, 1990, 351ff.

33 See especially the pioneering work by A. Hulsbosch, who died prematurely, *De Schepping Gods*, Roermond and Maaseik 1963.

34 J. Moltmann, *God in Creation*, London: SCM Press and New York: Harper 1985.

35 Cf. T. J. van Bavel, 'De kerkvaders over de schepping', *Tijdschrift voor Theologie* 30, 1990, 18–33. Within the pantheistic argument a correlation is produced between God and nature which regards the processes of nature that can be perceived as the outside of a divine reality which is hidden behind them. Everything becomes the expression of the divine life. God and evil can no longer be distinguished either; all is what it is and good as it is. Every tree can be addressed as if it were God himself. There is no longer any real freedom, because human action is always guided entirely by God. Spinoza was the sublime representative of this pantheism within Western culture. Within panentheism – which I myself find most attractive for the correlation between God and reality – there can be mixing and complete identification, if God is spoken of in too vivid terms, e.g. as a body, of which the cosmic forces are the power of expression. Then too the distinction between good and evil becomes impossible and our freedom disappears into the black hole of the divine energy. Thus with reference to God, thought models always imply a fundamental

analogy and an impossibility of comparison. I referred above to the quotation marks which within a panentheistic model of the being of things must be placed 'within' God and pointed to the nature of the relationship between the 'I' and its realm which together determine the personal core of the human being. 'Something like that' must also continue to apply to God.

36 Moltmann, *God in Creation* (n. 34), 86–93, 102.

37 Ibid., 118.

38 E.g. Gen. 8.22; Isa. 6.3; Job 9.5; 10.12; 38; Pss. 65.7; 104; 145.15; 147.8; Hos. 2.10; Ex. 3.6–22; Deut. 6.4–25. The main leitmotif is Prov. 8.22–31 and Wisd. 7.22–8.1, together with Job 28 and 38: the overwhelming wisdom and power of God in all things. Also the story of the sacrifice of Isaac in Gen. 22 and here above all Gen. 22.8 and 14 about God who himself will see to the sacrificial animal (*Deus providebit* in the Vulgate; here the LXX has only forms of *oraomai: opsetai, eiden*; the Hebrew is the same: *ra'h*: the meaning is, make to see, bring to view).

39 *Pronoia*, Wisd. 14.2; 17.2; Dan. 6.18; II Macc. 4.6; also in III Macc. 4.21; 5.30; IV Macc. 9.24; 13.19; 17.22; *pronoein*: Wisd. 6.7,13; Eccles. 3.4; Job 24.15; Ezra 2.28; Dan. 11.37; II Macc. 14.9 and III Macc. 3.24; IV Macc. 7.18. In the New Testament only Rom. 12.17 (= Prov. 3.4); 13.14; II Cor. 8.21 (= Prov. 3.24); I Tim. 5.8; Acts 24.2. In all cases it is a question of the concern of human beings for one another, that evil does not befall them.

40 Cf. C. van Sliedrecht, *Calvins opvolger Theodorus Beza. Zijn verkiezingsleer en zijn belijdenis van de drieënige God*, Leiden: Groen & Zn 1996.

41 A. Geense, 'Dieu y pourvoira. Perspectives oecuméniques d'une doctrine de la providence', in *Colloque Théologique de l'Église Wallonne*, 28 September 1991, Amstelveen: Improcep 1992, 15–29.

42 Calvin too and Beza himself, the most prominent spokesmen of the classical Reformation doctrine of election, continue to speak of a maze, a whirlpool and a labyrinth full of snares. The doctrine of election rests on two premises:
– a righteous God cannot be indifferent to evil;
– a believer who has made Christ his own and also his children who died prematurely and were not yet baptized must be certain of God's mercy.

The great, speculative tension and the intellectual maze arise where these two premises are understood in terms of causality. The first premise then comes into conflict with the doctrine that God is the cause of everything, because evil and sin are also part of God's creation; the second comes into conflict with the question of the guilt of those who have made no acquaintance with the gospel, those who have not been reached. A good, righteous and merciful God cannot cause evil or positively will the death and the damnation of the sinner, far less cause it. A good, righteous and merciful God cannot distribute opportunities so unequally that those who are innocently ignorant are cast out of salvation, the covenant and election. The core of this speculative strait-jacket is formed by too direct a connection between what people see happening in the order of salvation – conversion, faith, justification, sanctification, glorification of God's elect – and the guiding omnipotence of God, understood in terms of the analogy of causality. Although here there continues to be talk of the difference between God's hidden decision and the public implementation of it as a difference between first cause and second cause, the more time goes on, the more the character of the first cause is interpreted as a cause in a chain of causes. There is an original series which leads either to glorification or to rejection. 'The series of causes begins with God's honour and also ends with it. God is the first cause, and all that follows from this falls under the second or middle causes, in which then everything finally ends up with the last cause, the final cause, God's honour' (Kickel, quoted by Van Sliedrecht, *Theodorus Beza* [n. 40], 116). This causal series which connects everything with God's counsel as the source of all causes becomes a 'principle of transfiguring the world' (Van Sliedrecht, 141). So an attempt is made to 'wrench open the door of God's council chamber' (as Oberman objects against the synod of Dordrecht). For Thomas Aquinas, as of course for all of high scholasticism, there can be no question of a causal series in relation to God's action: God as *prima causa* is not just a first cause in a series of *causae secundae* but a source-cause on the meta-level. The *causae secundae* indeed come from God; not, however, as the effect from its cause, since we know that, but because in a mysterious way God makes us share in his all-embracing causality (Thomas, *Summa Theologica*, I, q. 22, a. 3c: '... *sunt aliqua media divinae providentiae: quia inferiora gubernat per superiora, non propter defectum suae virtutis, sed propter abundantiam suae bonitatis; ut dignitatem causalitatis etiam creaturis communicet.*' Cf. B. Delfgaauw, *Thomas van Aquinas*, Bussum 1980, 71–6). God uses human beings as his instruments, but the effect of that instrument in God's hand cannot be derived from the causality of the instrument: God can write straight with crooked lines, God can make sinners holy, and persecutors pillars of the church. But God cannot make transgressors holy at the moment of their transgression, nor the virtuous villains at the moment of their virtue. So there is a distinctive order of good and evil, sinful and holy, which is disclosed through Law and Gospel. How this order relates to God's righteousness and holiness, mercy and grace cannot, however, be indicated in terms of causality. Nor with a doctrine of merits nor with a doctrine of God's decrees. Both the doctrine of merits and the doctrine of God's double predestination are irresponsible extrapolations of the doctrine of *causae secundae*.

43   Thus H. de Lubac, *Le drame de l'humanisme athée*, Paris 1944.

44   W. Klever, 'De logica van het universum', in W. N. A. Klever (ed.), *Filosofische Theologie*, Baarn 1985, 40–64.

45   Thomas Aquinas, *Contra Gentiles*, I, II, c. 17: '*Quod Creatio non est motus neque mutatio.*'

46   E.g. Fifth Sunday in Ordinary Time, opening prayer: 'Father, watch over your family and keep us safe in your care, for all our hope is in you'; Second Sunday in Ordinary Time, opening prayer: 'Almighty and ever-present Father, your watchful care reaches from end to end and orders all things in such power that even the tensions and tragedies of sin cannot frustrate your loving plans.' Tenth Sunday in Ordinary Time, opening prayer: 'God of wisdom and love, source of all good, send your Spirit to send us your truth and guide our actions in your way of peace'; Twelfth Sunday in Ordinary Time, opening prayer: 'Father, guide and protector of your people, grant us an unfailing respect for your name and keep us always in your love'; Eighteenth Sunday through the Year, prayer after communion: 'Lord, you give us the strength of new life by the gift of the eucharist. Protect us with your love and prepare us for eternal redemption.'

47   *Liber Divinorum Operum* (*LDO*) 5, 24, in J. P. Migne, *Patres Latinae* (*PL*) 197, 913c, and 200.

48   *LDO, 5, 15, PL,* 197, 914d–915a.

49   *LDO* 4, 104, *PL*, 197, 888c. Quotations taken from J. van Laarhoven, 'Groen

licht voor de schepping: Visies van Hildegard van Bingen', *Tijdschrift voor Theologie* 30, 1990, 34–50: 44 (+ bibliography): there are similar but much more pessimistic texts in Alain of Lille in his *Planctus Naturae*.

50   M. Luther, *The Little Catechism*, First article of faith, in *Bekenntnisschriften der evangelisch-lutherische Kirche*, Göttingen: Vandenhoeck & Ruprecht 1986, 510. Cf. *The Great Catechism*, 75–6: 'This I mean and believe, that I am God's creature; that is, that He has given to me and constantly sustains body, soul and life, members small and great, all senses, mind and so on, eating, drinking, clothes, food, wife and child, servants, house and land and so on, and moreover makes all things serve us and our livelihood, sun, moon and stars in heaven, day and night, air, fire, water, earth and what it can produce, birds, fish, cattle, corn and all kinds of vegetation and also other bodily and temporal goods, viz., good government, peace, security. So one can learn from this article that no one of us has life or anything that is listed, of himself, however small and little it may be. For it is all summed up in the word "Creator".'

51   Huub Oosterhuis.

8. THE GOD OF THE LIVING: JESUS OF NAZARETH AS GOD'S MESSENGER

1   E. Schillebeeckx, *Jesus*, London: Collins and New York: Crossroad 1979; id., *Christ*, London: SCM Press and New York: Crossroad 1980.

2   W. Kasper, *Jesus the Christ*, New York: Paulist Press 1977.

3   H. Küng, *On Being a Christian*, London: Collins 1976.

4   Cf. G. Theissen, *Studien zur Soziologie des Urchristentums*, Mohr: Tübingen 1979; id., *The Shadow of the Galilean*, London: SCM Press and Philadelphia: Fortress 1987.

5   K. H. Ohlig, *Fundamentalchristologie. Im Spannungsfeld von Christentum und Kultur*, Munich: Kösel Verlag 1986.

6   C. J. Heyer, *Jesus Matters*, London: SCM Press and Harrisburg: TPI 1997, offers a survey of the investigation of the activity and message of Jesus of Nazareth over the last 150 years.

7   This is worked out consistently above all in the dogmatics of F. W. Marquardt, *Das christliche Bekenntnis zu Jesus, dem Juden*, I–II, Munich: Christian Kaiser 1990–1.

8   For the religious background of Hellenism and the expression 'To an unknown god', see P. van der Horst, *De onbekende god. Essays over de joodse en hellenistische achtergrond van het vroege christendom*, Utrecht 1988, 9–37. The expression can apply to the God of the Jews, whose name may not be mentioned; to an anonymous God to whom one appeals in order 'to make certain' in calamities but whom one otherwise would prefer not to identify; or to 'whatever god' one wants to mention in the pantheon 'for the sake of completeness'. The expression appears on inscriptions and in ancient Greek texts, usually in the plural. It then expresses the fact that as well as the known gods there are also all kinds of other gods and forces in play who dominate our life, or it refers to 'strange gods' from Asia and Africa, who are to be appeased with the Hellenistic gods.

9   Cf. E. Grässer, *An die Hebräer*, Evangelisch-Katholisches Kommentar zum

Neuen Testament XVII/1–2, Zurich: Benziger and Neukirchen: Neukirchener Verlag 1990/1993.

10 *Christology* is understood to be theological reflection on the confession that Jesus is the Christ, in other words the one anointed by God, i.e. the representative of God appointed king or leader of God's people who in the Jewish scriptures is already called *mashiach*, messiah. In general terms we can say that the Jewish messianic expectation is the expression of the eschatological hope of Israel: that one day there will be peace, justice and happiness for all peoples. This expectation of salvation takes on different configurations within Israel, of which the messianic expectation is one, but within the notion of a coming messiah there are many variables, even in Jesus' day: see J. Becker, *Messiaserwartung im Alten Testament*, Stuttgart: Katholisches Bibelwerk 1977; C. J. den Heyer, *De messiaanse weg. Messiaanse verwachtingen in het O.T. en in de vroeg-joodse traditie*, Kampen: Kok 1983; M. de Jonge, *Jezus als Messias. Hoe Hij zijn zending zag*, Boxtel: KBS and Bruges: Tabor 1990; G. Oegema, *De messiaanse verwachtingen ten tijde van Jezus*, Baarn: Ten Have 1991. The identification of Jesus as Messiah/Christ in fact represents a specific colouring of the Jewish messianic expectation which fits in anything but seamlessly. Indeed we find other honorific titles for Jesus alongside the Messiah/Christ title: Kyrios (as the Greek alternative for the Messiah king) and Son of God (as the Hellenistic form of the Messiah lawgiver and Moses redivivus). These four honorific titles of Jesus became one of the determining elements in the later christological disputes from the third and fourth centuries onwards, which put all the emphasis on the divine origin of Jesus, the epiphany of God which took place in him, and his authority (*exousia*) from God. However, there is also a line of thought 'from below upwards' which issues in a 'low christology', the rise of the figure of Jesus in hiding: as a Jew from the Jews, who inserts himself into the line of the prophets and the apocalyptic seers, a pious and righteous man, a suffering servant of God who is led to the slaughter, Elijah redivivus, the firstborn who is saved by God from the dead as a fulfilment of Isa. 49.9, and rehabilitated as righteous by God and 'adopted' among the crucified and accursed of all times. Both lines of thought are authentically New Testament. They cannot be played off against each other, though unfortunately this has happened time and again. Alongside this barren opposition there is yet another: that between christology and soteriology. Here the first is said to be about the person of Jesus and the second about his work. Because person and work, what he is and what he does, cannot be divided in the account of his life, this division of the theological argument is also extremely unfortunate. In the argument which follows – which is exclusively devoted to the question of God and thus does not aim at a complete christology – I try as far as possible to avoid both unworkable oppositions. For a number of soteriological models which are current within present-day Christian theology see R. Lanooy (ed.), *For Us and for Our Salvation. Seven Perspectives on Christian Soteriology*, Zoetermeer: Meinema 1994.

11 P. Schoonenberg, *De Geest, het Woord en de Zoon. Theologische overdenkingen over Geest-christologie, Logos-christologie en drieënheidsleer*, Averbode: Altiora and Kampen: Kok 1991.

12 *Nieuwe Rotterdamse Courant*, 12 March 1994.

13 *De Revisor* 1991, nos 11 & 2, 121.

14 See K. L. Schmidt, '*basileia*', in G. Kittel, *Theological Dictionary of the New*

Testament, I, Grand Rapids: Eerdmans 1964, 579–93. For the following see also R. Schnackenburg, *Gottes Herrschaft und Reich*, Freiburg: Herder 1959 ([4]1965); N. Perrin, *The Kingdom of God in the Teaching of Jesus*, London: SCM Press 1963; id., *Jesus and the Language of the Kingdom: Symbol and Metaphor in New Testament Interpretation*, London: SCM Press and Philadelphia: Fortress 1976; W. Pannenberg, *Theologie und Reich Gottes*, Gütersloh: Gerd Mohn 1971; E. Schillebeeckx, *Jesus* (n. 1); H. Merklein, *Die Gottesherrschaft als Handlungsprinzip. Untersuchung zur Ethik Jesu*, Würzburg 1976; B. D. Chilton, *God in Strength. Jesus' Announcement of the Kingdom*, Freistadt 1979; J. Schlosser, *Le Règne de Dieu dans les dits de Jésus*, Paris 1980; J. Moltmann, *The Trinity and the Kingdom of God*, London: SCM Press and New York: Harper 1981; H. Schürmann, *Gottes Reich – Jesu Geschick: Jesu ureigener Tod im Licht seiner Basileia-Verkündigung*, Freiburg: Herder 1983, and recently F. Bovon, *Das Evangelium nach Lukas (Lk 9, 51–14, 35)*, Evangelisch-katholischer Kommentar zum Neuen Testament III/2, Zurich: Benziger Verlag and Neukirchen: Neukirchener Verlag 1996.

15 Cf. A. Houtepen, 'Diakonia als Einladung Gottes', *Diaconia Christi* 30, 1995, no. 3/4, 3–45.

16 F. Bovon in particular in his commentary on the Gospel of Luke points to the dualistic background to the struggle with Satan and the forces of darkness in a number of passages of the New Testament. The *basileia* texts take on a polemical character through this emphasis, because all elements of violence are removed. They challenge the notion of a permanent struggle between God and the devil: this struggle is settled for good with the appearance of Jesus: Satan and the demons submit to the Son of Man. Cf. Chapter 3.

17 Schillebeeckx, *Jesus* (n. 1), 145f.

18 For an extensive discussion of the significance of the kingdom of God see also A. Houtepen, *People of God. A Plea for the Church*, London: SCM Press 1984, 125–41.

19 This is the theme of J. Derrida, *Aporias. Dying – awaiting (one another at) the 'limits of truth'*, Stanford: Stanford University Press 1993.

20 Roman Missal: Absolution.

9. THE HOLY *PNEUMA* OF GOD

1 Thus of course many texts in the New Testament where Jesus addresses YHWH directly as Father of Israel and his Father (e.g. Matt. 26.39, 42; Luke 10.21; 23.34, 46; John 11.41; 12.27; 17.1ff.) or where the relationship between Jesus and God is stated (Rom. 6.4; 15.6; I Cor. 8.6; 15.24; II Cor. 1.3; 11.31; Gal. 1.1; Eph. 1.3; 6.23; Phil. 2.11; Col. 1.3; 3.17; II Thess. 1.2; Titus 1.4; II Peter 1.17; I John 1.3; 2.22–3; II John 9; Rev. 3.21; 14.1, etc.).

2 There are systematic, innovating views e.g. in H. Mühlen, *Der Heilige Geist als Person*, Munich: Aschendorf [3]1969; J. Moltmann, *The Church in the Power of the Spirit*, London: SCM Press and San Francisco: Harper [2]1992; E. Schweizer, *Heiliger Geist*, Stuttgart: Kreuz Verlag 1978; A. van den Beek, *De Adem van God. De Heilige Geest in kerk en kosmos*, Nijkerk: Kallenbach 1987; P. Schoonenberg, *De Geest, het Woord en de Zoon. Theologische overdenkingen over Geest-christologie, Logos-christologie en drieënheidsleer*, Averbode: Altiora and Kampen: Kok 1991.

3   I cannot go at length here into this controversy, which moreover has been resolved in ecumenical dialogue. Cf. L. Vischer, *Spirit of God, Spirit of Christ. Ecumenical Reflections on the Filioque Controversy*, London: SPCK and Geneva: WCC 1981; J. Moltmann, *The Trinity and the Kingdom of God*, London: SCM Press and New York: Harper 1981, 178–87. Of course the Eastern Orthodox theology which refers to the Greek church fathers (Origen, Basil, Gregory of Nazianzus, Gregory of Nyssa, John Chrysostom) recognizes that the Gospel of John speaks of the Spirit who will be sent by Father on the intercession of Jesus (John 14.16, 26). Then Jesus is the advocate, the intercessor and helper or paraclete of human beings with God (I John 2.1; cf. John 17.12, 15).

He also remains in that capacity as the one who has risen to the right hand of God (Rom. 8.34; Heb. 7.25). But on the other hand it is the risen, glorified Christ himself who breathes the Spirit on the disciples (John 20.22). Then the Spirit is the *Paraclete*, the helper of believers, the support to their memory (John 14.26), though always as the extended arm, the mouthpiece of the risen Lord (O. Noordmans, *Gestalte en geest*, Amsterdam 1955, 233–6), his *alter ego* (J. Veenhof, *De Parakleet*, Kampen: Kok, 2nd edn, nd [1978], 21). But in John too this *Pneuma* is the *Pneuma* of the Father, i.e. of Israel's God. The whole tenor of John 14–17 is to indicate that the Spirit of the Father which has driven and inspired Jesus will inspire his disciples even after Jesus' disappearance from history, and also at his intercession with God. Thus it cannot be a communal 'product' of the Father and the Son, as if there could be any question of a double source. That is the way in which the Western formulation *qui ex Patre Filioque procedit* is often understood in the East. The Council of Florence made it clear that this means precisely the same as the formula *qui ex Patre, per Filium procedit*, which reflects the Eastern perspective (DS 1300–1302). The Christians from Orthodoxy 'united' with Rome also preferred the latter formulation with a reference to Florence and omitted the *Filioque* from the Nicene Creed: see the first of the articles of the Union of Brest: '... *postulamus, ne ad aliam confessionem stringamur, sed eam sequamur, quam in evangelii et sanctorum Patrum religionis Graecae scriptis traditam habemus, nimirum Spiritum Sanctum non ex duabus principiis, nec duplici processione, sed ex uno principio velut ex fonte, ex Patre per Filium procedere*' (cf. A. Houtepen, 'Uniatism and Models of Unity in the Ecumenical Movement', *Exchange* 25, 1996, 202–21). The importance of this whole debate only becomes clear in its consequences. Christianity shares with Israel (and all other religions) the same God whom Jesus calls his Father and by whom he knows himself to be sent. Therefore within Christianity the New Testament – the message and the narrative about Jesus – cannot be played off against the Old, nor can the church claim the 'New Covenant' in God's Spirit (Jer. 31.31) for itself alone, far less deny it to Jews. The Father and the Spirit are the two original names of God from which Jesus himself also lived and which legitimate his mission. All Christian mission therefore stands in service of the original belief in YHWH and needs to come to an understanding in a dialogical and theocentric way with all religious movements which seek to serve this one God.

4   These voices were heard above all at the World Council of Churches at Canberra in 1991, where the Korean theologian Chung Hyun Kyung spoke of associating the Christian *pneuma* tradition with the Asian and African tradition of ancestor spirits. For many this was a bridge too far. Perhaps we should say,

rather, that the pillars of her bridge were too weak: the association of God's *Pneuma* with the 'spirits' of the ancestors rests on an unhappy coupling of meanings which arise from the English 'spirit' and from an interpretation of the holy as the sacral in religious studies which I analysed in Chapter 5. African theologians seek the connection rather through the thought of the 'communion of saints' and a direct application of the New Testament language about God's life-giving Spirit, which raises from the dead (I Cor. 15). For Canberra see M. Kinnamon (ed.), *Signs of the Spirit. Official Report of the Seventh Assembly, Canberra, Australia, 7–20 February 1991*, Geneva: WCC and Grand Rapids: Eerdmans 1991; A. Houtepen, 'Der Heilige Geist als Quelle und Kraft des Lebens. Die pneumatologische Debatte in Canberra', *Una Sancta* 46, 1991/2, 92–107. The address by Chung Hyun Kyung is in her book *Struggle To Be the Sun Again*, Maryknoll, NY: Orbis Books and London: SCM Press 1990, 37–47.

5   Cf. G. L. Prestige, *God in Patristic Thought*, London 1956.

6   Throughout the Old Testament the '*ruach*' (wind, breeze, breath, sigh, in the Septuagint translated as *Pneuma*) of God' or 'the holy *ruach*' is the designation of God's presence and working as such. Whereas in the New Testament God is spoken of directly more than 1,200 times, the divine *Pneuma* is mentioned rather more than 200 times: 90 times we have *to pneuma hagion*, abbreviated to *to pneuma* in about the same number of times; 20 times *Pneuma* of God, the *Pneuma* of the Father or the *Pneuma* of the Lord, and only a few times the *Pneuma* of Christ (Rom. 8.11; I Peter 1.11), the *Pneuma* of the Son (Gal. 4.6) or the *Pneuma* of Jesus Christ (Phil. 1.19; cf. I John 3.24; 4.13). Jesus himself speaks of God as Father and *Pneuma*; here the association with the surprising and refreshing blowing of the wind is made explicit, especially in John 3.5 and 4.24. In Western languages, under the influence of the Latin *spiritus* and the Germanic *Geist*, this association is lost and a quite different language-field comes in: that of consciousness, inwardness, sensitivity, disposition. The Scandinavian languages speak of the 'Holy Breath' of God and in so doing have retained part of the original analogy. Because already in the Septuagint and the Greek texts of the Old Testament (e.g. Dan. 3.86) and in the Apocrypha (Enoch 22.3–13; Sib. Or 7, 127) and also in the New Testament *pneuma* is used as a synonym for *psyche* (the seat of consciousness, the will and the emotions), with which the human principle of life is at the same time identified, the *pneuma tou theou* also becomes an analogy of this and is thus interpreted anthropomor-phically as consciousness, power of the will, emotion; however, in this way it is also spiritualized. For the Old Testament terminology see R. Albertz and C. Westermann, '*ruach*', in E. Jenni and C. Westermann, *Theologisches Handwörterbuch zum Alten Testament* II, Gütersloh: Christian Kaiser/Gütersloher Verlagshaus 1994, 726–53. For the New Testament see '*pneuma*', in W. Bauer, W. F. Arndt and F. W. Gingrich, *Lexicon of New Testament Greek*, Chicago: Chicago University Press 1957, 680–5.

7   E. Schweizer, *Heiliger Geist* (n. 2), 23–4: 'In the Spirit God's work is experienced in the midst of a worldly, earthly or even political situation. Where else could human beings experience it? However, it is not understood as a personal experience but as an alien experience, which does not simply arise from one's own soul or spirit but from what it cannot as yet call "God", yet gradually does so with increasing awareness. So Holy Spirit has nothing to do with that higher ideal life which seeks to raise itself above the humiliations of the material: it is as near to the body as to the soul, to a person's bodily functions as

to their spiritual or mental ones. Israel used the same word for the Spirit of God as that which denotes the wind or the storm. God's spirit is as bodily, as concrete, as a storm wind.'

8   The Latin word *persona* derives from an Etruscan word which denoted the goddess Persephone. Her worship was an occasion for a carnival-like feast involving masks. Thus *persona* came to mean mask and hence the stage role in which the same actor can portray different characters by exchanging masks. But the application of this concept of *persona* to God very soon led to christological problems: people would not have it that in Jesus God played simply the role of a man. The theologian Sabellius, who spoke of three modes of appearance of God, was in fact condemned. All views which tend towards an exposition of the three names of God as so many roles or functions of God were also condemned in later times as modalism or Sabellianism. The analogy of different extensions of the same person, regarded as an extended person, which I used in Chapter 7, enter quite a different-language-field: that of the real scope of the person-in-relation, the social person.

9   K. Waayman et al., *Kansen voor spiritualiteit*, Baarn:Gooi en Sticht and Nijmegen: Katholiek Studiecentrum 1996.

10 H. Hermans, 'Het meerstemmig zelf. Op het raakvlak van psychologie en spiritualiteit', in K. Waayman et al., *Kansen voor spiritualiteit* (n. 9), 89–124.

10. THE ONE GOD AND THE MANY RELIGIONS

1   This chapter is a revision of a lecture for the Albert Dondeyne chair in Louvain and Bruges in 1995, now published in M. Lamberigts (ed.), *Vatican II, Terugblik en Toekomst*, Leuven 1996.

2   Cf. A. Camps, *Partners in Dialogue. Christianity and Other World Religions*, Maryknoll: Orbis 1983.

3   M. Foucault, 'Histories weten en macht', lecture of 7 January 1976, in *Te Elfder Ure* 25, 1991/1, no. 29, Nijmegen 1981, 559–72: 561: 'So what arose ten or fifteen years ago [since 1960–5] is – I would say – the increasing possibility of criticizing things, institutions, practices and arguments: a kind of general fragmentation of the ground on which we stand and also perhaps above all the most familiar, most solid ground which is closest of all to us, our bodies, our everyday activities.'

4   H. Fries and K. Rahner, *Einigung der Kirchen – reale Möglichkeit*, Quaestiones Disputatae 100, Freiburg: Herder 1983, 47.

5   D. Loose, 'Robinson redt het niet. Dialoog en ethiek', in W. Derkse (ed.), *Denken als dialoog. Reflecties over vraag en antwoord*, Kampen: Kok Agora 1994, 35–57. Taking up thoughts of Hannah Arendt, he writes: 'Thought is always discursive. It is a conversation with friends or with myself that never derives its meaning from the results obtained but from the activity of thinking itself. This does not survive the dialogue when it falls silent. The life of the spirit is dialogical, also and above all in reflection on the question of the good. Socrates did not understand his service of the truth to be a matter of handing on his insights to someone else. When he was called the wise man of Athens, he understood this to mean that he knew that he did not know. He did not hold any opinion, not even an opinion of himself, to be the truth. However, this did

not lead him to go and seek the truth elsewhere, against the opinion of the masses. This truth was found in considering opinions. The dialectic of his knowledge never destroyed *doxa* and apparent knowledge. It needed this opinion as a breeding ground. His knowledge is rather one that has been talked through, and in the process one's own knowledge and that of the other offer the prospect of a provisional truth which originally was not defended by either of the two conversation partners' (38). In this sense the activity of Jesus was like that of Socrates: he discloses and reveals the will of God in dialogue with Pharisees, scribes, the tax collectors, the temple establishment, the people on the streets and in the country, the Samaritans and those from outside Israel, but above all with the expectations of his own immediate disciples for salvation. Revelation does not destroy opinions nor ride over them, but takes them up in a new perspective. That is what Paul on the Areopagus also does. So do the apologists and missionaries of the first centuries. It is the legalistic fixation of the content of faith on church dogma and the gulf between dogma and lived-out faith which obscure this original maieutics of the dialogue. The pluralism of the truth then becomes a problem to be challenged, whereas it is an inexhaustible source of further discoveries about the truth.

6   E. Schillebeeckx, *The Church*, London: SCM Press 1990, 162.

7   Cf. R. Lane Fox, *Pagans and Christians in the Mediterranean World from the Second Century AD to the Conversion of Constantine*, Harmondsworth: Penguin Books 1988; A. Wessels, *Europe. Was it Ever Really Christian?*, London: SCM Press 1994; K. Armstrong, *A History of God*, London: Mandarin Books 1999.

8   Cf. L. Capéran, *Le Salut des Infidèles. Essai historique*, Toulouse 1934; W. Dietzfelbinger, *Die Grenzen der Kirche nach römisch-katholischer Lehre*, Göttingen: Vandenhoeck & Ruprecht 1962; F. A. Sullivan, *Salvation Outside the Church? Tracing the History of the Catholic Response*, New York and Mahwah, NJ: Paulist Press 1992. For a survey of the history of the reading see also B. Willems, 'Who Belongs to the Church?', *Concilium* 1, 1965/1, 62–71. In its original form, Cyprian's adage ran: *salus extra ecclesiam non est* (*Ep. 73 Ad Jubaianum*, *PL*, 3, 1110ff.; CSEL 3 [1], 214–15, 477 and 795). It is taken over in a slightly changed form by Fulgentius of Ruspe (642–527) (*De Fide ad Petrum* c. 43 CC 91 A, 711ff. [740–1]) and canons 70 (753), 73 (754), 79 (756), 80 (757) of the Council of Braga; in the Middle Ages it was attributed to Augustine. The Council of Florence gave the direction of the absolute necessity of the Catholic Church for salvation in 1442. In the confession of faith for the Jacobites we read: '*Firmiter credit, profitetur et nec Iudaeos aut haereticos atque schismaticos, aeternae vitae fieri posse participes; sed in ignem aeternum ituros, "qui paratus est diabolo et angelis eius" (Matt. 25.4) nisi ante finem vitae eidem fuerint aggregati* ...' (DS 1351). Here no good works nor even a martyr death help in the slightest: '*Neminemque, quantascumque eleemosynas fecerit, etsi pro Christi nomine sanguinem effuderit, posse salvari, nisi in catholicae Ecclesiae gremio et unitate permanserit*' (ibid.). Here Florence leaned vigorously on Fulgentius of Ruspe for support (cf. *PL*, 65, 3704A–B). Pius IX declared this doctrine church dogma in 1863 (DS 2867), but at the same time introduced nuances (DS 2866) that were endorsed by the schema *De Ecclesia* of Vatican I (1870) which was planned but not discussed; those who do not know Christianity or the church, through no fault of their own, cannot just be excluded from salvation (Mansi 51, 541–2; 570–1). Pius XII condemned an excessively vigorous interpretation (DS 3866–3873); Vatican II in effect took leave of it.

9   W. Cantwell Smith, *The Meaning and End of Religion*, London: SPCK 1978; id., *Towards a World Theology: Faith and the Comparative of Religion*, London: Macmillan 1981.
10 J. Baudrillard, *Les stratégies fatales*, Paris: Grasset & Fasquielle 1983.
11 J. Ratzinger, *Church, Ecumenism and Politics*, New York: Crossroad 1988, 154.
12 The most comprehensive survey of the different views is still, in my view, Paul E. Knitter, *No Other Name? A Critical Survey of Christian Attitudes toward the World Religions*, Maryknoll, NY: Orbis Books and London: SCM Press 1985; A. Camps, *Partners in Dialogue. Christianity and Other World Religions* (n. 2), is more critical and at the same time has a more practical orientation. J. Hick (ed.), *The Myth of Christian Uniqueness: Towards a Pluralistic Theology of Religions*, Maryknoll, NY: Orbis Books and London: SCM Press 1988 is instructive. There is also a good survey of the discussion in L. Swidler (ed.), *Toward a Universal Theology of Religion*, New York: Orbis Books 1987, and K. Cracknell, *Towards a New Relationship. Christians and People of Other Faiths*, London: Epworth Press 1986.
13 P. Teilhard de Chardin, *The Phenomenon of Man*, London: Collins 1959. But Teilhard continues to speak of Christianization and is very critical of e.g. the unitive thought of the Asian religions. See P. Smulders, *Het visioen van Teilhard de Chardin*, Bruges and Utrecht: Desclée de Brouwer 1962, 155ff.; U. King, 'Religion and the Future: Teilhard de Chardin's Analysis of Religion as a Contribution to Inter-religious Dialogue', *Theological Studies* 7, 1971, 307–23. As well as Teilhard de Chardin see above all also Alfred North Whitehead, Sri Aurobindo and in their footsteps Bernard Lonergan, who, according to P. Knitter, through their process thought have laid a philosophical basis under the idea of a 'unitive pluralism': Knitter, *No Other Name?* (n. 12), 7ff. For A. N. Whitehead see his *Religion in the Making*, Edinburgh: Macmillan 1926. According to Whitehead the great religions can be reduced to two views, depending on their conception of the human self and whether the idea of God is personal or impersonal: Christian and Buddhist. However, both must go through the third spiritual tradition of scientific experience and (process) metaphysics in order to rediscover their creative potential, to preserve themselves from dogmatism and idolatry and to grow into a religion 'in spirit and truth'.
14 K. Rahner, 'Christianity and the Non-Christian Religions', in *Theological Investigations* 5, New York: Crossroad Publishing Company and London: Darton, Longman and Todd 1966, 115–45; id., 'The Anonymous Christian', in *Theological Investigations* 4, New York: Crossroad Publishing Company and London: Darton, Longman and Todd 1966, 180–7.
15 R. Panikkar, *The Unknown Christ of Hinduism* (revised edition of his 1964 book), Maryknoll, NY: Orbis Books 1981; id., *Salvation in Christ: Concreteness and Universality. The Supername* (inaugural lecture at Tantur, Jerusalem, 1972), Santa Barbara 1972; id., *The Intrareligious Dialogue*, New York: Orbis Books 1978; id., 'The Jordan, the Tiber and the Ganges. Three Kairological Moments of Christic Self-Consciousness', in J. Hick (ed.), *The Myth of Christian Uniqueness* (n. 12), 89–116.
16 M. M. Thomas, *Man and the Universe of Faiths*, Bangalore: CISRS and Madras: CLS 1975; id., *Risking Christ for Christ's Sake: Towards an Ecumenical Theology of Pluralism*, Geneva: WCC 1987.
17 S. J. Samartha, *Courage for Dialogue. Ecumenical Issues in Inter-Religious Relations*, Geneva: WCC 1981; id., *One Christ – Many Religions. Towards a*

Revised Christology, Maryknoll, NY: Orbis Books 1991. For Samartha see E. Klootwijk, *Commitment and Openness. The Interreligous Dialogue and Theology of Religions in the Work of Stanley J. Samartha*, Zoetermeer: Boekencentrum 1992.

18 A. Denaux, 'Bij niemand anders is er redding (Hand. 4.12)', *Tijdschrift voor Theologie* 28, 1988, 228–46.

19 W. Pannenberg, *Systematic Theology* I, Edinburgh: T & T Clark 1991, 136ff.; cf. id., 'Toward a Theology of the History of Religions', in *Basic Questions in Theology* 2, London: SCM Press and Philadelphia: Fortress Press, 1971. Here the thought appears of a conflict over the total concept of reality: 'The unity of the history of religions has actually appeared in the historical interaction between the different religions; or, better, this process is still in progress today as a competition between religions concerning the nature of reality, a competition grounded in the fact that the religions have to do with total views of reality. Only in this way can they provide a basis for the order of human existence or, in another way, mediate salvation to man. By coming into contact with the devotees of other gods, however, they run into conflict with their religions, which can be smoothed out or peacefully settled in various ways: by the relativization of the universal claim of one's own as well as of the alien religion to merely that of a given circle of devotees; by means of interpretation or – under corresponding political conditions – even cultic fusion; and, finally, by displacement' (88). Within this rivalry of religions, by its historical dissemination and missionary activity throughout the whole world, Christianity has become 'the ferment for the rise of a common religious situation of the whole of mankind' (94). For the position of Jesus Christ as the new man see id, 'Die Auferstehung Jesu und die Zukunft des Menschen', *Grundfragen systematischer Theologie* 2, Göttingen: Vandenhoeck & Ruprecht 1980, 174–87.

20 H. Küng, *On Being a Christian* (1977), London: SCM Press 1995, 89–174; id., J. von Ess, H. von Stietencron and H. Becher, *Christianity and the World Religions* (1986), Maryknoll, NY: Orbis Books and London: SCM Press 1993; Küng, *Global Responsibility*, New York: Crossroad and London: SCM Press 1991, esp. 135ff. Küng points especially to the time-lags in different forms of the great religions: historical paradigms of Judaism, Christianity and Hinduism from different cultural periods continue side by side in the twentieth century. That makes dialogue more complicated, but at the same time increases the possibility of convergences.

21 J. Hick, *God and the Universe of Faiths*, London: Macmillan 1974; id., *The Myth of Christian Uniqueness* (n. 12); id., *God Has Many Names*, London: Macmillan 1980.

22 Knitter, *No Other Name?* (n. 12), 205ff.

23 A. Pieris, 'The Place of Non-Christian Religions and Cultures in the Evolution of Third World Theology', in V. Fabella and S. Torres (eds), *Irruption of the Third World: Challenge to Theology*, New York: Orbis Books 1983, 113–39.

24 M. Amaladoss, 'Gospel and Culture in Cross-Cultural Mission', in A. Houtepen (ed.), *Ecumenism and Hermeneutics*, Zoetermeer: Meinema 1995.

25 Katsumi Takizawa, *Das Heil im Heute, Texte einer japanischen Theologie*, Göttingen: Vandenhoeck & Ruprecht 1987.

26 W. Cantwell Smith, *What is Scripture? A Comparative Approach*, London: SCM Press 1993.

27 K. Schori, *Das Problem der Tradition. Eine fundamentaltheologische Untersuchung*, Stuttgart: Kohlhammer 1992.

28   I use this term 'epic' in the sense given to it by Paul Ricoeur in his *Time and Narrative*, Chicago: Chicago University Press 1984–8, taking up Aristotle's *Poetics*. The epic is more than the text of the narrative and also more than the narration or performance of it in the theatre. It is interwoven with the biography of individuals and peoples; it has a *clou* in what happens to human beings in their fate, their choice, their destiny. And as epic it works only in the way in which hearers, readers or onlookers take part in it, package it and shape it. Ricoeur calls this the threefold learning progress (*mimesis*) of prefiguration (the *clou*, the original fortune), configuration (the narration, the tragedy as text and drama) and refiguration (the reception, the emotion, the conversion, the following). Ultimately religions claim to offer a specific *clou* or key which determines the right of a particular narrative community to exist. It is at that level that the uniqueness of the Jesus event must be sought, but that cannot be attained separately, cannot be approached without concrete configurations and refigurations. That in Jesus the fullness of God has dwelt bodily and that with his whole person he makes up part of God's own being by virtue of resurrection from the dead is the specific core of the Christian epic, which as such is unique and does not have a direct parallel in any of the other living religions. Whether and how Jesus himself experienced and lived out this drama cannot be discovered, but it is not relevant to the *clou* of his gospel either.

29   Knitter, *No Other Name?* (n. 12), 7.

30   O. H. Pesch, *Das Zweite Vatikanische Konzil. Vorgeschichte, Verlauf – Ergebnisse – Nachgeschichte*, Würzburg: Echter Verlag 1993, esp. 291–310.

11. INFINITE GOD: TOWARDS A GOD WHO ALLOWS HIMSELF TO BE THOUGHT

1   E. Schillebeeckx, *Theologisch Testament*, Baarn: Nelissen 1994, 35.

2   Ibid., 171.

3   M. Heidegger, *Identität und Differenz*, Pfüllingen 1957, [8]1986, 45.

4   H. van Veghel, 'God en de roos. Heidegger en de god van de filosofie', in R. J. Peeters et al. (eds), *De Onvoltooid Verleden Tijd. Negen bijdragen tot een bezinning op traditie*, Tilburg 1992, 51–68.

5   Cf. W. Pannenberg, *Metaphysik und Gottesgedanke*, Göttingen: Vandenhoeck & Ruprecht 1998.

6   K. Rahner, *Hearers of the Word*, New York: Herder and Herder and London: Sheed and Ward 1969: 'We have recognized man as that existent thing who in virtue of his absolute transcendence stands in free love before the free God of a possible revelation' (139); 'Man is that existent thing who must listen for an historical revelation of God, given in his history and possibly in human speech' (161).

7   In his introduction to the Dutch edition of E. Levinas, *God en de filosofie*, The Hague: Meinema 1990, and in H. M. Vroom (ed.) *De god van de filosofen en de God van Pascal*, Zoetermeer: Meinema 1991 and in the collection *Langs de gewesten van het zijn*, Zoetermeer: Meinema 1996.

8   H. Adriaanse, *Vom Christentum aus. Aufsätze und Vortrage zur Religionsphilosophie*, Kampen: Kok Pharos 1995; A. L. Molendijk, *Aus dem Dunklen ins*

Helle. Wissenschaft und Theologie im Denken von Heinrich Scholz, Atlanta and Amsterdam: Rodopi 1991.

9   V. Brümmer, *Theology and Philosophical Inquiry*, London 1981; id., *What Are We Doing When We Pray?*, London: SCM Press 1984; id., *Over een persoonlijke God gesproken ... Studies in de wijsgerige theologie*, Kampen: Kok Agora 1988; id., *Liefde van God en mens*, Kampen: Kok Agora and Kapellen: DNB/ Pelckmans 1993. See the publications of the so-called 'Utrecht School' in the philosophy of religion, including G. van den Brink, L. van den Brom, M. Sarot, *Christian Faith and Philosophical Theology*, Kampen: Kok Pharos 1992 (with bibliography).

10   H. M. Vroom, *Waarom geloven? Argumenten voor en tegen geloof*, Kampen: Kok 1985; id., *Religies en de waarheid*, Kampen: Kok 1988; id., *Geen andere goden. Christelijk geloof in gesprek met boeddhisme, hindoeïsme en Islam*, Kampen: Kok 1993.

11   H. M. Vroom, 'De God van Abraham, de God van alle mensen', in id. (ed.), *De god van de filosofen en de god van de bijbel. Het christelijke godsbeeld in discussie*, Zoetermeer 1991, 129.

12   J. Derrida et al., *La faculté de juger*, Paris 1985.

13   C. Misch (ed.), *Der junge Dilthey. Ein Lebensbild in Briefen und Tagebücher 1852–1870*, Stuttgart ^{2}1960, 36, quoted in J. de Mul, *De tragedie van de eindigheid. Diltheys hermeneutiek van het leven*, Kampen: Kok Agora 1993, 26: '... that religion will not and cannot satisfy the need for knowledge.'

14   Cf. E. Schillebeeckx, *Theologisch Testament*, 87: 'Without the critical correction of the material world, the cosmos [and the intermediary of history with all its drama of life and death, injustice and catastrophe], any experience of inwardness can be suspected of being fiction. There is then only subjectivity, which risks being purely imaginary. New Age is in fact the climax of modern subjectivism, although at the same time it presents the unpaid bill of a one-sided concentration of the Christian churches on themselves, on liturgy and sacraments and the legalistic domination of church people.'

15   A. Finkielkraut, *De ondergang van het denken*, Amsterdam: Contact 1988 (= *La défaite de la pensée*, Paris: Gallimard 1987), 14: 'Instead of testing the facts by the norms of an ideal, he [Herder] demonstrates that these norms themselves have a genesis and a context; in short that they are themselves no more than facts. He sends the Good, the True and the Beautiful back where they come from; he drives the categories which are of all times out of the haven where they were complacently enthroned, to take them back to the corner of the earth where their cradle stood. Herder proclaimed that the Absolute does not exist; there are only values bound to places and principles which have arisen by chance. It is not the case that human beings are of all times and all lands: a specific kind of person belongs to each time and each land. Socrates: an Athenian from the fifth century before Christ. The Bible: a poetic expression of the Hebrew soul – originally determined by the circumstances. All that is divine is human, and all that is human, even the *logos*, belongs to history ... If no one is a prophet outside his country, from now on peoples need only take account of themselves ...' Humankind is 'none other than the sum of all particularisms which inhabit the earth' (23). Finkielkraut demonstrates with crystal clarity that the reference to the particular, unique, contingent, the situation and the facts becomes a new religion: one's own language, one's own land, one's own culture become the guiding thread of the estimation. The good is what is as it is in one's

own concrete biography. It is not metaphysics, which above all that is seeks the true form and cohesion of reality. It is the critique of metaphysics that leads to unbridled narcissism and racism. It is not the idea of God – which puts all nations under God – but the divinization of the nation – that leads to war, violence and xenophobia: 'After the abolition of metaphysics the truth exclusively lies in the duration of the existence of things' (27).

16   Otto Kallscheuer, *Gottes Wort und Volkes Stimme. Glaube, Macht, Politik*, Frankfurt: Fischer 1994.

17   R. Descartes, *Meditations on the First Philosophy*, in id., *Discourse on Method and the Meditations*, Harmondsworth: Penguin Books 1968.

18   Ibid., 113 and 122.

19   Descartes' great discovery, the basis of his universal mathematics, but also of his metaphysical views about the thinking self and spatial extension, is his insight into the relativity and the proportionality of the determination of place. At the end of his *Géométrie* of 1636 he writes: 'If one knows two or three terms of a mathematical series, the subsequent terms can easily be found.' In fact this is the summary of a number of discoveries from this time: the relative relationships and forces between the phenomena (as in the relationships between tones in the theory of harmony, in the description of the laws of hydrostatics, in the determination of position by the compass, but also in numerical relationships) which make superfluous an appeal to eternal principles or all kinds of purposive processes – teleology, God as *causa finalis*. Every place is an intersection of extensions or co-ordinates, every point an arbitrary zero point from which one can describe reality and its forces. It is this new universal mathematical discovery which determines the new view of the world far more radically than the shift from a geocentric to a heliocentric system or from dogmatic certainties to universal doubt. According to some scholars – e.g. J. H. van den Berg, *Metabletica von God*, Kampen: Kok Agora and Kapellen: DNB/Pelckmans 1995 – this could have been the content of Descartes' visionary discovery which he himself describes as a kind of divine experience, a miraculous insight (*fundamentum inventi mirabilis*), with place, date and time: Ulm, 10 November 1619 (a comparison with Pascal's *Mémorial* occurs to one here). Others, like S. Gaukroger, *Descartes. An Intellectual Biography*, Oxford: The Clarendon Press 1995, opt for a more scientific discovery, like the laws of the fracturing of light or insight into the possibilities of algebra to illuminate mathematical problems.

20   Ibid., 124.

21   Ibid., 124–5. Cf. A. Leijen, *Midden uit de oneindigheid*, Vught: Radboudsticht-ing 1995, 8, etc. Leijen points out that Descartes does not just speak about infinity in an extensive sense (the infinite extension of the *infinitum*) but also and above all in a perfective sense, 'an infinity which counts out my thought beyond itself and brings it near to reality, which infinitely transcends me. Infinity itself transcends my idea of infinity. The infinity which transcends my idea is the supreme perfection: God' (8). By becoming conscious of this position – 'I am a milieu between God and nothingness' – I become conscious of being supported by what precedes me and towards which I am on the way: '... it is above all the experience of myself as striving and willing, in which I discover that I am not the author of my own being'.

22   Ibid., 127.

23   J.-L. Marion, *Dieu sans l'être*, Paris 1982; cf. id., *L'idole et la distance*, Paris 1977; *Prolégomena à la Charité*, Paris 1986; *La croisée du visible*, Paris 1991.

24 'Hermeneutic of the icon means that the visible becomes the visibility of the invisible only if it receives the intention, in short if it returns in intention to the invisible', *Dieu sans l'être* (n. 23), 36.

25 L.-M. Chauvet, *Symbol et Sacrement. Une relecture sacramentelle de l'existence chrétienne*, Paris: Du Cerf 1988.

26 Ibid., 15.

27 Ibid.

28 E. Levinas, 'God and Philosophy', in S. Hand (ed.), *The Levinas Reader*, Oxford: Blackwell 1989, 167f., 174f.

29 Id., *Totality and Infinity*, Pittsburgh: Duquesne University Press 1969, 48ff.

30 Id., 'God and Philosophy' (n. 28), 177.

31 For the ethical dimensions of Levinas' concept of God and his ontology generally see R. Burggraeve, *Mens en medemens. Verantwoordelijkeid en God. De metafysische ethiek van Emmanuel Levinas*, Leuven and Amersfoort: Acco 1986.

32 J. Pohier, *God – in Fragments*, London: SCM Press 1985.

33 E. Jüngel, *God as the Mystery of the World*, Edinburgh: T & T Clark 1983; id., *Entsprechungen: Gott – Wahrheit – Mensch*, Munich: Christian Kaiser 1980; id., *Wertlose Wahrheit*, Munich: Christian Kaiser 1990.

12. REVELATION AND EXPERIENCE, HYPOTHESIS AND APOTHEOSIS

1 J. B. Metz, *Glaube in Geschichte und Gesellschaft*, Mainz 1977, 70.

2 N. Lash, 'Ideology, Metaphor and Analogy', in B. Hebblethwaite and S. Sutherland (eds), *The Philosophical Frontiers of Christian Theology. Essays presented to D. M. Mackinnon*, Cambridge: Cambridge University Press 1982, 70.

3 Cf. W. Pannenberg, *Wissenschaftstheorie und Theologie*, Frankfurt 1973, 299–348 (Theology as the Science of God): 'The idea of God as the reality which determines everything according to its concept is to be tested by the experienced reality of the world and human beings. If such testing succeeds, then it has not been done by an authority external to the idea of God, but the procedure then shows itself as according with the form of the ontological proof of God, as God's proof of himself. But as long as the starting point of the test of the idea of God by reality as it is experienced is still open, and that is the standpoint of finite knowledge, as a mere idea the idea of God remains a hypothesis over against reality as it is experienced. So it is part of the finitude of theological knowledge that the idea of God also remains hypothetical in theology and retreats before human beings' experiences of the world and of themselves, by which this testing has to take place. On the other hand, according to his concept God as the theme of theology already embraces the reality or experience by which the idea of God is to be tested, and thus defines the object of theology' (302). H. Kuitert, *Wat heet geloven? Structuur en herkomst van de christelijke geloofsuitspraken*, Baarn 1977, 140–59, speaks of 'search patterns'. Here he links up with the epistemological views of K. Popper in his *Conjectures and Refutations*, London: Routledge 1975, 33–59 (without mentioning these directly). Popper: 'The problem "which comes first, the hypothesis (H) or the

observation (O)?", is soluble; as is the problem, "Which comes first, the hen (H) or the egg (O)?" The reply to the latter is, "An earlier kind of egg"; to the former, "An earlier kind of hypothesis." It is quite true that any hypothesis we choose will have been preceded by observations – the observations, for example, which it is intended to explain. But these observations in their turn presupposed the adoption of a frame of reference: a frame of expectation; a frame of theories. If they were significant, if they created a need for explanation and thus gave rise to the invention of a hypothesis, it was because they could not be explained within the old theoretical framework, the old horizon of expectations. There is no danger here of an infinite regress. Going back to more and more primitive theories and myths we shall in the end find unconscious, inborn expectations' (47).

Kuitert calls such 'inborn expectations' 'primal faith'. In fact the hypothesis of God, as cherished in the three theistic religions of Judaism, Christianity and Islam, is already a far more developed 'search pattern' than the modern critique of religion has realized, precisely on the basis of accepting it in principle as a 'hypothesis'. This cautious approach of theological language about 'God' perhaps fails to do justice to the emotional *adhaesio* which should characterize belief in God. On the other hand, terms like 'hypothesis', 'expectation' and 'search pattern' indicate that it is more or less a 'wager' (as Pascal remarked). The acceptance of the hypothesis of God as the 'reality which determines everything' (Pannenberg's phrase) at least means that one can or must give one's life for it. And unfortunately people have been put to death for refusing to accept it. This last then conflicts utterly with the direction of the hypothesis, which, once again to use Kuitert's terms, is 'certain enough for one to be willing to die for it', but which does not give us the boldness 'to let others die for it' (ibid., 159). But the term 'hypothesis' also expresses what is distinctive in the religions mentioned, namely awe at the mystery of God which declares that for mortals to see God is taboo (John 1.18; I John 4.12). Because of this awe at the mystery of God, wherever I mention the human hypothesis 'God' I shall use quotation marks and omit these only when the sense makes it clear that this is a doxological statement, which ultimately can apply only to God. Only in the doxology can one 'free God from his quotation marks', as we saw with Marion in the previous chapter.

4   Thus H. Adriaanse, *Het specifiek theologische aan een Rijksuniversiteit*, Leiden 1979, 20.

5   Many theologians have quite wrongly begun to use the term 'secularization' – above all since Gogarten and Bonhoeffer – as a positive term. Thus already A. J. Nijk, *Secularisatie*, Rotterdam 1968, 60–7. One can be content with the situation which has arisen through secularization and which offers positive opportunites for a more responsible and committed faith that also keeps itself from the compulsion of the system and intolerance. But that does not yet rid the term 'secularization' of its negative and polemical content, which cannot be 'pacified' so easily. Cf. A. Houtepen, 'Secularisatie en katholieke theologie', *Civis Mundi* 24, 1985, 98–120; see Chapter 1 of this book.

6   The term 'hold' (*halten*) is used by G. Hermes in his *Einleitung in die Christ-katholische Theologie* I, Münster 1819, 261, as a translation of the scholastic *assensus*: the placing of faith in the sphere of the 'feelings' is attributable to Schleiermacher. For him, 'feeling' is what lies before the separation of subject and object and therefore offers more support than the analysing mind. Schleiermacher, too, is concerned with *adhaesio*. Cf. H. Berkhof, *200 Jahre Theologie. Ein Reisebericht*, Neukirchen 1985, 46–63.

7   Thomas Aquinas, *Summa Theologica*, II, II, q. 1, a. 6 (a quotation from Isidore of Seville).

8   Umberto Eco, *The Name of the Rose*, London: Secker and Warburg 1983, 491–3 and the conclusion, 501f.

9   G. Kaufman, *God, the Problem*, Cambridge, Mass.: Harvard University Press 1972.

10 J. L. Mackie, *The Miracle of Theism*, Oxford: Oxford University Press 1982.

11 C. Geffré, *Le Christianisme au risque de l'Interprétation*, Paris: du Cerf 1983.

12 J. Nolte, *Dogma in Geschichte. Versuch einer Kritik des Dogmatismus in der Glaubensdarstellung*, Freiburg: Herder 1981 (the term appears on 153ff.).

13 It is striking that despite a long philosophical tradition which is continued in the philosophy of religion about the limits to the possibility of human knowledge the term 'revelation' is absent from a large number of more recent philosophical lexicons. Moreover the theme is hardly discussed any more in the philosophy of religion; at least that is the impression given by a number of philosophers of religion at a symposium in Lund in 1984 on 'The Concept of Revelation' (Fifth European Conference on the Philosophy of Religion, Conference Papers). Almost all the speakers were dependent on the theological literature of recent decades, with the exception of T. A. Roberts, who was still completely orientated on John Locke (*Essay Concerning Human Understanding*, Book IV, ch. 34).

14 Despite all the criticism that he makes of the changing use of the concept of revelation and the historical distortions of it since the nineteenth century, P. Eicher, *Offenbarung. Prinzip neuzeitlicher Theologie*, Munich 1977, in the end remarks that 'revelation is the principle of unity in Christian thought *par excellence*', because 'the meaning of the word "God" in any theology is essentially determined by the term "revelation" and this expression in turn performs a function for any comprehensive understanding of reality' (586). This seems to me to fail to recognize the force of the Christian tradition in the first thousand years of its history and to neglect the major difficulties that the concept of revelation has posed in modern times.

15 H. Bouillard, 'Le concept de Révélation de Vatican I à Vatican II', in J. Audinet et al., *Révélation de Dieu et langage de hommes*, Paris 1972, 35–50, mentions the 1835 encyclical *Dum acerbissimus* of Gregory XVI, directed against the work of the German theologian Hermes and the French theologian Bautain, as the earliest church document in which the formal concept of revelation appears. This terminology was taken over by Pius IX and then authorized by Vatican I (ibid., 37). The content of faith had previously been indicated by other terms: *doctrina salutaris, via vitae* (Lateran IV [1215], DS 800–1), *evangelium* (Trent, DS 1501). In taking up this text from Trent, Vatican I replaces *evangelium* with *supernaturalis revelatio* (DS 3006).

16 Constitution *Dei filius*, caput 2–4 (DS 3004–3020). In DS 3020, *fidei doctrina quam Deus revelavit* is contrasted with *philosophicum inventum*. Nothing can be added to or taken away from this doctrine. For this constitution see H. Pottmeyer, *Der Glaube vor dem Anspruch der Wissenschaft*, Freiburg 1968, and A. Houtepen, *Onfeilbaarheid en hermeneutiek*, Bruges 1973, 153–86.

17 DS 3011: '*Porro fide divina et catholic ea omnia credenda sunt, quae in verbo Dei scripto vel tradito continentur et ab Ecclesia sive solemni iudicio sive ordinario et universale magisterio tamquam divinitus revelata credenda proponuntur.*'

18 J. A. Montsma, *De exterritoriale openbaring. De openbaringsopvatting achter de*

fundamentalistische Schriftbeschouwing, Amsterdam 1985. Cf. P. Tillich, 'Autorität und Offenbarung', in *Offenbarung und Glaube*, Gesammelte Werke VIII, Stuttgart 1970, 59–69.

19 D. Bonhoeffer, *Letters and Papers from Prison. The Enlarged Edition*, London: SCM Press and New York: Macmillan 1971, 280, 286, 329.

20 Montsma compares this Christian notion of revelation with that of the Mormons and describes it like this: '... revelation as a divine speaking which posits itself in human reality that makes possible an unassailable appeal to *Deus dixit*. This appeal concentrates on the formal category of revelation "from above", with which it removes itself from the field, the territory of investigation and testing', Montsma, *De exterritoriale openbaring* (n. 18), 3.

21 The German Duden gives a nice specimen of this view. Revelation: 'A piece of information which is given to human beings about God, his existence, will and activity in a quite definite extent about his secret being by those chosen to do so in communications, instructions and teachings which form the basis of any religion' (*Der grosse Duden* VIII, Mannheim 1964, 483).

22 The German word '*offenbaren*' has the assonance – also etymologically – of evidence, demonstration. It could be derived from a root '*bar*' as in '*Bahre*' = 'bier'. Revelation means 'put on the bier', thus J. R. Geiselmann, 'Offenbarung', in H. Fries (ed.), *Handbuch theologischer Grundbegriffe* II, Munich 1962, 242.

23 A. Oepke, 'Apokalypto', in G. Kittel, *Theological Dictionary of the New Testament* III, 3–92. Cf. Eicher, *Offenbarung* (n. 14), 28–41, and A. Sand, 'Die biblischen Aussagen über die Offenbarung', in M. Seybold et al., *Handbuch der Dogmengeschichte* I/Ia, Freiburg 1971, 126.

24 K. Waayman, *De betekenis van de naam Jahwe*, Kampen: Kok 1984.

25 C. Rowland, *The Open Heaven. A Study of Apocalyptic in Judaism and Early Christianity*, London: SPCK 1982, 61ff.

26 G. Dreyfus (ed.), *Traité de la Nature et de la Grâce*, Paris 1958, II, LVII, 205–6.

27 P. Stockmeier, '"Offenbarung" in der frühchristlichen Kirche', in *Handbuch der Dogmengeschichte* I/Ia, 27–87.

28 J. de Ghellinck, 'Pour l'historie du mot "revelare"', *Recherches des Sciences Religieuses* 6, 1916, 149–57. Stockmeier thinks that the idea of a closed revelation is expressed only in the 1907 decree *Lamentabili* in opposition to modernism (Stockmeier, '"Offenbarung"' [n. 27], 27).

29 Origen, *Comm. In I John* VI 5.

30 Stockmeier, '"Offenbarung"' (n. 27), 86.

31 Ibid., 64. Cf. G. Dautzenberg, *Urchristliche Prophetie*, Stuttgart 1975.

32 Thomas Aquinas, *Summa Theologica*, II, II, q. 1, a. 2.

33 H. Waldenfels, *Handbuch der Dogmengeschichte*, I/IIb, 57–76.

34 U. Horst, *Handbuch der Dogmengeschichte*, I/Ia, 117.

35 Eicher, *Offenbarung* (n. 14), 80ff.

36 Thus the title of a 1696 work by John Toland.

37 DS 2904–2914.

38 DS 3004–5.

39 T. M. Schoof, *Aggiornamento*, Baarn 1968; U. Gerber, *Katholischer Glaubensbegriff. Die Frage nach dem Glaubensbegriff in der katholischen Theologie vom I. Vatikanum bis zur Gegenwart*, Gütersloh 1966.

40 It is important here whether or not there is a lapse into neo-scholastic thinking: see P. A. van Leeuwen, *Openbaring, overlevering en Heilige Schrift in het Tweede Vaticaanse Concilie*, Nijmegen 1964, over the course of events in the composition of

the Vatican II constitution *Dei Verbum*. The debate after Vatican II plumbed sorry depths above all around H. Küng's *Infallible? An Enquiry*, London: SCM Press ²1994. Cf. A. Houtepen, *Onfeilbaarheid en hermeneutiek* (n. 16), 33–66, and id., 'Theologie en leerambt', *Kosmos en Oekumene* 14, 1980, no. 4.

41 Eicher, *Offenbarung* (n. 14), 120–62, aptly sums up the vocabulary of this way of thinking: authority, objectification, systematic thought, conceptualism, doctrine, proof.

42 Ibid., 581.

43 *Metaphysics* 980 b 28ff. For this and the following information I am basing myself on F. Kambartel, 'Erfahrung', *Historisches Wörterbuch der Philosophie* I, 609–17; A. S. Kessler, A. Schöpf and C. Wild, 'Erfahrung', *Handbuch philosophischer Grundbegriffe* (ed. H. Krings, H. M. Baumgartner, C. Wild) I, Munich, 373–86; D. Lange, *Erfahrung und die Glaubwürdigkeit des Glaubens*, Tübingen 1984, 7–27.

44 Kambartel, 'Erfahrung', *Historisches Wörterbuch* (n. 43), 610–11.

45 Ibid., 611; Lange, *Erfahrung* (n. 43), 16ff.

46 Lange, *Erfahrung* (n. 43), 11.

47 Ibid., 12ff.

48 Ibid., 14ff.

49 Kessler et al., 'Erfahrung', *Handbuch philosophischer Grundbegriffe* (n. 43), 375; Kambartel, 'Erfahrung', *Historisches Wörterbuch* (n. 43), 614.

50 Ibid., 377ff.

51 Lange, *Erfahrung* (n. 43), 21.

52 Pottmeyer, *Glaube vor dem Anspruch der Wissenschaft* (n. 16), 74–6, 238–40, 288–91, 295–99.

53 Kessler et al., 'Erfahrung', *Handbuch philosophischer Grundbegriffe* (n. 43), 379ff.

54 H. Küng, *The Incarnation of God. An Introduction to Hegel's Theological Thought as Prolegomena to a Future Christology*, Edinburgh: T & T Clark 1987.

55 For 'disclosure' see I. T. Ramsey, *Religious Language*, London: SCM Press 1957, 11–48. For the term *blik* see P. van Buren, *The Secular Meaning of the Gospel*, New York: Macmillan and London: SCM Press 1963, 85ff. He has taken it from R. M. Hare.

56 I have been guided here by A. Dulles, *Models of Revelation*, New York: Doubleday 1983.

57 W. Pannenberg et al., *Revelation as History*: London: Sheed and Ward and New York: Macmillan 1968.

58 Especially H. de Lubac and J. Daniélou.

59 Especially in the work of O. Cullmann.

60 Eicher, *Offenbarung* (n. 14), 491ff.

61 Constitution *Dei Verbum* 1, 6, 7.

62 Locke, *Essay Concerning Human Understanding*, Book IV, ch. XXXIV.

63 For what follows I base myself on E. Schillebeeckx, *The Understanding of Faith*, London: Sheed and Ward 1974; E. Biser, *Theologische Sprachtheorie und Hermeneutik*, Munich 1970; G. Siegwalt et al., *Écriture, Parole et communauté*, Paris 1977; W. Veldhuis, 'Ervaring, taal en traditie', *Tijdschrift voor Theologie* 22, 1982, 247–60. N. Lash, 'Ideology, Metaphor and Analogy' (n. 2).

64 Van Leeuwen, *Openbaring, overlevering en Heilige Schrift in het Tweede Vaticaanse Concilie*, (n. 40).

65 Cf. n. 22.

66   Pannenberg, *Wissenschaftstheorie und Theologie* (n. 3), 321.

67   Cf. A. Houtepen (ed.), *The Living Tradition. Towards an Ecumenical Hermeneutics of the Christian Tradition*, Zoetermeer: Meinema 1995.

68   E. Schillebeeckx, *Interim Report on the Books Jesus and Christ*, London: SCM Press and New York: Crossroad 1980, 11–12.

69   Id., *Christ*, London: SCM Press and New York: Crossroad 1980, 46.

70   M. Heidegger, *Introduction to Metaphysics*, New Haven: Yale University Press 1969, 86.

71   K. Rahner, *Hearers of the Word*, New York: Herder and Herder and London: Sheed and Ward 1969, 11: it is 'an analysis of the possibility of perceiving the reality of the revelation of God as that Being which in fact alone constitutes man fundamentally in his fully developed essence'.

72   Cf. P. Tillich, *Systematic Theology* I, London: Nisbet 1964, 40; R. Bultmann, 'The Concept of Revelation in the New Testament' (1929), in *Existence and Faith. Shorter Writings of Rudolf Bultmann*, ed. Schubert M. Ogden, Cleveland and New York: World Publishing Co. 1960, 79: 'Outside of faith, revelation is not visible; there is nothing revealed on the basis of which one believes. It is only in faith that the object of faith is disclosed; therefore, faith itself belongs to revelation.'

73   Cf. J. A. Montsma, *De exterritoriale openbaring* (n. 18), 19–74. In particular the gradual narrowing of the biblical and patristic imagery to the scholastic language of concepts and the nineteenth-century word book, to which the understanding of scripture runs parallel, is one of the causes for the increasingly rationalistic understanding of revelation. This is the main thesis of Biser, *Theologische Sprachtheorie und Hermeneutik* (n. 63), 21 and *passim*.

74   N. Lash, 'Ideology, Metaphor and Analogy' (n. 2), 72ff.

75   Cf. T. A. Roberts at the Conference of Philosophers of Religion in Lund, 1984 (cf. n. 13).

76   Cf. A. Houtepen, *Confessing our Faith Around the World* II, Faith and Order Paper 120, Geneva 1983, VI–IX.

77   N. Lash, 'Ideology, Metaphor and Analogy' (n. 2), 70.

78   Cf. E. van Wolde, 'Semiotik en haar betekenis voor de theologie', *Tijdschrift voor Theologie* 24, 1984, 138–67, who refers to this danger.

79   H. Kuitert, *Zonder geloof vaart niemand wel*, Baarn 1974, 28.

80   G. Kaufman, *God, the Problem* (n. 9), 226.

81   H. Albert, *Die Wissenschaft und die Fehlbarkeit der Vernunft*, Tübingen 1982, 162–3.

82   I. U. Dalferth, *Existenz Gottes und Christlicher Glaube. Skizzen zu einer eschatologischen Ontologie*, Munich 1984. Cf. Pannenberg, *Wissenschaftstheorie und Theologie (n. 3), 303ff*.

83   R. Bultmann, 'The Concept of Revelation in the New Testament' (n. 72), 78.

84   L. Gilkey, *Naming the Whirlwind. The Renewal of God Language*, Indianapolis: Bobbs-Merrill 1969; id., *Reaping the Whirlwind. A Christian Interpretation of History*, New York: Seabury Press 1976.

85   D. Bonhoeffer, *Letters and Papers from Prison* (n. 19), 341ff.

86   H. Küng, *Does God Exist? A Question for Today*, London: Collins 1984.

87   According to Kuitert it is even one of the most important backgrounds to the debate about revelation versus experience in church and theology: see Kuitert, 'Openbaring en ervaring, een misplaatste tegenstelling', in T. Schoof et al., *Meedenken met Schillebeeckx*, Baarn: Nelissen 1983, 43–53.

88   Cf. J. Sperna Weiland, *Romeins Schetsboek*, Baarn 1980, 40: 'Secularization implies that the thought which in former times rounded itself off figuratively into a world-view has become non-figurative; it is by no means fortuitous that in our time an art has come into being which "no longer represents anything". Around us lies the rubbish heap of the powerful creations of figurative thought and we are not sketching out any new pictures of the world. Among other things, that means that we can no longer understand God and human beings, nature and history, as well as our forefathers, that the past has become more enigmatic and the future more unsure.' Perhaps the fragmentation of existence consists more in the hypertrophy of the figurative: counting, measuring, weighing, with figures and letters (*figurae*), fill our culture. The non-figurative, e.g. in art, is an attempt to express what cannot be said, what is indescribable and perhaps a protest against the figurative occupations, fixations, clichés which hold our thought captive and get in the way of the experience of transcendence.

89   I have taken what follows from the article 'Geisteswissenschaften', in J. Mittelstrass (ed.), *Philosophie und Wissenschaftstheorie*, Mannheim, Vienna and Zurich 1980, I, 724ff.; A. Diemer, 'Geisteswissenschaft', in J. Ritter (ed.), *Historisches Wörterbuch der Philosophie* III, 211–15.

90   Aristotle, *Metaphysics* XI (K) 7, 1064 a–b, 284–6, Loeb Classical Library, ed. G. Cyril Armstrong, London: Heinemann 1933, 1935. This is about the theoretical science which Boethius called 'speculative'. It took a relatively long time for the term 'theology' to assume the later and more limited sense of the exposition of the Bible and dogma (*sacra pagina, sacra doctrina*). For church fathers like Clement of Alexandria (third century) and even for Augustine (end of the fourth century), as for Plato and Varro, *theologein* first of all meant the mythical activity of the Greek poets, and then the doctrine about the cosmic spheres and meteors, and finally the practical knowledge of the imperial protocol. See Augustine, *De Civitate Dei*, VI, 5: '*Tria genera theologiae sunt, i.e. rationis quae de diis explicatur: eorumque unum mythicum, alterum physicum, tertium civile.*' Thus literary criticism (especially the knowledge of the tragedies), natural science (the knowledge of the mysteries of the cosmos) and etiquette (the knowledge of the mysteries of the court) are embedded in the treatise on the divine. Theology and philosophy cannot in fact be distinguished in terms of method, but at most qualitatively: theology relates to the first or the true philosophy. Only Dionysius the Areopagite introduces a more limited use of the term. According to him the real, true theology coincides with the content of the Jewish and Christian scriptures or, in an even more limited way, with the doctrine of correct speaking about God (in addition to physiology as the doctrine of the creation and economy as the doctrine of grace, the church and the sacraments). Even then everything that can be known falls within the framework of the view of faith on reality, but the more time goes on, the more the strictly theological is about the doctrine of God in the strict sense. Thomas Aquinas works this out further and calls everything to do with the reality of the cosmos and society as such philosophy, whereas theology is directed towards the relationship between this reality and God (*Summa Theologica*, I, q. 1, a. 1). A debate then very quickly developed about the further delineation of the territory of theology, philosophy, geometry and other sciences. Cf. M. D. Chenu, *La théologie comme science au XIIe siècle*, Paris 1957; M. Grabmann, *Die Geschichte der scholastischen Methode* I–II, Graz 1957 (= Freiburg im Breisgau 1909); U. Köpf, *Die Anfänge der*

theologischen Wissenschaftstheorie im 13. Jahrhundert, Tübingen 1974; H. Dörrie, 'Spätantike Metaphysik als Theologie', in *Kirchengeschichte als Missionsgeschichte* IV, Munich 1974, 261–82.

91 For Alain and his significance for the development of theology see U. Köpf, *Die Anfänge der theologischen Wissenschaftstheorie im 13 Jahrhundert*, Tübingen 1974, 15ff., 52, 75.

92 *PL*, 210, 621ff.

93 In the *Summa 'Quoniam homines'* and the *Expositio Prosae de Angelis*. References in Köpf, *Die Anfänge* (n. 91), 18 n. 35.

94 *Regula* XCIX . Sicut homo per charitatem a thesi suae naturae in apotheosim gratiae ascendens est deificatus; ita Deus per charitatem ab apotheosi suae naturae in hypothesim nostrae miseriae descendens est humanatus. '*Nota quod aliud est thesis humanae naturae, aliud apotheosis, aliud hypothesis. Thesis dicitur proprius status hominis, quem servire dicitur, quando ratione utitur ad considerandum quid bonum quid malum quid agendum quid cavendum. Sed aliquando excedit homo istum statum vel descendo in vitia, vel ascendendo in coelestium contemplationem; et talis excessus dicitur exstasis sive metamorphosis, quia per hujusmodi excessim excedunt statum propriae mentis, vel formam. Excessus autem superior dicitur apotheosis, quasi deificatio; quae fit, quando homo ad divinorum contemplationem rapitur; et hoc fit mediante illa potentia animae, quae dicitur intellectualitas, qua comprehendimus divina; secundam quam potentiam homo fit Deus, sicut mediante illa potentia animae, quae dicitur intellectus, comprehendit invisibilia; per quam comprehensionem homo fit homo spiritus, sicut per speculationem rationis homo fit homo. Inferior vero exstasis est, quae et hypothesis, quando homo a statu humanae naturae demittitur degenerando in vitia; et hoc fit per sensualitatem, per quam homo fit homo pecus. Deus autem suam habet apotheosim, scilicet excellentiam suae naturae, a qua descendens exinanivit se, formam servi accipiens; se humiliavit usque in thesim nostrae naturae, imo usque in hypothesim nostrae miseriae, non quantum ad culpam, sed quantum ad poenam*', *PL* 210, 673–4.

95 Philo, *De somniis*, 2, 226, quoted in Biser, *Theologische Sprachtheorie und Hermeneutik* (n. 63), 53: 'If a thinking spirit is able to stand more firmly and no longer waver to and fro like a balance, then if it stands before God and where it sees God it will also be seen by God.' A comparison between this quotation and the introductory quotation from J. B. Metz shows that for all the wavering of position, continuity is not excluded even in theology.

EPILOGUE: GOD, AN OPEN QUESTION IN OUR APORIA

1 Following the *Te Deum* (the Ambrosian song of praise), the closing verse: *In Te Domine speravi, non confundar in aeternum* (= Isaiah).

Select Index of Names

SELECT INDEX OF NAMES